Modern Pentathlon
A Centenary
History: 1912-2012

by

Andy Archibald

Grosvenor House
Publishing Limited

Andy Archibald is hereby identified as author of this
work in accordance with Section 77 of the Copyright, Designs
and Patents Act 1988

The book cover picture is copyright to UIPM

This book is published by
Grosvenor House Publishing Ltd
28-30 High Street, Guildford, Surrey, GU1 3EL.
www.grosvenorhousepublishing.co.uk

A CIP record for this book
is available from the British Library

ISBN 978-1-78148-756-3

Contents

'Not to know what has been transacted in former times is to be always a child. If no use is made of the labours of past ages, the world must remain always in the infancy of knowledge.'

Cicero (106 BC - 43 BC).

Foreword

A quotation we're very fond of putting in pentathlon programmes is Aristotle's observation that 'the most perfect sportsmen are the pentathletes because in their bodies strength and speed are combined in beautiful harmony'. It's nice to think he's talking about us but strength and speed are found equally in evidence in many other sports. Skill and endurance might actually be considered more important qualities in our sport or, perhaps, skill sustained under demanding conditions. The Ancient Greek pentathlon wasn't directly the inspiration for our sport. With the exception of the final wrestling event (added much later) it was pure track and field (long jump, discus, javelin, sprint). These were the events that made up the pentathlon competition in which the famous American athlete, Jim Thorpe, triumphed in 1912 only to have his title rescinded (and then later reinstated) by some petty-fogging rule about professionalism. The only change to that original programme was a 1500 metre run that replaced the wrestling of the Ancient Greeks, thus turning it completely into a track and field competition. This is the athletic pentathlon that eventually morphed into the men's decathlon (ten athletic events) and women's pentathlon (five athletic events) which, in turn became the heptathlon (seven athletic events).

Neither is there any real truth in the legend that Modern Pentathlon originated in the Napoleonic Wars when a messenger rode through his enemies, picking them off with his pistol. When he was pulled off his horse, the legend has it, he swash-buckled his way out of a tricky situation with his sword, swam across the moat surrounding his destination and ran the final stretch to deliver his vital message. Then, presumably, he did the decent thing and expired honorably. Baron de Coubertin was, apparently, very fond of this story.

In 2012, Modern Pentathlon achieves its centenary as an Olympic sport. It has had an unbroken presence in every Olympic Games since 1912. That fact, apart from being a quite wonderful achievement, is little short of a miracle. To this day, there are many sporting professionals who won't be able to tell you which sports make up the Modern Pentathlon. As soon as they mention a jump and a throw, we have to begin educating them.

Amongst all the nations of the world, Great Britain is the only country to have had representatives in the Modern Pentathlon at all 22 Olympic Games since 1912. The great founders, Sweden, surrendered the sharing of this title by being absent in Beijing in 2008. France, Italy and the USA have all also been absent on but a single occasion. So it is appropriate, then, for a history of

Modern Pentathlon written in Great Britain to feature Great Britain's participation in this story. Since our international family is so close, others will recognise much of the British experience in their own beginnings.

For the UIPM (Union Internationale de Pentathlon Moderne), our governing body, the pressures to change, develop and modernise have been enormous. It wasn't enough to remind everybody that ours is the only sport specifically created by the founder, Baron Pierre de Coubertin, for the modern Olympic Games. The IOC told us, 'You're elitist, you haven't got enough friends,' so we invited dozens of other countries to join us and now pentathletes from every corner of the world take part. The IOC told us, 'Nobody wants to watch you,' and so we filled the stands at every Olympic event. The IOC told us, 'You're too expensive,' and so we learned how to make money and support our sport properly. The IOC told us, 'You're boring,' so we brought in the exciting one day event, now with its gripping combined run/shoot conclusion. We have jumped through every hoop waved in front of us and we are still here. And that is a triumph.

Who could have imagined in 1912 that the peculiar combination of riding, shooting, fencing, swimming and running, valued so highly by Baron de Coubertin, would last so long and remain so vigorously contested? This book, then, is a celebration of all that we have achieved in 100 years of competition and an opportunity to honour those who have been part of that story.

1912 and 2012 – A Brief Comparison

1912 Stockholm

Qualification process: No entry limit. Men only. Sweden entered 12. Of 32 entries, only 22 finished the competition.

Duration of competition: Six days.

Order of events: Shoot, swim, fence, ride, run.

Scoring system: Based on placing positions in each event – first gained one point, second two etc. The competitor with the lowest aggregate score and who completed all five events was the winner.

Fencing: 'Steam' (non-electric) epée in the open air. Decisions made by referee assisted by four judges. A round robin competition – each competitor fenced every other competitor once for the best of five hits (first to three). Winner of the competition was the one with the most victories.

Swimming: 300m freestyle in an open air, unheated 100m pool. Swum in unseeded heats. Fastest time overall won.

Riding: Competitors brought their own horses or organisers provided horses for those without. A 5000m cross-country course over 17 fixed jumps. Fastest time without fault won. 15 minute time limit. Speed of 500m per minute. Each rider began with 100 points. Points deducted for: refusal (2), second refusal (5), fall of horse

(5), fall of rider (10), each five second period over 15 minutes (2).

Shooting: 20 shots with a live ammunition pistol (unspecified bore) at a man-size target (1.7m high, 0.5m wide) with scoring centre marked from 10 (bull) to 7. Maximum target score: 200. For each shot, the target faced for three seconds during which the shot was fired. It then turned away for ten seconds to allow re-loading.

Running: 4000m cross-country over previously undisclosed terrain. Runners began at one minute intervals. Order determined by drawing of lots. Fastest time won.

2012 London

Qualification process: A series of qualifying competitions on five continents. Remaining places selected from the world ranking list. 36 men and 36 women will compete. Pan-America, Africa, Asia, Oceania, and Europe will all be represented.

Duration of competition: One day only.

Order of events: fence, swim, ride, combined event (shoot/run).

Scoring system: Performances in each event are converted to points. The competitor with the highest aggregate score is the winner. Competitors start the final combined event in the order in which they are placed after three events. The first to finish the combined event is the winner.

Fencing: 'Electric epée indoors on metal pistes. A round robin competition, each bout for a single hit. One minute maximum per bout. Winning 70% of bouts (25 out of 35 fights) = 1000 points +/- 24 points per hit.

Swimming: 200m freestyle in an indoor, heated 50m pool. Swum in seeded heats. A time of 2:30 = 1000 points +/ - 4 points for each 0.33 of a second.

Riding: Competitors ride horses assigned by random draw. All horses provided by the host nation. Competitors have 20 minutes to prepare horses for a show jumping course of 400m with 12 obstacles. Speed is set at 350m per minute. A faultless ride within time = 1200 points. Points deducted for: knockdown (20), refusal (40), fall of horse or rider (60). Only two refusals allowed at each fence.

Combined event (shoot/run): Competitors run 3000m, prefacing each 1000m circuit with shots with a laser pistol at five 59.5mm targets. Running may not recommence until all five targets have been hit. Competitors begin in order of their positions after three events. The first to complete the full course is the overall winner. An overall time of 12:30 = 2000 points +/- 4 points per second

Chapter One: 1912-1919

'Clilverd would have been placed much higher in the total if the horse provided for him by the Swedish Committee had been better.' BOA Report 1912

The planning

Baron Pierre de Coubertin (1863-1937), founder of the Modern Olympic Games and held to be the instigator of the first Modern Pentathlon competition, wasn't entirely acting on his own in this endeavour, even though his *Memoires Olympiques* (1931) might suggest otherwise. Purists, used to one event each day over five days, may grumble that the modern sport is not what de Coubertin intended. They'd be wrong. De Coubertin hoped for a test that could take place all in one day. In *Sport Pedagogy* he revealed:

'The brain-father himself is the first to admit that...the five events should follow each other in rapid succession without interruption so that the athletes compete with only the very short breaks they might need to change clothes. I have no doubt that we will achieve this.'

De Coubertin may have been prescient in that respect but some of his other ideas never saw the light of day. The 'brain-father', as he modestly called himself, would have liked the order of events to have been drawn just before the competition and the riding and running courses to have been kept secret - maps being issued two hours before the event began. He would have preferred to have included rowing rather than shooting, another physical event which would have been a poor alternative to the mental challenges of shooting. His proposed order was: run, ride, swim, fence and shoot. This seemed to him the ideal sequence for balancing the mental and physical stresses on the athlete. From a modern point of view, shooting would hardly be the most exciting event with which to settle the championship. And why conclude with the very event he thought should be replaced?

In many ways, de Coubertin was a dreamer, enthusing about grand schemes and loading them with weighty moral significance. What he had to accept, however, was always compromise. Luckily, one man knew de Coubertin's enthusiasms better than anyone. Luckily, for us, he was also the President of the Swedish Organising Committee for the Stockholm Olympic Games of 1912. That man was Colonel Victor Balck (1844-1928). Balck had been an important official in the Olympic movement since the outset in 1894 and the two friends were both committed to the concept of the modern Olympics. But it was Balck whose practical, organisational skill made sense of de Coubertin's more imaginative schemes and kept the Frenchman on the straight and narrow, Balck who took de Coubertin's fine ideas and shaped them into realisable events. It was, in many ways, the perfect team: de Coubertin, the Creative Director, waving his arms through the cigar smoke, eager to give birth to yet another work of genius and Balck, notes in hand, twenty years senior to de Coubertin, making practical sense of it all. Imagine the two men facing each other across the board room, handlebar moustaches bristling, each determined to find the best solution. There was also a bit of Swedish cunning in Balck's practicality, as we shall shortly see.

De Coubertin's enthusiasm for sport wasn't exactly formed on the playing fields of Eton but a similar place not a million miles away. His notion that sport was essential to the physical and moral development of the young was learned as an observer of Thomas Arnold's (1795-1842) teaching at Rugby School. Indeed, de Coubertin refereed one of the earliest Rugby internationals. In England, too, his attendance at and enthusiasm for the Much Wenlock Olympic Games held in Shropshire made him eager to do something similar but, naturally, on a grander scale. The Much Wenlock man, Dr William Penny Brookes (1809-95), had demonstrated to de Coubertin that not only was sport good for physical and moral development but it also had profound benefits for health.

So, when de Coubertin arrived for the inaugural meetings of the 1896 Olympic Games, a test of the all-rounder, the victor ludorum of sport, was very much in his plan. He was somewhat miffed, therefore, to find nobody interested. And so it remained for the next ten years or so. He had grown used to raising the subject whenever he had the chance, only to be depressed by the complete indifference of the committee. It wasn't until the IOC Congress in Berlin in 1909 that there was anything like a positive response. He proposed an event consisting of 'equestrian, running, jumping, swimming and wrestling' but allowed that fencing or shooting could replace wrestling. De Coubertin famously reported the committee's change of mind in his memoirs:

'I had already submitted the idea to the IOC on two previous occasions, and my proposal had always been greeted with a lack of understanding and almost hostility. I had not insisted. This time however the grace of the Holy Spirit of Sport enlightened my colleagues and they accepted an event to which I attached great importance: a veritable consecration of the complete athlete, the modern pentathlon was to comprise a foot race, a horse race, a swimming race, a fencing match, and finally, a shooting contest, which I would prefer to have had replaced by a rowing race, but this would have added greatly to the difficulties of the organisation, which was already quite complicated enough.'

One man in particular listened carefully at that meeting. Colonel Victor Balck stopped looking at the ceiling as he usually did when De Coubertin waxed lyrical and, for once, thought this pentathlon idea might be a going concern. He was in charge of the Swedish Committee responsible for providing the events for the Stockholm Games in 1912 so he agreed to take the idea away and report back at the Luxembourg IOC Congress in 1910. So what changed his mind? Why was he suddenly in favour of an idea he had previously rejected out of hand?

In 1906 at an unofficial Olympic Games held in Athens, a pentathlon event was introduced. It consisted of long Jump, discus, javelin, 200 metres sprint and graeco-roman wrestling. In the spirit of Ancient Greece, it was an elimination contest: only the top eight competitors qualified for the fourth event, the 200m sprint. Then, two more were eliminated and the final six wrestled for victory. Two features of this event stood out. Firstly, the gold and bronze medallists were both Swedes.

Secondly, this pentathlon was a kind of sideshow for the other athletic events; Hjalmar Mellander, the gold medallist, placed 4th in both the long jump and javelin; Istvan Mudin (HUN), the silver medallist, was 3rd in the discus, and the Swede, Erik Lemming, who took the bronze medal, was javelin champion in Athens and also won gold in the official Games of 1908 and 1912. One can imagine that Viktor Balck was well aware of the possibilities of a multi-event contest that would act as publicity for the other athletic events in the stadium, particularly since the Modern Pentathlon would take place in the first week of the Games. The fact that Sweden placed 1st and 3rd in the 1906 event might also have stirred the patriotic spirit of Colonel Balck and his team.

So, Balck took de Coubertin's ideas away from Berlin with him and reported back in Luxembourg the following year. The sport, he said, needed to be modified to suit the modern era. There was to be pistol shooting and not rowing, and fencing would be done with an epée and not a sabre. The fact that there already existed in Sweden a very similar combination of events might have had something to do with it, too. The Swedish Military Sports Federation was already using the named sports as part of basic training for Swedish army cadets.

De Coubertin was a French aristocrat but he had a reforming zeal that, if not quite socialist in conception, was at least partly democratic. One of the major initial difficulties was whether or not the organisers would be able to provide horses for the riding event or whether the athletes would have to provide their own. De Coubertin later recalled:

'I wanted horses to be provided by the host country and that athlete and horse would meet only moments prior to the beginning of the event. I think doing this would have fulfilled my dream of a competition that would be of great pedagogic value. Unfortunately, certain people persisted in opposing my concept, which has led to the organisers' totally forgetting the ideas that the creator of the modern pentathlon originally had for it.'

He was supported in this by the British committee member, the Reverend Robert de Courcy Laffan (1853-1927) who thought that if competitors brought their own horses it would 'not be a democratic contest of versatility'. Laffan, the donor of the Laffan Cup which to this day is contested in the British Men's Team Championship, was an important friend and supporter of de Coubertin. They first met in Le Havre in 1897 when Laffan spoke to Congress in fluent French about the spiritual values of sport. Coubertin later described Laffan as having 'come down from the heavens to help us' and welcomed this Headmaster of Cheltenham College on to his team. Later, as Rector of St Stephen, Walbrook, Laffan found time to act as BOA Secretary for 22 years. This apparently included the writing of over 11,000 letters in four languages in his negotiations for the 1908 London Olympic Games. He read the prayers at the Opening Ceremony of the Stockholm Games in 1912. So, frequently Laffan had intervened between committee members in order to calm the waters for de Coubertin. As a supporter, he had assured de Coubertin in a letter dated 14h December 1911:

'I hear of one or two competitors in the Modern Pentathlon who are training carefully for this novel event. I hope to hear of more as time goes on.'

Despite Laffan's solidarity with de Coubertin, Balck arrived at the 1911 IOC Congress in Budapest with the following ultimatum: 'The horses should be provided by the participants themselves. The Committee would completely reject a Modern Pentathlon if this resolution were not passed by the Budapest Congress as this is an essential prerequisite for Modern Pentathlon.'

De Coubertin raged and threatened rather impetuously to withdraw the cup which he had intended to present to the 1912 winner. Luckily, the grace of the Holy Spirit of Compromise stepped in and the rather unsatisfactory outcome was that those who could, would bring their own horses and that those who couldn't would have a horse supplied by the organisers. 1912 was the only Olympics in which this arrangement took place – from 1920 onwards the horses have always been supplied by the host country.

De Coubertin's egalitarian zeal was often tempered with interesting ideas about how this level playing field might be achieved. He wrote that:

'The Swedish concept is essentially aristocratic, and is meant for officers and gentlemen-riders. Although fairly willing to swim and shoot, for a cavalry officer, for example, to run across country on foot, would almost amount to debasement! This is the silliest of prejudices and one which I would gladly see uprooted by the pentathlon.'

All well and good so far, and, perhaps, one explanation of why running standards appear to have been so abysmally low in 1912. But then he goes on to suggest that the moral well-being of the lower classes might be substantially improved if they could only learn to ride a horse:

'On the other hand, a whole new category emerges. These are the habitués of athletic sports who frequent the shooting stand, the swimming pool or the arms room quite frequently and who, for the most part, have never had their own horses. Too often, horse riding itself remains foreign to them. This is a deplorable state of affairs which must end. The question of popular horse-riding must be resolved.'

He concludes, in fairness, that this startling approach to the education of those deprived of horse ownership just might be beyond the remit of his new sport: 'Obviously this will not be achieved by the rules of modern pentathlon but a similar institution could help a lot, especially if the democratic concept dominates in the end.'

From the autumn of 1910 onwards, Balck and his team worked on a suitable way to serve up this brand new sport. If the five events really had been an established part of Swedish military training, it is surprising how many of the team's deliberations seemed to be completely new. Firstly, their brief was to settle on five sports that tested 'endurance, resolution, presence of mind, intrepidity, agility and strength'. That was a difficult enough challenge but, then, secondly, to find five tests of equivalent value. Working with these rather abstract provisos can't have been easy. Thirdly, the order in which the events took place had to be considered. De Coubertin's idea of drawing lots for this immediately before the competition would have been an organisational nightmare and was rapidly dismissed on the grounds that it 'might unsteady the athletes'. To test the true champion, they argued, almost any order of events would be possible but for best results 'the difficulty in executing the tests should be the same for all the competitors'. None of this was really helpful. Anyone who has been caught in a sudden thunderstorm while riding, or found the pistol repeatedly jamming knows that 'difficulty' can vary from competition to competition, event to event, and person to person. None of these rather grand psychological considerations can have had much impact on the practical selection of events.

The chosen events

By the autumn of 1911, the order had been settled. It was to be shoot, swim, fence, ride, run. Each event was to be held on a separate day. Indeed, the fencing event was to be held over two days, taking the whole competition to six days in length.

Shooting

The shooting event would be done with pistols but there was no stipulation about what make or bore these pistols should be. The pistol simply had to be held in one hand and have open fore and back sights. This actually led to bores ranging quite widely in size (6.5 to 9.0mm), often very much larger than the 5.6mm / 0.22 in. requirement in later years. Such large bore holes may well have led to inaccurate readings on the target, it being easier to miss genuine strikes amid the gaping holes filling the target. Target distance was set at 20 metres initially although this was increased to 25 metres in order to balance the relative difficulty of the events. The man-sized target was 1.70m high and 0.5m across with scoring circles from 10 to 7. It would be a turning target that was visible for 3 seconds and then turned away for 10 seconds between shots. This was considered long enough for those using single shot pistols to reload.

Swimming

The challenge for the swimming event was that it should test an equal combination of endurance and strength.

300 metres was settled upon, though, judging from the swimming times in those days, 300 metres might have swung the balance towards endurance. The event would be swum in heats, there being no final, and the final positions would be settled only by time and not the relative positions in the heats.

Fencing

Amazingly, there was a short period in which it was seriously considered that the fencing event would be an open choice between epée, sabre and bayonet, competitors being free to fight with whichever weapon they chose! One of the committee was brave enough to say that there may well be 'grave difficulties in judging', to say nothing of the potential for permanent injury. As the least-practised of the three weapons (at least by officers, though not by other ranks), the bayonet was the first to be excluded but the committee were then tightly divided between epée and sabre. Eventually, epée ruled the day though the committee acknowledged there was 'much sympathy for sabre'. Regarded as less contentious by the committee, though more bizarre to the modern reader, was the decision to fight outdoors, the committee preferring 'fairly level ground' to platforms or wooden floors indoors. Each bout would not be for a single hit but scored as first to three or best of five. This explains the two days allocated to fencing in the programme.

Riding

The riding was, and probably remains to this day, the most complex and expensive of events to organise. Having established the uneasy compromise by which some competitors brought their own horses while others used horses provided by the organisers, there was still the requirement to establish what kind of test would follow. The general desire that horse, course, and rider should be strangers at the outset lingered on in these course plans. The ride would be an individual competition, point to point, that is, a fixed cross country course with obstacles and between 3000m and 5000m in length. It would be over a variable number of fixed jumps (maximum 30) at an expected speed of 500 metres per minute. Once again, the desire to balance tests of strength and endurance made the committee lean towards the longer course. They kept the distance flexible to allow for the varying terrain that might be provided. There were to be no bonus points for speed, but exceeding a time of 15 minutes would incur time penalties. However, since placing points would settle the outcome, to win you would need to ride fast. All this was agreed unanimously, unlike the proposal that there should be points for 'form in the execution of the ride'. The course would remain unknown to riders until a day or two before the competition when they would be able to walk the terrain but not have the jumps pointed out to them. In this way, general uncertainty might just lessen the advantage of having your own horse. Whether all twelve of the Swedish entries in 1912 trained vigorously throughout the early summer over this 'secret' course on their own horses is, however, not recorded.

Riding had a number of penalty points which were subtracted from each rider's nominal starting total of 100 points. These penalties applied to each obstacle. They were:

two points for 1st refusal or bolt
five points for 2nd refusal or bolt
five points for a horse falling
ten points for a rider falling
two points for every five second period over the course time limit of 15 minutes.

Running

Finally, the run was a relatively easy organisational task after the riding. It would be a cross country run over 4000 metres and, to preserve the individual challenge, runners would set off at one minute intervals, having drawn lots for starting positions. There seemed to have been a lingering air of the riding plans in the run: the length may well have been quite a variation on 4000 metres with the actual distance determined to suit the terrain. It is also unclear as to how much of the course was known to the runner before he started. Both these considerations should be borne in mind when looking at the times recorded.

The placing points system of scoring

There still remained one very important question: how were the organisers going to devise a system that gave equal importance to each event? What they settled on was a system that would remain in place for a further forty years despite its shortcomings. That was the place position scoring system. The pentathlete's finishing position in each event would be totalled -one point for 1st, two for 2nd and so on. The pentathlete with the lowest score at the end of the competition would be deemed the winner. It meant that an athlete had to complete all five events to finish in the final order. There were problems to this system though. What if you were the fastest swimmer in the world and beat the rest of the field by two minutes? Wouldn't you get any credit for this? No, was the answer. And what if there were 50 in the first event but athletes kept dropping out so that, say, only ten contested the final run? Would the positional points be re-jigged for the ten survivors so that, having come 50th in the shoot, that position would be adjusted to 10th after the final event. No, once again. All position points would stand regardless of who dropped out.

Most complicated of all was what would happen if there was a tie in an event. This was considered allowable ie. a tie in 3rd place, for example, would score one for 1st, two for 2nd, three each for 3rd= and then five for the next finisher and so on. A tie in the timed events (swim, ride, run) was unavoidable and no swim-off, ride-off or run-off was required but in shooting, a tie would result in an entire replay ie. four more series of five shots each for those concerned. In fencing, a one hit play-off was required between fencers who tied for first place or had an identical number of victories and hits against, otherwise position was decided by wins vs. hits against.

One peculiar quirk of the timing apparatus in the Modern Pentathlon was that the swim was timed in fifths of a second while the ride and run were timed to the tenth of a second. 1912 was the first time that any electronic timing had been used.

The competitors

The 1912 Olympic competition took place in Stockholm from the 7th to the 12th July in very hot weather. The temperature is sometimes cited as the reason for poor performance in the run but this, after all, was a temperate Swedish summer. There were 42 original entries, almost exclusively military and officer class. By the time the competition got underway, there were only 32 starters and, of those, only 22 finished. This may sound like a lack of stamina on the part of the athletes but it was much more to do with the nature of that first Olympic pentathlon – the competitors rarely were exclusively there for the Modern Pentathlon. As in the experimental Greek Pentathlon in 1906, competitors attended in order to take part in other sports but were, nevertheless, intrigued to dabble in this new Pentathlon. For some, a single event gave them a feel for what it was like, for others, a clash of events almost certainly forced their withdrawal. And once out of the competition, there was no way of rejoining it. As further proof of the experimental ethos of these games, there was no limit to the number of competitors a country could field. By 1920, the stipulation was four per country and from 1928 onwards, only three.

So the starters in Stockholm comprised no fewer than twelve Swedes, five Russians, four Danes, three British, two each from Norway and France, and a single competitor from each of the USA, Germany and Austria. The original entry list had included a further three Americans, a South African, and a Bohemian. They ranged in age from 21 to 53. The German, Carl Pauen, remains to this day, at 53, the oldest Olympic competitor in Modern Pentathlon. The local Stockholm newspaper, in previews, paid tribute to his 'evidence of elasticity at that age'. Since, however, he dropped out after the first event, the shooting, strictly speaking, his 'elasticity' was hardly tested and, not finishing the competition, he claims his title under dubious circumstances.

No fewer than 14 of the 32 starters represented their countries in other events, many with impressive medal pedigrees: The following other achievements by the 1912 pentathletes are listed below, their Modern Pentathlon positions preceding their achievements elsewhere:

Gösta Åsbrink (SWE) 2nd   1908 Gold in Team Gymnastics.

Georg de Laval (SWE) 3rd   1912 Silver in Team 50m Military Pistol.

Gustaf Lewenhaupt (SWE) 17th   1912 Gold in Team Show Jumping.

Hugh Durant (GBR) 18th   1912 Two Bronzes in Team 50m Military Pistol & 30 Duel Pistol.

Eric Carlberg (SWE) DNF   1912 Two Golds in 25m Small-bore Rifle Team & 30m Military pistol, 1908 Three Silvers in Small-bore Rifle Team, 50m Small-bore Rifle Ind. & 50m Military Pistol team.

Jetze Doorman (NED) DNF   Four Bronzes: 1912 Team Epée & Sabre, 1920 and 1924 Team Sabre.

Of course the twelve Swedes, having 'invented' the sport, dominated it completely. The first four placings in the event were all local boys, Stockholm born and bred. Indeed, eight of the top twelve finishers were also from Sweden. The impressive sporting credentials of these Swedes are indisputable but it is also a remarkable fact that almost every one of them lived a long life, mostly surviving into their late eighties during one of the most turbulent periods of European history. Indeed, the 1912 winner, Gösta Lilliehöök presented the prizes at the Swedish Championships as late as 1973.

The next largest contingent was the five from Russia. The interesting thing about these entrants was that four of them were Finnish, Finland being part of a Russian empire at that time. One of them, Oscar Wilkman-Vikema, later had the pleasure of competing for Finland in the 1920 Riding event. The Russian Finns made little impact in the event, although three of them did, at least, complete all five events. Boris Nepokupnoy, the only non-Finn, hailed from the vineyards of Tamagne in Southern Russia and did not finish.

The Danish team of four seems to have been drafted in merely as Sweden's closest neighbours. Only one finished and that was in last (22nd) place, some way adrift of the rest of the field.

The British entry

The British team members were all Londoners, two of them Brixton boys. None of the members of the team was highly-born, their roots being very middle-class – the sons of tobacconist, wine merchant and bank manager respectively. However, in the class-bound world of England at the time, there would have been a distinction between occupations, namely: wine merchant (upper middle), bank manager (middle), tobacconist (lower middle). In all cases, though, it is clear that their military careers gave them opportunities they might otherwise never have had. Interestingly, two out of the three men were not officers at the time of the Olympic Games, giving the lie to the assumption that competition was limited to the officer classes. All three members of the team were awarded gallantry medals in the war years.

The oldest member of the team was Squadron Sergeant Major (later, Lieutenant, DCM) Hugh Durant,

35, whose bronze medals in shooting at the 1912 Games are recorded above. His military career had already taken him to India and South Africa where he was making a name for himself as a marksman. He was an Orderly for King George V for which he received the Royal Victorian Silver Medal immediately after the 1912 Games. Sadly, he was killed in France in 1916.

Captain (later Major, MC) Douglas Godfree, 31, was born in Chiswick, West London. He'd already fenced sabre for GB in the 1908 London Games and did so again in 1912. He played polo, shot big game, and won racket and tennis tournaments. His obituary proclaimed 'there was no form of sport in which he did not partake'. He'd begun military life as a Gentleman Cadet at Sandhurst, as did so many early British competitors. Only a few weeks before the Games began, he was serving in Egypt. Like Durant, he served in India, and also in Mesopotamia, surviving the war to retire in 1927.

Finally, Bombardier (later Captain, MC, Croix de Guerre) Ralph Clilverd, 25, was in the Territorial Army when he competed in Stockholm. This should officially qualify him as the first ever civilian competitor (he was certainly listed as 'Mr Clilverd' in the order of start). Being a member of the Honorable Artillery Company allowed him to maintain other working contacts in London while getting the full sporting benefits of army life although, at the time, his civilian working life would have dominated his day. Clilverd's strength was his swimming - he won the swim in Stockholm, 30 seconds ahead of eventual bronze medallist, Georg de Laval. Clilverd may have benefited from the regular use of one of the London municipal baths. In the war he fought in Salonika and, after the war, he had an unusual job as a banker working on the liners travelling between Southampton and New York.

George Patton Jnr.

Among the other starting competitors, one man stands out: George Patton Junior, the famous American who went on to become General Patton, hero of the US 3rd Army in North Africa and Italy. Though glorified in the film *Patton*, revisionist historians are prone to making fun of him for his bluster and forthright confidence. Rusty Wilson, for instance, makes much of Patton's exaggerated version of his own successes in Stockholm. At Stockholm, Patton was a 25 year old Lieutenant and had made the long trip by ship to Europe, hardly the best preparation for a sporting contest. He had, nevertheless, trained rigorously every day on the *SS Finland* including spending several hours in a canvas tank swimming on the spot, his body tethered by ropes to the side of the pool. He arrived in Stockholm with his entire family and checked them all in at the Grand Hotel while the other American athletes remained on board ship. A wealthy man, he was determined to use the experience to advance his career saying, about the role of sport in his military life, 'in my business it is the best sort of advertising'. His great strength was his fencing in which he finally finished 4th. Indeed, he was so dedicated to the sport as a form of military training that, after the Games, he went straight to Saumur in France to study military sabre with the experts. With this experience behind him, he designed his own military sabre and rewrote the military sabre handbook on his return to the USA. Sadly, the days of the cavalry attack were numbered and, in this respect, Patton was a man out of his time. Given his later military fame, some like to mock Patton for his poor shooting performance in Stockholm, since he put 3 shots off target. But, there was a free choice of pistol and Patton's Colt had a much larger bore (0.38 in) than the pistols of his rivals most of whom used a 0.22 in. bore pistol. This meant that the holes on his target were sufficiently large to cause some confusion about quite how many bullets had made their mark. It is a tribute to Patton that he made no complaint whatsoever about this and, in his memoirs, fondly remembered the event with these words:

'The high spirit of sportsmanship and generosity manifested throughout speaks volumes for the character of the officers of the present day. There was not a single incident of a protest or any unsportsmanlike quibbling or fighting for points which, I regret to say, marred some of the other civilian competitors at the Olympic Games. Each man did his best and took what fortune sent like a true soldier, and at the end we all felt more like good friends and comrades than rivals in a severe competition, yet this spirit of friendship in no manner distracted from the zeal with which all strove for success.'

1912 Olympic Games: Stockholm (SWE)

The Modern Pentathlon in Stockholm took place in the first week of the Games in and around the newly built Olympic Stadium. Many commentators consider that 1912 was the first of the 'serious' Olympic Games and the design of the stadium matched this. The architect was Torben Grut, the father of the legendary Wille Grut, the 1948 Olympic Modern Pentathlon Champion and Secretary- General of our sport for many years. The 1912 Stockholm stadium remains in action to this day. It is used for international athletics meetings, football matches and rock concerts. At a current seating capacity of only 14,500, it is a little gem among sporting stadia. Grut's ambitious design set the tone for the magnificence of the event. In 1910 he wrote a piece for the Swedish Art magazine 'Konst' in which he described his ambitions for the park area outside the stadium in deeply poetic language:

'Here shall be an open air temple of Swedish granite sculpture, the very finest that we can produce. Severe and warlike rises the remainder of the northern Stadium. But in this little park, the sunshine playing through the crowns of oak in mystic clare-obscure, a vision shall be given of *Man* – of strength and beauty, carried monumentally on the lisener of the sturdy walls.'

The first event, the shooting, saw a wide range of arms in action. The Swedes used American Smith & Wesson target practice pistols; the Norwegians and German used German Parabellum automatic pistols; the Danes, Danish Army pistols; and Patton of the USA, as already mentioned, a Colt. It was the silver medallist, Åsbrink, the Swede, who won with 193. Georg de Laval and Lilliehöök, the other Swedish medal winners, tied for second place on 192. This involved a re-shoot of all four series, a rather extreme tie breaker. In this, both men scored much worse – 188 and 183 respectively but these final medallists had already established their strength in the very first event. In keeping with his reputation as a marksman, Hugh Durant took 4th place on 191. The other British competitors, Clilverd and Godfree, however, were well adrift with 172 and 166 respectively, Godfree putting two off the target completely.

Next day, the swimming event was held in the newly built swimming stadium. Swimming has experienced a sea change (quite literally) in so many ways since 1912. In Stockholm, the pool was 100m long and unheated. There were no wave-calming lane ropes. This was actually an improvement on past competitions, descriptions of which emphasise the mortal fear of swimmers dropped from boats into the stormy seas and challenged to race to dry land. Swimmers, if they trained at all, often trained in the sea or other open stretches of water and few seemed yet to have discovered that, if you lifted your arms out of the water alternately to propel yourself along, you could swim much faster. It was, apparently, the great Hawaiian swimmer, Duke Kahanamoku, who 'invented' the over arm crawl and used it to great effect in his swimming victories in Stockholm and Antwerp. However, in 1912 most of the pentathletes 'employed the trudgeon stroke' (a kind of side stroke with only one arm clearing the surface of the water) and the rest the breast stroke, probably with the head rarely dipping below the surface.

Nowadays, the first focus of the budding pentathlete is swimming. Learning to swim is like learning a new language; if you don't do it while you're young, you'll never master it. Anyone can learn to shoot, fence and ride to a reasonable level; some have even mastered running from very mediocre beginnings. But swimming is the qualifying event for a beginner in the modern sport. Interestingly, Sweden learned this quite rapidly; both Sven Thofelt and Wille Grut, the greats of Swedish pentathlon came from a swimming background. Not so the 1912 competitors.

The British pentathlete, Ralph Clilverd won the 300m swim in 4:58.4, an appallingly slow time by modern standards but understandable from the circumstances already described. The Austrian, Edmond Bernhardt, who was 2nd in 5:03.6, also represented his country in swimming, making Clilverd's swim all the more remarkable. Godfree finished a creditable 6th, though a full minute behind his compatriot but Durant managed to take more than 10 minutes to swim his 300m! He didn't take the wooden spoon though. That honour went to Vilhelm Laybourn (DEN) who at 12:09.6 would probably have been grateful to have been thrown a wooden spoon as a float.

The fencing event took two days to complete. It involved 351 bouts, each of them settled by the best of 5 (first to 3). All bouts, of course, were judged in the old-fashioned pre-electric 'steam' style by a president and his four assistants. This involved two judges on each side watching for hits landing on the fencer facing them. Each judge had one vote and the President (referee) one and a half votes in deciding whether each hit had been made or not. This is a far slower process than electric judging and partly explains the two days the event took to complete. By the start of this third event, only 27 remained in the competition. The winner of the fencing, Åke Grönhagen (SWE) won a remarkable 24 of his 26 bouts. The second placed fencer, a Frenchman, Jean, Comte de Mas Latrie, was only one victory behind him on 23 wins, with another Swede, James Stranne on 21 and Capt. George Patton of the USA on 20 to take 3rd and 4th places respectively.

A Swedish journalist wrote elegantly of his view of the fencing event that: 'Lt. Stranne and, in a still higher degree, a French representative, Comte de Mas Latrie, were more aggressive and lively in their work, yet without being wanting in watchfulness and in attention to the carriage of their weapons.'

The British trio placed 7th (Durant), 9th (Clilverd) and 17th (Godfree), Godfree, the 1908 and 1912 GB Sabre fencer, obviously having a bad two days in the fencing.

1912 Stockholm: The Comte de Mas Latrie (FRA) and future war hero, George Patton (USA) fight it out. Note the judges' positions and the elegance of the spectators in the background.

The BOA (British Olympic Association) Report on the Games, although stridently partisan in its tone, made no comment on our pentathletes' fencing. Not so the fencing report which whined 'we suffered somewhat by the rules and, it is believed, by the judging'. Since the Stockholm authorities had kindly allowed Clilverd to come out to Stockholm two weeks before the Games began in order to practice his fencing at the local clubs, this was perhaps a mean-spirited complaint.

So, after three events, the leaders were Georg de Laval (15 points), Gösta Lilliehöök (18 points), and Gösta Åsbrink (20 points), these three Swedes destined to be the medal winners but not in that order. Only just behind them on 22 points, however, was the best Briton, Ralph Clilverd.

The 5000m Cross-country riding event took place at Barkarby in North Stockholm. The majority of the competitors had brought their own horses. Two of the British trio had their horses sent out in advance, taking advantage of the Swedish authorities' generous covering of all costs while the horses were on Swedish soil. Only Ralph Clilverd, who lacked full military credentials, had to rely on the loan of a horse and this was to be a major disadvantage to him. There were 17 obstacles in all, made up of fences, ditches and bridges. No fewer that 13 of the 27 riders held onto their 100 point starting scores with no penalty. Ironically, since the organisers had intended to play down the time taken as a factor, the final order was dependent on speed.

Not surprisingly, the Swedes dominated with Grönhagen, Mannström, Georg de Laval and Lilliehöök taking the first four places, Grönhagen's winning time being 9:04.4. Only one man took longer than the 15 minute time allowed and that was Ralph Clilverd, the leading British pentathlete who had done so well in the first three events. As so often happens with unknown horses, it was one jump that caused all the trouble. Jump number eight lost Clilverd 37 points alone. He lost 20 further penalty points for exceeding the time limit. The BOA Report bitterly announced that Clilverd 'would have been placed much higher in the total if the horse provided for him by the Swedish Committee had been better,' although one wonders why he was not provided with a British military horse like the other two members of the team. Durant and Godfree, on their own mounts, were timed at 10:00.4 and 11:43.9 respectively. Georg de Laval, the eldest of three brothers in the competition, now led the field on 18 points, quite comfortably ahead of his fellow Swedes, Lilliehöök (22 points), the eventual winner, and Grönhagen (25 points).

The final running event produced such appalling times (between 19 and 24 minutes for 4000m) that commentators have sought to find an explanation. Yes, it was a hot day but a hot day in a Scandinavian country so that can hardly have been an excuse. The run began inside the stadium and was an out-and-back course through the immediate area of North Stockholm. The 1912 British Olympic Report claims that it was an 'extremely tough' course which was 'especially hard for the British runners who were not used to these hills'. Apart from this being a dismal preface to the great tradition of tough British running, it has to be pointed out, too, that the suburbs of Stockholm are not noted for their Himalayan topography. And while in the swimming pool it's true that the standards of the best swimmers in the world at this time were poor, it was far less true for running standards in which track times were entirely respectable. For instance, the British athlete who won the 1500m in Stockholm was timed at 3:56.8.

There are several reasons why the running appears to have been so poor and they don't have much to do with weather conditions or hills. Firstly, consider de Coubertin's comment that 'for a cavalry officer...to run cross country on foot, would almost amount to a debasement!' The competitors in the 1912 Modern Pentathlon were all pretty much cavalry officers or, at least, of equivalent disposition. It was possibly a matter of class to leave running to others while the real chaps hunted big game, played polo and fought duels. Secondly, there was no walk around the course beforehand and, apparently, no markers on the course itself. Competitors were given a map immediately before the start and had to calculate their way round. This would have been essentially orienteering without compasses! Photographs of the runners in the Stockholm event, however, do not show any maps clutched in the hand although the effects of the pleasant summer's day do show clearly on the faces. It seems unlikely that runners were left completely in the dark about the route, though. Thirdly, the course was said to be 'about 4000 metres in length'. It is likely that it was very much longer. As pointed out earlier, the exact distance will not have been a crucial issue and if the natural undulations around the stadium could have been put to more aesthetic use by adding a few hundred metres, that is likely to have been the outcome.

George Patton apparently 'started like a 100 yard sprinter but it was only by the employment of an incredible degree of energy that he managed to stagger past the tape'. He had been given a dose of 'hop' or pure opium immediately before the start and fainted at the

1912 Stockholm: Ake Grönhagen (SWE), the winner of the cross-country running.

end of the race. Having risked his life in this way, he took several hours to come round fully. The eventual winner on 19:00.9 was Gösta Åsbrink who hauled himself into the silver medal position with this run. Nils Haeggström (SWE) was 2nd and George Patton's incredible stagger got him into 3rd place. However, it was Gösta Lilliehöök's quiet 5th place in the run that won him the gold medal and lasting glory. Georg de Laval, who had had such a good lead after 4 events but slipped to 12th in the run, salvaged a bronze medal overall. In the official result presented some time afterwards, the British competitors were placed as follows: Godfree 10th, Clilverd 11th and Durant 18th.

If there had been a team competition and each team had consisted of three competitors and Sweden had been allowed to enter only one team (instead of four), the British team would have got the silver medal ahead of the only other complete finishing team, Russia. Sadly, team competitions didn't begin until 1952 so team glory in 1912 is merely a figment of eager imagination.

The first lady competitor?

The story of the 1912 Olympic Modern Pentathlon would not be complete without some account of the extraordinary tale of 15 year old British girl, Helen Preece. Helen was the darling of the show-jumping circuit. Even two years before, reports of the Horse Show at Olympia in *The Times* (June 18, 1910) recorded that: 'The riding of little Helen Preece was beyond all praise. It is not often we see such beautiful hands, or so much determination and judgment displayed by a girl of barely 14.' She drew 'the wildest enthusiasm from the audience' and, in November 1911, went on to win the $1000 gold cup at the Madison

Square Horse Show in New York, gaining herself an army of fans on both sides of the Atlantic.

It was an American newspaper, the *Louisville Herald* that broke the story of Helen's application to compete at the Modern Pentathlon in Stockholm. In those days private entries were possible. The article appeared on July 6th 1912, only the day before the first event took place and it reported confidently that Helen Preece had 'entered for several contests' but that her real ambition was to 'carry off the first prize in the great competition' – the Modern Pentathlon. Miss Preece is quoted as saying:

'I have obtained special leave of absence from my school in Hertfordshire, and my day's work now commences as early as 5 o'clock every morning, and only ends with bedtime at 8 o'clock. A varied program is mapped out for me each day, but it always includes riding, shooting, swimming, running and walking practice, and today I have been put on a special diet, also, so that I should be absolutely fit for the Pentathlon on July 11.'

She would have been four days late if she had turned up on the 11th but, in any case, she never competed. Her case would have roused widespread media controversy today but in 1912, the gentlemen of the Swedish Olympic Committee decided to reject her application which had been forwarded by the Reverend Laffan to the Swedish authorities. No grounds for refusal were ever given and what became of Helen Preece remains a mystery. Laffan's letter had said that, since only gentlemen may take part in Horse competitions, he assumed that would bar Preece from the Modern Pentathlon. He also pointed out, however, that swimming and tennis were already admitting ladies so some kind of precedent had been set. De Coubertin made his own position quite clear: 'I am personally opposed to admittance of ladies as competitors in the Olympic Games' but left the decision to the Swedish Organising Committee.

It was Kristian Hellström, the Secretary of the committee who reported that, at a meeting on 14th May 1912, the committee had decided 'not to admit ladies in the Modern Pentathlon'. No reason was given. Had the committee been under greater pressure to admit her, they might have cited the rule that demanded that all requests to ride horses provided by the organisers had to have been submitted by 1st April 1912 and that her application had come too late. In the event, the Stockholm games operated on such an ad hoc basis, such a ruling would probably have eliminated many of the gentlemen competitors, too. It was expedient, then, to give no reasons. De Coubertin, nevertheless, couldn't resist showing his personal involvement in the controversy while still managing to pass the buck when it came to making a decision. He wrote later in the *Revue Olympique*: 'The other day an application came signed by a neo-Amazon who wanted to compete in the Modern Pentathlon and the Swedish Committee, who was left free to decide in the absence of fixed legislation, refused that application.'

Two years later, at a meeting of the Modern Pentathlon Council of the BOA, it was noted that 'an application had again been received' from Mr. Ambrose Preece, Helen's father and a Job Master and Stable Manager. He asked once more about 'the possibility of ladies being eligible for the Modern Pentathlon Competition'. The response was that 'the Council disapproves of such a suggestion' and, furthermore, insisted that the BOA delegate to the Paris Congress of the IOC 'must oppose' such an idea. The motion was proposed by a Mr. Fowler-Dixon and seconded by Mr. Harold Fern, the man who was to go on to become President of FINA, the international swimming federation and serve as Secretary of the ASA for 50 years. Women swimmers had been admitted to the Olympic Games for the first time in 1912.

British Developments after Stockholm

The excitement of Olympic representation produced a welcome burst of interest in the sport after 1912. The Modern Pentathlon Committee of the BOA reported to the BOA Council Meeting several times in the summers of 1913 and 1914. In anticipation of preparations for the 1916 Berlin Games, they devised a scheme of selection. There were to be standards set in each event by the five different sports authorities. A 1st class standard would be worth three points, 2nd Class two points, and 3rd class one. In order to be considered a 'possibility', a pentathlete had to achieve a total of nine points over the five events. However, the committee still reserved the right to invite any athlete they thought had potential regardless of how he performed in the tests. They would begin this selection process during the winter months and, with touching optimism, asked the BOA to fund the scheme to the tune of £500, a massive sum of money in 1913.

Unfortunately, since Maj. Gen. Allenby of the Army Council refused military support, in the following year they were obliged to seek the use of the RAC club and Hurst Park facilities for their trials and revised their funding application down to £100. Had war not broken out a few months later, we may have been on the verge of a genuinely civilian participation in the sport but these best-laid plans were thwarted. Nevertheless, the advertisement placed in the BOA Report of 1912 had been an enticing one:

'The BOA Committee is charged with the discovery, selection, and preparation of candidates who are able to show sufficient reason for the consideration of their claims to be competitors representing Great Britain at the Olympic Games of Berlin in 1916 and appeals to all those who think of offering themselves as candidates for inclusion in the British Team for this event to communicate with the Secretary of the British Olympic Council, 108 Victoria Street, London SW.'

The Coming War

Since Berlin had been awarded the next Olympic Games in 1916, de Coubertin went to extraordinary lengths to deny that World War One might interfere with these plans. Long after hostilities had broken out, he persisted in the notion that the spirit of Olympic competition would heal all wounds. The temperamental de Coubertin seems to have had the good fortune of being managed by calmer members of the IOC committee throughout his life, friends to whom he would write letters revealing secret plots against himself. Among his confidantes was the Reverend Laffan who had tried to act as go-between in several delicate negotiations.

One of these involved the resignation of Theodore Cook from the IOC. Cook, an avid sportsman himself and the editor of *The Field* magazine, no longer felt he could represent the IOC if they were to persist in ignoring

German aggression to plan the Berlin meeting. Cook had no desire to embarrass de Coubertin and was quite happy not to publish his resignation but de Coubertin's paranoia could only see treachery everywhere he looked. He wrote to Laffan: 'You know what bitter enemies I have in France, you are aware of their recent attacks. What a luck for them to take hold of such a document as Mr. Cook's letter (of resignation). If it was published I would have to face an awful campaign of jealousy, hatred and contempt.' Having already explained Cook's position to de Coubertin, the normally placid Laffan became forceful in defending Cook despite risking his friendship with de Coubertin. Fortunately, no lasting harm was done.

It was clear that the Germans were proposing several changes to the Modern Pentathlon in Berlin. Sigfrid Edström (1870-1964), who was later to become IOC President (1942-1952) himself and another supportive friend to de Coubertin, wrote to the Baron in May 1914 to express his concerns:

'At Stockholm we arranged the Modern Pentathlon so that it gave the same chances to any gentleman, whether he was a military man or not. Thus the duel shooting was arranged with ordinary dueling pistols. Now Germany proposes that this shall be altered and army revolvers be used. If this is carried through it means a competition on an unequal basis, for the army revolvers of the various countries are very different. In fact, it will mean a competition not between the individuals but between the various systems of army revolvers used in the different armies. Furthermore, Germany proposes an addition re the riding competitions of the Modern Pentathlon, viz: that a single program of <u>fancy riding</u> should be added.'

Edström had also been a supporter of the compromise in 1912 which had allowed some pentathletes to ride their own horses. As it turned, out, however, the Olympic Games would not come to Berlin for a further 20 years. This did not prevent great eagerness being expressed by the Germans at the prospect of organising the games. Friedrich Karl of Prussia, winner of a Team Riding bronze medal in 1912, was so enthusiastic that he and 100 of his officers organised a big Pentathlon competition in 1914. This competition was won by Friedrich Karl himself. We will never know how good an athlete he might have become because he died in a French military hospital after being shot down. Just before dying, he wrote home to tell his family of the great kindness he had been afforded by his Australian captors.

The 1912 Games would be the last time that riders were allowed to bring their own horses. The Stockholm Olympic Games took place in an innocent age before catastrophic world events changed things forever.

Chapter Two: 1920-1928

"If Barton had won the riding, and with a bit of luck he might easily have done so, our team would have been easily second." BOA Report 1924.

The 1920s was a period of slow recovery after a devastating World War. Almost miraculously, three Olympic Games were held in Antwerp (1920), Paris (1924) and Amsterdam (1928) despite the debilitated state of much of Europe. It was the period in which the Modern Pentathlon Association of Great Britain was established and the first British Championship contested. Among those pentathletes who had survived the Great War, there was often an eccentric ebullience that has given us some real 'characters' to celebrate.

Antwerp 1920 – the organisation

There was much opposition to the holding of the Games in 1920. They had been awarded to Antwerp as a tribute to the Belgians' heroic struggle in the war but it was the gift of a poisoned chalice. The organising committee went bankrupt and many teams complained about the threadbare nature of accommodation and facilities. The Belgian committee couldn't even produce a report afterwards. Indeed it wasn't until 1957 that the Belgians cobbled together some kind of report from the documents left behind.

In Great Britain, there was a strong feeling that, since so many fine young athletes had died in the war, it was too soon to hold an Olympics. The acceptance letter to the IOC was apparently sent by mistake and the Reverend Laffan was among the minority who believed we should maintain a presence at the Games. The British government refused to contribute any money at all to the funding of the team and, by the end of April 1920, of the £30,000 public subscription target, a mere £1,700 had been collected. By comparison, the USA had raised $163,000 and provided a ship to take the athletes to Europe. France, Sweden, Italy and Spain all sent well-funded teams. By the time of the Games in August, however, over 250 British athletes went to Antwerp on funds that ran to no more than a total of £3000. The BOA came back with a deficit of £985 –so poor, in fact, that there was no official report because the BOA couldn't afford the paper to print it on. The newspapers reported only the bare results of the events without any embellishment and this despite the fact that Great Britain gained the third best medal haul behind Sweden and the USA. Germany, Hungary, Austria, Bulgaria, and Turkey, as the losers in the recent war, were not invited.

The British team

Teams in the Modern Pentathlon in Antwerp were now limited to a maximum of four from each country and, after 'Eliminating Tests' in Aldershot held between June 30th and July 2nd, the British Modern Pentathlon team selected was Edward Clarke, Hugh Boustead, Thomas Wand-Tetley, and Edward Gedge. Clarke was a Squadron Leader in the RAF and, at 31, comfortably the oldest, the others being 25, 22, and 24 respectively, and all army officers. When a meeting was held three years later (Sept 11th, 1923) at the Army School of Physical Training in Aldershot, members of the 1920 team had the chance to explain some of the difficulties they had faced. The purpose of the meeting was to prepare for the 1924 Games the following year and Captain Clarke (now of the East Surrey Regiment, and later to rise to the rank of Lieutenant Colonel), Captain Boustead and Captain Wand-Tetley were there to give their versions of the Antwerp experience in 1920. They regretted that they had only had three months notice of the event and that they had arrived in Antwerp only two or three days before the competition began which prevented them from:

stretching their legs over a piece of the country they might have to run across;

(ii) walking a line of country they might have to ride across and taking stock of the type of fence they might have to jump in the point to point;
(iii) taking swimming practice in the actual pool in which the swimming event took place.

They also had complaints about the shooting event:

'The Webley revolver was used in practice, it being understood that each country had to use its own service weapon. This was not so because any pattern revolver could be used: consequently if the team had practised and shot with the same revolver which, for example, the Swedes used (Smith and Wesson 0.22), the results obtained would have been far better than those obtained with the actual weapon used. Further, for some unknown reason, the actual target used in the competition was not used in practice and consequently our men were at a great disadvantage compared with other countries which had practised all through with the target used in competition.'

Interestingly, the team were quite wrong to make the additional claim that: 'this was the first time Great Britain had entered the competition. Consequently the team lacked that confidence that is born of experience.' To be oblivious to the efforts of our team in Stockholm in 1912 suggests a want of education. Little did our 1920 team know, however, that by making the effort to take part in Antwerp, they enabled Great Britain to maintain an unbroken representation at the Olympic Games to the present day.

1920 Olympic Games: Antwerp (BEL)

The competition in Antwerp took place from 24th to 27th August 1920 which suggests the shooting and swimming may have taken place together on the opening day. The order (shoot, swim, fence, ride, run) remained the same as in Stockholm but there were some organisational differences. The uncertainty expressed by the British team about what conditions they might have to face was probably quite widespread among all competitors. Only 23 entered the competition in Antwerp but 22 finished. There was, then, greater commitment to the competition than might have been seen in 1912 when many dropped out to participate in other sports, having 'had a go' at this new sport. Only Sweden, Denmark and Great Britain provided teams of four; France entered three, USA, Finland and Norway two each; and there was a single entry from Italy. There was far less involvement in other sports this time by the pentathletes; two fenced for their country - our own Thomas Wand-Tetley fenced foil as did Harold Rayner (USA) who won a Team Foil bronze medal, and the only Finn in the competition, Kalle Kainuvaara, went on to compete in the diving in which he had also participated in 1912. Only two of the competitors in 1920 had also competed in 1912. They were the eventual silver medallist, Erik de Laval (SWE), younger brother of Georg, the 1912 bronze medallist, and the Frenchman, Georges Brulé who, at 43, was the oldest competitor in Antwerp. Thomas Wand-Tetley at 22 was the youngest competitor.

Once again, Sweden dominated, taking the top four places in the competition. The Swedish Olympic report for 1920 noted that their fourth man, the powerfully-built Bengt Uggla would have done so much better had he not been hit on the cheek by a discharged cartridge just as he was about to fire.

The three medallists were head and shoulders above the rest of the field, there being 19 position points between third and fourth place. The 28 year old champion, Gustav Dyrssen, was embarking on a glittering career in 1920. He went on to gain a silver medal in the 1924 Games, a further team silver medal in Epée in 1936, won four National Fencing titles, including one at the age of 61, and was President of the UIPM for 21 years (1949-60). He was a Lieutenant-General in the Swedish army and commanded the Stockholm area for many years as well as being an IOC committee member. The Swedes were already discovering the value of a good run-swim. The wonder boy in this respect was 23 year old bronze medallist, Gösta Runö who, at 4:35.8, won the swimming event by over a minute from second-placed Dyrssen, himself a relatively strong run-swimmer. Runö also took the run in 14:09.4, the medallists all filling the top three places in that event. Sadly, Gösta Runö was only to live for a further two years. He died when the wing of his aircraft broke off during an acrobatics display. His memorial stone is now in the Swedish Air Force Museum.

The standard of shooting in Antwerp appears to have been very low indeed. The British complaints mentioned earlier may well explain some of this but, as well as the muddle over targets and weapons, the Belgian organisers inexplicably decided that the turning time for the targets should be reduced from three to two seconds per shot. It is quite possible that competitors arrived at the competition quite unaware of this change. The top score was only 181 by de Laval and no fewer than 15 of the competitors failed to achieve scores above 150. This included the entire British team.

The fencing was won by Jean Mondielli (FRA), though Dyrssen, the eventual champion, came 2nd. De Laval, winner of the shoot, also won the riding event in 9:35.2 and the times recorded suggest the course was somewhat shorter and easier than the Stockholm riding event had been for which 15 minutes had been set as the target. The original aim of the riding event had been that speed should play a minor role in the final result, speed being largely a measure of the individual capability of each horse. However, in both Stockholm and Antwerp the result was very much decided by time and this pattern was now set for the future.

It is claimed that the fencing event at all three Olympic Games in the 1920s was organised in pools with a semi-final and final. This was certainly true in Paris and Amsterdam but it seems very unlikely from the fencing position points that this was actually the case in Antwerp – there are no shared positions in the final fencing results which is one of the inevitable results of the pool system if no barrages for shared position take place. Barrages took place in Amsterdam but not in Paris. Much more likely was that the competition was a round robin as in Stockholm with each fencer taking on all the others in turn. The brevity of the competition suggests that the fencing event certainly wasn't as protracted as in Stockholm where the fencing took two days to complete and each bout was fought to the best of five. An allowance of five minutes per bout also persisted until after World War II which would also have made the event difficult to finish rapidly. Possibly Antwerp was the first occurrence of the one-hit competition as round robin. At the time, a double hit which occurs when both opponents hit each other simultaneously was counted as a double defeat. Since this was judged by the human eye rather than by electronic methods, it may well have been a controversial judgement at times. We do not know how often the double defeat was given in Antwerp but four years later in Paris no fewer than 32 double defeats were decided. In later years, when electronic judging developed, a double defeat was only recorded if fencers exceeded the time limit of three minutes without a decisive hit.

Two characters

Though the British team performed indifferently in Antwerp (Clarke 11th, Boustead 15th, Wand-Tetley 17th; Gedge 21st), it was a team that produced two very interesting characters. Firstly, Brigadier Thomas Wand-Tetley, CBE (1898-1956) had spent his war years as a prisoner of war during which time he studied various methods of physical training. Ending his army career as

Inspector of Physical Training, he developed many of the systems that prepared soldiers for physical fitness. He was particularly successful in developing the fitness of those who had been seen as failures in this respect elsewhere. He fenced foil for Great Britain in the 1920 and 1928 Olympic Games and was among those instrumental in setting up the sport of Modern Pentathlon in Britain between the wars.

Secondly, Colonel Sir Hugh Boustead, KBE, CMG, DSO, MC.(1895-1980) was another extraordinary man. He was serving in the Royal Navy in the Mediterranean when he heard of the death of his brother who had been fighting in France. He was so incensed that he deserted his post and travelled to South Africa where he joined a regiment that he knew would be heading for the fighting in France. Having made it to the battleground, he set about avenging his brother's death so effectively that he was commissioned and awarded the MC for his bravery. After the war he joined the Cossacks in Russia to fight against the Bolsheviks before captaining the Modern Pentathlon team in Antwerp. In his later career, he commanded the Sudan Camel Corps, climbed Mount Everest in 1933, expelled the Italians from Ethiopia and became a distinguished diplomat in the Middle East. His wonderful autobiography *The Wind of Morning* (Chatto and Windus 1971) is a Boys' Own Paper romp of the finest kind. In this excerpt he describes one evening in 1920 when he was a student at Worcester College, Oxford just before the Olympics:

'A splendid term ended with a memorable evening at the Commem Ball at Trinity with some enchanting young Danish girls. As luck would have it, I was called for by the President of the Imperial Boxing Association to fight that same night at the Holborn stadium. My fight was put on early as I had told the President I had to get back to Oxford... My Frenchman was a good deal heavier but rather fat, and I was able to knock him out in the third round, to an enthusiastic response. I hared off to Paddington and changed in the train into white tie and tail coat. I hadn't been marked in the bout... We danced till the sun was up, had bacon and eggs for breakfast and then went down to the Cherwell for a bathe.

A few days later I went to Aldershot for the Pentathlon trials. I was selected and asked to captain the team. We practised hard, ending up with a few days at Aldeburgh where we attracted some attention fencing with the epée on the front, the only suitable place I could find. In August we travelled to Antwerp for the Games but were beaten in all the Pentathlon events by the Swedes who had been training for it since the previous Olympics in 1912.'

The birth of the British Modern Pentathlon Association

British Modern Pentathlon as a formal organisation arose out of a state of embarrassment. The officers involved were well aware that, though they had attended the 1920 Games, British pentathletes had been under prepared, poorly supported and deserved better. In the autumn of 1923 a number of meetings took place to remedy this situation. At one such meeting at the BOA headquarters, 166 Picadilly, London on the afternoon of 5th November 1923 the proposal was made that there should be an application to the BOA for recognition and affiliation of the Modern Pentathlon Association. In all 1923 meetings, the minutes had been those of the 'Pentathlon

Committee'. By the first meeting of 1924 (28th January at Aldershot), the minutes bore the headline 'The Modern Pentathlon Association' for the first time.

Although the early development of the sport was necessarily a military exercise, the committee, even from the time of the 'Antwerp Post-Mortem meeting' on 11th September 1923 was all-inclusive in its brief. It felt that the military bodies should be involved: Navy, Army, RAF, the military training academies, but that the Police, the Civil Service and Oxford and Cambridge should also be included. Despite that willingness to involve everybody, it was the Aldershot Command that got things going. At a general meeting in October 1923 intended for those interested in Modern Pentathlon, no fewer than 48 officers attended. Col. AEW Harman, CB, DSO, the Chairman, explained the rules and there was great goodwill expressed from those in the different sports willing to offer their facilities and expertise. Col. RB Campbell, CBE, DSO, the manager of the 1920 team, arranged fencing facilities for anyone who wanted them, assured everyone that the costs for the 1924 Olympic team would be borne by the BOA and that entry to the sport was open to all ranks. When the subject of being excused regimental duty to train came up, Campbell was less generous; he 'pointed out that the keen man would always find time to train'. This clash in military circles between an officer's duty to his job and his desire to improve his sporting ability was inevitable and it was to be many years before the notion of full-time pentathlon training within the military world would be supported.

At a further 1923 meeting less than two weeks later, there were indeed representatives of the Police and of

Oxford University present. It was a very ambitious start: the general Committee would have representatives from all the invited organisations and there would be training centres set up in London, Aldershot, Tidworth, Oxford, Cambridge, Edinburgh and York. The first Pentathlon Championship would take place in March or April of 1924. In order to promote the sport, the organisers were keen to have medals struck to make awards for those who achieved various standards. This appeared to be more important than declaring an individual winner. The various Commands were instructed to hold high-speed competitions arranged, not with the athlete in mind, but according to the complexity of organisation. Thus, the programme would be: Day One: shoot, ride, run, swim. Day Two: fence. The standards were set for the various awards and named, in rising order, Standard, First Class and Special. Anyone attaining 'Special' would certainly have been a contender for the Olympic team. As a recruiting method, this approach has always been successful and various badge schemes in the ensuing years are testament to this.

The key players in this early development were Colonel RB Campbell (Chairman), Lieutenant LH Churcher (Secretary & Treasurer) with Lt.Col.ELW Henslow, MC, Capt. Walter Palmer, MC, and Capt FA Hewat, MC also in regular attendance. They chased up the reports from local Commands, bought two new Webley revolvers and 500 rounds of ammunition for the team and waited patiently for the arrival from the BOA's contingency fund of £10 per athlete to support the Olympic effort. The first President of the Association was Sir Philip Chetwode, KCB, KCMG, and, when Campbell later resigned as Chairman, Col. CE Heathcote, CB, CMG, DSO, replaced him.

First British Championship

The BOA Report for 1924 makes it clear that 'Centres were established at London, Edinburgh, Aldershot, York and Tidworth and for the first time in this country a championship called the Modern Pentathlon Championship of Great Britain was held'. This took place on May 20th and 21st 1924 in Aldershot and was the selection event for the Paris Olympics. Despite the efforts of the organisers to include athletes from every walk of life, only Army personnel and Sandhurst military cadets took part. The event was won by a Captain Horrocks (1895-1985), a man who was to become one of the legends of military history. Lt. General Sir Brian Horrocks, KCB, KBE, DSO, MC, LLD, as he was later to be titled, was Field Marshall Montgomery's right-hand man in North Africa in the Second World War and a man of great warmth and charm. His wonderfully entertaining autobiography, *A Full Life* (1960) includes a photograph of the 1924 British Championship competitors (16 of them) together with this account of his involvement:

'I was fortunate enough to win the championships in this country and so was selected with three others to represent Great Britain in the Olympic games which were held in Paris that year. For four months we were struck off all duties in order to train and at the end of this period I was superbly fit but the standard of performance in Paris was so high that I finished well down the order of merit.

Unlike certain other international contests this particular event seems to spread a spirit of friendship and co-operation among the competitors – a very important factor in the shrinking world of today.

At the conclusion of these 1924 Olympic games an international party was taken round Paris by one of the young French competitors in the modern pentathlon. He kept on looking at us anxiously and saying: 'Tell me-what really interests you, gentlemen?' As we had been in strict training for six months it was difficult to decide what forbidden fruit to sample first. Anyhow, it was a truly memorable night which resulted, I am afraid, in my running dead last in the final of the army mile a week later – much to the disgust of my regiment.'

Horrocks touches here on one of the most important qualities that Modern Pentathlon has fostered throughout its 100 year history – that of friendship and co-operation. The peculiar challenges of the sport bind together the athletes in an understanding that has always meant that a British pentathlete at an Olympic Games is likely to feel closer to a foreign pentathlete, that doesn't even speak the same language as he does, than he would to a fellow British competitor from another sport. The willingness to share advice about unknown horses, to lend equipment and coaching tips without regard to the advantage it might give in the competition has always been paramount. Horrocks echoes this sentiment elsewhere in his autobiography when he is talking about the rapport that existed between himself and his German captor but he might just as well be referring to the camaraderie of sport:

'All front-line troops have a respect for each other, but the further from the front you get, the more bellicose and beastly the people become. I have always regarded the forward area of the battlefield as the most exclusive club in the world, inhabited by the cream of the nation's manhood – the men who actually do the fighting.

Comparatively few in number, they have little feeling of hatred for the enemy –rather the reverse.'

Horrocks' great skill was his ability to communicate which made him popular as a soldier and, in retirement, as a TV presenter of military programmes. He, like Boustead, had fought against the Bolsheviks, having learned Russian as a prisoner-of-war. In later years, he was a familiar figure as Black Rod in the Opening of Parliament.

Horrocks was a comfortable winner of the first British Championship – 22 position points compared to 30 by the runner-up Lt. Scott. *The Times* recorded the first ten positions explaining that the first four would be selected for Paris. Since Paris was so easy to get to, however, a full squad of eight pentathletes, a Manager (Lt. Henry Churcher) and a Trainer (QMSI S.Usher) travelled. Though Lt. DFC Scott was 2nd and Lt. HV Kearon 4th in the trial, the team was made up of Horrocks (aged 28), David Turquand-Young (Gentleman Cadet from Sandhurst and 3rd in the competition at the age of 19), Sgt. Maj. George Vokins (aged 28) and Lt. Frederick Barton (aged 24), both of whom had shared 5th place in the national competition. As well as Scott and Kearon, the traveling reserves included Lt. HN Charrington and Lt. WA Goddard.

Besides Horrocks, the other great character in the team was David Turquand-Young, DSC (1904-84) or 'Turkey' as he was known. He was later to go on to win the British Championship in 1928 and compete in his second Olympics where he finished a very creditable 6th, an achievement not to be improved upon by a British pentathlete at the Olympics until 1972. However, 'Turkey' was even more famous as an international rugby player. He played for England five times in 1928-9 as second row, a position usually reserved for the heaviest of players. He went on to fight with honour in World War II as a Lt. Commander in the Navy. Perhaps his immortality was best assured, though, by his caricature appearing on one of the Wills's cigarette cards, sought after by every schoolboy in England. The picture is of an elegant pencil-moustached man-about-town who exudes a casual confidence. The back of the card reads:

'D. Turquand-Young, a good-looking, whole-hearted forward, and an England player in 1928 and 1929 is 6ft. 1 in. in height. This makes him particularly useful at the line-out and he applies nearly 13 st. weight in the scrum. He is a real 'goer' in the open, fast, tireless and always on the ball. Known everywhere as 'Turkey,' he was at one time an officer in the Royal Tank Corps and played for The Army. He is now in business, and during the season 1928-9 acted as captain of the Richmond XV., who profited by his skill and enthusiasm.'

Since Turquand-Young had left the army to work for his father's firm of Chartered Accountants by 1928, like Clilverd in 1912, he was the second British civilian competitor. However, it was to be very many years before anyone could truly claim such a state, such was the utter reliance on the military to organize everything. Well into the 1980s, civilians were dependent to a very large extent on military facilities and organization for their sporting opportunities.

Managing the rules

To honour the retiring President of the IOC, Baron de Coubertin, the 1924 Olympic Games were held in Paris.

De Coubertin had already learned to live with changes to his original conception of the five events but he baulked, as did many others, at the way in which the hosts of each new Olympic Games seemed to feel entitled to adjust events to match their own views of Modern Pentathlon. There was a danger that this constant meddling with the sport by each new Olympic Organising Committee would spin out of control. Modern Pentathlon really needed its own international federation so that rules could be established and sustained by a committee that had the interests of Modern Pentathlon at heart and had not just been seconded from one of the component sports. Although the IOC was ultimately in charge of organising the competition every four years, the constituent members had many other duties to attend to beside the Modern Pentathlon.

The first attempt to deal with this problem did not occur until just before the 1928 Games in Amsterdam. The formation of CIPMO (Comité Internationale du Pentathlon Moderne Olimpique) at least gave the sport's administration to a separate IOC committee. This new committee was made up of two IOC members, two representatives from each of the five constituent sports and a secretary and treasurer. The first committee consisted of five Frenchmen, three Swedes, two Hungarians, an American, a Belgian (new President of the IOC, Henri de Baillet-Latour) a Dutchman and a German.

This development was largely inspired by Tor Wibom who became instrumental in blocking impromptu changes proposed by Olympic committees. Wibom was the manager of the victorious Swedish team in Antwerp, Paris, Amsterdam and Los Angeles, and also became the very first President of the UIPM (1948-49). On January 14th 1928, he wrote a letter on behalf of the Swedish Military Sports Federation, inviting officials from Belgium, Denmark, Great Britain, Finland, France, Holland, Italy, Norway, Czechoslovakia, Germany (readmitted to the Games in 1928), and the USA to join his fellow Swedes in this project. In this letter he pointed out that constant modifications of the rules did little to encourage those who had devoted so much time and hard work to competing. He continued:

'But the most serious defect of this lack of stability of the rules of the competition lies in the fact that the different participating countries have never, to my knowledge, had the opportunity to express their views on the desirability of successive changes; it has often been only a few months before the Games that the rules were communicated to them.

It is not only the rules of the shooting event that have been subjected to a variety of changes; but those of the riding event and, recently, those of the cross-country running... Thus, in the shooting event, the period during which the target appears, fixed at three seconds in 1912, was reduced to two seconds in Antwerp and, at the Paris Games, it was decided firstly to fix it at two seconds, then at three seconds, but this latter decision wasn't taken until March 1924, and actually the whole event was recently changed from duelling pistol (with a moving target) to precision pistol (fixed target) where the time allowed (for each shot) is virtually unlimited – one minute per shot.

In the case of the riding course, it is mainly the time allowance that has varied from one competition to the next. There has been a tendency to give exaggerated importance to speed, which, to some extent, depends more on the individual qualities of the horse than in the rider's ability to complete the course...

There are those, too, who would modify the rules of cross-country running in such a way that the start, which formerly took place at one minute intervals between each competitor, would now become groups of four to six runners with an interval of three minutes between each group.'

So Wibom's concerns were really twofold – 1) that the rules be made consistent and decided by the participating countries; 2) that the test of the pentathlete be a test of the individual against the elements as envisaged by de Coubertin rather than a series of races. The struggle to maintain these priorities has, in truth, been with the sport throughout its history. The rapidity of the 2012 one day competition may well have been closer to de Coubertin's original conception of the sport but adaptation has become a necessary feature of survival.

1924 Olympic Games: Paris (FRA)

The 1924 Olympic Modern Pentathlon took place from 12th to 17th July. The shooting was held on the 12th (a Saturday) in Versailles, Sunday was a day off, and Monday was the day for the swimming at the open air 50 metre Tourelles stadium together with the Eliminating round of the Fencing at Colombes. Tuesday concluded the fencing, the riding was on Wednesday in Fontainebleau, and the competition ended on the Thursday with the running over the very fast Hippodrome du Grand Parquet course back in Colombes. The tradition of widespread venues for the pentathlon events was, thus, well-established, the endurance developed over long bus journeys between events being one of the unacknowledged requirements for success in Modern Pentathlon.

Of 41 provisional entries, 38 took part, the Swiss and Argentinian withdrawals leaving 11 countries still represented. There was no official team competition but, had there been, among the seven teams of four, Sweden, France and Great Britain would have placed best. Had three-man teams been recorded, the order would have finished 1) Sweden; 2) Denmark; 3) Finland; 4) France; 5) Great Britain; 6) Netherlands; 7) Belgium; 8) USA; 9) Italy – a very healthy representation of countries at only the third meeting of the sport. This absence of a team event did not put the organisers off; in the Official Report for 1924, each sport is prefaced by the flags of the best three teams. In a fairly random system, the Modern Pentathlon team result is based on the first six individual placings -ten points for 1st and five, four, three, two and one for the remainder. This gave the order: 1) Sweden 19 points; 2) France 3 points; 3) Finland 2 points.

The individual competition was won by the 25 year old Swede, Bo Lindman, by a sensational gap of 21.5 placing points over the silver medallist, the reigning Olympic Champion, Gustav Dryssen. Only the great Wille Grut (1948) has beaten the rest of the field by a greater margin than Lindman did. Like his predecessor, Dyrssen, Lindman went on to take the silver medal at the next Olympics to make way for the next Swedish champion and repeated this position in 1932 where he also fenced in the Swedish epée team. One might almost think that these great Swedish pentathletes were too gentlemanly to win twice in a row and did the decent thing by conceding their titles to a fellow Swede at the next occasion while still, nevertheless, putting on an impressive show. Like Dyrssen, too, Bo Lindman, by then Lt. Col. Lindman, went on to serve the sport by being Treasurer and then Secretary of CIPMO at the crucial stage of the formation of the UIPM at Sandhurst in 1948.

It wasn't all plain sailing for Lindman and Dyrssen, however. Both men shot poorly to begin the competition in only 9th and 20th positions (170 and 160). Once again, the quality of shooting was very poor. Otto Olsen (DEN) won with a meagre 186. One feature of the shooting at that time was that the number of shots on target was a greater deciding factor than the final total. This meant, for instance, that Turquand-Young (GBR), who put no shots off but achieved a mediocre 168 total finished 10th whereas Marius Christensen (DEN) who put one shot off, finished 12th even with a better overall total of 170. Spare a thought, though, for the two Czechs, Karel Tuma and Jindrich Lepiere, who finished in the last two places overall and managed target totals of only 68 and 55 out of 200, Lepiere having 14 shots off-target out of 20. Look on these two men kindly, however, as taking the first faltering steps towards the huge success that the Czech pentathletes enjoy today.

The standard of swimming remained very poor in Paris. Lindman's time of 5:18.6 was good enough to win but was still 20 seconds slower than the British pentathlete, Clilverd, had achieved in Stockholm in 1912. Dyrssen was in 4th place and Turquand-Young, just three weeks past his 20th birthday and the baby of the competition, came in 3rd. Only nine men swam faster than six minutes. Lepiere (TCH) once again took the wooden spoon with a time of 8:49.8.

The fencing event was underway the same day as the swimming and fencers were initially drawn in four pools of nine or ten fencers, the top five in each qualifying for the semi-finals. Each semi-final allowed five men to progress to the final and contest the top ten places. This rather cumbersome process with its inevitable barrages (play-offs) and sharing of position points surprisingly remained the norm for the next four Olympic Games. The pool system was not without its shocks: Lindman scraped through the first round losing five of his nine bouts but settled down to match Dyrssen in the semi-finals. In the final, it was Dyrssen's experience that gave him 1st place, the aptly-named Italian, Gaspare Pasta, came 2nd and Lindman 3rd. Only George Vokins of the British team made the final, finishing in 10th place but one of the judges at the event was a young George Dyer who later became Commandant of the Army PT Corps and was significant in advancing the early life of British pentathlon. He donated the Dyer Cup which was to be the prize for the best individual in the British Championship for many years to come.

Despite the long-held desire to prevent speed from being the deciding factor in the riding event, the first 23 places were decided by time. True, competitors were introduced to their horses a mere five minutes before riding them, but a general aim in the riding event was establishing itself –since it is impossible to provide 38 horses of comparable ability, it is better to reduce the impact of the riding event on the overall competition. This is a solution that has worked in the modern point-scoring sport but, where time was almost the single distinguishing factor, position points were much affected by the natural ability of each horse. There were only nine instances of refusal at a fence and five eliminations. Two of those eliminations were the British pentathletes, Turquand-Young and Barton. Barton was particularly unfortunate. The BOA Report reveals that, as he approached the final jump, he was 30 seconds ahead of the rest of the field and was without fault. The three most difficult jumps were all in the final 40 yards of the course and, at the very last of these, Barton's horse refused three times. Though he succeeded in crossing the finishing line, the three refusals were sufficient to eliminate him. It caused Henry Churchman (the writer of the report) to exclaim 'If Barton had won the riding, and with a bit of luck he might easily have done so, our team would have been easily second'. Turquand-Young, one of the biggest men in the competition, had drawn the smallest horse. The little brute still managed to throw him at one point and ensure his elimination. The bogey time for the course was ten minutes, each second faster than this being worth two points. The winner was Henrik Avellan (FIN) in 8:26.0 but Dyrssen and Lindman were chasing him home in 3rd and 4th places. The best Britons were George Vokins in 8th place and Brian Horrocks in 12th.

The final running event took place at the hippodrome where the paddocks and lawns laid out for show jumping events made for smooth running. The course remained unknown to the athletes and unmarked until immediately before the event but the combination of easy terrain and, possibly, a slightly short measure made for some outstanding times. Lindman assured himself of the title by winning in an astonishingly fast time of 12:40.0 with Christiaan Tonnet (NED) on 12:49.0 and

Brian Horrocks (GBR) coming 3rd in 13:07.0. Poor Jindrich Lepiere (TCH) came last in every single event but we can be sure, at least, he had the friendship and support of his fellow competitors. Indeed, perhaps one of the great losses of modern sport has been that the demanding qualification systems now in place for major competitions have eliminated the athlete for whom taking part is all.

The final result in Paris was a predictable Swedish whitewash. Bo Lindman, the new champion, inherited his title from the silver medallist, Gustav Dyrssen, and the bronze medal went to Bertil Uggla, older brother of Bengt who had taken 4th place in Antwerp. Bertil Uggla, incidentally, had already won a bronze medal in the Pole Vault at the 1912 Olympics and represented his country in foil and epée too. The British team placed 7th (George Vokins), 13th (David Turquand-Young), 19th (Brian Horrocks) and 28th (Frederick Barton), the highlights for the team being Horrocks' 3rd place in the run and Turquand-Young's 3rd and 5th places respectively in swim and run. Since Lindman had won on the strength of his victories in the run and swim, this particular combination strength was starting to prove essential to success in the sport.

The British Team Manager, Henry Churcher, concluded his BOA report on the 1924 event with stirring enthusiasm. Suggesting it was a pity that the team had been entirely military personnel, he wrote: 'The competition is such a fine one that it must be for the benefit of every country to have hundreds and not just a mere handful of its young men perfecting themselves with a view to becoming expert, or at any rate proficient, Pentathletes.'

GREAT BRITAIN'S TEAM IN THE MODERN PENTATHLON.

1924 Paris: The British team (l-r: Fred Barton, George Vokins, Brian Horrocks, David Turquand-Young).

Inertia and regeneration

The jump start that British Modern Pentathlon had experienced during the winter of 1923/4 seemed now to evaporate into nothing. After the 1924 Games, the minute book was not used again until March 1927 when the prospect of another Olympic selection gave the sport much needed impetus. It was decided 'that every endeavour should be made to get together the best possible representatives' for Amsterdam 1928, rather overlooking that there had been no British Championship since 1924 and no organisational development in that time either Once again, Capt. Churcher, the Secretary, was obliged to send letters to every possible source of talent and the hope was expressed that the BOA would pay for postage since 'the Association had no funds'. There was, however, a statement of the Association's kit inventory which was available for training:

Item	Number	Total value
Fencing jackets	6 @ 10/- each	£3-00
Fencing pants	3 @ 10/- each	£1-10/-
Fencing epées	8 @ 5/- each	£2-00
Fencing bags	4 @ 5/- each	£1-00
Fencing masks	8 @ 5/- each	£2-00
Fencing gloves	8 (no cost)	
Revolvers	2 (no cost)	
Rounds of ammunition :	400 (no cost)	

Total cost: £9-10/-

Note: in pre-decimal British money, 20 shillings (20/-) were worth one pound (£1).

Aside from the preparations for Amsterdam, one matter that took up the committee's time was considering the offer of a rather grand cup by the Reverend Laffan. The cup was described by the BOA secretary as being 'a very massive one which stands 18 inches high'. Laffan had been presented this cup by the IOC in recognition of his many years of service to them and had laid down in his will that the cup should be presented to Modern Pentathlon. When he died in 1927, his family passed on the cup to the BOA who were naturally concerned that there should be a regular competition for this cup and that it would 'do good for the Association' before handing it over to the Modern Pentathlon committee. This was exactly the inspiration needed and marked the reinstatement of the British Championships in 1928 and the beginning of annual competitions. The 'Laffan Cup' has been awarded to the winning team in the British Championships ever since. Even so there was doubt expressed at the Pentathlon Committee meeting in November 1927 by Major Dubs, the Weapons Training Officer, about the likely level of interest in the sport in the future He considered that: 'No doubt, this year, there would be any amount of people very keen on the Olympic Games but...would it be possible to retain sufficient interest in other years between, after the games were over?' Lt.Col. Dyer assured him there would and 'this was the general opinion of the meeting'.

That same letter from the BOA offering the Laffan Cup contained less good news. The BOA was not going to offer any funds for training for 1928 even though they had in 1924. Rather optimistically the letter continued 'as you were fully equipped in 1924 it is quite possible that you do not require any further equipment'. So the paltry kit list above – basic fencing equipment and a couple of misfiring Webley revolvers - would be all our plucky chaps could expect to use in their quest for Olympic glory. The BOA also announced that entry to the Olympics would now be open to NCOs and 'men', providing strict rules about amateur status were followed. Since George Vokins had competed in Paris at the rank of Sergeant Major and the non-commissioned Durant and Clilverd had competed in 1912, this is a slightly puzzling announcement. But it reminds us of the class divide that existed in the early days of the Olympic Games. Officers and gentlemen were welcome but less so the working classes, many of whom were excluded because they had accepted paltry sums of money for working as lifeguards, games instructors or by competing in local wrestling or running contests.

Money, of course, has always been a key issue in Modern Pentathlon. Although the sums mentioned in

1928 were trivial by modern standards, they were nevertheless critical to the survival of the sport. Even though the Association (with funding from the BOA in 1924) had lavished £123 on preparations for the previous Games, they conceded that, since they had some kit already, the expenditure for preparing the 1928 team would need to be no more than £67. A summary of financial requirements was succinctly set out by Col. Heathcote: 'The Chairman pointed out that they would require an annual income of £100 to run the Association with success each year, giving a small balance which could be kept for the extra required during the Olympic Games year.'

How was this money to be raised? Membership subscriptions wouldn't be enough. Fund-raising football matches were considered worth trying as were appeals to the constituent sports bodies and military organisations. Rather surprisingly, it was declared that: 'The Army Council are not keen on the Olympic Games, but they would probably consider the Modern Pentathlon if it was put to them properly, owing to the military value of it.'

The training plan for the 1928 selection process was elaborate. Once again there were to be eliminating contests all over the place – Edinburgh, York, Colchester, Tidworth, Aldershot, Portsmouth, Devonport, Cranwell, Hounslow, Shorncliffe, Woolwich, Sandhurst, Oxford, Cambridge, Weedon, Rhine Army and Northern Ireland. How many of these places actually held competitions is unknown. The holding of full pentathlon competitions in all of them seems very unlikely. The top two placings in each competition were to qualify for the All-British Competition. The top six in that competition would begin intensive training for the Olympics 'from the last week in June'. A final trial would then take place on the 20th July and the team would leave for Amsterdam five days later.

The British Championships of 1928 (only the second to be held) took place on the 21st/ 22nd May. There were 39 entries but only 16 competed. The winner was a civilian, David Turquand-Young, late of the Royal Tank Corps. Lt. Alfred Goodwin was 2nd, RSM George Vokins was 3rd and Lt. Lance East 4th. The top six were selected for intensive training but George Vokins, our best performer at the 1924 Games, was unable to give up the time and withdrew from the squad. On 20th July, as promised, *The Times* announced that the team for Amsterdam would be David Turquand-Young (aged 24 and our only Paris Olympian), Alfred Goodwin (aged 25) and Lance East (aged 27). The trainer was Sgt. Inst. TS Hill and the Team Manager was Capt. WP Bradley-Williams, the Hon. Secretary and Treasurer of the Association and a Chief Instructor at the Army School of Physical Training. Though not mentioned in the report, a reserve, Lt. WA Turner, who became British Champion in 1931, also travelled to Amsterdam.

1928 Olympic Games: Amsterdam (NED)

The Amsterdam Games were held from 31st July to 4th August and once again there was some travelling to be done between events. The order was shoot, swim, fence, run, ride, each event being held on a different day. The slight adjustment to the order, putting the riding last, has been used from time to time in later years. It allows the competition to conclude with some pomp and ceremony for the organisers. For the pentathlete, its main merit is that a disastrous ride in a final event will, at least, not have dissuaded the rider from continuing to try hard in the other events. It is very rare to find an over-confident pentathlete who still has the riding event to face.

15 countries entered a total of 38 competitors. The entry for each country was reduced from four to three athletes but there were no fewer that eleven teams with the full complement of three. Germany, Hungary and Austria were admitted to the Games for the first time since the Great War had ended though Austria withdrew its single competitor. Denmark entered two and Hungary and Portugal one each. It seemed extraordinary in the circumstances that there was no team event at the Olympic Games until 1952. Such a competition, computed from the total individual scores of each team, requires no further organisation and there was eagerness expressed for a team event by most of the countries represented in Amsterdam. The British team manager even believed that a team event would be preferable to the individual competition. Seven of the entries had competed in Paris four years earlier, the most notable of these being the Olympic champion, Bo Lindman, and the British champion, David Turquand-Young.

The shooting event took place at Zeeburg and it was raining during the early details. However, the standard compared to previous competitions was very impressive. The event was won by Heinz Hax (GER) with an outstanding score of 196. Six other men beat the Paris winner's total with Otto Olsen (DEN), 194, and Ingvar Berg (SWE), 191, taking 2nd and 3rd places. Tucked in behind the leaders were Alfred Goodwin (GBR), 188, and Sven Thofelt (SWE), 187, a man who would become one of the greatest names in Modern Pentathlon history. The rule which counted the number of shots on target as more important than the overall score showed up quite markedly in favour of the defending champion, Bo Lindman on this occasion. He shot very badly (158) but with all 20 shots on target. This gave him a higher placing (15th) than Hermann Hölter (GER) who scored 179 but put one shot off. Heinz Hax, the winner of the shooting event, was a fascinating character. He won a silver medal in Rapid-Fire Pistol (25 metres) at each of the next two Olympic Games in Los Angeles and Berlin. He rose to the position of Major General in the German army, receiving the Knight's Cross with Oak Leaves for his bravery in 1945. Unfortunately, at the German surrender, he was handed over to the Soviet authorities and sentenced to 25 years hard labour. After ten years in a Soviet work camp, the German President negotiated Hax's release and he finished his career in the German army during peacetime.

The swimming took place next in the Olympic pool. There was a cool wind and the water was choppy. The event was won comfortably by Eugenio Pagnini (ITA) in 4:37.6. Thofelt was 2nd in 5:02.4 and Lindman, already well behind after his poor shoot, placed 5th. The best British athlete was Turquand-Young in 7th place, East and Goodwin both taking well over six minutes for their swims. In his report, Bradley-Williams acknowledged the British weaknesses and declared 'to do any good in this event one must be able to 'crawl' or 'trudge' the whole distance of 300 metres.' Obviously, such versatility in the water was still beyond the British team.

The fencing event was once again based on the pool system but this time barrages were fought until there was a clear distinction in placings. There were no shared position points as there had been in Paris. Lindman made a shock exit in at the pool stage ending up in a barrage with Hax, East and Goodwin for 21st place. First round winners were Mayo (USA), Otto Olsen and Helge Jensen (DEN) and Zenon Mallysko (POL). All four men went on to the final and it was the experienced Helge Jensen who won the event ahead of Helmut Kahl (GER), a Berlin policeman, and the young Richard Mayo (USA) who was to go on to even greater success four years later in Los Angeles. Thofelt was 4th. Turquand-Young made the semi-final but ended in 15th place.

Afterwards, Bradley-Williams considered that 'the fencing was not of a very high standard and the winners were mostly those who were good at the 'flêche' (a running attack).' Purists who felt that fencers should be more elegant, and there were a number of this mind among the pentathletes in Amsterdam, argued that the epée should be replaced with the sabre to 'eliminate the element of luck'. By this they meant that, because one had to establish right of way in sabre and the target was limited, the element of skill was greater in sabre than in epée where the whole body was the target and no right of way needed to be established. Luckily, the epée has remained the weapon of choice for pentathlon to the present day. Certainly the element of luck may well have been greater in epée before the advent of electronic scoring, but the use of the epée means that a beginner has a chance to beat the champion at a single hit. There are many ex-pentathletes whose greatest moment in the sport happened when they stumbled forward on the piste and, by mistake, hit an Olympic Champion on the toe. It's another of the egalitarian wonders of our sport.

The running event took place at Hilversum, some way south east of Amsterdam, starting and finishing in the local stadium but moving over heavy sand and heather outside. The event appears to have been poorly organised. For some reason, the committee wanted to time each runner on a separate watch and, because they didn't have enough watches, they ran the event in three heats with runners leaving at one minute intervals in each heat. The run was won by Stefan Szelestowski (POL) in 14m 14.4, followed by Tauno Lampola (FIN) and Lindman (SWE), 3rd. Turquand-Young and Goodwin of Great Britain finished 9th and 14th respectively but Lance East turned his ankle just outside the stadium and hobbled home in 30th position.

The final riding event was even further away from Amsterdam at the military camp in Amersfoort. The course was relatively easy with only a big drop at the 6th fence causing worries. The horses were good Irish-bred jumpers. Only a period of ten minutes was allowed for warming-up and once again it was time alone that separated the first 14 finishers. Ingvar Berg (SWE) was the winner in 8:04.8, with Heinz Hax (winner of the shooting) 2nd and Carlo Simonetti (ITA) 3rd. Both Turquand-Young and Lance East had clear rounds, East's round being particularly impressive because his swollen ankle had prevented him walking the course beforehand. This meant he rode it knowing nothing at all about the jumps he was to face.

The final overall result was that the 23 year old Sven Thofelt (SWE) became the new Olympic Champion. After a terrible shoot and fence, Bo Lindman, the defending champion had somehow fought his way into 2nd place. For the first time, someone other than a Swede won a medal – the Berlin policeman, Helmuth Kahl, took the bronze medal for Germany and pushed Ingvar

Sven Thofelt (SWE) 1928 Olympic Champion and UIPM President 1960-1988.

Berg, the third Swede, into 4th place. With David Turquand-Young going one position better than George Vokins had in Paris for Great Britain and taking 6th place, another 'first' was born – two of the first six places went to 'civilians' rather than military officers.

The finishing position points totals of the top athletes were not impressive – Thofelt (47), Lindman (50) and Kahl (52). Compare that to Lindman's winning score of 18 in Paris and the evenness of performance in Amsterdam becomes apparent.

There was no official team result but, just for the record, it would have finished:

1. SWE (155)   2. GER (180)   3. ITA (241)   4. NED (248)

5. FIN (253)   6. USA (256)   7. GBR (262)   8. POL (329)

9. FRA (373)   10. BEL (390)   11. TCH (421).

Who has ever taken part in a Modern Pentathlon competition and not thought 'if only'....?' The five events are so various, so brimming with hazards, that no one ever has the perfect competition. Many a mediocre competitor might have been a champion if only he had been at his best in all the events of the same competition. Bradley-Williams' report contains the comment that 'if Turquand-Young had had the score and placing (in the shooting) of Goodwin, he would have been the winner of the Pentathlon.' He went on to bemoan the lack of preparation and experience of the British team compared to other countries and concludes: 'The competitors should be trained to swim over the full distance, and should use the crawl or trudge stroke. They should also be able to run up to four or five miles, and furthermore, must be of the right disposition for the competition, namely, not in any way excitable or nervy.'

The new champion, Sven Thofelt, had a mighty sporting career and an even greater impact as administrator. He took 4th place in the Modern Pentathlon in both 1932 and 1936, adding a silver (1936) and bronze medal (1948) in the Epée Team event to his 1928 gold. He won 11 national titles in swimming, fencing and modern pentathlon and he rose to the rank of Brigadier General in the Swedish army. Most important of all, Thofelt was the UIPM President from 1960 to 1988. A big man, he spoke English and French impressively and he managed to combine a seriousness of purpose with a twinkle in his eye. Modern Pentathlon owes him the greatest of debts for its continued existence.

Chapter Three: 1929-1939

'If McDougall has sufficient practice in fencing and shooting before 1940 he should be in the first three in Tokyo (1940).' BOA Olympic Report 1936.

Another terrible war halted the pace of rapid developments in the sport during the 1930s. In Great Britain, annual championships took place with regular committee meetings to manage them. On the international stage, CIPMO had been established in order to lend stability to the organisation of the sport. Two further Olympic Games took place despite the Great Depression and the rise of Nazism, and there were, for the first time, international competitions in addition to the Olympic meetings.

The evolution of the British MPA

The stalled development in the period between the Olympics of 1924 and 1928 was not repeated. The MPA committee was determined to keep the sport moving after Amsterdam. Bradley-Williams, 1928 Team Manager and Secretary, was assisted by Col. ELW Henslow, OBE, MC, the MPA Chairman, and Lt. Col. GN Dyer, DSO, in getting things moving. One particular meeting on 7th November 1928 brought up a number of issues that would be relevant in the years before the 1932 Olympic Games in Los Angeles.

There was some irony in that, at the same meeting as the MPA endorsed CIPMO (and therefore its control of the rules), the committee set about changing the way competitions would be run in Great Britain. One such change that turned out to be very unpopular with the athletes was the addition of penalties in the riding 'for bad horsemanship and style'. In competitions since 1912, each rider began with 100 points and lost points for refusals, falls, etc. This new rule allowed the Chief Judge to deduct as many as 80 of those 100 points if, in his opinion, the rider wasn't elegant enough. An outcry at the British Championships in 1929 had this reduced to 50 penalty points the following year, later to 20 and then, finally, the measure was removed completely. It would only have taken one Chief Judge who saw himself as a buttress against 'falling equestrian standards' to ruin a perfectly good ride with these arbitrary penalties. Throughout the history of Modern Pentathlon there have been sensible tests to check that a rider will not injure himself or harm the horse but these measures need to happen before the riding event and not as part of the event itself.

One very significant change was a decision to disqualify anyone who didn't complete all five events. The exact wording of this clause was as follows:

'Any Competitor who fails to complete the course in Swimming and Running, or is absent from any event, will be disqualified, and his placings will not be considered in that or any subsequent event of the Competition, either as an Individual, or a member of a Team. This disqualification will not affect the placings of the Competitor in previous events in which he has competed.'

It appears from the wording here that, as long as the competitor begins the riding, fencing, and shooting events, he is not 'absent' and his final score will count. The inability to complete an event for whatever reason has, for the greater part of our history, not resulted in the individual's overall result not being counted. In 1930, the concept of 'disqualification' was not properly distinguished from 'elimination' and this led to serious disputes over the issue which finally boiled over at the 1953 World Championships (see Chapter 5). Thereafter, a more sensible approach was taken. Nowadays, the rules of the UIPM make clear that 'elimination is a penalty for a mistake concerning the rules of the game that has not been committed deliberately' while 'disqualification is a penalty for deliberately attempting to circumvent or deliberately circumventing the rules of the game.' It is a critical distinction.

There were compensatory rule changes too, however, and, on a cross country course far from home, the following rule would have been welcome:

'In the Riding Competition, if a Competitor has a fall at an obstacle and loses his horse, he may, with the sanction of the Judge, re-mount, if his horse has been caught, and continue the ride or may use a spare horse which will be brought up to him. No time will be allowed him and he must continue from where he fell.'

Other lesser changes to the rules were made. In shooting, the ammunition was to be provided by the competitor and the phrasing 'Army pistol or pistol of any make' described the weapon to be used. Later on, as a result of changes to the way the Royal Tournament was organized, the fencing event once again reverted to best of three rather than just a single hit. This effectively doubled the length of the pentathlon competition from two to four days and allowed the fencing arrangements to become intrusive.

In 1928, too, the BOA asked the MPA if they would be sending a team to Los Angeles in 1932. There was a strong push from the BOA to persuade the Americans to move the event to the East Coast so that Europeans could travel there more easily. This rather ignored the heroic efforts American teams had made to come to Europe in tip-top condition for the previous four Olympic Games. They had devised all kinds of strenuous land-training substitutes during the passage across the Atlantic. It was about time Europeans made similar efforts but the committee members were pessimistic: 'It would be useless sending a Team as they were certain to lose all their training in so long a journey, unless they were there for some weeks before the Games, which would be out of the question.' Thankfully, a change of heart took place by 1932 and this feeble stance was replaced by something a little more ambitious.

The seemingly paltry sums of money which the MPA were raising to run the sport in the early 1930s were, nevertheless, the lifeblood of its existence. In late 1928, the MPA had a mere £16-17s-10d (£16-80) to its name and took the radical step of selling all its equipment to raise enough funds to run the British Championships the following year (1929). It was estimated that a British Championship would cost £15 to run. The pile of old fencing kit and Webley pistols was valued at £19 total so that, by the same time the next year, they had a kitty of £27-8s-2d (£27-40). The subject of membership fees was raised and Col. Dyer opposed these, considering he might get some Army money instead. This plan clearly failed because, although the fund was sustained at £30-5s (£30·25) in 1930, by early 1932 (Olympic year), it had fallen to just £9-8s-3d (£9·40). At this stage, Col. Dyer reluctantly accepted that subscriptions were necessary and set the entry fee for the British Championships at 10s (50p) per team and 5s (25p) per individual. Even then, he was still holding out for the Army grant that would make such charges unnecessary.

The British Championships

The numbers competing in the British Championships rose gradually each year – 18 in 1928, 26 in 1929, 27 in 1930, and 34 in 1931. They were dominated by the Royal Military Academy at Sandhurst. Indeed, there were attempts to limit Sandhurst to Company teams rather than college teams in order to give the others a chance. Col. Dyer, time and again, wisely postponed such a move. At Sandhurst, the enthusiastic Capt. Campbell was responsible for training many cadets in the sport. He was, incidentally, the son of the famous 'Rajah' Campbell who donated the cup for the best cadet in the British Championships. Dyer knew that Campbell would know best how to handle the situation by balancing the strengths of his various teams. It was quite clear that Campbell regarded Modern Pentathlon as an excellent training regime for his cadets. This was largely why such an emphasis was placed, not on the winner, but on the number of awards given to the competitors for achieving standards. These awards reached a peak in 1931 when 12 Special, 44 1st Class, and 94 Standard awards were made at the British Championships (awards were made separately in each event). The business of committee meetings was often taken up with the discussion of these awards. The committee added to the list of awards those near-misses who, through injury or bad luck, had just fallen short of the standard set.

From 1929, teams (of two or three –best two to count) competed for the Laffan Cup and from 1930, individuals battled for the Dyer Cup. The MPA had promised the BOA that, for such a prestigious trophy as the Laffan Cup to be awarded, there must be a minimum of four teams competing. From 1929, the British Championships have had an unbroken run (apart from the war years, 1940-46) until the present day. The Olympic Qualifying Competitions of 1924 and 1928 should fairly be regarded as having been 'British Championships' and so Brian Horrocks (1924) and David Turquand-Young (1928) rightfully take their places at the head of the list. It was the 19 year old Gentleman Cadet Vernon Barlow who, while still at Sandhurst, burst upon the scene and took the 1929 title. He repeated the feat in 1930 as a Second Lieutenant in the King's Shropshire Light Infantry. One report on the 1930 championship declared 'It is interesting to note that Lieut. Barlow's points were very nearly equal to 2nd place at the last Olympic Games'. Since position points were entirely dependent upon the quality of the field, however, this was not a very sound observation of Barlow's real ability. Second place in 1930 went to William Clapham, another cadet, whose later obituary in *The Times* (1941) regretted that he had been killed in action. A friend, a Mrs. L More, wrote of him: 'I knew him as a fine fisherman, good shot, and the keenest of deer-stalkers, and it was only in 1938 that I met him and his beloved 'Skipper,' striding down George Street, Edinburgh, on their way north to stalk what I fear now may have been his last stag.'

The British Championship for 1932 was also, in part, the selection trial for the Olympic Games. Though the BOA's fund-raising had been much more successful than in the past, to send a team to Los Angeles would be very expensive. A cost of £10,800 was estimated, about £150 per person (an enormous sum of money in those days) and Modern Pentathlon was originally allocated only two competitors. There were 42 entries for the Olympic trial and British Championship (12-14 May) from which a squad of five was selected. The new champion was Lt. Percy Legard with G.Cdt. JA Dene, 2nd (repeating his 1931 place), Lt. Turner (the 1931 Champion) 3rd, G.Cdt. Jeffrey MacDougall, 4th, and Vernon Barlow (1929 and 1930 Champion), 5th. Performances were unimpressive with MacDougall putting four shots off target and only Legard turning in a decent run (13: 42). Nevertheless, the report to the BOA played fast and loose with the truth revealing that 'it is thought that Great Britain has a very good chance of victory in this event'.

Whether this bogus claim won more funding or whether the Army stepped in with additional sponsorship is not known but a team of three with two officials represented Great Britain at the Olympic Games in Los Angeles. Paying scant attention to the finishing order in the British Championship, the team selected was Percy Legard (aged 26), Vernon Barlow (22) and Jeffrey MacDougall who, at 20, was the youngest in the Los Angeles competition. Since both Legard and MacDougall went on to further represent Great Britain in 1936, this may well have been a shrewd selection. The Team Manager was, once again, Capt. Henry Churcher (the Association Secretary) and Capt. Roger Ames, who would be our manager in 1936, went along as judge and official.

Los Angeles – the preparations

On July 13th, *The Empress of Britain* set sail for New York with the bulk of the Olympic competitors, including the Modern Pentathlon team, on board. There was a new optimism about staying in shape: 'all five events could be practised (on board) because the ship contained a beautiful swimming bath and two gymnasia containing mechanical horses'. Having crossed the Atlantic, the team took an entire floor of the Royal York Hotel in Toronto for a two-day workout before taking the Canadian National Rail to Chicago. Changing to the Santa Fe Railway, the team proceeded to Los Angles via Albuquerque and Winslow to arrive at their destination a few days before the Opening Ceremony. The plan was to have a few hours break at each of the stops for 'working out'. Since Albuquerque was 5000 feet above sea level, however, members of the team were forbidden from doing anything more taxing than walk and take shower baths.

Though Los Angeles had been awarded the Games nine years beforehand, the Americans had not anticipated the Wall Street crash of October 1929 and its effect on the economy of the whole world. 13 million Americans were unemployed and President Hoover refused to attend the Olympic events. Six months before the Olympics began, not a single country had replied to invitations to attend. Hardly any tickets had been sold until Hollywood stars –Mary Pickford, Douglas Fairbanks Jnr, Charlie Chaplin and Marlene Dietrich – agreed to entertain the crowds. Since IOC members had to pay their own way, only 18 out of the 66 attended. Nevertheless, the Games were a huge success, the facilities outstanding, and, best of all for the American economy, they made a profit.

Modern Pentathlon competitions held far from Europe inevitably result in a reduced entry. For the 1932 Games, there were 26 entries originally from 11 countries. Petrus Grobbelaar from South Africa was unable to make it but 25 other pentathletes took part. Mexico was new to the event and Portugal and Hungary, who had sent their first tentative single entries to Amsterdam, were back with greater numbers. Hungary's full team entry marked the beginning of a triumphant history during which they replaced Sweden as the dominant Modern Pentathlon force. There were also full team entries from Sweden, Germany, USA, Italy, Mexico, and Great Britain. There were two entries from Portugal and a single entry each from France and the Netherlands.

The Swedish team had a daunting pedigree. Sven Thofelt, the 1928 champion was there, as was Bo Lindman, the 1924 champion and 1928 silver medallist. Lindman had lost training through an injury en route to Los Angeles and his unreliable shoot would always make his final result unpredictable. The new face on the team, although at 32 he was no beginner, was Johan Oxenstierna or, to give him his full title, Count Johan Gabriel Oxenstierna af Korsholm och Wasa. A tall, elegant aristocrat, Oxenstierna was to go on, in 1949, to replace Lindman as Treasurer of the UIPM. He also served as naval attaché in London during the war when his coded messages were intercepted by a treacherous clerk back in Sweden who passed on the vital secrets to the Nazis.

Sweden's nearest rivals should have been Germany but none of Germany's previous Olympic team was in Los Angeles. Instead, they sent a young team. The oldest, at 27, was Helmuth Naudé, who along with his team mate, Konrad Miersch (25), was to die fighting in World War II. Miersch's son, Ekkehard, was to swim for Germany in the 1956 Olympics. The third, youngest (23) and, at only five feet (152 cm) tall, tiniest member of the German team was Willi Remer who went on to put in the best German performance (5th).

The home team, USA, had no real previous form but, as well as home advantage, they had one veteran of the 1928 Games, Richard Mayo, to carry their hopes. At West Point Military Academy, Mayo had been a good runner and fencer but, in Amsterdam his poor riding had placed him last. So, during 1931, he spent the entire year training at the Cavalry School in Fort Riley, Kansas. He was a career soldier and retired in 1956 as a Brigadier General.

The Hungarian team members were a versatile crew. Elemér Somfay had already won a silver medal in the 1924 Track and Field Pentathlon. The other two team members, Imre Petneházy and Tibor Benkö also fenced in the Individual Epée event in 1932 where they each lost 3-0 to none other than Bo Lindman and Sven Thofelt respectively. The two Portuguese entries also had other Olympic experience in 1932, Rafael de Sousa in the 25 metres Rapid Fire Pistol and Sebastião Herédia in the Individual Foil.

The British team was led by Percy Legard. *The Times* commented on his British Championship win that his 'physique is almost perfect, and he was not in the least exhausted after a stiff three days' programme'. He might have shot better 'but for curable impatience' and hopes were clearly very high for this 1929 British Ski-Jumping Champion. Legard had been born in England but spent the first 15 years of his life in Sweden honing his winter sport skills. As well as competing in the Modern Pentathlon in both 1932 and 1936, he also competed in the Winter Olympics of 1936 (combined cross-country skiing and jumping) and 1948 (winter pentathlon). He rose to the rank of Lieutenant Colonel. In his autobiography, *Monkey Business* (Quiller Press, 1993), Monkey Blacker paid tribute to his friend and fellow pentathlete:

'Percy Legard, blond and well-built, was half-Swedish and was, exceptionally, much keener on skiing than hunting, spending his winters on the snow. Long before Eddie the Eagle of modern ski-jumping fame was hailed, incorrectly, as the first British ski-jumper, Percy was jumping regularly with, I suspect, rather more success than the Eagle, and certainly more glamour, for he was very good-looking. He was extremely versatile, and spoke several languages; a natural athlete, he played regularly in dance bands and painted in oils. But he had no powers of application; he was so relaxed and so anxious to rush off to the next party that he really never became more than a jack of all trades. However the Modern Pentathlon might have been invented for him...'

The other double Olympian in the team was Lt. Jeffrey MacDougall, DFC, who had been born in Buenos Aires and died on active service in 1942. He had been seconded to the RAF as a Wing Commander and was awarded his DFC for his rôle in a night attack over France.

1932 Olympic Games: Los Angeles (USA)

The Los Angeles competition was a great success for many reasons. Firstly, it was the first time the so-called 'classical' order was used. Ride, fence, shoot, swim, run was to become the standard sequence for many years to come and it has the greatest appeal, moving as it does from the least predictable outcome (riding) to the most predictable (running). Secondly, the facilities were excellent and thirdly, it was one of the closest fought Olympic battles in the history of the sport. The competition ran from the 2nd to the 6th of August, one event per day.

The riding event was held at the Riviera Country Club in Pacific Palisades. The riding course was just under 5000m in length with 15 very mixed cross-country jumps (water trough, farm wagon, railroad crossing, etc.) A bogey time of 10: 51.8 was set which only seven riders failed to better since the standard of horses was very high. The winner was Bo Lindman (SWE) in 8:07.4, who nudged out the newly expert, Richard Mayo (USA), by three seconds. Mayo appeared to have ridden the whole course devil-may-care without a crash helmet, not an unusual sight in the early days of the riding event. Third place went to Vernon Barlow (GBR) with Percy Legard (GBR) in 5th place. Oxenstierna (SWE) separated the two Britons in 4th place. Sadly, the third Briton, Jeffrey MacDougall, accompanied the two Mexicans in getting disqualified, in his case, for riding outside the markers and jumping the wrong jump. Where, in future years, he would have received 0 points and been out of the competition, in 1932 and, indeed, while position places were in operation (until 1954), he merely shared

24th place with the Mexicans and was by no means cut adrift. The big shock of the event was that the defending champion, Sven Thofelt, fell badly and broke two ribs. He managed to finish the ride in 15th place and miraculously battled on through the whole competition.

The fencing event was held in the impressive State Armory Building and was organised as a round robin competition. Gone was the luck of the drawing for pools, gone were the awkward play-offs for placings. Even the double defeat, so devastating in previous contests, was modified by a system that scored two points for a win, one for a double defeat, and zero for a loss. The winner, amazingly, was the injured Sven Thofelt (SWE) with 35 points. Bo Lindman and the Italian, Francesco Pacini shared 2nd place on 32 with Mayo just a single point behind them. Though he did manage to hit Thofelt, Legard was down in 18th position with MacDougall and Barlow even worse. The manager, Henry Churcher, echoed earlier sentiments about sabre being preferable to epée since it involved less luck. One would have thought the British team might have been glad of any luck coming their way after such a poor showing.

The shooting event was won by Richard Mayo with an impressive 197 (49, 49, 50, 49). This gave him a comfortable lead in the overall competition though Oxenstierna, who had fenced poorly, managed 194 for 2nd place. Apparently, Oxenstierna was lucky to have been allowed to take part. He had been taking a couple of practice shots in the nearby woods before his event when a policeman arrested him. Luckily, Oxenstierna managed to persuade the policeman to let him do the shooting event first. The policeman watched, decided Oxenstierna was probably not a criminal, and departed. Thofelt was in 9th place with 188 and Lindman, so often a nervous shot despite his past overall successes, put one shot off in the second series and finished with 167. The British team had a sound, middle-of-the-field performance: Legard (187), MacDougall (185) and Barlow (184).

Thofelt added a swimming win to his fencing triumph with a time of 4:32.4, refusing to acknowledge the effect of the broken ribs. Gradually, standards were improving in the swim with six men, including MacDougall, swimming faster than five minutes. Lindman and Mayo were well down the field, though Mayo continued to lead after four events with 21.5 pts. Oxenstierna, whose best event had been his shoot, was 2nd with 25 pts, Thofelt 3rd on 26 pts and Lindman, back in 4th place with 31.5 pts, seemed to be out of the running.

The final running event took place at 9am at the Sunset Fields Golf Club. About two-thirds of it was on the fairways but the rest involved climbing a very steep hill. The times suggest the course was a tough one but at last the British team came into its own with Legard winning by a full half-minute from his team mate, MacDougall. The winning time of 15:12.2 was a slow one and the hot favourite, Mayo, suffering badly from a pulled Achilles tendon, saw his strong lead melt away in the final event.

It was Oxenstierna who was crowned the new Olympic Champion having won none of the events but having stayed in contention throughout. His placings were ride (4th), fence (14th), shoot (2nd), swim (5th), and run (7th). Lindman repeated his 2nd place from the Amsterdam Games, a quite remarkable recovery after his dreadful shooting, and Mayo hung on for the bronze medal although he must have been desperately disappointed to have been injured when he was leading the field so comfortably. Another disappointed man was Thofelt who missed a medal by half a point to lose his title and finish 4th. These 4 men were comfortably ahead of the rest of the field and their final points were:

1. Johan Oxenstierna   (SWE)   32

2. Bo Lindman   (SWE)   35.5

3. Richard Mayo   (USA)   38.5

4. Sven Thofelt   (SWE)   39

The British competitors finished 8th (Legard), 14th (Barlow), and 15th (MacDougall).

Although, once again there was no team competition, it seemed that everyone had calculated team results. Often, these calculations were based on adding the final positions together but it is more consistent with later methods to add the points accumulated over five events. On this basis, the team result would have been:

1. SWE 106.5   2. USA 155   3. GER   158   4. GBR   176
5. HUN 182   6. ITA   194

Though Sweden had continued to dominate the sport, this competition marked a change in fortune for the home country, USA, and, since Berlin would host the next Games, Germany too. The British team had acquitted themselves well and established what was to become a lasting tradition –good at running, bad at fencing – that was to recur in many future competitions. One remarkable feature of the three medallists in Los

Angeles was their longevity. Oxenstierna lived to be 95 years old, Lindman, 93, and Mayo, 94: not a bad advertisement for the health-giving aspects of the sport.

Great Britain between Olympic Games

Back in Aldershot, a regular, reliable pattern to organisation was emerging. Every May or June, a British Championship was held. It was dominated by Gentlemen Cadets from Sandhurst, AM Askwith winning in 1933 and GJC Bowen in 1934. Numbers were generally stable, though an outbreak of mumps at Sandhurst in 1933 reduced entry numbers to 25 that year. The three hit bouts prolonged the fencing event to a day and a half within a four day competition. Percy Legard won the 1935 title and, later that year, an interesting shoot/swim/fence day was held in Aldershot as part of the winter training programme. Astonishingly, it was won by David Turquand-Young the 1924/1928 Olympic veteran and hopes were expressed that he might try out for the Olympic team in 1936. However, in the 1936 Championship, it was Jeffrey MacDougall who pushed Legard into 2nd place. Both men's Olympic reputation had already secured their team places in Berlin. The 3rd placed Archie Jack completed the 1936 Olympic team. Sadly, David Turquand-Young's hopes of an Olympic comeback were squashed - he could only place 8th. The 1936 British Championship was also the first time an RAF team took part; they finished an impressive 3rd in the team event.

There was a growing awareness that real improvement could only come with experience against foreign pentathletes and with specific training in the weakest event, namely fencing. An invitation from

Sweden for 'four officers' to compete in their August 1934 competition was, unfortunately, refused by the British Army authorities but in the winter of 1935/6 efforts were made to provide fencing experience for our Olympic 'possibles' by having matches against established fencing clubs. The Epée Club, London FC, RAC, Bertrands, Grosvenor FC and Masks were all approached with this proposal.

1936 Olympic Games: Berlin (GER)

The organisation of the Berlin Modern Pentathlon was an entirely military affair. As a result, the horses had been trained over the course at the Döberitz military drill grounds for a year, the shooting targets were electrically operated for the first time, and scores were transferred to large scoreboards within minutes of an event finishing. The Germans prided themselves that their exemplary first-aid service wasn't required on even a single occasion. The only setback came in the fencing event: the Germans decided to return to holding it outdoors. It rained heavily and there was a delay of three hours while the event was moved inside the House of German Sport. This was particularly problematic because it was the very first time that the electric judging system with metal pistes had been used.

In his book, *Berlin Games* (John Murray, 2006), Guy Walters notes the collective eagerness of German organisers and supporters to be admired by the rest of the world. This made it quite difficult for visiting athletes to be harsh in their judgements of the Nazi way of doing things. Modern observers are frequently astonished that a regime already well-established in its oppression of Jews was not more openly reviled by the athletes.

Hindsight has certainly changed the way the Nazi regime is viewed but it should also be remembered that an athlete is so focused on the task he has set himself at an Olympic Games, it is in his own interests to close his mind to all extraneous information, no matter how disturbing. There were serious attempts at a boycott of the Berlin Games, however, and a British team set off to compete in the 'Alternative Olympics' in Spain. Unfortunately, they arrived in Barcelona to coincide with the Spanish Civil War breaking out. The Games were cancelled and the British team had to return home promptly.

The competition in Berlin took place from August 2nd to the 6th. There were originally 19 countries entered but Canada, Portugal and Spain withdrew before the Games opened. This left 16 countries competing of which only Greece, Mexico, Austria and Peru did not have the full complement of three. Attending for the first time were Brazil, Greece, Peru and Switzerland. Rather surprisingly, only three competitors out of 42 were returning Olympians –Sven Thofelt (SWE) and the two Britons, Percy Legard and Jeffrey MacDougall. Some pentathletes still took part in other sports: Sven Thofelt, Rezsö von Bartha (HUN) and Fritz Weber (USA) fenced in the Epée events and Anisio da Rocha (BRA) rode in the Three Day Event. At the Winter Olympics that same year, Percy Legard had also raced in the Nordic Combined event and Karl Leban (AUT) in the Speed Skating. In keeping with military efficiency, all the competitors were listed by rank. Of 42 entries, 39 were officers, one was non-commissioned (a German, Herbert Bramfeld), and two were civilians – Alfred Guth (AUT) and Alexandros Baltatzis (GRE).

The 1928 Champion, Sven Thofelt was hoping to do better than his 4th place in Los Angeles but the hot favourite was a 27 year old German 1st Leutnant, Gotthard Handrick. He was known as a strong shot and fencer but, as Charles Leonard (USA) wrote in his diary, 'he is known all over Europe as a poor rider'. Leonard led a strong American team which, aboard the SS Manhattan from New York, had been worked to the bone by their coach, the 1932 Bronze medallist, Dick Mayo, who stood muffled in overcoats on deck while his team battled in a pool 'watered directly from the icebergs'. Apart from Leonard, in the US team were Fritz Weber, an outstanding epéeist, and Dodd Starbird, who, despite breaking a metatarsal bone in his foot on board ship, took part in all five events. They had trained together for a full year in anticipation of the Berlin Games. The Hungarian, Nándor von Orbán, had reportedly won a 'European Championship' the previous year but fuller details of that event cannot be found.

The British team was, unusually, among the most experienced, Percy Legard and Jeffrey MacDougall having both competed in Los Angeles. The third member of the team, at 33, was actually the oldest. Lt. Archie Jack, like MacDougall, had been born in Buenos Aires. He trained at RMA Woolwich and Cambridge and went on to lead a colourful and varied life –boyhood friend of the spy, Donald Maclean, he became a Special Operations saboteur, blowing up bridges in Serbia for which he was awarded the MC. He spoke fluent Hindustani, led mountain warfare training in Lebanon and Palestine and, in retirement, took part in ocean racing competitions. The Team Manager in Berlin was Roger Ames.

The first event, the riding, took place on Sunday 2nd August. The riders had walked the course the previous Friday and, to retain 100 points, each rider had to ride a faultless round inside a time of 11:06.7. Since 1912, the penalties had differed very little. Now the penalties were:

three points per refusal
six points for each second refusal;
six points for a fall of horse;
twelve points for a fall of rider;
half a point per second over time.
One significant addition was a swingeing 50 point penalty for a third refusal but this was less harsh than the previous penalty for this failure which had been elimination.

The horses and the course in the competition, a mixture of sand, woods, hill, and stream, had been prepared to perfection which led the British IOC representative and 1920 team member, Lt. Col. Wand-Tetley, to grumble 'the course is too simple and is not a test of real horsemanship'.

A later allegation was that Gotthard Handrick actually rode his own horse to victory. As a member of the Swedish Swimming team, Wille Grut was watching the riding event in Berlin. In his autobiography *Om jag minns ràtt?* -If I remember correctly- (1994), he notes:

'In Berlin the horses were out of sight of the place of the draw and that means that nothing would have been easier than to use a walkie-talkie to inform the team about what number a German had drawn - and to put that number on the appropriate horse. I remember that the ultimate victor Gotthard Handrick won the riding. Was it due to superior riding skill or thanks to German "cunning" in the draw?'

The official report doesn't support this allegation, however. It states that: 'The horses, each bearing a number, were brought to the paddock at 7.30am and the participants arrived at 8am. The drawing of lots for the horses took place at the paddock after which each rider was weighed and then given 15 minutes for trying out his horse.'

Certainly, Charles Leonard considered Handrick's fast round as one of the 'breaks of the game' which led Guy Walters (*Berlin Games*) to conclude 'there was no suspicion –nor was there any evidence – that the Germans had cheated'.

Film of the riding event shows the horses being driven at breakneck speeds – Handrick (GER) and Mollet (BEL) can be seen making liberal use of the whip. Leonard (USA), who casually tossed his crash helmet aside as he set off, found himself on a horse that was slightly slower than the rest and regretted not driving it on harder. Those were the days of a very different kind of riding in which the horses were pushed to levels far more stressful than would be allowed today. The death of a horse at the end of a race was not an unknown experience. Once again, in Berlin, the horse's speed was the deciding factor. No fewer than 27 riders were fault-free. The winner was Silvano Abba (ITA) in 9:02.5 with Handrick and Mollet sharing 2nd place in 9:09.6. Even though the British team only had six penalty points between them and were all inside the time limit, they finished 17th, 29th and 30th. No wonder Wand-Tetley was so scathing about the ease of the course.

The 23 year old Raoul Mollet, though he finished well down the field, became an important figure in Belgian sport. In Berlin, his good looks caught the eye of Leni Riefenstahl whose film *Olympia* features him twice. At the end of the riding event he is seen combing his hair and grinning. He took part in the Equestrian events in 1948 having been a German prisoner through the war. He then became President of the Belgian Olympic Committee where his sensible ideas about National Sports representation at the IOC and the limiting of committee numbers caused Avery Brundage to block Mollet's membership of the IOC. It must have given Mollet special pleasure that his protégée, Jacques Rogge, is now the IOC President.

It seems to us today extraordinary that anyone would hold the fencing event outdoors. It was the only mistake the German organizers made and resulted in a three hour delay as they moved all the electric equipment indoors out of the rain. Amusingly, the detailed account of the daily weather conditions in the Official Report omits any mention of Monday 3rd August. The event was not finally completed until 11pm that evening. For the modern pentathlete of 2012, used to bouts of a single minute, it must also seem extraordinary that five minutes were allowed for each bout right up until 1960. It made for a very long fencing day. It was Fritz Weber (USA) who took the fencing event by a single point from Handrick (GER) with Thofelt (SWE) in 5th place. Handrick, therefore, retained his lead after two events. The British team played their now traditional supporting role in fencing, providing a solid base in the lower half of the table.

The shooting event was set up for maximum performance –electrically operated turning targets placed in sunlight with the firing end in the shade. It was won in spectacular fashion by Charles Leonard (USA) with a first-ever 'possible' of 200 out of 200. Leonard had been given his first rifle at the age of only six, had a shooting range in his basement and, as long as he 'avoided the water tank' was encouraged by his father to aim at any target that took his fancy. In Berlin, Leonard used a Colt 0.22 pistol but mounted on a slightly heavier 0.38 frame. Rivals were surprised by his three pound trigger pressure –they expected something lighter. He was also quizzed about whether he used drugs to steady his performance. He wrote in his diary 'I do <u>NOT</u> use dope'. Pentathletes were allowed only two 'sighters' before the competition and Leonard put one of these out of the bull. But there was no stopping him once the competition began. Dressed in a pressed shirt, silk tie, blue jacket and beret since 'shooting is a gentlemanly game', he proceeded to hit the bull 20 times in succession and was afterwards invited to cut out and keep the centre of the target as a souvenir. It was framed on his study wall for the rest of his life.

1936 Berlin: Charles Leonard (USA) wins the shooting with a perfect 200.

Leonard's team mate, Weber, finished 2nd with 194 but Handrick's 4th place (192) kept him comfortably in the lead overall. Thofelt shot 190 and Abba (ITA) 188 to stay in contention. Archie Jack was the best British performance on 187 with Legard (180) and MacDougall (173) some way behind him. The British, however, earned the admiration of the Belgian team. The Belgians only had two pistols for their team of three and one of those was confiscated by the German authorities for being too old (and, presumably, dangerous). The British team kindly loaned the Belgians one of their own pistols so that they were still able to compete.

The swimming was held in the apparently 'frigid water' of the Olympic Swimming Stadium. The event was attended by none other than the German Chancellor, Adolf Hitler, whose busy programme allowed him only a brief visit. No wonder then that the Official Report proudly proclaimed 'this event was completed within an hour'. The swim was won by the youngest competitor, Hermann Lemp (GER) in a new Olympic record of 4:15.2. Second place went to 'European Champion' Nándor van Orbán (HUN) in 4:23.4 with Thofelt (SWE) 3rd in 4:34.9. The British trio all finished between 5:00 and 5:20 and seven of the field still took longer than six minutes to complete the 300 metres.

With only the running to go, the leaders were:

1. Handrick (GER)   17.5   2. Thofelt (SWE)   23
3. Leonard (USA)   32

4. Orbán (HUN)   39.5   5. Abba (ITA)   40.5
6. Lemp (GER)   46.5

The cross-country running took place at Wannsee Golf Club and involved a difficult route through steep ravines, forest glades and meadows. Though comfortably in the lead, Hendrick, in Leni Riefenstahl's film *Olympia*, is seen to be in a dream-like state at the start and, when given his starting orders, appears to spring into action from complete stillness. This contrasts markedly with the other competitors who warm their muscles with their hands and prance on the spot in anticipation. The event was won by the Austrian pentathlete, Karl Leban, in 13:17.4 and the British runners, Legard and MacDougall, who had placed 1st and 2nd in Los Angeles, came 4th and 6th respectively in Berlin. MacDougall, apparently, had 'the leather of one of his shoes burst' on his run. He stopped twice to try to remedy the problem but, 300 metres from home, kicked off the shoe and ran barefoot. Even more impressive was Dodd Starbird (USA) who, despite his painful broken metatarsal bone, managed to complete the competition with a 7th place in the running. While Charles Leonard toured Europe for a few weeks after the Games, Starbird, his team mate and friend, had to return home promptly with his foot in plaster. So close were the two team mates that, in later years, Leonard's daughter married Dodd Starbird's son.

Though he only placed 14th in the running, it was enough for Gotthard Handrick to win the Olympic title by 8 placing points. Handrick was to become a fighter pilot after the Games fighting for the fascists in the Spanish Civil War and, as a Major in the Luftwaffe, he was awarded the German Cross in Gold. He survived the war. Hitler was so pleased with Handrick's Olympic victory that, the very next day, Handrick was promoted to Hauptmann. The silver medal went to Charles Leonard (USA) who, like Handrick, only finished outside the top ten in one event. Leonard, too, had a successful military career in Japan and Korea after training at West Point Military Academy. His record in the shooting would, of course, never be beaten although targets would change shape in future years and so new records would be set. In 1958, on a trip to Germany, Leonard met Handrick once again. Leonard retired as a Major General and died aged 94 in early 2006. He was buried in Arlington Cemetery alongside his brother, a Navy Admiral.

The bronze medal went to Silvano Abba (ITA) who edged Sven Thofelt (Sweden) into 4th place by 1.5 place points. Thofelt's running was a disaster. He was not known as a good runner, even though the film of the Games shows him to be running well enough, but he placed 24th, a full two minutes behind the winner, dashing all hopes of a medal. Abba was the only one of these four men who died in World War Two. He was killed at the Battle of Izbushensky near Volgograd as one of the 700 riders of the Italian Savoy Cavalry who made the last cavalry charge in military history. The British team finished 13th (Jeffrey MacDougall), 19th (Percy Legard) and 31st (Archie Jack). The three medallists were presented with laurel leaf crowns soon after the running event but the medals were presented the next day in the Olympic stadium.

Though, once again, there was no team competition, calculations reveal a great deal about the shift in national prowess. Both USA and Germany had impressed in 1932 but Sweden had still dominated. In Berlin, everything changed. Thofelt's disappointing 4th place was still not as disappointing as the performances of his Swedish team mates, Georg von Boisman (10th) and Ebbe

1936 Berlin. The medallists: Charles Leonard (USA) silver, Handricke (GER) gold (giving the Nazi salute) and Silvano Abba (ITA) bronze.

Gyllenstierna (16th). The final 1936 team results would have been:

1. USA	186	2. GER	188	3. SWE	223
4. HUN	240.5	5. ITA	248.5	6. FIN	310.5
7. GBR	314.5	8. NED	336.5	9. BEL	345
10. FRA	396	11. BRA	497		

Wand-Tetley, in his report to the BOA, proudly recorded that: 'Field Marshal von Blomberg (German War Minister), at a dinner attended by all military officers at the Games, stated that he considered the Modern Pentathlon to be a very practical training and of great value in fostering those qualities necessary for an active officer.'

1937-1939

The British MPA was determined to prepare immediately for the next planned Olympic Games in

Tokyo in 1940. Wand-Tetley suggested to the BOA that a grant to support the MPA might be provided by the Army Sports Control Board. He proposed running competitions in two tiers –one for the 'elite' top 15 and another for the fledgling cadets coming into the sport. He also felt that inviting foreign teams to compete in home competitions was essential and that any British pentathlete with any promise be sent on a three month fencing course at Aldershot. He concluded by saying that Jeffrey MacDougall showed sufficient promise in Berlin that 'if he has sufficient practice in fencing and shooting before 1940 he should be in the first three in Tokyo.'

A request to the BOA for a grant of £50 to invite foreign teams was refused but the MPA still planned to invite one foreign team each year from one of France, Holland and Denmark. In 1938, a Dutch team lost to a British team composed of Sqd.Ldr.GN Tindall-Carill-Worsley, 2nd Lt.RA Hofman (British Champion in 1937 and 1938), and G.Cdt. PJD Coleman (who won both the swimming and the running events). The Army Sports Control Board kindly provided £10 for the 'entertainment' of the Dutch guests. During 1938, the membership of the MPA rose from 39 to 69 and the Chairman, Col.GL Brown 'brought up the question of mechanisation affecting future competitions'. He believed 'in all probability the horse would be substituted by the motor bike in future competitions.' This was not as far-fetched as it sounded. An article had appeared in a Hungarian newspaper in June of the previous year announcing that there would be a German competition in which 'the participants were permitted to choose between horse riding or a 7500-metre motocross race on a very hard course.' There is no record of the event having taken place, though.

In 1939 it was Sweden who was to be MPA's invited team and a proposal was made that they should be sent a plan of the riding course in advance so that they would have an opportunity to practice on a similar course. Money was tight, and Col. Brown suggested, quite reasonably, that other services should be asked to subscribe - £10 from each of the RAF, Navy, Marines and Territorial Army, and £5 from the Universities. Since the ASCB once again provided £10 for entertaining the guests, he also proposed that: 'similar entertainment to that which was provided to the Dutch team last year would be suitable (for the Swedish team). Those responsible for the entertainment last year were asked if they would repeat the same again this year.' What kind of wild night out was paid for with the princely sum of £10 is, sadly, not recorded.

The 1939 British Championship was won by another Gentleman Cadet, CG Wylie but the best laid plans of the MPA were interrupted by far sterner international events. Many young athletes reaching peak performances in 1939 were to have their sporting careers abruptly taken away in the war that followed. The same was true in other countries. In 1939, Charles Leonard had returned to West Point to prepare for the 1940 Olympic Games but by September 1939, those Games were cancelled. In 1938, there had been a team competition in Hungary with six representatives in each team where Bollden (SWE) swam an amazing time of 3:56.6 for the 300 metres. The Hungarian, Orbán, won the competition and Bolgar and Gyllenstierna of Sweden placed 2nd and 3rd. The team competition marked a first-ever triumph for Hungary over Sweden and a hint of things to come. It was also the first competition for Claes Egnell (SWE) who featured regularly in these pre-war competitions but who had to wait until 1952 for his own Olympic success having broken his leg just months before the 1948 Games. In 1939, a competition in Stockholm was won by Garvs of Germany but, in 3rd place, the great Swede, Wille Grut, about whom we will hear much more in the years ahead, was making his debut ahead of his compatriot, Egnell.

After the Berlin competition, it was the Germans who were the first to propose that the Modern Pentathlon might benefit from a points rather than a placing system. Though this would not be realized until 1954, changes were definitely underway. These changes would have to be put on hold for the duration of the war but, by 1939, Modern Pentathlon had developed a life outside the Olympic Games and was alive and well in many more countries than it had been before.

Chapter Four: 1946 – 1950

'If the horse-riding has to be cut out from the Competition, the only suitable substitute is motor-cycling.' MPAGB minutes, 1946.

After the war

Despite the devastation of World War II, the sport began again with much more impetus than it had after World War One. The neutrality of Sweden and Switzerland during the war allowed those countries to lead the way in a rapid revival. However, the riding event, problematic from the very start in 1912, now rarely passed unmentioned in committee meetings around Europe. Horses, so integral to past warfare were now redundant. Tanks and other vehicles were replacing horses as fighting machines. So, since the sport was still overwhelmingly military, providing competition horses was becoming a problem. As the numbers of competitors grew, the tough 5000 metre cross-country riding course became an organizational headache. Each horse could only endure a single ride and that necessitated one horse for every pentathlete taking part in the competition.

British revival 1946-48

Regular MPA committee meetings resumed on 4th July 1946 and were chaired by a man who was to become one of the very greatest influences on the sport in Great

Britain. Brigadier Leslie Wieler, CB, CBE (1899-1965), had lost his right arm in a direct attack on his tank in North Africa; he was the only survivor. He went on to become Vice-President of the UIPM, a position he held from the body's inception in 1949 until his death in 1965. He was the leading force behind the planning of the events at the 1948 Olympic Games and, in the 1950s he was instrumental in getting schools, universities, and pony clubs to take part in the sport, thus creating a solid base for civilian participation. One recruitment ploy he particularly enjoyed was getting his secretary to call schools and universities. The secretary would ask 'Will you take a call from the Governor of the Tower of London?' This was Wieler's official position. Wieler would then take the phone and, while the listener gulped in awe, insist the school or university concerned should get a team together for the British Championships. MPA membership numbers increased rapidly.

In 1946, despite a real push to include civilians, the MPA was still a military organisation. This arrangement became formalised when the constitution was revised. The new document declared that the President would be the Director of Military Training (Maj. Gen. Sir Charles Keightley, KBE, CB, DSO); the Chairman, the Inspector of Physical Training (Leslie Wieler); the Vice-Chairman, the Commandant of the Army School of Physical Training (Col. RW Littlehales); and the Secretary/ Treasurer, the Chief Instructor, ASPT (Maj. R St. G. Harper). Far from making the sport a closed shop, this plan encouraged continuity. There was a great deal of movement between jobs in the aftermath of the war, and, by linking committee responsibility to a military office rather than an individual, the survival of Modern Pentathlon was assured.

In those post-war meetings there were other well-known figures: Alfred Goodwin of the GB 1928 Olympic team (now, Lt. Col. Goodwin, OBE) was there as official adviser. Major Percy Legard of the Northern Command and 1932 and 1936 Olympic team member enquired whether the 'electrical fencing-judging machine' he'd sold to the MPAGB before the war was still available. Capt. Leslie Lambert, well-known pentathlon administrator during the next 40 years, was already adding his voice, as was Maj. George Gelder whose fencing expertise benefited the MPA for many years.

The riding problem

Not surprisingly, committee plans at this time were largely taken up with preparations for the 1948 Olympic Games. Six month training courses for Olympic hopefuls were proposed and it took little time for Aldershot and Sandhurst to be named as the likely Olympic sites. Providing horses would, however, be a problem; organisers would have to rely on a few military horses and also approach private owners for the loan of their horses. All this meant a great number of delicate negotiations over the next two years – influential horse owners needed to be co-opted onto the committee and good relations maintained with stables. The situation was so precarious at times that the minutes recorded: 'If the horse-riding had to be cut out from the Competition, the Committee agreed that the only suitable substitute was motor-cycling, but they felt that it would be far better to modify the rules of the Horse-riding event to suit the standard of the available horses.'

This genuine consideration of a motor-cycling alternative persisted for many years. It only really died a death in the early 1960s. The then IOC President, Avery Brundage, a supporter of Modern Pentathlon, told UIPM President, Sven Thofelt, that the replacement of horse riding, an established Olympic sport, with motor-cycling, a non-Olympic sport, would inevitably exclude Modern Pentathlon from the Olympic Games. That finally put paid to motor-cycling as an alternative.

Modifying the rules

At the 1947 British Championships, the first since 1939, a number of modifications were made to the riding event. There were only 16 fences, none of them above 3'6" (107 cm) in height. The disqualification rule was deleted and no bonus points were given for riding faster than the 10 minute bogey time. In this way, both inexperienced riders and less able horses might stand a better chance of completing the course without mishap. Elsewhere, the FIE (Fédération Internationale d'Escrime) had recently declared that fencing would henceforth be an indoor sport. The effect of weather conditions on electrical equipment had to be considered. Finally, still with civilian participation in mind, a definition of what constituted a team was established. It read: 'Three competitors (two to count), all of whom must belong to the same School, Regiment or Educational establishment. The three members must be nominated before the start of the competition.'

The 1947 British Championships

The 1947 British Championships took place in Aldershot over two and a half days from 10th to 12th September. The event order was ride, swim, shoot, fence, run. There were 47 competitors (a record), all of whom completed all five events. This sensational achievement was largely brought about by the new protective riding rules which were a masterful way of stimulating the interest of large numbers of potential competitors immediately after the war when the army still had the power to do so. No fewer than 25 competitors completed the riding under the time limit. No rider was rewarded for having gone faster than the time limit so a rather bizarre sharing of top spot resulted in all 25 riders receiving 11.5 place points each. That meant that the seven riders who were just over the ten minute allowance shared 26th place, setting them at quite a disadvantage for having been just those few seconds slower. One of this latter group was the new British Champion, Lance Corporal Andy Martin whose 55 place point total edged out the runner-up Major Percy Jones who got 57.5 points. Martin's place positions were Ride 26, Swim 3, Shoot 11, Fence 6, and Run 9. He was to retain his title the following year and be selected for the 1948 Olympic team. To have someone below officer class take the British Championship not once but twice seems to have been a healthy blow for equal opportunity at the time. Martin's father was, however, a brigadier – a point humorously made by his surviving team mates today (both officers) when surprise is expressed at this breakthrough.

Martin was also a member of the winning two-man team of the 5th Royal Inniskilling Dragoon Guards. His team mate was Major CH Blacker, MC, who was to become a legendary figure in the world of sport and in military circles. General Sir Cecil Blacker, GCB, OBE, MC (1916-2002) was known to all as 'Monkey' Blacker. A fellow officer cadet at Sandhurst had decided Blacker looked like an ape and Blacker was too confident a man to be easily taunted and embraced the nickname as his own. Monkey became a member of the 1951 Modern Pentathlon World Championship team and his career beyond that was one of dazzling variety. He was a novelist, a painter, a Grand National jockey, an international show jumper and an entertaining raconteur. He was even Regimental Boxing Champion while commanding that same regiment. His military career, both in the field and in political negotiations included the Dunkirk evacuation, effecting political changes east of Suez, dealing with the IRA in Northern Ireland, and managing the military policies of succeeding Labour and Conservative governments. Like other early characters in Modern Pentathlon, he was nonchalant about the sport. In his autobiography, *Monkey Business* (Quiller Press, 1993), he describes his early pentathlon experiences:

'I could run and ride. I had often fired a pistol. I had never fenced. I could swim but only after a fashion… A stroke resembling that of a shrimp, achieving little forward movement with maximum effort, earned me a time over the required lengths that I was too ashamed to reveal. I realized I must learn the 'crawl'.'

Blacker later found himself working at the Ministry of Defence in London where he: 'swam at lunchtime in the RAC baths, joined the London Fencing Club, shot my pistol and ran round the running track at the Duke of York's Barracks. I rose up the ranking table and at the end of 1951 was selected for the British team of four to compete at the World Championships in Sweden.'

Another notable sportsman competing in the 1947 British Championships was Major Derek Allhusen. Allhusen was to win Olympic team gold in the 1968

Three-Day-Event in which he also took individual silver. He was then 54 years old and a grandfather (his grandson, Nick, was the Cambridge MPC captain in 1992). In 1948, he also took 6th place in the first and only Olympic Winter Pentathlon which consisted of a 10km cross-country ski race, downhill skiing, and a fence, shoot and ride. Allhusen was offered an MBE after his triumph in Mexico but apparently turned it down because his teammates had not been given the same honour.

The international scene

Sweden's total domination of Modern Pentathlon before World War II had been dented a little by Germany and the USA in the 1930s. In particular, Gotthard Handrick's individual triumph for Germany in Berlin in 1936 must have hit the Swedes hard. But Germany had been crushed in the war and Sweden had been neutral. After the war, Sweden became top dog once again and took that responsibility very seriously, not least by being instrumental in the formation of a lasting international body. Germany returned to international competition in 1952.

In October 1947, a team competition took place in Sweden and the result was a clear predictor of the new order: 1. Sweden, 2. Hungary, 3. Finland, 4. Switzerland, 5. USA, 6. France, 7. Great Britain.

The individual event used two scoring systems alongside each other, the traditional placing points and the newly experimental points system modelled on the decathlon scoring system in Finland. It was significant that the two systems produced different outcomes:

Placing points: 1. Karácson (HUN)   2. Grut (SWE)
3. Gahr (SWE)

'Decathlon'style points: 1. Grut   2. Gahr
3. Karácson

1948 Olympic Winter Pentathlon

This event was experimental and 1948 was its only appearance in the Olympic calendar. 14 competitors took part and all the medals were won by Sweden. A surprise winner was 21 year old Gustav Lindh who, when interviewed in the year 2000 revealed that he 'did not mean to win', having expected one of the other Swedes, all many years his senior, to take the title. No one made much of a fuss of him when he got back to Sweden and his abiding memory is a salutary lesson for anyone hell-bent on lifelong celebrity: 'I gained some nice friends. We still exchange Christmas cards today - 52 years later.' The silver medallist was Wille Grut but the greatest loser was the favourite, Claes Egnell who broke his leg badly in the Downhill Ski-ing. That injury ruled him out of the Summer Olympic Modern Pentathlon in London for which he had also been a strong favourite.

The Winter Pentathlon event had been mounted as a 'demonstration event' at St. Moritz but, despite enthusiastic promotion by Sweden, it never gained a foothold. Only six countries were involved and the idea of riding in a Winter Olympics was unattractive to the FEI (Fédération Équestre Internationale). Despite a proposal for a 1950 World Winter Pentathlon Championship in USA or Switzerland, there was no room in the international programme for two Modern Pentathlons. Winter Biathlon (Cross-country skiing and rifle shooting) did take off in 1955, though, and for many years, the UIPM was named the UIPMB to include responsibility for the Winter Biathlon. It seemed to make some sense that multi-sports organisations might have mutual interests but it was not an easy relationship. Outside Sweden, modern pentathletes knew little about Winter Biathlon, though a Royal Marine, Rod Tuck, competed for Great Britain in the 1964 Olympic Winter Biathlon competition as well as being a pentathlete. The UIPMB bulletin reached a point where the summer issue was full of news about Biathlon (of little interest to pentathletes) and the winter issue was full of news about Modern Pentathlon (of little interest to biathletes).

1948 British Championships (Olympic Trials)

This event was held on April 20th to 24th over five days in the classic order. It was, in part, a rehearsal for the Olympic event but the nature of the entry necessitated modifications. There were 52 entries with no fewer than 15 teams represented. Though the event was sponsored by the Army Sports Control Board, a plea for donations appeared on the cover of the programme and all individual entries were charged 5/- (shillings) each with a further 5/- for each team entry. Aldershot's oddly-shaped municipal swimming pool, Bisley range, and Sandhurst (fencing and running) were tested as Olympic venues but the riding event fell far short of a preparation for the bigger event.

The shortage of horses and the fear of damaging those few they had before the Olympic event resulted in a highly modified riding event. The programme made it clear that this was not the usual cross-country event but merely one intended to 'test the ability of the competitor to ride and jump'. The Polo Ground at Aldershot was set out with just 8 jumps over a distance of 1,200 yards and a maximum time limit of five minutes was allowed. If the rider outran this time by a single second, he was disqualified. This draconian rule succeeded in eliminating 20 of the 52 riders from the competition and awarded all of them 52 placing points, a starting score certain to prevent success in the rest of the competition. Points were deducted from the starting score of 100 points for refusals and falls but, as if the rigid time limit wasn't difficult enough, the Chief Judge was allowed to deduct up to 100 points for poor style. So the dreaded and unpopular 'style' penalty, so reviled in the past, raised its ugly head once more. It was used extensively – even the winner, Lt. Michael Lumsden, a distinguished point to point rider, lost two style points and, among those lucky enough not to have been already disqualified, as many as 70 style points were deducted.

Though fencing was for a single hit, bouts still lasted five minutes and the field was divided into two separate pools in order to reduce the length of the day. Though the first four places were settled with a barrage, most other placings were shared in pairs. The running course was not revealed to competitors before the start. At the conclusion of the competition, the top ten were named as the Olympic Training Squad. Andy Martin retained his British title, this time by 12 place points from Michael Lumsden. Peter Duckworth was 3rd and a naval competitor, Geoffrey Brooke, took 4th place. These four were selected to go to the pre-Olympic international meeting in Thun / Berne in May. The man who had led the field until the running event was the 42 year old Percy Legard, veteran of three Olympic Games (1932,

1936, 1948-winter). His great comeback was thwarted at the final hurdle, however, when he slipped to 5th place overall.

The Berne Pre-Olympic Meet

This event gave a strong indication of the state of play before the Olympic Games. It took place from 12th to 15th May in the order shoot, swim, ride, fence, run and was won comfortably by Wille Grut. He never placed higher than 3rd in any event but his total of 36 was 28 points ahead of his compatriot, Sune Wehlin, a strong runner. The Hungarian, Lászlo Karácson, was 3rd but his Olympic performance was to cause a sensation for other reasons than his final result in Aldershot. The best British performances came from Geoffrey Brooke (19th) and Andy Martin (24th). The team positions were 1. Sweden, 2. Hungary, 3. Switzerland, 4. USA. Great Britain finished in 9th place though a judicious calculation based on finishing positions in each event boosted their placing to 6th in a report in *The Times* which confirmed the Olympic team as L/Cpl. Andy Martin, Lt. Michael Lumsden, Lt. Geoffrey Brooke, RN and Capt. Peter Duckworth.

1948 Olympic Games: London (GBR)

Janie Hampton's book, *The Austerity Olympics* (Aurum Press, 2008) gives a clear sense of what the 1948 Games were like. In post-war Britain, there was a shortage of practically everything –food, building materials, accommodation and, most importantly, money. Foreign countries chipped in with materials where they could but everything was very much 'make do and mend.' While most competitors from around the world stayed in huts in Richmond Park and had to bring their own towels with them, the pentathletes were accommodated at New College, RMA Sandhurst in what must have seemed the height of luxury.

The 1948 Games marked the end of sport as the preserve of the gentlemen. At last the class divisions were breaking down and, under a new Labour government that had just introduced the National Health Service, opportunities were extended to every class. Though initially sceptical about the ability of the Games to make any kind of money, the Labour government quickly decided to use the Games as an encouragement to tourism. The ploy worked and the Games made a profit. There were not many sponsors but the British male competitors were all kitted out, courtesy of Coopers' Outfitters, with a brand-new free pair of Y-front underpants each. They were the envy of their foreign rivals, apparently, who queued around the block to purchase a pair each of their own.

Personalities at the 1948 Games

Among the pentathletes were, as always, some interesting characters. The only competitor returning from the 1936 Games was the Belgian, Raoul Mollet who had a difficult ride and withdrew after the first event. The Swedish team consisted of Capt. Wille Grut, now the firm favourite; Lt. Sune Wehlin, a very strong runner, and, a late selection in the absence of the injured Claes Egnell, Lt. Gösta Gärdin. The strongest Hungarian was Capt. László Karácson who had won the Hungarian Championships in 1946 and 1947. His teammates were István Szondy who, in the early 1950s would play a central rôle in Hungarian success, and Frigyes Hegedüs, perhaps best known for his later manual of training, *Modern Pentathlon* (Corvina Press, 1968). The American, Major George Bissland Moore had been a track star at West Point Military Academy and acquitted himself honorably in World War II, having won two Bronze Stars, a Purple Heart and a Legion of Merit award. Roberto Curcio (Italy) was, at 35, the oldest competitor. He went on to be an important committee member of the UIPM and for many years was the power behind the Italian Modern Pentathlon Association. In 1982 he was to become involved in a major scandal involving the doping of horses at the World Championships in Italy (See Chapter 8). Lauri Vilkko (Finland) would go on to gain medals at the next three World Championships and the 1952 Olympic Games. Finally, 1948 marked the Olympic appearance of Karel Bártu, who later coached the Czech team to a silver medal at the 1976 Olympic Games. His son, Jan Bártu, who won a team silver and individual bronze at that Games, is, of course, the current Great Britain Performance Director.

This was an era of brief pentathlon lives. None of our 1948 team had long sporting careers. Neither Andy Martin, our best all-rounder, nor Michael Lumsden, the expert rider, continued in the sport beyond 1948. A new difficulty emerged for those pentathletes like Martin and Lumsden who were leaving the army – getting time off work to compete was often out of the question; the civilian world wanted its pound of flesh. Interestingly, Andy Martin's rank of Lance Corporal would, in fact, have excluded him from the Equestrian events at the 1948 Olympics. The FEI, despite protests, insisted that all competitors hold officer status. This resulted in a farcical situation where the winning Swedish team was disqualified. The Swedes had temporarily promoted Sgt. Gehnäll Persson to Second Lieutenant for the duration of the Games. Unfortunately, Persson rode round in his sergeant's cap which gave the game away. France was awarded the gold medal instead. By 1950, even the FEI had come into the modern world and dropped this divisive rule from its statutes.

Two characters

Lt. Cdr Geoffrey Brooke, DSC, (1920-2009) had a remarkable naval career. In 1941 he was on board *HMS Prince of Wales* when it was sunk off Singapore. In the following weeks he made a daring escape from the Japanese by boarding a Yangtze river steamer which was fire-bombed and machine-gunned throughout the journey. He organized the rescue of other survivors and, in a series of small dilapidated open boats and rafts he made a 1,600 mile journey from Indonesia to Sri Lanka and eventual safety. Brooke wrote two books about the experience, *Alarm Starboard* (1982) and *Singapore's Dunkirk* (1989). He also wrote an unpublished history of Modern Pentathlon which he completed shortly after the Olympic event in 1948. It must have been hard enough for Brooke to train for his sport since he was a naval officer but there is some irony in the fact that he was such a terrible swimmer (6:29.6 in the Olympic event). He obviously made up for this weakness in many other ways.

Though he was the non-competing member of the 1948 Olympic team, Peter Duckworth was to become our leading pentathlete after the Games. He was British Champion the following year and placed 9th in the first

World Championships that same year. His sporting career was cut short by a serious shrapnel wound when fighting in the Korean War in 1951. He went on to become the central figure in the MPAGB, managing our National teams and driving the sport forward in Great Britain with strategies for raising money and for more effective training. Most of all, he always took time to write to young pentathletes coming into the sport with words of encouragement. That there are a number of such letters still stored away today is testimony to how importantly his encouragement was regarded. In one such letter to a young naval officer, Michael Egan, Duckworth touched on one of the great advantages of the sport. He wrote: 'To my mind the great thing about this game is that you and I can indulge our taste for competition in five events in which, outside the framework of the Modern Pentathlon, we couldn't begin to or would not dare to. Because of this we can find umpteen other sportsmen of similar mind with whom, regardless of our standard in this event or that, we can do battle.'

Though recently bed-ridden after a stroke robbed him of his daily fitness regime, Peter Duckworth remains full of lively conversation about Modern Pentathlon.

The competition

The Modern Pentathlon began with the riding event on Tweseldown on a gloriously sunny Saturday 30th July. In keeping with Christian tradition, the Sunday was a rest day and, in keeping with British tradition, the remainder of the competition was conducted in pouring rain from Monday 1st to Thursday 4th August. Of the 47 competitors, 42 took part as members of full teams of three. Represented in this way were Argentina, Belgium,

Brazil, Czechoslovakia, Finland, France, Hungary, Italy, Spain, Sweden, Switzerland, USA, Uruguay and Great Britain. There were, additionally, two Chileans, two Mexicans, and a Cuban taking part. This was a sensationally diverse field from so many countries so soon after the war and pentathlon officials in London were determined not to let such an opportunity for forming a new international organization pass them by.

After months of anxiety about the riding event, the organisers achieved the late 'acquisition' of fifty horses from Germany. This, together with the 'dozen or so' loaned or hired horses, assured a strong field. The 5000 metre course had 22 fixed jumps and was thought to be somewhat easier than the 1936 course in Berlin. It, nevertheless, proved a better test of horsemanship - instead of 25 riders being fault-free, only nine competitors were inside time and without faults at Tweseldown.

Wille Grut set a hot pace in the overall competition by winning the ride in 9:18.2. George Moore (USA) placed 2nd in 9:22.7 and Michael Lumsden provided the GB team with the highlight of its competition by coming 3rd in 9:29.0. One of the favourites, the Hungarian, Karácson, suffered a bad fall in the riding event and broke his collar bone. He spent the night in hospital but returned for the fencing event in the morning with his right arm bound to his side. Karacson had been considered one of Wille Grut's main rivals before the competition began but Grut was confident of his own superior preparation. An interesting link between the two came in later years – Grut's Hungarian wife had previously been married to Karácson. Another of the Hungarians, Frigyes Hegedüs also failed to complete the course. This devastating start to the Hungarian efforts may well have played some part in their failure to attend the first three World Championships (1949, 1950 and 1951). They had learned their lesson, however, by the time of their return in the 1952 Olympic Games where they staged a revolution in their fortunes. In his book *Modern Pentathlon*, Hegedus is generous about the sportsmanship of the British team at the riding event and includes the following little moral tale. In the draw, one of the British team (Michael Lumsden) drew a horse that he knew well. Feeling this would give him an unfair advantage over his rivals, he asked the jury to allow him to pick another one. The jury members were suspicious that he had picked a poor horse and was doing his best to avoid riding it. They refused his request and Lumsden went on to gain a clear round and finish in 3rd place.

In the fencing event, Wille Grut shared 1st place with Aëcio Coelho (BRA) who also took part in the Three-Day-Event at the 1948 Games. They each won 28 bouts, two clear of George Moore in 3rd place. This left Grut on two place points and Moore on four after two events, both well clear of the rest of the field. The best British fencer was Brooke who took 13th place with 20 wins although Lt. Col. White, the manager, felt that 'the British team had more than their fair share of double hits'. Karácson (HUN) had fought bravely all day with his right arm strapped to his body. He was naturally a left-handed fencer but his total of 21 victories was, nevertheless, an heroic achievement.

In the shooting at Bisley, there were nine competitors who shot 190 or better compared to only five in Berlin. The 190s included Wille Grut whose final series placed him 5th behind the winner, Bruno Riem (SUI), 194; Werner Schmid (SUI), 193; Frigyes Hegedüs (HUN), 193; and Lauri Vilkko (FIN), also 190. True, there was no one of Charles Leonard's stature to get a perfect score, but the general standard was getting better. Karácson, though a strong shot with his right arm, found the enforced use of his left arm at Bisley just too much to bear. He only put a single shot off target and scored 173 but that, sadly, was to be the end of his competition. Grut disappeared into a distant lead overall, having accumulated only seven total place points after three events. Moore still held on to 2nd place even though he'd only placed 21st in the shooting. Bruno Riem's fine 194 victory moved him up to 3rd place overall.

The heavy rain that had begun towards the end of the shooting event persisted relentlessly throughout the swimming at Aldershot Municipal Baths the next day. A 25 metre section had been boarded off so each swimmer had to swim 12 lengths in cold and murky water. Despite the weather, 600 spectators turned out to cheer the pentathletes. Even the previous week's sunshine had failed to warm the water so a fast swim seemed to be unlikely despite rumours of two sub-four minute swims having recently taken place in Sweden. Once again, it was Wille Grut who took 1st place, his third victory in the competition. His time of 4: 17.0 was four seconds better than the runner-up, Istvan Szondy (HUN) who swam 4:21.1. Lauri Vilkko (FIN) was 3rd. Overall, despite the sizeable gap between them, the leading two remained the same: Grut (8 points), Moore (43 points). The newcomer to the Swedish team, Gösta Gärdin, had moved into 3rd position (44 points). No one could catch Grut now.

The weather brightened up for the final running event over rough ground at Sandhurst. A big hill kept the times slow – only three men broke 15 minutes: Sune Wehlin (SWE) who won in 14:09.9 and the two Finns, Lauri

Vilkko and Viktor Platan. George Moore and Gösta Gärdin came just behind them in 4th and 5th places respectively which protected their hold on the silver and bronze medals overall. The British team produced a mediocre performance: Martin (20th), Lumsden (34th) and Brooke (37th) but had at least kept up some kind of British tradition by all finishing in the top 20 in the running event.

Though, for the final time, there was no official team competition, everyone had made the relevant calculations. The finishing team positions would have been:

1. SWE (167)   2. FIN (221)   3. USA (224)
4. SUI (272)   5. FRA (316)   6. ITA (321)
7. ARG (329)   8. ESP (367)   9. GBR (385)
10. URU (408)   11. BRA (476)

1948 London: The medallists (l-r: Wille Grut (SWE) gold, Bissland Moore (USA) silver, and Gösta Gärdin (SWE) bronze).

Grut's overwhelming domination of the 1948 Olympic Games was a feat that can never be repeated. With a total placing score of only 16, he was a full 31 place points ahead of the silver medallist. He won three of the five events outright. Of course, such a sensational victory was bound to draw the attention of the media. Even in 1948, newspaper reports tried to turn him into Mr Perfect. It was said that he would avoid standing next to a smoker even outdoors (quite difficult to do in 1948) and that the only break he ever took from his rigorous training schedule was to escort his sons to church on Sunday morning. Grut was having none of this and made his views perfectly clear: 'In Sweden, an engineer or an agriculturalist only gets a paragraph in the papers, while a man who kicks a ball gets himself splashed over six columns. I don't approve of that. So many people now want only the gay life. This is why I am retiring. I set out to do a thing and I did it. Now I shall start out on a new phase of my life.'

Perhaps even more significant than his breath-taking victory in 1948 was his enormous influence on the sport as Secretary-General of the UIPM from 1960 to 1984. Grut managed the Swedish team until 1960 before devoting himself to serious UIPM business. Grut's father, Torben Grut, had been the architect who designed the 1912 Olympic Stadium and who had written so poetically about his ambitions for the stadium (See Chapter 1). Wille had been a good student and was all set to study medicine at Cambridge when the collapse of Ivar Kreuger's business empire in 1932 robbed the Gruts of all their money. So enormous was Kreuger's influence that he controlled 64% of the entire Swedish Stock Exchange and thousands were bankrupted by the collapse. Instead, Wille Grut became a soldier. That cost his family nothing and set him underway on a highly successful sporting and military career.

As a young man, Wille represented Sweden in the swimming at the 1936 Berlin Olympics where he also watched the pentathlon events. In witnessing Handrick's win which brought to an end the unbroken success of Sweden did he vow revenge for his home country? Whatever his motivation, he became Swedish Modern Pentathlon champion five times between 1939 and 1948. By the time he arrived in London for the 1948 Games, he was only a month short of his 34th birthday. Grut no doubt gained training opportunities through Sweden's wartime neutrality, but Grut's sporting career would have been even greater had the world not been at war and he had been able to compete in international competitions. He later rose to the rank of Lieutenant Colonel in the Swedish army and was a much-admired leader of his men. Like every other Swedish Olympic champion before him, Grut was a member of the prestigious Royal Svea Artillery Regiment. In his early training, Bengt Uggla, who had placed 4th in the 1920 Olympic Modern Pentathlon, told him, 'Play sport until the day you die, but do not let sport be the death of you'. Grut remembered this and, at 97 years old, has only recently cut down on his daily swim and gym workouts. He lives in the Swedish lakeside town of Ostersund. A highly intelligent and affable man, Wille Grut has smoothed the way for the survival of Modern Pentathlon in the modern era, as will be very evident in the coming chapters. Of the respect due to the great administrators of Modern Pentathlon, our sport owes him the most.

The New Union and the beginning of annual World Championships

On 3rd August 1948, a meeting of those involved in the 1948 Olympic Modern Pentathlon took place at Sandhurst, on the penultimate day of the competition. 17 nations were represented. From the Americas came Argentina, Chile, Uraguay, Brazil, Mexico and the USA. From Europe came Great Britain, France, Spain, Italy, Switzerland, Austria, Hungary, Czechoslovakia, Finland and, of course, Sweden. All were unanimous in approving the formation of FIP (Fédération Internationale de Pentathlon Moderne). This new organisation would represent the interests of all the national bodies, co-ordinate their efforts and instigate an annual World Championship, the first to be held in Sweden in 1949. The new committee consisted of Tor Wibom (President), Leslie Wieler (Vice-President), Sven Thofelt (Secretary) and Bo Lindman (Treasurer). To have the British organiser of the Olympic event on a committee with the three celebrated Swedes was an honour for Great Britain and there is no doubt that Wieler's easy, considerate manner was helpful to the committee in the years ahead. Once Wibom had established the organisation he had planned for so long, he graciously surrendered the presidency to Gustav Dyrrsen, the 1920 Olympic Champion, who would remain President of the UIPM until 1960. The existing organization, CIPMO, had been concerned solely with the administration of an Olympic competition every four years. Although there were two representatives from Modern Pentathlon on this committee, the rest were made up of representatives of the constituent sporting bodies. Frequently, however, these representatives had no experience of nor affection for Modern Pentathlon whatsoever.

Once the FIP was established, the immediate road ahead was not as smooth as it could have been. Already there were enemies of the sport. An American submission to the IOC in 1948 declared 'It is generally agreed that the Olympic Program is already far too long,' and then suggested Modern Pentathlon be dropped because 'participation in this event is by a very limited number in only a few countries.' This same submission also proposed deleting Women's High Jump, Long Jump, and Shot Putt as well as many gymnastic events so was unlikely to gather much support. Tor Wibom came away from the founding Sandhurst meeting sufficiently confident to write to the governing bodies of each constituent sport inviting the nomination of an expert to liaise with the FIP and attend its meetings but without voting rights.

There were flies in the ointment, however. Two Frenchmen, Le Commandant Georges Hector of the FEI (Fédération Équestre Internationale) and Armand Massard of the FIE (Fédération Internationale d'Escrime) were determined not to relinquish any of their powers to the new upstart organization. Hector wrote an oily letter congratulating Wibom on the formation of the FIP and insisting that CIPMO now be disbanded in favour of the new organisation. He also proposed a number of alterations to the FIP statutes; Wibom's French wasn't really up to the job, he implied, and he, Hector, would happily correct him. Imagine Wibom's outrage to find that, at the CIPMO meeting that followed, Hector spoke vehemently against FIP. To add salt to the wound, neither Wibom nor Lindman, the two Modern Pentathlon representatives on CIPMO had been invited to this meeting. At this same meeting, Massard, who was of the opinion that, since France didn't have a National Modern Pentathlon Association, no other country should, spoke out against the formation of the FIP. Neither Massard nor Hector had attended the 1948 Olympic Modern Pentathlon and knew very little indeed about the sport. A series of angry letters from Lindman to Otto Mayer, the IOC Chancellor in Lausanne, ensued. It was IOC President, Sigfrid Edström who intervened on behalf of his Swedish colleagues. He and Bo Ekelund, the Swedish IOC representative, read through the new statutes of the FIP carefully and pronounced themselves highly satisfied. Edström wrote to Mayer: 'I have told Mr Thofelt (Secretary) that the old committee (CIPMO) will not be needed any more and that the federation of Modern Pentathlon (FIP) will be recognised by us.'

Extraordinarily, this highly satisfactory conclusion was greeted in a rather curmudgeonly way by Lindman. He disputed that the IOC had any power to make such a decision. When Edström gently pointed out that any new federation would have to be ratified by the IOC, Lindman argued that Edström was 'entirely wrong' about this and that the IOC's sole decision was whether to include a sport in the Olympic progamme or not. This seems to us today a foolhardy stance for Lindman to have taken, especially in the light of Modern Pentathlon's continued battle for inclusion over the years. Luckily, Edström was a big man and took no offence. Indeed, in late 1949, by which time Gustav Dyrssen had replaced Tor Wibom as President of FIP, Edström stepped in to quell the Frenchman, Massard, who was still resentfully making waves. Edström wrote to his Chancellor in Lausanne:

'My dear Otto, Enclosed please find a letter that I have just received from Massard. It seems that we will fight about this matter also. Since now an international federation for Modern Pentathlon has been formed with 17 countries with such a splendid president as General Dyrssen and such an energetic secretary as Col. Lieut. Thofelt it seems to me that we ought not to raise any more trouble about this matter. Each federation will have a member in the council of this new international federation of Modern Pentathlon. All competitions will take place after the rules of this federation and it will also arrange all world championships and competitions. Why shall it then not take care of the Olympic Games? I know that Massard and de Polignac will have a talk with you ahead and I wish to warn you.'

If there was any revenge to be had by the thwarted Frenchmen, it took place at the IOC meeting in Paris in late 1949 when the FIP would be formally ratified. Despite Edström having used the word 'federation' throughout the above letter, the FIP committee members were aware that there would be pressure to refuse the use of a word that copied the titles of (and, therefore, appeared to confer the same powers as) the other established constituent sports. So Bo Ekelund, the Swedish representative, was dispatched to Paris with the instructions that only 'in the case of emergency' should the FIP allow the word 'union' to replace 'federation'. The Frenchmen demanded to be appeased and so the UIPM (Union Internationale de Pentathlon Moderne) was born.

The birth of the points system

Wibom's 1948 manifesto contained a number of proposals. Apart from the formation of an 'international pentathletic league', other stated ambitions were: an annual world championship; the instigation of team competitions; the establishment of a winter pentathlon; a full amendment of the rules; and the use of a new scoring table to replace the place point system.

A points system had actually been proposed by CIPMO many years before in Berlin 1930. The Germans tried it out in the late 1930s and Sweden had been operating a dual points and placings system for about five years. Wibom declared that the placing system gave 'accidental and incorrect classification' and, even worse, it 'makes it possible for competitors to help comrades by dishonorable means, which is impossible under the points system.' The 'dishonorable means' is possibly a reference to an accusation made by the Swedish journalist, Torsten Tegner, In the recriminations that followed Sweden's very poor showing at the Berlin Olympics, Tegner accused Erik Drakenburg, the Swedish Team Manager, of instructing the other two Swedes in the team to run slower than Sven Thofelt in order to boost his position in the competition. When runners depart at one minute intervals, well-separated in the field, it is extremely difficult to achieve such a plan and, in any case, Ebbe Gyllenstierna and Georg Boisman ran far quicker than Thofelt in the competition. The journalist, popularly known as 'TT', might have felt guilty about such wild accusations, though, because he went on to sponsor Wille Grut's early training.

Cheating, then, was not a defect of the placing system. A better argument for disbanding it was that, under the placing system, it was possible to run ten minutes faster than anyone else and still only have a single point advantage for your expertise. That said, some would argue that if Modern Pentathlon is truly a test of the all-rounder, extreme expertise in a single discipline should not be overly rewarded. Perhaps the real spirit of Modern Pentathlon resided in the placing system after all. An interesting exercise is to apply the placing system to the modern sport; you will be frequently surprised what little difference it makes to the final order.

As with most innovations, the Swedes had found that there was initial opposition in Sweden to the points system but by the time of its first official use at the World Championships in 1954, practically everyone was fully behind it.

The points system was founded on the following initial standards:

Riding (5000 metres cross-country):

1000 points maximum. Bogey time: 10 minutes +/- 1 point per second.

Refusal penalties: 1st – 40 points; 2nd -60 points; 3rd – 90 points.

Penalties for a fall of horse or rider: 60 points.

NB. All fences were fixed so knockdowns were impossible.

Fencing: 1000 points for winning 75% of bouts.

Score per bout determined by formula 1300 /number of bouts.

A minimum of 20 bouts required or two hits per bout used.

Shooting: 1000 points for 195 out of 200 +/- 20 points per target point.

The number of hits on target would now be irrelevant; only the total target points were considered.

300 metres Swimming: 1000 points for 4 minutes +/- four points per second.

4000 metres Running: 1000 points for 15 minutes +/- three points per second.

This was a format that would remain essentially the same for many years to come. The nature of the riding would change and the standard of swimming and running would improve sufficiently to demand a change of the 1000 points position but the main formula was set effectively from the outset. Wibom was very clear about the effect of the new points system on the riding event: 'Riding is somewhat downgraded in comparison with other branches, the reason for that is that, in our estimation, one can <u>never</u> have at one's disposal in pentathletics horses which are of exactly equal worth'.

Concern about the vagaries of the riding event was also raised by Sven Thofelt at about the same time. The Frenchman, Massard, wrote proposing that the order revert to a previous version in which the riding had been the final event. Thofelt replied: 'From experience it has been shown that horses are never exactly equal, and that consequently the equestrian competition depends very largely upon luck. We have found that it is very unfortunate for a competitor who has done good work in the three or four tests to lose all his chances in the pentathlon on account of a bad horse.'

Like a wild stallion, the riding event clearly needed discipline and this was the newly-born UIPM's attempt to bring its effect on the whole competition under control.

1949 (First) World Championships: Stockholm (SWE)

The inaugural 1949 World Championships took place late in the season (16-20 October) in Stockholm. Wille Grut, as organizer, was there to welcome the 21 pentathletes that took part. Nine of them were Olympic veterans, the other twelve were part of the new order. As in 1950 in Berne, where only 19 attended, the competitors came exclusively from Western Europe. Indeed, the Swedish *Dagbladet* rather meanly described it as: 'A World Championship in modern pentathlon which is actually a European Championship and a European Championship without Hungarians – the Swedish class Karácson – and naturally without the Germans.' This was a disappointing start after Grut's hard work. Limited financial resources were partly the problem for other countries but a number, too, were waiting to see the outcome of these opening attempts before committing themselves. A team event was officially established for the very first time and in 1949 and 1950, Sweden won gold and Finland the silver. In 1950, Switzerland, the previous year's bronze medallists were pushed into 4th place by the Italians. Other participating nations were Great Britain (4th in 1949, 5th in 1950), Belgium and France.

The first individual World Champion was a blond, good-looking Swedish sergeant called Tage Bjurefelt who could, reputedly, run 400 metres in 48 seconds. He had won the Swedish Championship at his first attempt. Like Grut, the 1948 Olympic Champion, Bjurefelt won three of the five events outright – the riding, the shooting (a poor 183) and the running. He then promptly disappeared forever from the world of Modern Pentathlon! He was, apparently, 'unfit' a year later in Berne and so failed to defend his title. He will forever be the first World Champion but the brevity of his sporting career is mystifying. Like so many soldiers of the time, the pressures of military life may have drawn him away from competition or, alternatively, a new civilian career may have been unsupportive of his sporting talents.

He managed to push the impressive Finns, Vilkko and Platan into 2nd and 3rd places with the Olympic bronze medallist, Gosta Gärdin taking 4th place.

Bjurefelt may have stolen the thunder in 1949 but, back in 6th place, only weeks into a pentathlon career, having been spotted swimming in a Stockholm harbour, was Lasse Hall, the man who would become the first double Olympic Champion (1952 and 1956). Hall, from Karlskrona, was a carpenter by trade and therefore a civilian. So great was his potential, however, that swift arrangements were made for him to be employed by the Swedish Admiralty and his training monitored and developed by the best in the land. The investment paid off handsomely. Only a year later, Hall was World Champion, a feat he repeated in 1951 before taking his first Olympic title in Helsinki. As we know, some good fortune is a prerequisite for consistently great performance in Modern Pentathlon, but Wille Grut characterized Hall's strengths as 'will power, endurance and an ability to come back after failure', qualities that we can recognize in only the best of our sportsmen and women.

The 23 year old Hall took the 1950 world title in Berne with a commanding 19 point total. For a relative beginner, he impressed everyone by winning the fencing event and then, in a 25 metre pool, was the first man to break four minutes for the swimming. His time of 3:55.0 was 17 seconds ahead of the runner-up. Diulio Brignetti (ITA) won the silver medal (28 points) and Lauri Vilkko (FIN), the previous year's runner-up, took the bronze (33 points).

Hylton Cleaver –Modern Pentathlon journalist extraordinaire

One of the spectators won over by watching the London Olympics was the eccentric and brilliant *Evening*

Standard reporter, Hylton Cleaver. As a successful writer of schoolboy yarns and detective novels, Cleaver knew how to tell a story. For him, hyperbole was merely a working tool and when he became enthralled with Modern Pentathlon, he applied the same stylistic devices to his reporting of the sport. Take for instance, his report on the plucky Frenchman, André Lacroix. Having broken his wrist and twisted his ankle in the riding event, Lacroix nevertheless completed the whole competition much to the amazement and admiration of fellow competitors. Cleaver described the accident as follows: 'Lacroix found his horse apparently kneeling down for him to mount again, but unfortunately kneeling on the rider's arm, which is now in plaster.' Lacroix's heroic battle clearly caught Cleaver's imagination and he rarely missed the opportunity to turn him into a character from one of his schoolboy yarns. Reporting on a fencing event the following year he described Lacroix as a' black-moustached, sharp-chinned, ferret-eyed d'Artagnan.'

The Swiss winner of the shooting event, Bruno Riem, caused something of a sensation when asked to pose for photos afterwards. On a still-crowded range, he lifted his pistol and quite without warning fired a live shot. The press report read: 'He may have been able to knock ash off a cigarette but it was an alarming experience. He must have missed Duckworth by no more than a foot and the Englishman leapt back thoroughly scared.'

Mad dogs and Englishmen

The British team's placing of 4th and 5th respectively in 1949 and 1950 was essentially the best of the also-rans. In Stockholm, a flu-ravaged Peter Duckworth, fourth member of the Olympic team was our best performer in

9th place, with new man, Jack Lumsdaine (RAF), who swam the majority of his race back stroke, behind him in 13th. Geoffrey Brooke bowed out of his competitive career in 16th place. A year later in Berne, it was Lumsdaine, having replaced Duckworth as British Champion, who took 9th place with Duckworth 16th and Ted Marsh 18th. But these are the bare bones of the story. As so often happens, it is the also-rans who have the most interesting adventures.

Here's Cleaver, once again, with his account of Ted Marsh's last minute arrival in Berne to replace the injured Michael Howard:

'Britain's reserve man, Captain Ted Marsh, called for from England yesterday, had left Oxford at 8 a.m. wearing riding breeches, boots, spurs and service dress; drove by car to Northolt and says that when he reached Berne the Customs had only time to ask whether he was carrying cartridges when senior officials brushed everyone aside, crying: "Make way there for the captain." Orders had clearly come from the highest level to send him through.

After a 45 minutes' car ride he was allowed time to inspect the jumps on foot, was given one brandy and hoisted into the saddle. He rode the course courageously enough, and afterwards, although soaked to the skin, postponed a bath or food in order to hurry away for a practice swim in the local baths. That spirit represents for me the great appeal of the Pentathlon. Even then, before turning in, after more than 12 hours in rather uncomfortable kit, he found time to visit Corporal Howard, whose stay in hospital, to the dismay of our team, who have not much money, is costing £2 a day. Nobody quite knows how this is going to be paid; but obviously it will be.'

The whole British operation seems to have been destined for disaster. The Team Manager, Errol Lonsdale had arrived in Berne with Michael Howard ahead of the others. Lumsdaine, a fighter pilot in the war, had commandeered an old bi-plane and persuaded Peter Duckworth to accompany him in it to Berne, sharing the costs. Running out of petrol over France and with a chunk of the tail fin hanging off, Lumsdaine landed to re-fuel. Unfortunately, he'd chosen an airport at which a major French military exercise was taking place. The control tower fired Verey light flares warning him off; he fired a flare back and landed. Ignoring all protests, the 6ft 3in (191cm) Lumsdaine marched through the crowd demanding his plane be serviced promptly. In recalling the incident, Duckworth declares: 'I have never in my life met a man so utterly fearless as Jack Lumsdaine.' The big Flight Lieutenant got his way and they arrived in Berne in time for the competition. Meanwhile, Howard had been knocked unconscious in a fall from a horse in training and was in hospital, leaving Lonsdale to fill the empty third team place himself had it not been for the last minute arrival of Ted Marsh.

Jack Lumsdaine, who had grown up in Shanghai with an Australian father and American mother, was a versatile performer and the best British pentathlete from 1949 to 1954. As an airman, he also competed in, and won, an extraordinary multi-tasking event arranged by the French each year, the *Pentathlon Aeronautique International Militaire*. A team of two (one pilot, one crew) was to fly from Paris to Vichy on a specified route, shoot, move dropped weights from one end of a pool to the other, fence, score basketball hoops via obstacles, conduct a 12 km evasion exercise wearing a 25 lb backpack, crawl under wire, negotiate a tunnel 50 cm in diametre, cross a policed frontier, carry a comrade 100m, scale a wall, and reach a destination by map reading. This Lumsdaine and his partner, Sq. Ldr Podevin, another established pentathlete, did with great success. This description may, of course, be another example of Cleaver's hyperbole (elsewhere he described the event as 'involving escaping from prison') but it seems entirely consistent with the times and the pentathletes of that extraordinary generation.

Chapter Five: 1951-1959

'If a little luck comes our way (and I think I can fairly say that it never has before) we should have at least one individual highly placed.' Errol Lonsdale, British Team Manager 1952.

The decade of the 1950s broadened participation in Modern Pentathlon throughout the world. With its own international body now established, this was the first decade of the modern era of the sport. Pentathlon careers generally became longer and the commitment to individual and national success was much more serious. There were, however, also unexpectedly brief appearances at the very highest level revealing the difficulties of sustaining a job, military or civilian, while continuing to compete. At international level, this period marked the arrival of the Soviet Union on the world sporting stage. By 1960, World Championships and Olympic Games had been held in North and South America, Asia and Australia, and nations from the African continent – Tunisia, Morocco and South Africa –had also participated. On a domestic level, a concerted effort to involve schools, universities and pony clubs paid off and significant civilian participation on a larger scale began.

1951 British Championships

Grand plans for a pentathlon competition to take place in Hyde Park during the Festival of Britain seem to have come to nothing. The prospect of shooting live rounds in such a crowded public space probably ended discussions early on. The British Championships of 1951, however, had 72 competitors and was won by the Royal Marines team. Indeed, Naval and Air Force pentathletes tended to rule the roost in the early part of the decade. Of the 72, John Majendie, a Kent policeman was the only 'civilian'. This was a forerunner to much more extensive Metropolitan Police involvement later in the decade. Majendie was the MPAGB Secretary for many years and, at the age of 91, was recently presented the prestigious *Times/Sternberg Award* for organising annual Normandy landing reunions. Future British champions, Don Cobley (RAF) and George Norman (Army) were making their first appearances and a Capt. CG Wylie, who had won the British Championship as a Sandhurst cadet in 1939, also competed. The appearance of World Champion Lasse Hall at the British event raised expectations. The Swede won the competition but Peter Duckworth regained his British title, finishing just behind Hall. Sadly, Duckworth, at the peak of his career, was denied another World Championship; days after the British event, he was on his way to fight in Korea. That left a British team of Jack Lumsdaine, Jervis Percy and Monkey Blacker to place 4th of the eight teams that competed in Hälsingborg, in the south of Sweden.

1951 World Championships: Helsingborg (SWE)

After the rather limited entry of the first two years of this competition, the established European teams were joined in Hälsingborg by Denmark, a surprisingly strong team from Brazil and an unexpectedly weak team from the USA. There were 27 pentathletes in total. The fact that it was once again the Swedes who hosted the World Championship only two years after launching it and that it was held very late in the year (21-25 October) was because Spain, the original hosts, had withdrawn. With only 19 member countries, not all of whom had willingly paid their subscriptions, the sport was relying rather too heavily on the fine band of Swedish ex-champions to hold the sport together.

The riding event was half the usual distance which enabled everyone to achieve some kind of score. Torsten Lindqvist (SWE) won the riding, as he did the fencing. In the shooting, Eduardo de Medeiros (BRA), won with a score of 195, a considerable improvement on the previous two years in which the slightly smaller targets introduced in 1948 were proving challenging. The farcical rule whereby a man who hit the target 20 times was given a better placing than one who hit it 19 times regardless of target score was fully exposed for its weakness when Helwigh (DEN) was placed higher than Taalikka (FIN) –the Dane scored 152 with 20 shots on target while the Finn missed once but still managed 185 (33 target points better than his rival!). This rule was changed soon after the competition. Lasse Hall, the defending champion came into his own with a swim of 3:53.0 and his compatriot Wehlin won a difficult (or overlong) run in a very slow 15:40.0. The final result was predictable: Hall retained his title edging out Lauri Vilkko (FIN) by two place points and Lindqvist took the bronze medal. Also predicable was the team competition with Sweden retaining its title comfortably from the Finns. The impressive team from Brazil took the bronze medal, 52 placing points ahead of the British team. Team member Monkey Blacker records in his memoirs:

'Considering the amateur way in which we had prepared we were pleased to finish fourth out of the nine competing teams, though the Swedes, Finns and Brazilians, all far more professional in their attitude, beat us easily.'

Lumsdaine had finished 9th, Percy 12th and Blacker 16th. The highlights were Percy's 3rd place in the riding and 4th place in the final run.

1952 British Championships

These were held over five days at the usual Aldershot venues and appeared to be quite inconsequential in selecting the team for the Olympic Games that year. Even though the British competitors were joined by Lacroix of France and Minder of Switzerland, the new champion was John Hewitt of the Royal Marines who led his team to retain the Laffan Cup but personally never finished higher than 5th in any event. The runner-up was George Norman, 3rd place went to Jim Wood and a rather unfit Jack Lumsdaine was 4th. However, the team that was selected for Helsinki consisted of Lt. Hewitt, Flt.Lt. Lumsdaine and Lt. Jervis Percy who had finished only 17th. All of them were officers. Sgt. George Norman of the Army PT Corps, however, was relegated to 4th man and Marine Cpl. Jim Wood's 3rd place appears to have been entirely overlooked, though he was part of the training squad.

The Team Manager Maj. Gen. Errol Lonsdale MBE (1913-2003) became a tremendous servant to Modern Pentathlon. He had fought in Sudan, Korea, and Malaya and became both MPAGB President and a member of the UIPM executive board. As a former Transport Corps officer, his greatest love was actually trains and he has the distinction of having a train named after him. He was

John Hewitt rides to victory in the 1952 British Championships at Tweseldown.

also enterprising as a fund raiser for the BOA. He did a deal with Rothmans which ensured that the more people who smoked, the more money would come into the BOA coffers. Not a sponsorship deal that would win many friends today. Lonsdale was reserved in his optimism about how his team would do in Helsinki: 'If a little luck comes our way (and I think I can fairly say that it never has before) we should have at least one individual highly placed'. And, just as he expected they might be, his cautious hopes were soon dashed.

1952 Olympic Games: Helsinki (FIN)

Although the 1949 and 1950 congresses had been attended by only 9 and 14 countries respectively, 23 countries attended the 1952 Congress in Hämeenlinna, the small town in which the Modern Pentathlon was held. It was there that the decision was made that the points system would succeed the placings system from 1954 onwards.

There were 15 teams competing in the first official Olympic team event. Hungary had returned having missed the first three World Championships. Uruguay, Mexico and Portugal sent teams and there were individuals from Argentina, Chile, and South Africa. Germany was welcomed back into the sport for the first time since 1936. Above all, the 1952 Games marked the debut of the formidable USSR team.

For those young enough not to have experienced the Cold War between the West and the Communist bloc it may be difficult to understand the bitter enmity created by this division. Traditionally, the Soviet Union was scornful of the Olympic Games. With some justification, it regarded the organisation as a refuge for bourgeois attitudes and elitism. The exclusion of the working classes through its draconian rules about amateurism and tight control of opportunity for them to compete had been built into the Olympic ethos no matter how much its officials lauded the aims of 'sport for all'. Though Stalin's attitudes had been consistent with the Soviet stance, the development of sport in the Soviet Union as a unifying team activity for young working people led him to see the value of international sport as a means of convincing the world of the virtues of the socialist approach to life. When the Soviet Union attended the Helsinki games, its leaders insisted that the Communist bloc countries be accommodated separately from other countries. The Soviet athletes selected had been carefully picked to represent correct Soviet attitudes abroad and tainting them with too much Western experience would not do. Wille Grut tells a tale of having visited a sauna during the Helsinki games expecting to find it empty. It turned out to be packed with Soviet athletes. One of the coaches spoke a little German and having asked the Olympic Champion, 'Bist du nicht Wille Grut?'and got an affirmative answer, he invited Grut back to the Soviet camp to drink tea – a rare experience which Grut remembers with great pleasure.

Of the 51 competitors in Finland, 11 of them had been at the previous Olympics including great Finnish hope, Lauri Vilkko, who had placed 4th in London. In fact, 22 members of the field were eventually to retire as multi-Olympians. The most important of those was the 22 year old Armenian, Igor Novikov (1930-2007) who was to dominate the world stage in the late 1950s, becoming World Champion in 1957, 1958, 1959, and 1961. Novikov competed in four Olympic Games but, astonishingly, was never Individual Olympic Champion. When he retired, he led a training school in Yerevan and became President of Soviet Modern Pentathlon (1977-91) and UIPM President (1988-92).

A few competitors took part in three Olympic Games during this period: the Chilean, Nilo Floody, and two of the Mexicans, Jose Perez and Antonio Almada. Had it not been for the Swiss boycott of the 1956 Melbourne Olympics over the Soviet invasion of Hungary, Erhard Minder and Werner Vetterli, the 1954 World Championship silver medallist, would surely have done the same. Vetterli went on to be a TV presenter and politician in his home country. Another notable entry in 1952 was Australian swimming coach, Forbes Carlile, whose most famous swimmer was Shane Gould (1972 Olympic Champion). He celebrated his 90th birthday in 2011. How Carlile managed to compete at all is a mystery

– Australia didn't hold a National Championship until just before its own Olympic Games in 1956.

The favourites for the first-ever team victory were surely the Swedes. Lasse Hall was reigning World Champion, Thorsten Lindqvist had won bronze the year before, and at 36, the oldest man in the competition, Claes Egnell had one last chance to make up for missing the 1948 Games as the result of a broken leg (he had, however, competed in the 25 metre Rapid Fire Pistol in London). Next favourites were the home team, Finland, who had won the silver medal at each of the last three World Championships. Lauri Vilkko was to win the shooting event with an impressive 196. He was a soldier who would reach the rank of Colonel before retiring in 1985. Olavi Mannonen, just 22, was to go on to achieve his greatest success at the 1956 Olympics. He later became Chief of Police in Helsinki. Olavi Rokka was a young lawyer, eventually to become a Civil Judge. Finally, the Hungarian team were to some extent an unknown quantity. Only István Szondy was returning from the 1948 team who had performed so disappointingly. New boys were Gábor Benedek and, at 19, the youngest in the competition was Aladár Kovácsi. Both would achieve great things in the future but would 1952 be too soon for them? Since the Hungarians had absented themselves from all three World Championships held so far, nobody knew.

The riding took place on the afternoon of July 21st. 64 horses had been selected from an original pool of 120. Some had been bred in Finland, others bought from Sweden. They had all been subjected to a systematic training progamme which had begun in 1949 and all 64 of those horses selected had completed the course without fault and within the time limit. Despite the day being wet and chilly, the riding produced a better overall performance than had been the case at Tweseldown four years earlier: 22 within the time limit compared to 14 and with fewer obstacle faults. Lasse Hall, though World Champion, was still a relatively inexperienced rider. He was late in the draw and, as he warmed up, he noticed that his horse appeared to be lame. He appealed to the jury who, by a narrow margin, 4-3, voted for a re-draw. Wille Grut takes up the story:

There were six spare horses, and just before Hall was about to pick out one of the six numbers, an elderly, very distinguished lady spoke to me in Swedish and said that Hall should draw number six. That number would give him the mare Laarina, a horse that was totally superior to all the horses that participated in the first draw. According to the rules, all the horses are supposed to be equally good and Laarina was therefore "too good". I said to Hall: "Lasse, draw number six!" He put his hand in the bowl with the six numbers and scooped up number six. A pure miracle one might say.'

So Hall took his opportunity and was the fastest of the field, beating the Finnish mounted policeman, Olavi Mannonen, into 2nd place by 21 seconds with the Hungarian, Szondy, taking 3rd place.

The next day the fencing event ran for ten hours. The surprising winner, by a comfortable four victories, was the 34 year old Brazilian, Alysio Borges. The Hungarians did well with Benedek 2nd and Szondy 4th. Even the teenager, Kovacsi, came in 10th. Sweden had shared the team points with Hungary (Egnell 3rd, Lindqvist 6th, Hall 7th) but the Finns had done disastrously, only managing 19th, 37th and 38th places.

The shooting was a triumph for Lauri Vilkko who won comfortably with 196. Two South Americans took the next two places – Alberto Ortiz (URU) 190, and Hernan Fuentes (CHI) 188, both men being experienced Olympic competitors from their participation in 1948. Finland was right back in the competition now having easily beaten the Swedish and Hungarian efforts. In fact, the next best teams in the shooting were USA and Chile. Having had one large slice of luck in the riding, Lasse Hall had another in the shooting. He turned up to the range 25 minutes late for his detail. Luckily for him, a Soviet protest had held up the event sufficiently that Hall was in time for his delayed competition. Though he only shot 182, he still lay in 3rd place behind the Hungarians, Benedek and Szondy after three events.

The swimming took place on another grey and chilly day. The temperature of the pool was 18°C which explains why everyone swam below their best. Even Hall only managed to win in 4:05.4 and was six seconds ahead of the Eduardo de Medeiros (BRA. Generally, though, the standard of swimming was improving inexorably. Despite the conditions, 21 swimmers beat 4:45 as opposed to only 12 in London in 1948. The American Thad McArthur finished 3rd with Novikov and Szondy 4th and 5th. After four events, Hall and Szondy were tying on 24 points and Benedek had 27. The team competition was equally close: Hungary had only a three point lead on Sweden.

The final running event was a hard one with precipitous gradients worked into the course and many of the runners paced themselves poorly. For instance, Vilkko was three seconds ahead of McArthur at the halfway stage but 25 seconds adrift of him at the end.

McArthur proved himself to be an excellent run-swimmer, winning the run by 20 seconds from Gabor Benedek in 14:20.4. This hauled him into 8th place but still placed him well outside the medals. Great Britain's momentary success in a mediocre overall performance came with Jervis Percy's 3rd place in the running. The Olympic medallists were well clear of the rest of the field by the end. Lasse Hall won the first of his two Olympic titles with a well-paced run in which he placed 8th. He had 32 points in total, seven ahead of the silver medallist Gabor Benedek. Istvan Szondy, the most experienced Hungarian, took the bronze medal, a great improvement on his poor showing in London in 1948 and the youthful Igor Novikov placed 4th some way behind the medallists. He had never recovered from a poor ride and mediocre fence but, like the Hungarians, he was to come back from meagre beginnings to great strength in the future.

The team event was won by Hungary, 16 points clear of a disappointed Swedish team. Since all three Hungarians, like the individual winner, Hall, were civilians, the 1952 competition marked a radical change. This was the beginning of the slow shift in emphasis in which a military sport would eventually become overwhelmingly civilian in character. Finland grabbed the bronze medal by a hair's breadth –two points ahead of the USA. The Soviet Union finished 5th in its first outing, ahead of Brazil. Great Britain placed a lowly 10th. The Hungarian victory was a sensation. The Swedes had never forgiven themselves for losing the individual title for the first time in 1936 but now they were at a crossroads. Apart from a highly controversial victory at the next World Championship in 1953, they were never again to win the team event. Now, Hungary and the Soviet Union would become the real powers of Modern Pentathlon for decades to come.

1953 World Championships: Rocas de Santo Domingo (CHI)
Controversy in the team event

It was ambitious of the UIPM to ask South America to host the 1953 World Championships so early in the development of the sport internationally. Argentina expressed some interest in becoming hosts but eventually the event took place in Rocas de Santo Domingo, Chile in early December. There were only two European teams in attendance- Sweden and Hungary – together with Werner Vetterli of Switzerland and a single British entry, Jack Lumsdaine, who, since he tested aircraft for commercial companies, was able to justify going down to Chile on a test flight. The MPAGB did not have the funds to send George Norman, the 1953 British Champion, to Chile. The rest of the field (23 competitors in all) consisted of teams from Argentina, Chile, USA, Brazil and Uruguay.

The individual title was won comfortably by the Olympic silver medallist, Gabor Benedek, with his Hungarian compatriot Szondy, the Olympic bronze medallist, moving up to 2nd place. The American Bill Andre took the bronze medal. Lasse Hall was in Chile to defend his world title but was clearly not in peak fitness and finished only 11th. He even failed to win the swimming event which was won by Hermanny of Brazil in 3:57.9. Benedek took the riding and running prizes while Nilsson of Sweden won both the fencing and shooting.

The team event was inevitably a battle between the two European teams, Sweden and Hungary, with

Sweden desperate to regain the domination it had lost in Helsinki. They had produced their strongest team (Hall, Lindqvist and Nilsson) for this event and, when the Hungarian, Karoly Tasnády, rode outside one of the markers in the riding event, Sweden were hopeful of victory. However, Tasnády, even with a penalty, finished in 21st position in the ride and the strong running and swimming of the Hungarians saw them to a comfortable victory -116 points to the Swedes' 142 with Argentina taking the bronze on 154 points.

What happened next was something that the Hungarians have never quite been able to forgive the Swedish team. The Swedes launched a protest that Hungary should be disqualified from the whole competition since Tasnády had broken the rules by riding outside the correct marker in the first event. At first, the jury dismissed this protest but, having persuaded Brazil to support them, the Swedes eventually won the vote and Hungary, the true winners, were disqualified and Sweden given the team victory. This partially justified but pedantic interpretation of the rules was to have ramifications in the future.

The tension over this episode rankled for so long that in the 1970 *UIPM Bulletin*, a full 17 years later, Sven Thofelt took the opportunity to defend the decision and his own integrity in an extraordinary article. Istvan Szondy, then the German coach, had, said Thofelt, 'spread a rumour' and 'depicted me as a person morally below the standard'. In defending the action of the 1953 jury, Thofelt reminded readers that Tasnády had certainly been disqualified in the riding in Chile. Since Tasnády had already been awarded points and a placing after the event, this was a rather thin argument. Thofelt's real justification for the disqualification lay in Rule 111 which stated: 'No prize is to be given to a competitor who neglects, who is disqualified or who does not take part in one of the five tests. This rule is also applicable to the team of the competitor.'

Despite the original intention that only those who completed all five events should count in the final total, this had not been the case for some years and was evident in the results as far back as 1932. There had certainly been a failure in the UIPM rules to distinguish between 'disqualification' and 'elimination', an omission which wasn't remedied in the statutes for many years. Eventually, the statutes made this distinction clear: 'Elimination is a penalty for a mistake. Disqualification is a punishment for a deliberate attempt to contravene the rules.'

Clearly, Tasnády had not deliberately ignored the markers. The competitors, and especially the Hungarians, must have returned home with a very bad taste in their mouths. Had the situation occured a year later in Budapest, the controversy might never have arisen since it was the first time the points system was used. Tasnády would have received zero points for his elimination in the riding and, though all three Hungarians would have had final scores, the loss of 1000 points to the Swedes in the first event would never have been made up. At the UIPM Congress in Melbourne in 1956, the offending Rule 111 was dropped from the statutes. If a competitor was 'disqualified' (eliminated) in any single event, his final score and that of his team would still stand. That Congress also added a rule whereby, in the event of an injury in the riding, a team's fourth man would be allowed to continue in the rest of the competition. He would, however, begin with a zero score for the riding event.

The riding event, a persistent thorn in the side of organisers, had received another shock just before the competition in Chile had begun. Sven Thofelt received a startling letter from Lt. Col. Donald Hull, the secretary of the USMPA. It read:

'I would like to point out to you that very soon the United States of America will not be able to send a team to Modern Pentathlon competitions where horsemanship and fencing abilities are required. Our young officers and soldiers no longer have an opportunity to ride or to fence. The American Army is now completely mechanized and there are no more horses in the Army. There are only a limited number of horses in civilian riding clubs and they are not available to our pentathletes. The sword is no longer carried by American officers and only a decreasing number of American schools continue to teach the use of the epee. We have had to start from the very beginning in training individuals for the Modern Pentathlon event in the 1952 Olympic Games and at the present. We may be able to develop a team for 1956, but certainly not after that.

I suggest that serious consideration be given to substituting the riding and fencing events in the Modern Pentathlon. I think that an obstacle course might be considered as an appropriate substitute for the riding course. A dummy grenade throw could take the place of the present fencing competition. It is believed that obstacle courses and grenade throwing are a part of the training schedule of every Army, so that the substitute of these two latter events would maintain the Modern Pentathlon as a military type activity.'

The letter may seem to take the function of Modern Pentathlon as a military training exercise a little too literally but it asked a very practical question – why would military institutions bother to maintain riding stables when horses no longer had a military function? The modification of the riding event that was to be central to developments over the next few decades perhaps began with this central problem. After all, military pentathletes still consituted the overwhelming majority of participants.

1954 World Championships: Budapest (HUN)
The new scoring system

Budapest played host to the World Championships for the first time but the city was to become such a frequent and popular venue that, in many ways, it has become the home of Modern Pentathlon. Typically, the British team grumbled about the postal services and the money exchange rate but had to acknowledge that it was nice to see some big crowds for a change and that standards of performance were constantly improving, even in the British team. After the competition, Errol Lonsdale, the British Team Manager put his finger on the real quality of Modern Pentathlon:

'It produces such splendid sportsmen, and unlike some other forms of sport, has also created most excellent friendly relations amongst all the nations who take part. In fact one of the most pleasant things about the annual world championships of the Modern Pentathlon is the opportunity provided for sportsmen of many nationalities to meet and renew old friendships.'

To this day, the very large numbers of ex-pentathletes who continue to administer the international sport is testimony to this special feature of friendship in the world of Modern Pentathlon.

Hungary provided some excellent horses, all stallions, at Orkeny, an old cavalry training centre, 60 km outside Budapest. 21 riders out of 34 beat the time allowance but there were still five pentathletes who, for the first time, received zero points, among them Olavi Mannonen (FIN) who would win the silver medal the following year. There was no sign of Olympic Champion, Lasse Hall this year but a new name from Sweden was about to burst on the scene. The 19 year old Björn Thofelt, proudly watched by his father, Sven, narrowly lost the riding event to Szondy (HUN). The fencing victory was shared by Vetterli (SWI) and the irrepressible Lacroix (FRA) and the shooting (192) by Szondy and Johnson (USA). No one swam faster than four minutes in the lovely Margaret Island pool but Vladimir Cerny (TCH) won in 4:05.6 with Igor Novikov (URS) just behind him. After four events, young Thofelt had a 200 point lead on Szondy. It was another hard run, won by Bertil Haase (SWE) in 14:24.0, in which Thofelt came 12th and completed a sensational overall individual victory with 4,634.5 pts, beating Vetterli and Szondy into 2nd and 3rd places. An unknown Czech competitor, Vladimir Cerny was 4th and the defending World Champion, Gabor Benedek, was back in 5th place in front of his home crowd. In the team event, however, Hungary (Szondy, Benedek, Tasnády) had a comfortable victory over Sweden who had also been beaten to the silver medal by Switzerland.

The British team placed 7th, narrowly edged out by newcomers, Austria, but ahead of France and two other newcomers, Czechoslovakia and Romania. George Norman, who had retained his British title in 1954, was 12th, Sgt. Dai Rees of the Royal Marines (fourth man who had replaced the sick Jack Lumsdaine at the last minute) was 22nd and Sgt. Don Cobley (RAF) 28th.

Bjorn Thofelt's victory on Hungarian soil was a wonderful achievement for such a young first-timer. It is interesting that, even by using the old placings system, he would have won comfortably (Thofelt 32, Szondy 43, Cerny 48, Vetterli 50).

The new points system was regarded as a definite step forward by almost everybody but it was far from perfect. By allowing additional points above 1000 for going faster than the time allowance, the riding was given disproportionate importance. It was also encouraging riders to drive the horses too hard; this would not be popular with those generous enough to lend the horses in the first place. Szondy won the riding with 1192.5 points whereas the top score in the fencing, where 1000 points was the equivalent of 75% victories, was only 877. Since the original intention was to downgrade the importance of the riding, this scoring had a detrimental effect on the overall points system. Additionally, 195 as the bogey score for 1000 points in shooting was well beyond the ability of the competitors. Even the winner only scored 192. The standard of swimming would improve rapidly over the coming years but at only +/- 5 points a second and with a bogey time of four minutes, there was little differential or high scoring for some years to come. The running event (1000 points at 15 minutes +/- 3 points a second) was appropriately scored but would require a big improvement in standard before any high scores were seen. Indeed, the later moving of the running bogey to 14:15.0 recognised this improved standard of running.

Changes can be made very slowly in a committee-based international organisation. The next issue of the statutes in 1957 remained a thin booklet with very few changes made and none at all made to the scoring system. To give some idea of how very slowly things can move, the first UIPM discussion of the possibility of Modern Pentathlon competitions for women took place in 1955. The first World Championships for women took place in 1981, 26 years later!

1955 British Championships

Hylton Cleaver, the *Evening Standard* journalist, continued to campaign in his articles for more civilian participation in the sport but, though there were 72 entries in the championships held in late September, only John Majendie, the policeman and a schoolmaster, Mr. D. Thompson (who came 9th) were civilians. The RAF had won the team event for the previous two years and there were grumblings that the Army teams had to compete by unit whereas the RAF and Navy could enter fully representative teams. The RAF this year won by a mere five points from the Household Cavalry. George Norman (Army), champion for the previous two years, was beaten into 2nd place by Don Cobley (RAF) and Reg King (Army) took 3rd spot. Three weeks later, the World Championship team consisted of Cobley, King and Gordon Walker (who had come 4th in the British Championships).

1955 World Championships: Macolin (SUI)

Once again, the World Championships returned to Switzerland, this time to Macolin. The Swiss team was a strong one and here was a chance for them to do great things on home soil. There were 14 teams competing in Macolin including Cuba for the first and only time. Cuba managed to beat Germany, now competing in its first World Championship since the war. Lasse Hall returned to the competition after his absence in 1954, and the current Swedish World Champion, Björn Thofelt was this time the absentee. Among the favourites, therefore, were Szondy (HUN) and Vetterli (SWI) with the impressive Novikov (URS) still to make a lasting mark on the sport despite his fine 4th place at the Helsinki Olympics.

As it turned out, the riding was something of a farce with half the competitors scoring fewer than 400 points and nine of them, including the hapless Novikov, scoring zero points. Only Great Britain's Don Cobley managed to outdo Novikov's misery with 1660 penalty points to Novikov's 1620. Fortunately for the tail-enders, the top score, shared by Szondy and Mahler (FRA) was only 846, the bogey time having been rather inexpertly calculated in an attempt to limit the excessively high scores seen in 1954. Both winners rode 9:07.3 but were penalised 154 time faults. Don Cobley's personal agony lasted 23 minutes. Other big names set at a disadvantage by the riding event were Lasse Hall (603.5 pts) and Werner Vetterli (554.5 pts).

Vetterli duly won the fencing event from Bertil Haase (SWE) with Szondy and O'Hair (USA) taking the shooting with 194. Frigyes Hegudus reveals in his book, *Modern Pentathlon* that Szondy was such a nervous shot that: 'He was known to be unable to get a single minute of sleep during the night preceding the shooting event even with the help of the strongest sleeping pills.' This is an interestingly innocent revelation in the light of later concerns about the use of tranquillisers in the sport.

Lasse Hall showed he was back at full fitness a year before defending his Olympic title with a winning swim of 3:57.0. Vladimir Cerny (CZE), another victim of the riding (105 pts) and 4th overall the previous year, came 2nd in the swim with 4:06.4. Another tough running course resulted in a victory for Bertil Haase (SWE) in 14:28.0 with Great Britain's Don Cobley storming through to 2nd place, ten seconds behind.

The unexpected overall winner was Konstantin Salnikov (URS) whose relatively unspectacular performance showed the virtue of consistency (Ride 793.5; Fence 804; Shoot 920; Swim 912; Run 1024). Salnikov had come 17th the year before in Budapest but wasn't selected for the Soviet Olympic team in 1956. So, this first ever Soviet champion, like the Swedish World Champions, Tage Bjurefelt and Bjorn Thofelt, seemed to have a brief but brilliant career. Salnikov also helped the USSR team to its first team medal –a silver behind the strong Hungarians. The home team, Switzerland, managed to claim the bronze medal ahead of Sweden who in turn were just 1.5 points ahead of the USA team.

Individually, Olavi Mannonen (FIN) took the silver and Aladar Kovacsi (HUN) the bronze, only three points ahead of Bertil Haase. Szondy's terrible run (16.28.0) dropped him to 5th place. Though he came back to share a team medal in 1958, this was Kovacsi's only individual World Championship medal and he would not be selected again for the Olympic team the following year. The British team finished 12th (Walker 30th, Cobley 34th and King 41st).

The 1956 Olympic Games: Melbourne (AUS)

There were many problems attached to holding the first ever Olympics outside the Northern hemisphere: Melbourne had won the Games by a single vote; it was being held during an Australian 'summer' (November) so the event took place very late in the year for most athletes; stadium construction in Melbourne was going very slowly; there were boycotts over the Suez Canal disputes and the Soviet invasion of Hungary; the strict Australian quarantine laws meant that the equestrian events had to be held in Sweden; and finally, Australia was so far away – even by plane it was a 30 hour journey from Europe. As far as Modern Pentathlon was concerned, Australia had only held its first National Championship in April 1956 and had formed a governing body not long before. There were doubts that Australia would have the experience to run a major event. Fortunately, since horses were provided by the organisers in Australia, Modern Pentathlon was not banished to Sweden and was a fully-fledged member of the Australian sporting celebration. The general feeling was that, although preparations seemed to be slow, when the event arrived, everybody was impressed by the efficiency and the friendliness of the organising committee.

There were entries from 18 countries, 13 teams and 5 individuals so that 40 pentathletes started the competition. Among them was defending Olympic Champion, Lasse Hall, who had only qualified for the Swedish team at the last minute when he won the National Championship. Ten of the field had competed in Helsinki including Olavi Mannonen (FIN), Igor Novikov (URS) and Gabor Benedek (HUN). There was no Szondy or Kovacsi in the Hungarian team and the selection of relative unknowns, Janos Bodi and Antal Moldrich, seemed to be taking something of a gamble for the Team Champions, although Moldrich had the previous year won the Hungarian Championship. The oldest competitor was Nilo Floody of Chile, aged 35 and competing in his third Olympic Games. At 33, the Swede, Bertil Haase, was the next most senior while, at the other end of the age range, 16 year old Australian, Sven Coomer, was thrown into the lion's den in front of the home crowd on the strength of his swimming ability. Sven, primarily a skier, went on to make a living in Aspen, Colorado, where he invented and still sells a popular zip-fit liner for ski boots. Finally, Gerardo Cortes, Sr, of Chile is a notable entry in 1956 because his son, Gerardo Cortes, Jnr, also competed in the Olympic Modern Pentathlon in Seoul in 1988.

It's the taking part that counts –the British achievement

Before looking at the outcome of the 1956 Olympic Games, we should stop a moment and consider a different kind of achievement. Great Britain is the only nation in the world to have competed in every single Olympic Modern Pentathlon competition from 1912 to 2012. Indeed, with the sole exception of Mexico 1962, it has always been represented at World Championships, too. It's true that real success for the British team has been very thin on the ground until comparatively recently but, often, the actual physical difficulty of getting to the championships would have deterred lesser beings. Great Britain is not alone in this achievement but, as a tribute to all those from any part of the world who have merely attended a big competition and been proud to get there, consider the plight of the British team in Melbourne.

The Team Manager, Lt. Col. OG (Geoffrey) W White, DSO OBE, wrote a 20 page report on the Melbourne experience which is a mixture of comically old-fashioned attitudes and sheer, gritty determination to do the job properly. White, a decorated veteran of the war against Japan in Burma, had already published a book about his wartime experiences ('*Straight on for Tokyo*') and was not a man to take difficulties lying down.

The BOA had assured the MPAGB that they could only afford to send a single pentathlete to Melbourne. In such circumstances, squad training would seem to be unnecessary. Not until late July of 1956 did the BOA change its minds and allow three pentathletes and a manager to travel. Furthermore, the BOA wanted the names by early September. It was never easy to negotiate the release of military personnel but by late August, ten 'hopefuls' were in training, assisted by ex-Olympian, John Hewitt, who had recently broken his leg in a point to point race. The team had to be selected before the British Championships when the exhausted selected athletes might well lose to fresher athletes- a precarious position for the selectors. Fortunately, the team selected consisted of the 1955 British Champion, Sgt Don Cobley (RAF); CSM George Norman, who regained his British title in the 1956 competition; 20 year old Cpl of Horse, Tom Hudson and the non-travelling reserve was SSI Michael Howard, all of whom, fortunately, performed well in the British Championship. The complete absence of officers in the team was a thorough break with the past and threw Lt. Col. White into some confusion. Since White was quite sure the lower ranks lacked the 'mental stamina' of the officer classes, he engaged a Dr Kemp, a Scientologist, to work with the team and give them a psychological boost. These services, like anything that came the team's way, were given completely free.

The team, then, set off for Melbourne after about nine weeks' training. Meanwhile, the USA team had been training hard together in Texas for nearly two years and the Soviet Union had a programme of intensive training for a large squad that had been underway since Helsinki.

The flight to Melbourne took four days with seven refuelling stops and three nights spent in the air. The team had no training for eight days and, when they were itching to begin, they had to wait several more days for air freight to arrive with all their kit. Meanwhile the Australian Navy kindly loaned them two epées, two masks, and two jackets (no gloves) to share. Training involved clocking up over 1000 miles in just a few days in a loaned Austin A50 provided for transport. The team members were out from 7am until 7pm each day. When their single shot Webley pistol arrived, they practised on a windswept coastal range where, despite their mental training, White declared: 'our Pentathletes at times became most continental in their exhibitions of temperament on the firing point.'

When one of the team needed penicillin to treat 'foot rot' and had to miss the Opening Ceremony, even Lt. Col. White lost his cool. In his advice to future managers, he snarled: 'Team Captains must take NOTHING for granted, not even the ability of a three stripe NCO and Olympic Athlete to look after his own feet.'

With the prospect of the team being robbed of a chance to compete through the injury, Michael Howard had been hurriedly flown out by RAF carrier and arrived in Melbourne just a few hours before the riding event began. As it turned out, the original team members were all able to compete and Howard had to watch from the side lines. Howard nevertheless competed in the fencing events in Melbourne. Having been in the Modern Pentathlon squad since 1950, he now went on to compete in three Olympic Games (1956, 1960, and 1964) in fencing, winning a team epée silver medal in Tokyo. Back at the riding, since other ranks, unlike officers, did not have appropriate riding uniform, Moss Brothers had provided uniforms of a light tropical material for the team. The day of the riding was chilly and misty. Even our plucky chaps must have had a sense of foreboding as the competition began.

The competition in Melbourne

Nearly 100 horses had been bought and trained by the Victoria Police Force a couple of miles away from the Oaklands Hunt Club where the event took place. 45 horses were selected for the event and the other horses made available for training. Many riders were surprised by the power of the selected horses, having been practising on lesser beasts in the weeks before. A huge crowd watched the event. Only six riders beat the ten minute time allowance and only four of them scored above 1000 points. At the other end of the field, 24 of the starting entry of 40 scored fewer than 700 points with eight zero scores and four men hospitalised. The British team achieved a grand total of just 335 (Cobley 315, Hudson 20, Norman 0). All three had falls but Hudson, who was kicked in the head by his horse, still managed 'a gutful finish'. The hospitalised pentathletes included the 1954 World Champion, Bjorn Thofelt. Thofelt's saddle slipped twice and, the second time he was dragged along the ground for some time. Astonishingly, though concussed, he remounted and finished the course, barely conscious, before being taken to hospital. The early elimination of both Thofelt and, therefore, the Swedish team, from the competition was a real disappointment and marked the end of an era for that great Pentathlon nation. After Hall's retirement, it was to be 11 years before Sweden won any kind of medal again. The winner of the riding event was George Lambert (USA) whose team had such an unassailable lead after a single event (USA 3020, Finland 2572, USSR 2457) that they became instant favourites to win the competition.

The comfortable winner of the fencing was the young Rumanian, Cornel Vena, with the remarkable score of 1,111 points, 148 points clear of the runner-up, Wäinö Korhonen (FIN). Vena had been a rower at university and had only taken up Modern Pentathlon in 1953. His fencing scores in 1954 and 1955 had been unimpressive but his win in Melbourne turned heads. He appears to have retired after the competition – another case of a bright flame too promptly extinguished. The Hungarian team, who had a poor start in the riding, showed the value of consistently good fencing scores and won the team event ahead of the USSR. Even with the chaos inflicted by the riding scoring, of those who finished in the top ten at the end, eight had achieved similarly high placings in the fencing.

The shooting event was at the Williamstown Rifle Range by the sea and was subject to high winds. The electrical turning targets broke down at one point and had to be pulled manually. The event dragged on, each detail taking as long as 90 minutes because, after every series fired, everyone tramped down to the targets - photographers, journalists, jury d'appel and the general public. There appeared to be little range control. Again, eight of the top ten shots went on to finish in the top ten overall and the event was won by Antonio Almada (MEX) with 193, just ahead of the big names, Benedek and Novikov, both of whom shot 191. The British scores were Cobley and Hudson 173 and Norman 162. The Rumanian coach shook his head in wonder at the Webley single shot pistol they had been using. After three events, the Finns, Korhonen and Mannonen led the field from Gabor Benedek. Lasse Hall, who had shot a poor 181 was in 4th position.

Hall came into his own again with a 3:54.2 swim but there was a new wonder swimmer in the USSR team –Ivan Deryugin swam 3:46.7. The home crowd were treated to a 3:57.4 swim by 16 year old Sven Coomer and the Hungarian, Antal Moldich also swam below four minutes so the barriers to progress in swimming were at last coming down. Even in the British team, the swimming performance was 1:39.0 better than the 1952 team and 1:43.0 per man better than the 1948 team swim. Tom Hudson's 4:02.0 was a British best. The USSR team beat the USA team into 2nd place in the swimming but, after four events, the Americans still retained the overall lead they had launched with their wonderful riding start. Individually, Lasse Hall's swim had moved him narrowly into the lead ahead of the two Finns.

It was a return to the Oaklands Hunt Club for the final running event, a testing race across creeks and ploughed fields. After all the difficulties they had experienced, it was a moment for the British team to be proud. Don Cobley won the running event in a superb time, 13:35.5, beating his rival Bertil Haase (SWE) by 13.5 seconds. This was a 'fastest ever' performance and went a long way to easing the British disappointments of the previous days. Lasse Hall, in 8th place, managed to retain the lead and win an unprecedented second Olympic title with Mannonen and Korhonen of Finland taking silver and bronze. Once again Novikov took a disappointing 4th place but he was to become the first consistently great World Champion in the immediate years ahead. He did, however, lead the Soviet team in Melbourne to the first of many great team victories over the coming years. The USA's team of a soldier, a sailor and a civilian who had trained hard and attended every competition they could over the previous two years, deservedly took the silver medal and Finland the bronze. The Hungarians had been too damaged by the riding event (Moldrich scored only 95 points) to manage any better than 4th place but, as Lt. Col. White pointed out, only weeks before 'the Hungarians were fighting a battle in Budapest armed only with Pentathlon pistols'. The Hungarian uprising against the Soviet Union was much on everybody's mind.

UIPM's relationship with IOC President, Avery Brundage

In 1952, Sigfrid Edström retired as IOC President and was replaced by the Chicago businessman, Avery Brundage. Edström had, of course, been a powerful ally of Modern Pentathlon. He had been part of the organisational team for the very first Olympic event in Stockholm in 1912 and, as a Swede, had close personal ties with men like Gustav Dyrssen, the UIPM President, Sven Thofelt and Wille Grut. Since his death, Avery Brundage has been painted very much as a pantomime villain with his obsessive defence of amateurism, his supposed anti-semitism and his Nazi loyalties. Brundage, however, was a good friend to Modern Pentathlon. He had been an Olympic athlete himself, competing in the 1912 Athletic Pentathlon where American Indian Jim Thorpe had won impressively. After Brundage's death, it was revealed that it was he who had been personally responsible for informing the IOC that Jim Thorpe had previously played 'professional' baseball, thereby getting him disqualified. However, because of his own Olympic experience, Brundage had a soft spot for Modern Pentathlon. UIPM Officials frequently consulted him and got supportive replies. Brundage was very pleased to supply a supportive statement that was extensively used in Modern Pentathlon publicity. It read:

'Among the most coveted medals in the Olympic Games, and rightly so, are those for the prestigious Modern Pentathlon. Here is an event that is truly Olympic in every sense of the word, requiring ability in five exhausting events of five different sports, It has also the distinction of having been invented by the Baron de Coubertin himself. The winner is a real champion and becomes one of the heroes of the Games.'

In the 1950s, Brundage's support was sought on several occasions. Firstly, the 1957 World Championships had been scheduled to be held in Mexico. As late in the year as July, the Mexicans withdrew and Gustav Dyrssen turned to Brundage to see if he could use his influence to change the Mexicans' minds. On this occasion, nothing could be done and, once again, the Swedes had to step in as last-minute hosts. Gustav Dyrssen was himself an IOC member as, later on, was Sven Thofelt and this coveted position came with its own financial difficulties. Members were expected to fund their own trips to congresses and competitions. At one point, Dyrssen wrote to Brundage to apologise for his absence from the Tokyo congress in

1959. He wrote that the journey would be 'too expensive for a farmer after two years of bad weather and poor crops.' But Dyrssen was a loyal supporter of Brundage. At the 1954 World Championships, at Brundage's request, he had provided all competitors with a questionnaire about their training habits. This was intended to expose any 'professional approach' or contravention of the strict amateur laws in sport. Everyone was happy to participate in the quiz although the Soviet team insisted on having their answers checked by embassy staff first. The 'amateur' obsession of Brundage became a nuisance to Modern Pentathlon as well as other sports. Three weeks was considered the maximum permissible stretch for full-time training before athletes were deemed professional. Brundage hounded some athletes over this, particularly his own countrymen and yet appeared to be able to do nothing about the many athletes training full-time within the Soviet bloc.

Another significant issue affecting Modern Pentathlon was that, although a team competition had been instigated in the 1952 Olympic Games, a single medal was awarded to each team in that event. This seemed unfair since the Equestrian events and Gymnastics also had team events which depended on the accumulation of scores in the individual event, just like Modern Pentathlon, and yet medals were awarded to the teams in those events. This situation was not resolved until well into the 1980s. However, when Brundage was eager to reduce the number of competitors and events in the Olympic Games, Modern Pentathlon was able to argue that, since the team event did not add to the number of individuals in the competition, our team event was no burden on the increasing number of competitors.

Brundage himself was much opposed to team sports which, in Brundage's 'confirmed opinion, can never remain amateur at an international level because of national pressure for victory.' He argued that this had been very much the attitude of his predecessors, too. There were, however, other pressures on Modern Pentathlon. Understandably, one of the arguments for allowing a sport to stay in the Olympic Games was that it should be 'widely practised by at least 25 countries'. With 32 member countries in 1958, Modern Pentathlon could comply with that demand but Sven Thofelt had a rather elitist argument to back up the relatively small number: 'Modern Pentathlon is a very complicated and expensive sport and designed by the Founder for the very best sportsmen in the world. It lies in the nature of the sport that it can't be widely spread.'

There is some logic to this argument but it became less and less convincing as the years went by and public access to sporting opportunity became the driving force for Olympic participation. An interesting parallel was drawn between Modern Pentathlon and the Decathlon event. Thofelt argued that, though the component events of Decathlon, like Modern Pentathlon, were widely practised, the Decathlon event was more specialist and yet this 'finest and best of all the track and field events' would be the last to be eliminated from an Olympic programme. Modern Pentathlon should be considered in the same way.

The Winter Biathlon, for which the UIPM had some responsibility, was much more difficult to justify as a 'widely practised' sport. Brundage didn't like the tiny numbers that competed or its military roots. In many ways, Modern Pentathlon survived because it could claim to be slightly less elite that Winter Biathlon and the two sports were often discussed together as a package in the UIPM/ Brundage correspondence.

The 1957 Sofia IOC Congress had upset the UIPM by demanding that Modern Pentathlon and Kayak Canoeing be dropped from the Olympic Games. Thanks to Brundage's intervention, Modern Pentathlon was to survive but with an upper limit of 60 competitors allowed for the Games in 1960. This was not an onerous limit since numbers competing at previous Olympic events had not yet approached such a total. Throughout the history of the IOC, host countries have been determined to formulate their own plans about the way sports should be operated. This was usually in contradiction with the IOC's wishes and the IOC would have to remind the hosts that they had no right to make such changes. The formation of the UIPM came about largely to protect against such a situation and maintain some consistency of rules from one Olympic Games to the next. Indeed, the UIPM declared in its 1957 statutes that rule changes should only take place in the year immediately following an Olympic Games.

Modern Pentathlon for all in Great Britain

The late 1950s proved to be an exciting time in the development of Modern Pentathlon beyond the military in Britain. As a result of the political tumult in Hungary, a number of Hungarian emigrés arrived in Britain, pentathletes among them. Indeed, there was a team of Hungarian refugees competing in the 1957 Army Championships in only the second year of that competition. Directly from that influence, the Cheltenham club was formed by Joe Buscko, another Hungarian refugee. His team included triple Olympian, Robbie Phelps, who soon formed a breakaway club, Spartan, in nearby Gloucester. Spartan was to become a British Champion Team. From the same club, Robbie's nephew, Richard, became, in 1993, Britain's only male World Champion.

The Metropolitan Police began to organise competitions at Imber Court and at Oxford and Cambridge universities, the beginnings of what would become a long tradition were underway. Anthony Wieler, son of UIPM Vice-President Leslie Wieler, started up a team at Oxford and Colin Peace, who had come into Pentathlon competing for the Navy, began a team at Cambridge together with yet another Hungarian refugee, Zoltan Mezei. Colin Peace became a huge influence in Modern Pentathlon, establishing the Pony Club, taking the role of British Team Manager in the mid-sixties and stimulating the sport at all levels with his enthusiasm. He now lives in Canada where he is a Professor of Veterinary Surgery.

There was also, for the first time, a schools event – a tetrathlon with rifle shooting replacing pistol and no riding event – that was established by John Felix at Whitgift School and taken up enthusiastically by a number of other schools throughout the country. On the back of the interest gained in the sport by the holding of the World Championships in Aldershot, the schools made their debut in the 1959 Army Championships as guests just a year after Oxford and Cambridge had made an identical debut. These developments were arranged with brisk efficiency by Peter Duckworth. By the early 1960s, both the Varsity match and the Schools' Tetrathlon had become independently-run competitions in their own right. At the same time, Biathlons were also a very successful way of getting athletes to dabble in the sport. In 1957 a shoot/run biathlon was held at Windsor with great success.

At the top end of the sport, Don Cobley had established himself as our only world-class pentathlete. After his fine run in Melbourne, he placed 6th, 10th and 11th respectively in each of the next three World Championships. Tom Hudson beat Cobley in the British Championships in 1957 and 1958 but then, just as he was making his mark, his pentathlon career came to end. Pat Harvey, a 21 year old lieutenant from Guildford, who was to achieve his best performance at the Rome Olympics, had a reliable, all-round ability but the team suffered badly from a lack of international experience and a failure to establish any kind of regular squad training. Peter Duckworth who returned to become Team Manager for the 1959 World Championship was very clear about these shortcomings and frustrated at the inability of the MPAGB and the military authorites to change things. Even the preparations for Rome 1960 were half-baked in ambition –a weekend together maybe once a month. Duckworth was well aware, too, that new pentathletes needed to be found from the worlds of running and swimming. The USA squad had contained one man, Arnold Sowell, who had placed 4th in the 1956 Olympic 800 metres.

The Leading Teams 1957- 1959

One man and one team completely dominated Modern Pentathlon in the late 1950s – Igor Novikov and the Soviet Union. Novikov, together with team mates Alexander Tarassov and Nikolai Tatarinov made it three victories in a row. Though the length of the cross-country riding course was decreasing, the wide discrepancy between results in that event made the consistency of the Soviet team all the more impressive. The exaggerated prominence of riding scores in the first points scoring event in 1954 had been overcompensated from 1955 onwards and the event was yet to settle into some kind of parity with the other events. Switzerland disappeared from prominence and the Swedish team were no longer certain medallists but Finland and Hungary and, to some extent, the USA, provided competition to the mighty Soviet machine. It had become the pattern to hold World Championships late in the year – October was usually guaranteed to produce challenging weather conditions in most countries.

1957 World Championships: Stockholm (SWE)

For the third time in only seven years, the Championships returned to Sweden thanks to the late withdrawal by Mexico, the original hosts. Bjorn Thofelt, in his final World Championship did his best to erase the bitter memory of his elimination in Melbourne. He won the riding with 996 points but then a miserable 580 fence and 658 run pushed him down into 11th place overall. Novikov's victory by 324 points over his Soviet team mates was even more impressive because he began with only 668 points in the riding. A world record 1140 in the fencing, a 194 shoot, a 3:59.1 swim and a 976 point run (still good enough for 5th) showed his complete superiority over the rest of the field. Tarassov took the silver with a strong run at the end and Tatarinov the bronze, giving a clean sweep of the individual medals to the Soviet team. The second team home, 1400 points behind the winners, was Finland, a good result since only Korhonen remained from their great post-war team. He placed 4th just ahead of the Hungarian, Ferdinandy, who had been fourth man in the Hungarian team in Melbourne. With Bodi and Szabo, he took the bronze medal in the team event ahead of Sweden. Don Cobley's 6th place for Great Britain was a marvellous achievement. He had begun with only 732 in the riding but then fenced an excellent 930 and then finished in 3rd place in the running behind Stanislav Przybylski (POL) and Nikolai Tarassov. The other Britons, Tom Hudson and Clive Eldridge had begun so poorly in the riding event that they never recovered and finished 29th and 35th of the 38 competitors.

1958 World Championships: Aldershot (GBR)

Ten years on from hosting the 1948 Olympics and the formation of the UIPM at Sandhurst, Great Britain hosted its first World Championship using similar venues although the swimming was held in the indoor Aldershot army pool. Once again, Novikov and the Soviet team triumphed easily though they were split individually by a new face from Finland, Kurt Lindeman, who took the silver medal. Lindeman's scores were solidly reliable and his impressive final run pushed Don Cobley into 2nd place in front of his home crowd. In the team event, Hungary took 2nd place, leaving Finland in 3rd but their success in Aldershot was significant for a far greater reason. Their team was composed of Imre Nagy (5th) and Aladar Kovacsi, 11th, (his final performance before retiring to become a successful gynaecologist). But a new name, in 6th place, was the 20 year old András Balczó, a man who was to become, in many people's opinion, the greatest pentathlete ever. Interestingly, it was as a run-swimmer that Balczó came into the sport. He won the swim in 3:48.3 and was 5th in the running although his first ever fencing score of 592 would raise a lot of eyebrows in the light of his prowess at this event later on –he was soon to become Hungarian Epée Champion. The British team were Don Cobley (11th), Pat Harvey (25th) and Tom Hudson (29th) in his final outing. They did, however, comfortably win the running event – Cobley (2nd), Hudson (4th), Harvey (9th) to give the home crowd something to celebrate.

1959 World Championships: Hershey (USA)

The 1959 World Championship was held around the largest chocolate factory in the world. The Pennsylvania

Three great military names plan the organization of the 1958 World Championships at Aldershot (l-r: Lt. General Sir Brian Horrocks, Brigadier Leslie Wieler and Field Marshal Sir Gerald Templer).

hosts made everybody very welcome but the events were marked by a cheery inefficiency that sometimes stretched the patience of the visitors. Once again, Novikov retained his title, impressively winning the running event for the first time and placing 3rd in the swim. Having established strong technical events, his coaches were clearly paying more attention to the potential high scores available in the physical events. The Soviet Union won the team event (Tarassov 3rd, Tatarinov 15th) but Finland was, this time, only 600 points adrift. Still only scoring 615 in the fencing, Balczó took the silver medal though the Hungarians were only able to take 5th place. The USA took a deserved bronze medal, 500 points ahead of Sweden. The entry of 39 was a strong one and showed the possibility of having a full complement of athletes no matter where in the world the competition was held. The British team were thwarted once again by the vagaries of the riding event. Cobley managed an overall 11th place after his horse had landed on top of him in a fall. Pat Harvey and Peter Little could only place 34th and 35th places with zero and 384 points respectively in the riding event.

The high turnout in Hershey had a lot to do with preparations for the Olympic Games in Rome the following year for which Novikov was a clear favourite. But the 1960s were to become the Balczó era; the great Soviet champion, Novikov, would be forced to concede his throne to the young Hungarian. In Great Britain, the 1960s would mark the arrival of Jim Fox who would make his mark even more impressively than had Don Cobley, the most successful of the British pentathletes in the 1950s.

Chapter Six: 1960-1969

'If we were like the Soviet Union and could call on 50,000 pentathletes at any one time or like the USA who spent $50,000 preparing their team for Moscow, we'd be the champions.' *Weekend* magazine article 1961

The 1960s was a decade of spreading world-wide participation. Olympic Games were held in three different continents which provided new challenges – a lack of infrastructure in Tokyo, a lack of oxygen in Mexico City. The rule of Igor Novikov and the Soviet Union was challenged by Hungary and, in particular, Andras Balczó. The instigation of a World Junior Championship extended top level competition to the young but now, almost on a permanent basis, Modern Pentathlon was fighting to justify its existence to an IOC increasingly under pressure to reduce the number of sports in a swelling Olympic Games. Radical restructuring of the riding event took place. Though the IOC were now financially benefitting from TV money, Avery Brundage, the President, remained determinedly 'amateur' and was reactionary in the face of most new developments.

1960 Olympic Games: Rome (ITA)

The Italians took every opportunity to build the new stadia in proximity to the historical elegance of Ancient Rome. The venues for Modern Pentathlon were, however, as usual, widely dispersed – the riding in Passo Corese, 40 km north of Rome, the shooting in Lazio and the running at the Acqua Santa Golf Course on the Appian Way, south east of the city. Only the fencing and swimming were in the central stadia. This was the first time that an upper limit was placed on the number of pentathletes taking part. Sixty athletes were entered, representing 23 nations and these included, for the first time, Tunisia and Morocco. The competition began in scorching dry heat on Friday 26th August and ran over six days, since a Papal decree had insisted that Sunday (the day after the fencing) be a day of rest.

The team competition would inevitably be a battle between the USSR and Hungary. The Soviet team consisted of the established athletes, Novikov and Tatarinov, now aged 30 and 32, and a new team member, Hanno Selg, 28, an Estonian ski champion who, nowadays, runs his own bus company in Tallinn. The Hungarians included their regulars Balczó and Nagy, and selected as third man, Ferenc Nemeth, rather than the 1959 and 1960 Hungarian Champion Ferenc Török. Imre Nagy reveals in his memoir that the Hungarian coaches were not allowed to travel with the team to Rome and were replaced by 'faithful communist party members'. This meant that the team arrived only the day before the start of the competition, raising false hopes among their rivals that they might not show up at all. Björn Thofelt (SWE), the 1954 World Champion was making a final attempt to redeem himself after his 1956 disaster. Many other pentathletes in the Rome competition showed versatility by competing in other Olympic events during the 1950s and 1960s, too: Antonio Almada (MEX), Udo Birnbaum and Frank

Battig (AUT), Jose Perez (MEX)- Epée; Neville Sayers (AUS), Naji El-Mekki (MAR) - Rapid Fire Pistol; Peter Lichtner-Hoyer (AUT) – Equestrian; and Ralf Berckhan (GER) – Canoeing. Kurt Lindeman (FIN) competed in Foil and Epée events (where, incidentally, he comfortably beat Christopher Bland (IRL), Oxford MPA Captain and later, Sir Christopher Bland, the BBC Chairman).

Two other entries deserve special prominence – Dieter Krickow (GER) later became Secretary-General of the UIPM (1988-92) where he made enormous contributions to the technical development of the sport and the 21 year old, Peter Macken (AUS), who was competing in the first of his five Olympic Modern Pentathlon competitions (1960-76). Finally, Okkie van Greunen (RSA) was to be the last South African to be allowed to compete in the Olympic Games until 1992. The movement against the anti-apartheid laws in South Africa was becoming more strident in the 1960s. Though the UIPM received assurances from the IOC that it would be acceptable to receive South Africa for competitions until 1963, after that the South Africans were cast out and it would become very risky for teams to compete against them. Certainly, at club level, those risks were occasionally taken in later years and, at such meetings, the South Africans were always warm and generous hosts.

Passo Corese became, in later years, the centre of Italian Modern Pentathlon and was a lovely site for the riding event. The 70 Sardinian horses were strong and well-trained and the course (4,500 metres with 25 obstacles) was not overly demanding. The result was that the scores were high but some of the embarrassment of recent chaotic results in World Championships was erased. 34 of the 60 entries scored over 1000 points with

Sergio Escobedo (MEX), an Army Colonel, who would head the Organising Committee at the 1968 Games, winning in the break-neck speed of 7:41.0, 24 seconds ahead of George Lambert (USA). This gave him 1237 points. Among the leading competitors, only Novikov (982 pts) and Selg (967 pts) of the USSR lost ground but, although the Mexicans were 300 points ahead, Hungary and the USSR were only seven points apart in 5th and 6th places. Peter Duckworth, the British Team Manager commented that, in the riding event, speed was so much of the essence that 'each competitor should ride with a stop watch strapped to one wrist.' This emphasis on speed was a bad thing for Modern Pentathlon. It was too hard on the horses and had been regarded as detracting from riding skill since the sport's beginning in 1912. In the immediate aftermath of the Rome Games, this problem would have to be dealt with once and for all.

The fencing event took place at the Palazzo dei Congressi in the centre of Rome. It was won by Imre Nagy (HUN) with 1000 points, one hit ahead of his team mate, Ferenc Nemeth and Bob Beck (USA). Balczó was suffering from a shoulder injury sustained in a fall in the riding event and only managed 885. This was better, however, than the favourite, Novikov's, poor score of 839. In the tense match with the Soviet Union, the Hungarians considered a double defeat better than a risky attack that might result in a loss. In the first bout, Nemeth forced a double defeat with Tatarinov which so infuriated Novikov that he threw caution to the wind in his first bout and Balczó had little trouble finishing him off. The Hungarians won the match 5-3. In his report, Duckworth created a beautifully optimistic picture of the mediocre British fencing skills by saying of Pat

Harvey, 'having baffled several opponents, his point failed to fix and he himself was hit.'

After a day of rest, the shooting took place 70 km outside Rome at the Umberto I Range in Lazio. Though often shooting into the sun, the standard was good and the winner with 195 was Escobedo who added to his victory in the riding event by beating Mazur (POL) and Beck into second and third places. Pat Harvey managed a very creditable 4th place with 191. Hanno Selg (URS) had, apparently shot 196 but was penalized 12 target points for an infringement.

After three events, the competition leader was Sergio Escobedo ahead of Bob Beck and Antonio Almada (MEX). This remarkable Mexican performance kept the team in bronze medal position until just before the final event. The very high standard of skills shown by the Mexicans in the first three events was, sadly, cancelled out by the extremely low standard of their physical events –Escobedo swam 5:02.0 and the Mexican team finished 9th and 16th respectively in the swimming and running events.

Andras Balczó won the swimming in 3:45.0, just two seconds in front of Novikov and eight ahead of Jack Daniels (USA). Bob Beck also swam under four minutes which, with only one event remaining, gave him the lead overall, almost 100 points ahead of Antonio Almada and Ferenc Nemeth (HUN).

The final running event took place on a parched Acqua Santa Golf Course where the heat was a powerful limiting force. Igor Novikov won the run in an impressive 13:38, ten seconds ahead of Balczó but neither of these great pentathletes managed to win a medal, their skills on the first three events having been below their usual standard. Balczó was 4th and Novikov 5th. Instead, Ferenc Nemeth's 7th place in the run secured him overall victory with the first ever 5000+ score in an Olympic or World Championship competition. Though Imre Nagy was behind Nemeth in the running, he too moved up the field into silver medal position and Bob Beck's 24th position in the run still enabled him to hang on to the bronze medal. It was such a very close finish that only 62 points separated the top five pentathletes. Almada and Escobedo of Mexico, who had led the field after two and three events respectively, finally finished 17th and 22nd.

With Hungary in 1st, 2nd and 4th places individually, the team gold medal was undisputed with USSR taking the silver and USA the bronze medals. Finland, Poland and Sweden followed and Great Britain placed 7th, content in the knowledge that 10 teams were behind them including the Mexicans who had performed so impressively in the early part of the competition. Individually, Pat Harvey had performed best with a good 11th place. Don Cobley was 24th and Peter Little 26th.

The British team had arrived in Rome almost two weeks before the competition and appreciated the necessary adjustment to the temperature this allowed (although the Hungarians arriving the night before the start didn't seem to have done them any harm!). The British training had been inconsistent throughout the winter and involved a great deal of travel. The team selected, Pat Harvey (Army), Don Cobley (RAF), Peter Little (RAF) with Len Collum (Army) as fourth man, had undergone none of the disasters of previous British teams. They had swum personal bests and achieved steady scores elsewhere. Peter Duckworth recognized that future success would depend on ready-made run-swimmers and civilian participation, to say nothing of a bit of civilian money. But the nature of 'amateur' sport was shot through with casual desultory arrangements. While Avery Brundage, the IOC President policed Western sportsmen to ensure nobody took their training too seriously, the Communist bloc countries were developing models of 'professional' sports organisation that would form the prototype for success in Modern Pentathlon competitions for years to come.

Modern Pentathlon in the Soviet Union

In 1961, the year in which the first ever World Championships to be held in Moscow took place, an article appeared in the *UIPM Bulletin*. The details explained in no uncertain terms why the Soviet Union ruled supreme in the sport. Since the war, Modern Pentathlon had been quietly developing in the Soviet Union, even though its first appearance internationally was not until the 1952 Olympic Games. Every one of the fifteen republics had its own Modern Pentathlon federation and twenty cities had a specialized sports school. Modern Pentathlon was overseen by five senior coaches and 200 assistant coaches. Annually, the Ukraine Championships had 70 entries and the Russian Championships, 60. There was a standardized categorization of all pentathletes –the Junior Squad must achieve 1700 points in three events, and then the Seniors rose gradually through the following categories, each graded by the number of points achieved in five events: Grade 3: 2800 points; Grade 2: 3400 points; Grade 1: 4000 points; and Masters: 4,400 points. Such a government-backed system was far beyond the wildest dreams of most other national federations in the world who considered themselves lucky to be able to get in a few hours practice together whenever their pentathletes were free from other duties. In the years to come, a competition in Moscow or Budapest in which large numbers of home competitors took part would be a far tougher proposition to a foreign athlete than even the Olympic Games.

1961 World Championships: Moscow (URS)

The British team prepared for Moscow by training in West Germany beforehand where, in competition, they beat the German and Swiss teams. They had also worked out that, by this route, they could all get to Moscow and then back to England for less than a total of £350. Sadly, on August

Igor Novikov (URS) World Champion 1957, 1958, 1959 and 1961.

3rd, the border between East and West Berlin was closed and the political situation forced the team to travel to Moscow via Aldershot. This probably explains the long list of faults that Peter Duckworth found in the Soviet administration of the Moscow event –broken lifts and windows, missing plugs, ceaseless misinformation – everything appeared to be designed to create maximum discomfort for the British team. He does however, in his report, point out that the greatest number of disapproving whistles from the crowd in Moscow was reserved for the Germans and the Americans. The loss of both Don Cobley and Pat Harvey from the team (Harvey's new civilian employers were completely unsympathetic to his sporting ambitions) and the financial restrictions imposed meant that only a three man team flew to Moscow together with manager, Peter Duckworth. They were Peter Little and Len Collum from the Rome team and Sgt Mick Finnis (Army) as the new recruit.

There were 42 competitors from 14 countries in Moscow including the first ever entry from East Germany. Though the three East Germans did not make an impact in this, their first competition, over the coming years they became a powerful presence in Modern Pentathlon.

The first sensation of the opening riding event was that the Olympic Champion, Ferenc Nemeth, fell from his horse in the collecting ring and was badly injured. The fourth Hungarian, Ferenc Török didn't have enough time to prepare properly and, in pouring rain, had to leap on to the horse in his tracksuit and ride the course in Nemeth's place. He scored a paltry 52 points. Nemeth, despite being Olympic Champion was never Hungarian Champion and never competed for Hungary in a major competition again. In Moscow, however, the Hungarian recovery from such a setback was impressive – they even managed to win the silver medal in the team event. The riding course was 3500 metres with a big hill in the middle and the Soviet organisers produced 64 throughbred horses for the event. Unlike Rome, Moscow produced only five 1000+ rides, three of them being the Soviet team, Igor Novikov, Ivan Deryugin (who had not been in the team since his gold medal team performance in 1956), and Boris Pakhomov, an outstanding run-swimmer.

A surprisingly low score of 904 in fencing was, nevertheless, good enough for Novikov to win the event and he and Balczó shared 2nd place on 195 in the shooting behind Cerny (CZE) who scored 197. It was Deryugin (3:43.0) who nudged Balczó out in the swimming but Balczó beat Novikov by two seconds to win the run. Balczó had begun the competition with a 900 riding score and the 175 point lead this surrendered to Novikov was too much to catch up even though he performed strongly in the other events. So a Soviet whitewash gave Novikov his 4th and final world title. Deryugin took silver and Balczó the bronze. Though new to the team, Pakhamov still managed 4th place. This, of course, gave the Soviet Union victory in the team event almost 2000 points ahead of the Hungarians, a gap unlikely ever to be reproduced. USA once more took the bronze medal ahead of Finland.

The British team finished a miserable 13th. Len Collum was eliminated in the riding, Little got only 392 in the fencing, and, according to Duckworth's report, Finnis in the shooting 'explored every complete ring on the target except the centre one'. The cry that Great

Britain was 'the best of the true amateurs' was beginning to sound rather hollow. Exaggerated differences between the British and other Modern Pentathlon nations started to appear in the press. 'If we were like the Soviet Union and could call on 50,000 pentathletes at any one time or like the USA who spent $50,000 preparing their team for Moscow, we'd be the champions.' According to *Weekend* magazine, 'we reckoned we'd done it on 2s 7$^1/_2$d a man!' In the same article, John Majendie is quoted as saying, 'It's a bit of a slog...but I notice that once a chap takes up the pentathlon he never gives it up.' Luckily for British Pentathlon, gritty determination did at least keep everyone going.

1962 World Championships: Mexico City (MEX)

The money situation was so desperate in the UK that this was the only World Championship that Great Britain has ever failed to attend. Though the programme listed 18 countries including the Dominican Republic, 14 teams were actually in Mexico for the event which was celebrated alongside a Mexican Youth Games in late November. It was a chance for the experienced Mexican team (Escobedo, Almada, Perez) to have a final stab at glory and, if proof were needed of the ubiquity of the sport, all six continents were represented. Sadly, yet again, the competition was scarred by the awful inequalities of the riding event. 16 riders failed to achieve even 600 points, among them Balczó (560), Novikov (488) and Pichushkin of the Soviet Union (320). The Soviet team found themselves more than 800 points adrift of the leaders, USA, after the riding. All the more impressive, therefore, that USSR came through to win the competition, Novikov scoring 1042 to win the fence and Pichushkin winning the difficult run at high altitude. This gave the Soviet team a winning total of 13,204, this time a tiny margin of only 13 points ahead of Hungary. Paul Pesthy (USA) collapsed in the thin air 200 metres from the finish and there was a dispute as to whether he had been helped to his feet or not. He managed to cross the line before losing consciousness. This enabled USA, to hold on to the bronze medal, pushing the disappointed Mexican hosts into 4th place. Individually, it was new Soviet team member, Edward Sdobnikov, who took the gold medal. He elbowed the 34 year old Novikov into 2nd place. Novikov's 324 deficit to Sdobnikov after the riding was too big a gap to make up. Balczó's awful ride kept him in 4th place overall and it was his team mate, Ferenc Török who took the bronze. The report in the *UIPM Bulletin* quite rightly pointed out that 'the riding event in Modern Pentathlon has decided the whole event too often.' The truth of this was never more obvious than in the riding scores of the top six finishers overall:

Sdobnikov (812), Novikov (488), Török (832), Balczó (560), Jackson - USA (876), Nagy (796).

And these were the best pentathletes in the world! It was time for a radical reappraisal and a surprise announcement was to force this necessary change in a hurry.

An announcement about Tokyo 1964

Modern Pentathlon officials were shocked to read in their newspapers in 1961 that the Japanese had decided to eliminate Modern Pentathlon from the Olympic Games. Protests to Avery Brundage brought back the reassurance that only the IOC could make such decisions and not the host country. Indeed the Tokyo Organising Committee soon issued an apology: 'We deeply regret our informal decision to be submitted to the IOC Session in Athens has been reported by news agencies as if we had officially decided.'

The Japanese had understandably had difficulties planning the riding event. Their association had been founded as far back as 1955 in readiness for the bid to host the Olympics but no activity of any kind had taken place until September 1959. One of the problems in developing Modern Pentathlon in Japan was that, legally, only the Police and the Self-Defence Force were allowed to handle guns. So, 36 members of those two organisations, mostly run-swimmers, took part in the first competition in Japan. The Tokyo Olympics depended for their funding in part on the Horse Racing industry which, coincidentally, was the only source of horses the pentathletes had. With only race horses to ride, the two Japanese pentathletes who had attended the Rome Olympics had never attempted to clear a jump before leaving Japan. All things considered, Kazuhiro Tanaka and Shigeaki Uchino had done pretty well in the riding event in Rome, scoring 922 and 751 respectively.

At the UIPM Congress in Rome, the Japanese had submitted a proposal requesting that the clause in the UIPM statutes denying organisers the use of race horses and steeplechasers be suspended. Understandably, they had no other way of organizing the Tokyo event. The Japanese also pressed for the maximum number of competitors for Tokyo to be fixed at only 40. The reaction of the UIPM was commendable. Rather than rant and rage against the injustice of this, they made some very sensible changes to the riding event. The riding distance was reduced to 1000-1500 metres; the speed was also reduced from 500 to 400 metres per minute and no additional points were given for beating the bogey time; at least half the jumps would, for the first time, be moveable; and, by reducing the maximum number of competitors to 50 (it was 60 in Rome), the horses would be able to go twice. Sven Thofelt proudly proclaimed that the Tokyo event would cost less than 10% of the costs in Rome. Through these measures, the riding event and its role in the sport was preserved.

Brundage puts his oar in

Avery Brundage seized the opportunity at this stage to put pressure on Modern Pentathlon officials. Since he had appeared to act on behalf of the sport, he now felt able to call in a few debts. In a letter to Sven Thofelt, Brundage wrote: 'Yours is a fine sport, involving the all-round philosophy of the Olympic Movement and I am sure you want to avoid criticism of any kind.'

This particular letter happened to be drawing attention to the eternal threat of 'professionalism' which Brundage abhorred above all others but it is a sentiment that he might just have easily used about the riding in Modern Pentathlon. The riding event was, and always would be, a problem. There was extreme pressure on the sport's leaders to make changes. Once again, the motorcycling option reared its ugly head and, in an attempt to fight for the survival of Modern Pentathlon in whatever form, a number of rather unctuous letters were sent to Brundage. One such letter came from Wille Grut, the newly-appointed Secretary-General of the UIPM. He told Brundage: 'I think it is high time for us to make this change to another sport that requires courage, cool judgement and determination.' Adding a moral element to the proposed shift to motorcycling, Grut added:

'The youth in Stockholm is steadily getting physically degenerated and with that may follow moral degeneration. These boys who are now in the claws of materialism could ride motor bikes and find a healthy outflow for their energy and would be transformed into good sportsmen by learning to know the other four events of Modern Pentathlon.'

This was a fine attempt by Grut to appeal to Brundage's known affection for the character-building possibilities of sport. However, the proposed alternative of motorcycling was doomed from the start. Apart from the unhealthy emphasis on mechanization that motorcycling required, Modern Pentathlon would only be allowed to include a new sport which was already one of the chosen Olympic sports. Brundage, himself made suggestions: 'Why don't you consider a rowing, gymnastic or weight lifting event? The single scull, I think, would be a good replacement.'

The UIPM Congress, however, was unanimous in voting to retain the riding event in whatever form it could and particularly strong support came from Eastern Europe and South America where riding facilities were still plentiful.

1963 World Championships: Macolin (SUI)

It was left to the Swiss to show the world that Modern Pentathlon could manage the riding event properly and put the new rules into practice. It was the third time Switzerland had hosted the World Championships in the mountains 35km outside Berne. The traditional order of events was changed in Macolin and the riding became, on this one occasion, the penultimate event despite fears that another farcical riding event immediately before the final run would send out a very bad message to the world about the health of the sport. The 1500 metres course had 20 obstacles set over pleasant fields. The horses, for the first time ever, went twice, the afternoon rider often doing better than the morning rider on the same horse. There were no additional points given for riding fast and so the course was very much a test of the rider's skill rather than the horse's brute force. It was exactly what was needed to restore confidence in the event. The result was that only 90 points separated the top twenty riders and only 72 points separated the next ten. This didn't mean that the riding event was a foregone conclusion, though. Seven riders scored zero including Peter Lichtner-Hoyer (AUT), considered to be one of the finest riders in the sport. Another loser on that day was a 21 year old Jim Fox in his first ever World Championships. He scored 358 points in the riding and joined a long list of great pentathletes who had similarly made an inauspicious start to their careers. For anyone starting out learning to ride, it is reassuring to know even the greats had their difficulties. What do the following world champions have in common: Igor Novikov, Björn Thofelt, Pavel Lednev, Boris Onischenko, and Janusz Peciak? Answer: They all had zero scores in the riding event in a World Championship or Olympic Games. The new MPAGB President, Major General Ronnie Bramwell Davis, CB, DSO was Chef D'Equipe in Macolin and wrote to Fox's commanding officer at REME:

'He himself (Fox) made an awful nonsense of the riding… His horse ran out about half way round and he had three refusals at a comparatively easy obstacle during which time he lost his stirrups. Instead of getting properly under control he tried to ride the rest of the course without stirrups and of course went from bad to worse. I won't go on any more as I could write two or three pages.'

The competition in Macolin was to mark a power shift between the reigning champion, Igor Novikov, and the man who would replace him as king, Andras Balczó. For once, neither man lost the competition on the riding and, in the other events, incrementally Balczó crept ahead so that, by the end, when he won the running event, there was no dispute about who was the new World Champion. It had taken him since 1958 to get there, but Modern Pentathlon was now ruled by Andras Balczó. He would be five times World Champion and, between 1958 and 1972, he would never be out of the top six. Every one of the top six in Macolin was from Hungary or the Soviet Union with Ferenc Torok taking the silver and Novikov the bronze. Hungary regained the team title from the

Jim Fox, ten times British Champion and 1976 Olympic team gold medallist.

Soviet Union and, for the sixth year running, USA took the bronze medal. Rapidly making their mark now were the East Germans who took 4th place.

The British team of Sgt Mick Finnis (Army), Capt Rod Tuck (Royal Marines) and L.Cpl Jim Fox (Army) finished 27th, 29th and 41st. Their 10th place in the team competition was, however, better than Finland and Switzerland, both countries having more impressive pentathlon pedigrees. Finnis had, bizarrely, broken his dental plate on the first shot of the final series. Fox had become British Champion that year in the absence of the injured Finnis who was therefore unable to defend his title. The management of the team had been taken over in December 1961 by Capt. Gordon Richards who, based in Bielefeld in Germany, had built his team around him there, enlisting Finnis, Collum and Fox in full-time training in Germany. The hard work was all too much for the fledgling Fox who was hospitalised and, by the end of 1962, returned to Arborfield to train. Richards' report on the World Championships shows a clear exploration of the team's possibilities but there was no real justification for his belief that the bronze medal in Tokyo was 'in the bag'. He noted that the Hungarians had extensive competition experience which the British could never match and his report concluded with a very odd list for which he offered no illuminating comment: Average age of Hungarian team: 26 (all married); Average age of Russian team: 28(all married) Average age of British team: 26 (none married).

Had he stumbled upon a theory of Modern Pentathlon success that nobody else had considered?

Richards was not a negotiator. He was a man who did things his way or not at all and it takes courage for a national body to entrust such a man with full responsibility. The MPAGB was not prepared to do that and when Bramwell Davis announced to Richards in Switzerland that the training base for the coming Olympics would be Arborfield and not Bielefeld, Richards walked out and never returned to the sport. His resignation letter expressed contempt for 'weekend pentathlon supporters' which is the way he characterized the management. He was probably right about the partial commitment of an essentially amateur organization. From time to time, someone, like Richards, comes along who could certainly make a difference to the sport but whose approach is so uncompromising that those 'supporters' who have given considerable time and effort to keeping the sport going feel pushed out and unappreciated. It requires proper funding to entrust a 'messiah' with the job of training a team and the MPAGB would persist in living from hand to mouth for many years to come.

The case of the missing superstar

Though World Champion, the most important absentee from Tokyo was Andras Balczó. Even in early summer of that year he was winning international competitions but then, together with his Hungarian teammate, Istvan Mona, he was jailed for a year for smuggling Swiss watches into Rumania. The Iron Curtain was the perfect backdrop to stimulate trading activities for those sportsmen lucky enough to be able to travel abroad. You can be sure Balczó and Mona were not alone in seeking to plug a gap in the trading market and Western athletes were also sure to take saleable supplies with them whenever they went into the Eastern bloc. It meant that Hungary's top pentathlete would miss the Olympic Games. This was an extraordinary action for the Hungarian government to take but the decision to jail him may have had something to do with Balczo's uncompromising character.

Andras Balczó (1938-)

Andras Balczó was born in Kondoros and grew up in Nyiregyháza in North East Hungary, the son of a Calvinist pastor. He came to Budapest at the age of 18 as a typewriter mechanic and two years later was visiting Aldershot for his first World Championship. Though World Champion for the first time in 1963, divorce from his first wife, the jail sentence and the missed Olympic Games must all have contributed to a low period in his life. For those of us lucky enough to have seen this tall, elegant, calm athlete in action, it comes as a surprise to learn from Sándor Dávid's book, *Balczó*, (Sport 1973), that Balczó was a man wracked with

Andras Balczó (HUN): Olympic Champion 1972. World Champion 1963, 1965, 1966, 1967, 1968.

anxiety and insecurity about his own sporting genius. After the Rome Olympics where the team members were deprived of their coaches, Balczó resolved to be his 'own coach and trainer'. He was a member of the Csepel club, the Metal Workers' Union, and this set him apart from the Honved, ex-military team, which dominated Hungarian pentathlon at the time. Ferenc Török, a lawyer and, in more recent years, a politician and UIPM Vice-President, was Honved's top man.

Though Balczó became an agnostic Christian during the early years of his time in Budapest, a 'road to Damascus' moment brought him back to the church and his outspoken attacks on the Communist regime and, in modern times, on the more liberal 'euro' government in Hungary have made him, in many ways, the black sheep of the Modern Pentathlon world. After Olympic victory in Munich in 1972, Balczó retired but, despite his fame (a biographical film, *Kuldetes* –'Mission', was made about his life), was given no significant role in the Modern Pentathlon world. He worked in an undemanding job at the National Horse Breeding Inspectorate until he walked out entirely on the whole set-up, insisting he would have nothing more to do with the sport in which he had been a hero. He refused all approaches from his Hungarian pentathlon colleagues thereafter and it is only recently, in his seventies, that he has softened a little. He attended the 50 year reunion of the Rome Olympics and has recently been pictured with other Hungarian champions. In 1973, Balczó married Monika Csaszar who, at 17 years of age, had won a bronze medal in Gymnastics in Munich. Together they have produced twelve children, Balczó joking that he 'became a father of many children because of the lack of self-restraint'. Nowadays, he is a leading member of the Jobbik (JMM) political party and has a strong anti-abortion stance. Right-wing in attitudes, the party is, nevertheless, Hungary's third strongest political movement. Balczó enjoys talking to young people about his faith and beliefs. It is a great shame that he was deprived of contributing his expertise to future generations of pentathletes.

1964 Olympic Games: Tokyo (JAP)

After all the apprehension about the riding event in Tokyo, the Modern Pentathlon there was a great success. 37 competitors took part, consisting of 11 full teams and individuals from Korea, Chile, Brazil, and Italy. The Australian racehorses used had all been trained over jumps for the previous eight months and the course was neat and flowing. 11 competitors scored the maximum 1100 points and only five pentathletes scored less than 1000, the lowest score being 940. While skilled riders may have felt somewhat cheated by this lack of differentiation, the event ensured that the final result would not, for once, be the outcome of savage injustice in the opening ride.

The fencing event was won by Ferenc Török with a score of 1000, ahead of his experienced Hungarian team mate, Imre Nagy. Third place was taken by the well-known Austrian pentathlete, Rudi Trost, for many years the Berlin and Germany fencing coach. In his book, *Modern Pentathlon*, Frigyes Hegedus mentions that, during the hottest part of the day of the fencing event, Török, who was having an unbroken set of victories, took off his plastron to cool off. When he attempted to carry on fencing without a plastron, 'one of the overzealous judges made him put it on'. Török was so rattled by this that he lost his concentration and had a string of defeats before regaining his winning form.

The standard of shooting was extremely high with 18 pentathletes shooting 190+. The winner was Albert Mokeev (URS) with 198 though Novikov had a respectable 196. Otto Török, Ferenc's brother and the third member of the weakened Hungary team, had a disaster in the shooting. He failed to fire a shot and then fired twice on the following target to incur a penalty of 20 target points. This gave him only 168 and that, coupled with his mediocre 795 in the fencing was the end of Hungary's team hopes. The swimming provided an unprecedented clean sweep for Sweden. Their team (Bo Jansson, Rolf Junefelt and Hans-Gunnar Liljenwall) came 1st, 2nd and 3rd with Jansson winning in 3:45.2.

The final running event took place in Chiba on the Kemigawa Golf Course. It had rained heavily the previous night and the ground was very soft with a gruelling 'up and down' hill route. The first three to finish were Mokeev (URS) in 13:48, Jim Moore (USA) and Peter Macken (AUS). But it was the small wiry frame of Török in 5th place that wore the gold medal by the end of the day. He needed resuscitation afterwards and the medal ceremony was delayed accordingly. He'd managed to gain 30 points on Novikov who took the silver and Mokeev took the bronze. In 4th place was Peter Macken (AUS), the five-time Olympian who was producing his greatest performance in his second Olympic Games. The team event was won comfortably by the USSR and the USA took the silver medal just 16 points ahead of the hapless, depleted Hungarians.

The British team of Mick Finnis, Jim Fox, Robbie Phelps and, fourth man, Rod Tuck had arrived in Tokyo two weeks before the competition, full of hope. They had competed in an unprecedented five international matches that season with some success. Fox was competing in the first of four Olympic Games and Phelps would compete in three. Highlights were Robbie Phelps' 8th place (820 points) in the fencing. This was a particularly satisfying retort to Bramwell Davis' claim that Phelps was 'considered utterly hopeless by our Olympic fencers'. Mick Finnis shot 194 to take 8th place and Jim Fox beat his personal best by 20 seconds to place 4th in the swimming (3: 49.5) and 4th again in the running event. Lowlights were certainly Fox's 'paralytic' fence of only 280 points (he lost his first 11 bouts) and Phelps' disappointing shoot of only 181. Their final positions were Finnis 21st, Phelps 25th, and Fox 29th which put them back in 9th position as a team. For Capt Paul Stevenson, the Team Manager (and future Major General), it was a desperate disappointment. He highlighted the importance of fencing and shooting experience in his report and implored the MPAGB not to leave preparations for the next Olympic Games until the last minute again.

Post-Tokyo rule changes

During the latter part of the 1960s some very sensible rule changes were made. In riding, crash helmets became obligatory and weights were added to the saddle for any rider weighing less than 75kg. In fencing the percentage of victories needed for 1000 points was reduced from 75% to 70% and a double defeat only applied if the fencers concerned exceeded the time limit without a decisive hit. In shooting, misfires as a result of faulty ammunition were no longer penalized, competitors were allowed five practice shots instead of two, and, now that automatic pistols were so widely used, the time the targets were turned away was reduced from ten to seven seconds. There was also a change in the 1000 point mark from 195 to 194 and there was a difference of 22 pentathlon points per target point compared to 20 points previously. In swimming, the 1000 point bogey was reduced from 4:00 to 3:54 but the number of points per second was increased from five to six in 1965 and then to eight in 1968. This gave a significant new advantage to the successful swimmer and brought new blood into the sport from swimming clubs around the world. Finally, in 1965, the 1000 point running time was dropped from 15.00 to 14:15 but the tariff remained at three points per second.

Also, 1966 marked the first introduction of anti-doping control. This fascinating subject will be dealt with more fully in the coming chapters but competitors had for some time been drinking alcohol to steady their nerves before shooting. The objection to this had little to do with worries about 'cheating' – remember that nobody had objected when George Patton had been injected with opium before his run in the 1912 competition. The real concern was, quite rightly, that a drunk pentathlete and a loaded pistol do not make for a very safe combination. Someone was in danger of getting accidentally shot. In his 1963 World Championship report, Gordon Richards had recorded that 'the Australian team's apparent inebriation caused some marked comment from many Chefs D'Equipe. (Alcohol) was never envisaged by Baron de Coubertin and its use has been officially deplored.' In 1965, when a shooting detail was delayed, Herbert Polzhuber (AUT) found time to drink so much that he was disqualified for being out of control on the range. Official doping control began a year later and consisted of breathalysers to detect alcohol and some blood and urine samples at other times throughout the sports, although small quantities of caffeine were the only 'drugs' detected. There was an acceptable blood alcohol level of 40mg/ml which, according to rumour at the World Championships in Melbourne (1966), was equivalent to 'four Australian beers taken an hour before shooting'. Some teams brought their own breathalysers and took full advantage of the 'prescription' suggested. Not until 1968 would an official disqualification be made, though.

In 1967, the establishment of a Technical Committee enabled a proper consideration of the rules and led to the inevitable development of a more detailed rule book. The 1950 statutes were composed of 44 little pages; the modern rule book runs to well over 200. In his wonderful history of fencing (*By the Sword*, Macmillan, 2002), Richard Cohen records that in 1992, an official, noting the size of the FIE rule book asked René Roch, the FIE leader: 'There are six hundred or so rules in your book, M. Roch - 75 to 80 percent of them measures against cheating. Does your sport have a problem?' A sport with many rules does not have a problem; it is merely realistic about human nature. To a large extent, all rules are inevitably measures against cheating. The officials of any sport are constantly required to outwit the creative imaginations of its athletes. Cohen argues elsewhere that 'all games are played in continuous tension between their formal rules (or laws) and a shifting convention of what players find acceptable.' This is a more subtle, and accurate, description of what actually happens in all sports. It could be said that those who cry 'cheat' and heap moral opprobrium on athletes at every turn suffer from a reductive and authoritarian view of the world. It is, no doubt, helpful for the rule makers of our sport that so many officials were once athletes themselves. Finally, at the Mexico Congress in 1968 the UIPM became the UIPMB (et Biathlon) and the link with Winter Biathlon remained until 1993.

1965 World Championships: Leipzig (DDR)

One additional rule added at the 1965 Congress was that the host country must guarantee visas to all visiting pentathletes. This need arose because East Germany had refused visas to a number of military personnel. The British team was therefore only able to send Robbie Phelps, a civilian, and the USA team, who had been such a force for so many years, was unable to participate at all. The Leipzig event was an important one: it celebrated 800 years since the founding of the city and was the first time that both Senior and Junior World Championships were held in the same place. It also marked the establishment of East Germany as a powerful Modern Pentathlon nation. Large paying crowds attended the events in Leipzig in late September.

Unlike in Tokyo, the riding event was a tough one. The course was largely show-jumping in style with 23 jumps and some good, strong horses. However, only three men scored over 1000 points and there were 17 riders who scored fewer than 400 points. Of these, ten scored zero, including Pavel Lednev (URS) who only weeks before had won the Hungarian Championships. Among the unlucky was Robbie Phelps whose single fall cost him 470 points in time lost.

The winning fencing total of 1026 was shared by Igor Novikov (URS), at 36 years old competing in his last World Championships, Olympic Champion Ferenc Török (HUN), and Rudi Trost (AUT). Phelps, despite losing his first five bouts, scored 844 and took the scalps of Balczó and Török en route. Phelps then won the shooting event with 197, a record that remained for many years. Peter Macken (AUS) had shot 198 but was penalized for firing outside orders in the practice. With two events to go the battle was between Török and Novikov who each had 3000 points but Balczó won both the swim and the run so convincingly that he overhauled them both to win his second world title. Novikov took the silver and Török the bronze. In the team event, the Hungarians (Balczo, Török, Mona) were once more the winners and the Soviet Union (Novikov, Mokeev, Lednev) came second. The hosts, East Germany, took the bronze medal to the delight of the crowd. This was the final appearance of the Russian pentathlete, Albert Mokeev, who, sadly, died at only 33 years old in 1969.

Junior World Championships in the 1960s

Leslie Wieler, the UIPM Vice-President, died in 1965 and the trophy he had previously donated to the World Junior Championship became the Leslie Wieler Challenge Cup. Young pentathletes who were no older than 21 in the year of competition were invited to take part. The riding course was easier and the running course shorter than in the senior competition. In 1965, the riding event was the penultimate event in this competition and the overall winner, Janos Bodnar (HUN) had fallen badly and had his arm in plaster for the running event. However, he managed to hold off Björn Ferm (SWE) to win the title and the Hungarian team also beat the Swedes into 2nd place. Ferm was, of course, to become Olympic Champion only three years later.

It is interesting that, over the years, winning at junior level has not been a guarantee of future success. There is a short list of men who have been both World Junior and Senior Champion –Kelemen (HUN), Starostin (URS), Fábián (HUN), Svatkovsky (RUS), Balogh (HUN), Moiseev (RUS), Marosi (HUN) and Karyakin (RUS). Some pentathletes have, of course, enjoyed successful sporting careers that they began in their teens but others have made no impact at all at senior level. Perhaps, without extensive coaching support, a career in Modern Pentathlon can only be sustained for a limited period. Perhaps, in some cases, early success can lead to a complacency that undermines the fullest development of the individual. With the modern wide range of structured age group competitions, however, it seems likely that more and more young athletes will have extended adult careers.

In 1966, the Junior World Championships were held in Bratislava where a unilateral decision by the organisers, urged on by the Hungarians, changed the running tariff from 2.5 points per second to 4 points a second. This resulted in a team win for Hungary. The previous system would have given East Germany the victory. Unilateral though the decision was, it was soon generally adopted. Over the distance of 3000m, four points is much more in keeping with the senior tariff of three points per second over 4000m. The event was won by Peter Kelemen (HUN), later to be the 1970 Senior World Champion. The winner of the fencing event was Hans Jacobson (SWE), already World Junior Epée Champion and later to take an Olympic epée team gold medal in Montreal. Jacobson actually shared his World Junior Epée title with Jacques Brodin (FRA) in extraordinary circumstances. In a barrage for first place, both men ran out of time on equal hits in three separate fights. After the second they were warned that, if it happened a third time, they would share the title, and that is exactly what they did. A number of leading epéeists in the world have started their sporting lives in Modern Pentathlon, especially among the Swedes and Hungarians. The great Hungarian coach, Béla Rerrich was responsible for the Swedish domination of world fencing at this time and his pupils, Björn Ferm among them, won World Championship and Olympic medals from 1968 through to 1984.

In 1967, the World Junior Championships were hosted by the British in Aldershot and were won by the 20 year old Hans-Jorg Tscherner (DDR), the only married man in the competition. It was the first triumph for the East Germans; it was also, remarkably, the last. When they finished outside the medals a year later at the Mexico Olympics, the East German Modern Pentathlon team was ruthlessly disbanded by its sporting masters. Having grown used to winning in all world sports, the East German authorities were not prepared to wait the year or two it would have taken for their pentathletes to develop into champions. National honour was at stake.

Though no World Junior Championships were held in Olympic year (1968), László Pethö won in 1969 in front of his Budapest home crowd.

1966 World Championships: Melbourne (AUS)

The choice of Melbourne as venue for the 1966 event prompted some remarkable travel plans by the UIPM.

Having made a good deal with the Pan Am travel agents, a group of 20 (pentathletes, officials and wives from Sweden, Germany, Finland and Great Britain,) set off from Frankfurt on 25th October to travel to Melbourne via San Francisco, Honolulu and Sydney, sightseeing en route and returning via Hong Kong and Bangkok. It's amusing to imagine today's top competitors preparing for a World Championship in such a way.

The competition began in early November with 10 teams and 31 competitors. The riding was a flat course with dykes and water jumps. The horses were good thoroughbred hunters and 22 riders scored more than 1000 points with seven gaining the maximum 1100. Of the very few casualties, Robbie Phelps lost 615 points as the result of time penalties for a single fall in the water with nobody handy to catch the departing horse. The fencing was won comfortably by Balczó (1111 points) and Jim Fox's score of 926 was a rare fencing success for Great Britain. Testing of blades was so strict that the event was delayed by two hours, so many competitors had fallen foul of the rules. The British team had 9 out of 12 weapons rejected. The shoot was won by Istvan Mona (HUN) with 195. The use of breathalyzer testing for alcohol appears to have reduced overall performance by quite a few target points. However, Balczó's lead was unassailable by this stage. He finished 2nd in the swim behind Jim Coots (USA) - 3:39.0 but won the running, beating an established track star, Orlin Larsen (USA) into 2nd place. The running event was over treacherous country with the hurdling of barbed wire being an unexpected ingredient. Luckily, no lasting injury was sustained and Balczó took his third World Championship, almost 300 points ahead of silver medallist, Viktor Mineev (URS) and Török took the bronze. The Hungarians comfortably retained their team title with USSR in 2nd place and the East Germans holding off the USA for the bronze medal. The British army competitors Jim Fox and Barry Lillywhite had only managed to compete at all as a result of a late military flight to Melbourne. Robbie Phelps and Team Manager, Colin Peace, had been part of the UIPM Grand Tour. The team finished 9th out of the 10 teams but for Jim Fox it was the big breakthrough that everyone had been anticipating. He finished 5th overall and was now establishing himself as one of the top pentathletes in the world.

Troubles in the USA

With Avery Brundage as President of the IOC, his fellow Americans were required to be exemplary in all matters. This caused some problems for the USMPA. Immediately before Tokyo 1964, Brundage was pursuing complaints against the training centre in San Antonio. Firstly, the 'amateur' rule that stated that more than three weeks' continuous training should be considered professionalism was enforced. Both George Wilson, USMPA Secretary, and Wille Grut, the UIPM Secretary-General, had attempted to explain to Brundage that military training and Modern Pentathlon were often indivisible. Grut had already told Brundage that the physical quality of recruits in Sweden was so low that Modern Pentathlon training was regarded as an essential character and physique builder for the raw soldier. George Wilson explained that, in the USA, such training was 'considered important to the career of the military man and in no way curtails or interrupts military careers'. Another complaint made to Brundage was that civilians in the USA, who, after all, paid through their taxes for all military facilities, were being denied the use of such facilities and therefore at a disadvantage. This was patently untrue. More than 20 civilians frequently trained in San Antonio with their military counterparts throughout the 1960s and 14 civilians and 13 military men took part in the 1968 Olympic trials. Brundage insisted he had several sources for these complaints but by 1969 was prepared to accept that they had been generated largely by one man, 'an overzealous father whose son was not selected as a member of the US Junior Modern Pentathlon team.'

The USA was not alone in this persecution; any newspaper article suggesting a 'professional' approach to training in Western Europe would lead to another Brundage interrogation. Meanwhile, the truly professional approach (in its most positive sense) of the Eastern European countries was left to take its course, Brundage being unable to exert the same political influence in those countries.

1967 World Championships: Jönköping (SWE)

It was back to Sweden once again for the World Championships. 60 competitors took part and heavy rain contributed to some wildly inconsistent riding scores. Among the five zero riders was another future World Champion, Boris Onischenko (URS), and many others had low scores (only nine over 1000 points). Of the survivors, the winner was Jim Fox, the only 1100 of the day. Jim, like Andras Balczó became a great horseman in the process of his pentathlon career and, more importantly, a great lover of all things equestrian and this triumph put his indifferent start in the sport well behind him. Of the other leading pentathletes, Balczó,

Ferm and Török all remained in contention alongside the other two Soviet athletes, the Lithuanian, Stasis Shaparnis, and the recalled 1962 World Champion, Edward Sdobnikov. Török won the fencing (1114), Mona the shooting (197) and Kutschke (GDR) the swimming (3:30). The run was a hard one and won by Shaparnis (13: 39) who despite problems in the shooting event (736) still managed to take the silver medal overall, 10 points ahead of Björn Ferm (SWE). The winner was, of course, Balczó, with his team mate Török in 4th place. Jim Fox, for the second consecutive year, placed 5th and cemented his position as one of the world's best. The team event was easily won by Hungary although, had Onischenko not scored zero in the riding, the Soviet Union may well have beaten them. Instead, they took the bronze medal with the Swedish team (Ferm, Jacobson, Liljenwall) making a welcome return to the medals, taking the silver on home soil, two of the team actually performing in their home town.

The British team (Fox 5th, Phelps 22nd, Howe 37th) finished an impressive 5th, a big improvement on recent years' performances. Lt. Mike Howe was to be fourth man in Mexico the following year and thereafter would be drawn away from Modern Pentathlon by military duties. In 1974, he was shot dead in Cyprus in a tragic misunderstanding. Sitting in an open army truck approaching a Turkish/Greek check point, he was casually playing his guitar. The innocuous instrument was mistaken for a rifle and the border guard opened fire on him.

The Team Manager from 1967 through to the Olympic Games in 1972 was Major Monty Mortimer and he had gained the team valuable experience by entering them for as many international competitions as possible. He certainly instilled a military discipline in his team but his relationship with Jim Fox was, at times, tense, and probably not helped when Mortimer wrote in his annual report that the only limits to Fox becoming an Olympic medallist were his 'slightly immature approach to competition and his volatile nature'. Mortimer was quite determined and undiplomatic, too, in his objection to doping. In 1972, his rage over this subject made it to the national press and, even at the start of his managerial career in 1967, he reported:

'The UIPM have taken on the task of testing for drugs in the World Championships and Olympic Games. As yet they are not quite sure what they are doing or how to do it and whilst this situation exists the Eastern European nations will always be one jump ahead. There is no doubt the the Russians, Hungarians and East Germans have a very sound plan for drugging their teams for the shooting event at least and whilst this continues we will be at a three hundred point disadvantage. It should be clearly understood by all British competitors that only shooting scores obtained without the use of alcohol will be considered when national teams are selected.'

British Modern Pentathlon in the 1960s

The British Championships in 1960 had set a very bad precedent for the rest of the decade. Although Peter Little won the title, the organisers made such a mess of the timing in the running event that *The Times* reported the event with the punning headline 'Little successful in Pentathlon'. MPAGB President, Field Marshal Sir Gerald Templer (1898-1979), KG, GCB, GCMG, KBE, the no-nonsense scourge of the Communist uprisings in

Malaya, was quoted as saying 'We have always taken great pride in producing meticulously accurate results. But things have gone wrong today in a really big way. It doesn't give me any pleasure to have to say that.' The quaking timekeepers gave the title to Little with Don Cobley and Jo Buscko 2nd and 3rd but, as the REME band ran through its complete repertoire, murmurings from the competitors were beginning to drown them out. Jo Buscko, the founder of the Cheltenham club was a Hungarian refugee and, despite his success in the early 1960s, was often left out of teams travelling abroad because of the risk to his own security. In 1972, Buscko was instrumental in training the young Canadian team he brought to Munich for the Olympic Games.

Len Collum and Mick Finnis won the title in 1961 and 1962 respectively but the rest of the decade was Jim Fox's dominion with the exception of two occasions. In 1964 the Olympic team had been training so hard that they allowed an outsider, Sgt. A 'Willie' Wilson, RAF, to outdo them at the British Championship. Naturally, there were representations from the RAF as to why Wilson had been excluded from the Olympic team. As in previous Olympic years, the BOA had demanded names early in the summer and the British Championships came too late for inclusion as a selection competition. Mike Thomas and Tony Flood were also frequently in the reckoning for team places. In modern times, now that the international programme is so highly formulated, the British Championship holds little prestige. It is a domestic competition in which the elite international athletes rarely take part. The other occasion when Jim Fox did not win was in 1969 when he took a sabbatical from the Army. Appropriately, the popular champion that year was Robbie Phelps, the man who spent his entire career in the shadow of Jim Fox. Such was that shadow that Fox cast over all his rivals that it might be easy to underestimate Phelps' great achievement.

Robbie Phelps, MBE (1939 -)

Phelps, a scrap metal merchant from Gloucester, came into the sport in 1959, like so many, from swimming. Starting out in the Cheltenham MPC, he soon formed Spartan MPC based in Gloucester. He maintained an unbroken run from 1964 until 1973 as a member of every British World Championship and three Olympic teams during those years, a record only beaten by his nephew, Richard. Not one to retire from anything, he has competed in more than 45 British Championships, been an official at four further Olympic Games and, at the age of 71, came 6th in the World Masters' Fencing Championship. There are very few living pentathletes in Great Britain who have not benefitted at some time from Robbie Phelps' practical advice.

Jim Fox, OBE (1941 -)

Fox was born in Woodborough, Wiltshire and grew up in Portsmouth. He was a boy soldier and became the driving force behind the successful REME team of the 1960s and 1970s. For a fuller account of his life, there is no better source than David Hunn's biography, *Smelling of Roses* (Ward Lock, 1980) – you will still find copies available on www.amazon.co.uk. Jim won the British Championship ten times and competed in four Olympic competitions (1964-76) placing 4th in Munich (1972) and winning a team gold medal in Montreal (1976). His best World Championship performances were 1975 (3rd), and 1966 &

1967 (5th). After retiring from Modern Pentathlon in 1976, he was granted a commission in the army and, as Capt. Fox, took charge of the MPAGB Centre of Excellence. There has been no better spokesman for the sport and, when he became Chairman of MPAGB in the late 90s, his public popularity and important connections enabled the sport to survive difficult times. He was forced to resign this position to deal with the effects of Parkinson's disease which he developed soon after. Though Jim Fox's sporting credentials are impressive, he is admired every bit as much for the way in which he has dealt with the effects of this terrible disease as for his sporting success. He has always turned heads whenever he has entered the room, but it is his personality that wins everyone over. To have taken part in competition with Jim Fox will always be a great memory for the many who did so.

The Pony Club and other British developments

One important development in British Modern Pentathlon was the initiation of the Pony Club Tetrathlon (ride, air pistol shoot, swim, run) in 1966 by Colin Peace. This was a response to the establishment of the British Junior Modern Pentathlon Championship in that same year and born of a desire to keep teenagers busy at Pony Club camps. The Pony Club entered two teams every year in the British Junior and produced many fine pentathletes, of whom Danny Nightingale, member of the 1976 Olympic Gold medal team, was probably the most successful during that period. In more recent times, of course, all our women Olympic medallists, along with many other current pentathletes, owe their beginnings to the Pony Club.

In 1968 Rod Tuck edited an MPAGB Yearbook and established an important means of communication in the sport. In the same year, a Highland Pentathlon was held at Aviemore. This consisted of skiing, curling, rifle shooting, swimming and running and the event continued annually well into the 1980s. As with Winter Biathlon, it was an event that pentathletes occasionally dabbled in but which largely catered to a different clientele.

Taking part in a sport dominated by Communist bloc countries provided British pentathletes with insights that they would otherwise never have had. The Cold War persisted throughout this period. In the summer of 1968 a British Universities team visited Czechoslovakia. After the event, they were leaving a Bratislava bar just after midnight when they were amazed to find the streets full of Soviet tanks – a full invasion was taking place. After a couple of attempts, our team managed to flee across the border to safety but the MPAGB Yearbook report of the trip, with typical British detachment, makes no mention of this little difficulty. At the same time, our current MPAGB Chairman, Tony Temple, was a newly-qualified law student and hoped to go to Budapest to train in Modern Pentathlon. He was visited at home by Foreign Office officials who told him he must not go because he would be instantly arrested and exchanged for 'one of their spies.'

1968 Olympic Games: Mexico City (MEX)

The high altitude brought many to Mexico City well in advance of the mid-October competition. The British team, thanks to the loan of a VW Minibus had twice spent two week periods at Font Romeu in the Alps. More impressively, the Swedish team members had been hosted by the Swedish Embassy Attaché in Mexico at whose private villa they could train throughout the winter.

Among the 48 athletes competing, many were multiple Olympians – Peter Macken (AUS) and David Bárcena (MEX) -five times (Bárcena in the Three Day Event for three of them); Jim Fox (GBR) and Pavel Lednev (URS) - four times, and a number of others who were three times Olympians – Boris Onischenko (URS), Andras Balczó (HUN), Robbie Phelps (GBR), Mario Medda (ITA), Jorn Steffensen (DEN) and Hans-Gunnar Liljenwall (SWE).

The riding event was cross country in style with occasional steep banks. 27 riders achieved better than 1000 points and five of them, including Björn Ferm (SWE), gained the full 1100. Top names to lose out in the ride were Onischenko (995) and Török (920). Only one pentathlete scored zero; Hans-Jurgen Todt (FDR) has gone into history as the man so frustrated by his luck that he set about his hapless horse with his crash helmet and had to be restrained by his team mates. In the British team, only Phelps did badly with a score of 795.

First place in the fencing was shared by the Hungarians, Mona and Török on 1046 with Balczó scoring a disappointing 931. Ferm, Fox and Lednev had 885, 862 and 839 respectively. None of the leading competitors won the shooting but Ferm, Balczó and Lednev were equally matched on 934 points (191). The great run-swimmer in the competition was Karl-Heinz Kutschke, an East German policeman with 'a liking for beat music'. He won both events – a swim of 3:33.5 and a run of 13.45 in the hot, oxygen-starved atmosphere compounded by the midday sun. Perhaps it is significant that, helped by the change from five points per second to eight points per second, the top five in the swimming event (Kutschke, Ferm, Lednev, Balczó, Onischenko) became, for the first time, the top five pentathletes overall but not in that order. With the run to go, Ferm had a 23 second lead on Balczó and the advantage of setting off last in the draw. Since each runner set off at one minute intervals, this meant he was informed at every turn of his faltering advantage over his rival. At the half-way stage, Balczó had pulled back 19 of those 23 seconds but Ferm's altitude training had served him well. In the second half of the race, he held off Balczó by just 11 points to deny the four times World Champion his first Olympic title. Despite losing 200 points to Kutschke on the running, Lednev held his East German rival off and took the bronze medal. So Ferm became Sweden's 8th Olympic Champion, following in the golden footsteps of Lillehöök (1912), Dyrssen (1920), Lindman (1924), Thofelt (1928), Oxenstierna (1932), Grut (1948) and Hall (1952 and 1956). In later life, Ferm, now a grandfather, has become a successful businessman in South East Asia. He acknowledges that being Olympic Champion did his business success no harm but that the event all seems a very distant memory to him now. He has no plans to retire though – that is, apparently, a direct effect of the attitude of mind he developed as a pentathlete. Hungary took the gold medal in the team event ahead of the Soviet Union. Sweden won the bronze medal but suffered the first disqualification in Modern Pentathlon when Liljenwall was found to be above the alcohol limit after the shooting event. That resulted in a surprising re-award of the medal to France who had originally finished 4th, having never achieved such heights before. They were only nine points ahead of the USA.

There is no hiding Monty Mortimer's bitter disappointment in his team report on the British performance (8th of 15 teams). He described it, somewhat hyperbolically, as 'our greatest failure of all time'. Money for competition was always short but the team had attended six international competitions with some success, thanks to a Sports Council grant of 50% of costs. Fox had won in Fontainebleau and beaten Balczó for two consecutive years at the REME Championship. Individual performances (Fox 8th, Lillywhite 30th and Phelps 38th) fell short of expectation in the case of each member of the team, though, and Mortimer was inconsolable.

1969 World Championships: Budapest (HUN)

The post-Olympic year is often regarded as anti-climactic but a return to Budapest for both Senior and Junior World Championships would always be a big occasion. Jim Fox had left the Army and gone off to pursue civilian life in Jersey, thanks to a job offer from his old team mate, Mick Finnis. How would the British fare in his absence? More importantly for other countries, Ferm, the new Olympic Champion, still only 25 would continue to compete until 1972. Could he match Balczó on Hungarian territory?

Show jumping was introduced for the first time and, until 1973, faults were penalized by time additions – seven seconds for a knockdown. Only seven competitors cleared 1000 points, among them Balczó and Onischenko. Ferm scored only 935. However, it was Ferm who won the fencing with 1078, sufficiently far ahead of the other two to jump back into the competition. A poor shoot by Ferm gave Onischenko the lead though it was Peter Kelemen (HUN) who won the shooting with 196. It remained a three man race to the very end with Onischenko winning the swim and Balczó the run. Everyone who attended remembers the chant of 'Balczó! Balczó!' from the huge crowd who encouraged him every step of the way. Balczó won his fifth consecutive World Championship, Onischenko was 2nd and Björn Ferm 3rd. However, it was the Soviet Union who triumphed in the team competition, beating the Hungarians into 2nd place with the West Germans taking the bronze comfortably ahead of the USA. The British team (Phelps 13th, Stevenson 28th and Darby 44th) finished 9th and the decade ended for them with the yawning gap clearly left by the absence of their best competitor, Jim Fox.

Chapter Seven: 1970-1979

'If. If's a bloody great thing. If I'd got over that fence, if I hadn't shot late... Well, there's no if – you either do it or you don't.' Jim Fox interviewed by Norman Harris 1971

In the 1970s, Balczó gave his glorious farewell performance and Pavel Lednev took over his mantle. In the British camp, the 1976 Olympic gold medal was as considerable a break with past traditions as it was possible to make. When, after endless delays, women were allowed to hold their own competitions, early British domination of those events gave the impression, albeit briefly, that the Modern Pentathlon map had changed. The retirement in 1972 of IOC President, Avery Brundage ushered in a new era in which his obsessional concerns about amateurism were replaced by a more professional approach to sports organization and training. The MPAGB employed its first full-time staff and the UIPM membership grew to encompass 50 national bodies.

1970 World Championships: Warendorf (FRG)

The strength-sapping sand of the running course provided a dramatic conclusion to this competition. The riding event had given Peter Kelemen (HUN) a 135 point lead over his compatriot, Balczó, and 60 points over

Boris Onischenko (URS). Balczó and the veteran 1960 bronze medallist, Bob Beck (USA) shared the spoils in the fencing with 1022 points but Onischenko won the shooting (196) and, with good swims from all the leading athletes, it was Onischenko who set off on his run in the lead. The man from Kiev had given his all in the first half of the run but staggered in a state of collapse down the final stretch, often losing his balance and falling on the soft sand. He was overtaken by both Hungarians, Kelemen and Balczó, Kelemen holding off the five times World Champion by just 11 points to take an unexpected title with Onischenko in bronze medal position. With Pal Bakó (HUN) in 4th place, the Hungarians comfortably beat the Soviet Union to take the team gold medal. The host country, West Germany, took the bronze just ahead of the USA. Jim Fox made a promising return to the sport after his year's absence by coming 10th. Robbie Phelps was 19th and Jim Darby 38th. Barry Lillywhite had had a bad traffic accident in June of 1970 and had therefore been unable to compete.

1971 World Championships: San Antonio (USA)

Despite the jumps being 'festively decorated with flowers from a local cemetery', the rain and mud ensured that the horses at Fort Sam Houston caused several problems: Balczó rode 855, Fox 830, and only seven of the 40 competitors achieved over 1000 points. Zsigmond Villányi (HUN), the current Junior World Champion, had a dream start to his competition -1095 for riding and 972 for fencing, for which he shared 2nd place with Onischenko. It was Balczó who shared first place in the shooting (195) with Risto Hurme (FIN) and Leonid Ivanov (URS) and the young Dutchman, Rob Vonk, set a world record in the swim of 3: 21.9. However, Onischenko was determined not to allow a repeat of his previous year's running disaster. Showing startling fitness, having begun the competition with only 990 in the riding event, he comfortably held off both Villányi and Balczó to take a deserved World title. Balczó won the running easily but it wasn't enough to pull him back and he took the bronze and Villányi the silver.

It was a double celebration for Onischenko whose Soviet team overhauled Hungary by just 17 points with the USA taking bronze and West Germany 4th place, a neat reversal of the previous year's fortunes for the hosts. The British team (Fox 19th, Phelps 21st and Lillywhite 27th) finished 7th of the 12 teams. One interesting feature of these years between Olympic Games is the absence of Mexico bronze medallist, Pavel Lednev, from the Soviet team. Having fallen out with the coaching officials, he was left in the wilderness during this period. It is a puzzling history for a man who was to become one of the great champions. He made his debut in Leipzig in 1965 (20th), competed in Melbourne in 1966 (11th), won the bronze in Mexico in 1968 but was missing from the team in 1967, 1969, 1970, and 1971.

1972 Olympic Games: Munich (FRG)

Though he had been beaten to the World title for the previous two years, nobody doubted that the 1972 Olympic title had Balczó's name on it. In this, his final competition before retirement, there was a strong feeling in Munich that, for anyone else to take the title would be a moral affront to the sport. The defending champion, Björn Ferm was there as were Onischenko, Villányi and Lednev but Peter Kelemen, the 1970 Champion was only fourth man in the powerful Hungarian team and had to give way to Pal Bakó.

Munich was a magnificent setting for these Games. 59 individuals and 19 teams took part and the competition was run very efficiently. The riding event, held at Riem, a little out of the city marked the final fading of the sport's cross-country history. Though entirely a show-jumping course, a water trench, rustic poles and a striking artificial hill added to the challenge. The horses, however, were outstanding and more than half the field gained over 1000 points. Jim Fox was, however, one of only four maximum 1100 rides. Among those leaders, he was joined by defending champion, Björn Ferm with Balczó and Lednev both on 1060. Unexpected losers in the riding were the Soviet pair, Onischenko (945) and Shmelev (920) and young Hungarian star, Villányi (975).

One of the most memorable sights of the riding event came from the only zero rider, George Skene, a member of the teenaged Canadian team whom Jo Buscko had brought to Europe that summer on the adventure of a lifetime. 17 year old George was clearly fighting hard to control his strong horse. Having survived half the course, he disappeared over the hill and there was a period of silence. Suddenly, a horseless Skene appeared on the brow of the hill, took off his helmet and saluted the crowd –a most dignified conclusion to his scoreless riding effort.

So often the fencing result signals the likely overall winners and, on this occasion, the top four in the fencing were the final top four. After 14 hours and 58 fights each, Onischenko emerged the winner with 1076 points to reduce the deficit he had been left with after the riding. Balczó scored 1057 and Lednev and Fox shared 3rd place with 1019. This was a magnificent effort from Fox and a score never bettered by a British pentathlete in Olympic competition. It put him into the overall lead, just two points ahead of Balczó.

Though Mario Medda (ITA) was the top scorer with 198, the shooting of the Soviet team was quite incredible – Onischenko 197, Lednev and Shmelev 195. Balczó was the subject of a protest; in his second series, a judge claimed that he had fired twice on one target turn. Had this protest been upheld, Balczó would have lost 220 points and, with it, his Olympic title. It was extraordinary to watch this great pentathlete sitting quietly to one side as if he hadn't a care in the world while officials decided his fate. There was sufficient doubt (and maybe deference, too) on the part of the judge to accept that he might have been mistaken and Balczó's 193 was allowed to stand. Poor Jim Fox's lead evaporated as he shot 188 with an opening series of only 44. The underperformance of the British team in the shoot (Phelps 182, Lillywhite 175) caused Team Manager, Monty Mortimer, to rage:

'You saw the Russian shooting in the next stand to Jim. He looked as if he were taking a morning stroll; not in the least interested in the electronic scoreboard. I simply do not believe that any young athlete can shoot like that unless he has had a needle of some sort. The Hungarians are ahead of the world in pharmaceutical development and the rest of the Eastern European countries are not far behind. The International Olympic Committee have rules concerning the use of drugs, depressants and stimulants. They have a list of banned drugs. But it doesn't take long for scientists to produce drugs that are not on the list and administer them in such minute quantities that it would take a pint of blood to detect them.'

The fact of the matter was that, in Sapporo earlier that year, the IOC and the UIPM had agreed that only alcohol testing would be used after the shooting event in Munich. However, at an ad hoc meeting of national managers and officials in late August, Wille Grut gained general agreement that urine tests for tranquillisers would also be used. When these tests on the athletes showed 14 of them as 'positive', Thofelt pressed Grut to sort out the problem. It was agreed jointly by the IOC and UIPM that the ad hoc meeting of officials had had no real jurisdiction and that such testing was, therefore, of doubtful value. In a rather embarrassing climb down, Grut had to explain that 'UIPMB did not ever officially ask the IOC Medical Commission to add 'tranquillisers' ... I should not have allowed a non-competent meeting of team captains to charge me to forward their opinion... I now feel that this task has not been one for which I am properly trained ... I very much regret the loss of time and money I seem to have caused your commission.' Months later the UIPM decided to take no action and the IOC endorsed the UIPM decision through a series of semi-logical justifications. None of the 14 'positives' was ever named. Mortimer's claim was shot through with a misunderstanding of drug procedures but his sense of moral outrage was celebratedly British and at least produced the headlines the British love most.

The swimming event was won by Chuck Richards (USA) in 3:21.7 with Veikko Salminen (FIN) and Rob Vonk (NED) following him home. Among the top competitors, Shmelev swam 3:32, Onischenko 3:38, Ferm 3:40.4 and Lednev 3: 42.8. Jim Fox failed to make any improvement on his 8th position with a disappointing 3:51.2. This meant that, going into the final running event the leaders were: Onischenko 4215, Lednev 4193 and Balczó and Ferm both 4133. Jim Fox had a total of 4011.

The running event started and finished in the main Olympic stadium but involved a tough first half including an awkwardly angled bank along the top of a hill. Balczó had seven seconds on Jim Fox at the halfway stage and fought hard to the finish with his stock of energy depleting with every stride. He pulled back the advantage Onischenko and Lednev had on him and crossed the line in 12:42 as Olympic champion at last with 5412 points. No victory could have been more popular. The Olympic title had eluded the great Igor Novikov before him despite his illustrious record and it seemed as though the same fate might befall Andras Balczó but, as the Hungarians celebrated by tossing him in the air, Balczó was able to retire a hero. Onischenko (5335) took the silver medal and Lednev (5328) took the bronze medal as he had done in Mexico four years earlier. Jim Fox was still fighting for a medal despite his poor showing in shooting and swimming. His magnificent run of 12.35 was enough to win the event but not a medal. He finished 4th overall, just 17 points behind Lednev. In three of the five events, he was faultless and he had had two shots so close to the line in the shooting that they had to be gauged. Had either one of them been a millimetre closer, he would have had that medal. If...if....

The team event was won comfortably by the Soviet Union with Hungary 2nd and Finland (Risto Hurme, Veikko Salminen and Martti Ketelä) clinging on to a ten point lead over USA to claim the bronze. Great Britain finished 9th, at least managing to beat ten other teams.

Resolving the drug situation

The confusion over testing in Munich produced widely different opinions though not the level of moral condemnation that one might have expected. In *The Pentathlete* immediately after Munich, I wrote:

'Notions that a 120 shot will suddenly shoot 198 are totally unfounded. Shooting is an acquired skill and, while tranquillisers may eliminate nervousness, they certainly do not improve a person's shooting skill. Tranquillisers are harmless and would guarantee that at least everyone starts on an equal level. After all, the argument against alcohol was not so much over its calming properties as the potential danger of semi-inebriates on the firing point. There is no such danger involved in the use of tranquillisers and, unlike other drug usage, there is no danger to oneself involved.'

This stance raised some eyebrows so I was surprised and pleased to receive an unexpected endorsement from Wille Grut who wrote:

'Andy Archibald's points of view on the doping matter are interesting and I agree with him. I have suggested to Professor Prokop to join me in a short visit to Professor Med. Beckett in London in February (1973) on which occasion I hope to come very close to the truth in this complex question. Maybe I will come to the conclusion that it IS possible to organise a 'watertight' control... I think that we will NOT come to such a conclusion and the logical step to take would then be to ALLOW CNS depressants as they are fairly harmless and do not produce 'carelessness' on the shooting-range. To collect and analyse 59 urine samples in Munich cost 20,000 Deutsche Mark. I think that it is a waste of good money, if we cannot guarantee that all sinners are detected.'

Grut's reponse was pragmatic and, as the man most concerned with enabling the sport to function, his real concerns were over cost and reliability. He found in his meeting in London that it was not possible to be confident about testing and that the cost was prohibitive. The result was that testing for tranquillisers ceased from the 1974 season onwards. Years later, Grut realised that a better approach was to create a situation where tranquillisers would be counter-productive. Put the shooting event immediately before the run or the swim when the tranquillisers will still be working and, at a stroke, their value is nullified.

The responsibility for enforcing the rules of a sport, of course, belongs to the organisers. In Modern Pentathlon this is ultimately the job of the UIPM. But it can often be an enormous and, more importantly, a costly job. Many of the confusions over ultimate responsibility in the past have resulted from a mismatch between IOC and UIPM rules and responsibilities on drug taking. Nowadays, we are free of those concerns and WADA (World Anti-Doping Agency) controls all drug matters.

Pavel Lednev (1943-2010)

Like his predecessor, Igor Novikov, Lednev, a Ukrainian from Lvov, was never to win the individual Olympic title. For the next few years, however, he would be unbeatable. He was World Champion in 1973, 1974, 1975 and 1978, and rarely out of the medals from his debut in 1965 alongside Novikov, to his final Olympic effort in Moscow in 1980 alongside Starostin. Though

Pavel Lednev (URS): World Champion 1973, 1974, 1975, 1978.

entirely focused on the task in competition, Lednev was an easy-going extrovert who knew how to enjoy himself. In retirement, as a UIPM official, he was an affable conversationalist and, doubtless, an inspiration to many. His relatively premature death in November 2010 (aged 67) was much mourned.

1973 World Championships: Crystal Palace (GBR)

Great Britain's hosting of the World Championships was expected to take place in the Aldershot area but the committee broke with tradition and organized an impressive event in South London instead. There was surprise and some doubt when the shooting range was set up against the crumbling walls of the great Crystal Palace Exhibition site which had burned down so spectacularly in 1936 but, in the end, the event went without a hitch. Urine tests for tranquillisers were used after the shooting event though Errol Lonsdale, Chairman of the Organising Committee, lamented that 'it seems very sad that we need to have an organization set up for this sordid business'. His main objection, though, was delightfully British – he felt that the poor officials who had to carry out the tests would miss all the fun of the competition. He exhorted the athletes, therefore, to pee as quickly as possible please.

The riding event was held at possibly one of the loveliest sites ever used for a World Championship. A hilly wooded area in the park allowed undulations and turns that hinted at the old cross-country style but was entirely a show-jumping course, designed by Alan Ball. It was a problem getting sufficient good horses but, as Wille Grut pointed out, these horses were all 'the precious property of private people' and must be treated with respect. About five of the horses were not really good enough even with the removal of the water jump the day before. The most high-profile victim of the inconsistency in horses was Janusz Peciak (POL) who scored zero here just three years before becoming Olympic Champion.

Despite the rules against this, sensible host countries will naturally have encouraged their athletes to train over the jumps in the correct order for months before the big day. Those athletes will also have ridden and got to know the competition horses over a period of months, sometimes years. Indeed, many of the horses will have been their regular training mounts. Not so we British. In *Smelling of Roses*, David Hunn tells the tale of General Lonsdale's meticulous guarding of the secrets of the riding course at Crystal Palace. It was quite clear that the British were going to set an example to the world on this. In reality, the prospect of getting to know the horses in advance was blocked more by financial circumstances than anything else since the generous benefactors from all over the country had necessarily all brought their charges along at the last minute.

The effect of the variable standards of the horses in the riding was not wholly damaging; 28 riders scored 1000+ but there was also a good number of riders scoring much below that. As luck would have it, these seemed to be divided fairly evenly between teams, many teams having one rider with a poor score. In the case of the all-powerful Soviet Union team, it was the 1971 World Champion and Olympic silver medallist, Boris Onischenko, who gained only 928 points. The next day, however, the Soviet scores in the fencing – Lednev 1069, Onischenko 1046, Shmelev 977 – made it quite clear who the overall winners would be.

The West German team dominated the shooting (Thade 196, Köpcke 194, Werner 191) and the young Canadian, Jack Alexander, set a new best in the swimming of 3:18.1. After four events, the three Soviet competitors, together with Risto Hurme (FIN) and Heiner Thade (FRG), led the way. Onischenko's ride had left him at a disadvantage to the powerfully-built Vladimir Shmelev who placed 2nd in the running behind Shoji Uchida (JAP). It was Pavel Lednev who led the total Soviet rout of the competition, though, to become World Champion for the first time. Shmelev was 2nd and Onischenko 3rd. Of course the Soviet Union ran away with the team competition by 900 points but the Germans took the silver with a fine performance in which they individually placed 7th, 8th and 9th. The Hungarians had had an appalling start to the competition with Horváth riding 766 and Maracskó 810 but, with Kelemen in 5th place overall, they secured the bronze medal.

After his fine 4th place in Munich, there were great hopes that Jim Fox might win a medal but he had a very poor competition by his standards especially in fencing and shooting. The British team finished 8th (Fox 11th, Peter Twine 34th and Robbie Phelps 38th). Phelps had been brought in at the last minute when Adrian Parker, about to debut in his first World Championships, broke his collarbone in a riding accident in training.

In his UIPM report, Wille Grut made comparisons of the difference between the top score and the average score in each event in both 1972 and 1973. Though there were fluctuations depending on the riding standard and the difficulty of the running course, it was in fencing, so often the predictor of the overall winners, in which the gap was largest. The differences for 1973 were: riding (193), fencing (302), shooting (246), swimming (248) and running (190).

1974 World Championships: Moscow (URS)

Having come 1st, 2nd, and 3rd the previous year and now competing on home soil, it was unlikely there would be any change to the leader board; the Soviet Union would dominate. For the third time the World Junior Championships was held alongside the Senior. The UIPM had decided that testing for tranquillisers was too expensive and uncertain and so they were taken off the list of prohibited substances. Wille Grut noted that the average score in the shooting that year rose from 799 (1973) to 880 (1974). Was this a direct result of the rule change? The Soviet authorities had provided 80 horses for the event but a viral disease in the stables the week before meant that only 41 were available and each had to go round four times in two days (the Junior competition was held the next day). Once again, fortunes in the riding were mixed. 17 achieved 1000+ but there were casualties, too. The Hungarians, on average eight years younger than the Soviet team, once again took the lion's share of this misfortune: Maracskó (870), Kancsal (814) and Villányi (876) set themselves an insurmountable problem in the team event after the first day and it was little short of a miracle that they fought back heroically to win the silver medal. By contrast, the Soviet team performed well: Lednev and Shmelev each had a single knockdown and Onischenko scored 978 points.

The fencing was won by Onischenko (1063) with Lednev two hits behind (1021). In the shooting, the same German team (Werner, Köpcke, Thade) for the second year scored astonishingly well -196, 194, 192. In the Junior competition, Britain's Peter Wall (now General Sir Peter Wall, KCB, CBE, ADC Gen, Chief of the General Staff, and the professional head of the British Army) shot 197 to win that event. After three events, Lednev led from Onischenko, John Fitzgerald (USA), and Jörg Steffensen (DEN). Steffensen, a great raconteur and talented artist, had, apparently, spent the previous two weeks on a cycling holiday with his wife in Finland! Unfortunately, both Fitzgerald and Steffensen were hit by a stomach virus during the competition which severely affected their run/swim events. Another Canadian, John Hawes won the swim in 3:21.2 though in the Junior competition, Vladimir Galavtin (URS), the eventual champion, swam 3.15.54.

Shoji Uchida (JAP) once again won the running event in 12:59. Fox, starting exactly one minute behind Fitzgerald, made the decision to set out very fast and catch his rival as soon as possible. This task he achieved and he finished 2nd in the run. The final result was that the Soviet team had a clean sweep of the medals, in exactly the same order as in Crystal Palace –Lednev, Shmelev, Onischenko. Behind them were two Hungarians –Maracskó and Kancsal – who had fought back magnificently after their poor rides. Jim Fox finished 6th: 1100 in the riding event would have given him the bronze medal but, as usual, he was not alone in trying to suppress that one little word 'if' in his mind. Perhaps most justified in wondering 'if' was the Hungarian team who had bettered the Soviet team in four of the five events. Their disastrous riding, however, put paid to team glory. They finished 2nd to the Soviet Union. Rumania came 3rd just three points in front of the West Germans. Apart from Fox, the British were unimpressive. Peter Twine finished 44th and Andy Archibald 48th.

1975 World Championships: Mexico City (MEX)

Late in the season but offering some hint of the likely outcomes for the coming Olympic Games, the Mexico competition was notable for several reasons. By beating the Soviet team, the Hungarians re-established themselves as real contenders for the Olympic gold. The replacement of Boris Onischenko in the Soviet team with Leonid Ivanov (not in the team since 1971) proved a disaster. Ivanov scored only 332 points in the riding and finished 40th overall. The toughness of the competition showed itself particularly in that only three men scored 1000+ in the running event, the best of those being Britain's Adrian Parker. Finally, the competition marked a sea change in the fortunes of the British team. Jim Fox finally climbed on to the podium as the bronze medalist and, in finishing 4th overall with the same points as West Germany but better running results, the British team that would compete in Montreal made a significant breakthrough. True, it was not a predictor of gold or silver medals –the Soviet Union and Hungary had taken possession of those for evermore, or so it seemed – but a bronze medal in the team event in Montreal was now a real possibility.

There were some surprising absentees in Mexico in late November. Rumania, Poland and Czechoslovakia failed to attend. Astonishingly, too, the South American countries were absent having regarded the Pan-American Games, held two weeks earlier, as more to their liking. Of the 46 entries in the riding event, seven scored 1100. Among them were Kancsal and Fox. Fox had drawn a small horse, comically called "Mickey Mouse", but which proved to be every inch capable of carrying a big man. Peter Ridgeway (AUS) impressively won the riding event for the second year running. Lednev won the fencing with 1068 and this event once again was the most reliable final predictor; the first three in fencing made up the first three overall. Axel Stamann (FRG), a Berlin policeman, won the shooting with 198. John Hawes repeated his Moscow swimming victory (3:26.4) and the run was won by Adrian Parker who, unlike everyone else, appeared to be immune to altitude. Most teams had come several weeks early to Mexico to acclimatise. Not so the British who managed to win the run without any altitude training. To give some idea of Parker's powerful finish, with 1000 metres to go he was ahead of Jim Fox in the running by 16 seconds. At the finish he was 40 seconds ahead, also beating the impressive Mike Burley (USA) and comfortably ahead of Uchida, winner for the previous two years.

The final result gave the gold medal to Lednev for the third year running. Tamas Kancsal was 2nd and Jim Fox

3rd. A mistake by the officials initially gave the bronze to Maracskó. The shouts of delight when the error was amended were testimony to the enormous popularity Jim Fox enjoyed throughout the world. At last he had got the medal he deserved. So the Hungarians reversed the trend in the team event ahead of the USA who also beat the Soviet Union into 3rd place. Great Britain's 4th position was no freak result and there were many areas still to improve upon. Parker finished 11th in his first World Championship but Danny Nightingale, who had performed very poorly in fencing and swimming, placed only 33rd.

Before leaving Mexico, we must record the efforts of Trond Woxen of Norway who epitomises the great spirit of 'taking part' better than anyone. Trond competed in three World Championships (1971, 1974, and 1975) and finished last in each of them. In Mexico, he had been offended to find out that fellow pentathletes had conducted a pre-competition tote in which entrants bet on the total points Trond would achieve in the competition. Quite a few, quite accurately as it turned out, put their money on Woxen getting zero points in the whole competition. Sure enough, Woxen was eliminated in the riding and broke his ankle in the fencing and so was unable to continue. At the concluding dinner, however, he made a speech castigating those who had had such little faith in his ability and he awarded them the 'Smelly Fish of Norway' for their lack of optimism. Trond went on to be a successful music producer in the USA. In a modern world in which high standards are expected throughout the sport and every opportunity for qualification contested, we miss him.

1976 Montreal. Great Britain win gold (l-r: Jim Fox Adrian Parker, Danny Nightingale).

1976 Olympic Games: Montreal (CAN)

Perhaps the comment to be savoured the most about Great Britain's extraordinary gold medal in this competition came from Wille Grut, a man who knew the sport better than any other. He wrote: 'As to my opinion, this was the most honourable victory out of all others in the history of the Olympic Games in Modern Pentathlon.' Coming from the man who had won his own Olympic title in 1948 by a mile, this was praise indeed.

Naturally, the team competition would be between the Soviet Union and Hungary; nobody else had won it since 1953. The Soviet Union had brought back the 39 year old Boris Onischenko after his absence the year before together with three times World Champion, Pavel Lednev and Boris Mossolov, the 1971 World Junior Champion. Vladimir Shmelev was unexpectedly made fourth man. The Hungarians, still a young team, retained their 1975 winning line-up of Maracskó, Kancsal and Sasics. In competition for the bronze medal would probably be West Germany (Esser, Werner, Köpcke), USA (Fitzgerald, Burley, Nieman), and Great Britain (Parker, Nightingale, Fox). The Czechs (Bartu, Adam, Starnovsky) were outsiders and hadn't even attended the World Championships the year before. Pavel Lednev was hot favourite for the individual title.

The riding event took place at Bromont, 85 km outside Montreal but a lovely site. Missing from the start were the Dutch and Mexican teams, and, most surprisingly, the strong Rumanian team who had taken the bronze medal two years earlier. Michael Proudfoot, the British Team Manager, put in a protest that the course was too easy but no changes were made. The result was that 35 of the 47 riders scored 1000+ and 13 of those 1100. Since this group of 13 contained Jim Fox and Adrian Parker, perhaps in hindsight, the British protest was best ignored. Despite this generally high standard, there were, once again, casualties. The Hungarian team had a terrible start with scores of 866, 972, and 934 which left them with much to make up. Jiri Adam of the young Czech team had a bad fall and gained only 794. Even worse for his team, he carried his injuries throughout the competition. A very strong fencer (he is one of our top referees these days) he made up for losses the next day and went on to win the shooting event with 198.

The fencing event, most notable for Onischenko's disqualification (more of this later) and the consequent elimination of the Soviet Union team, blew the competition wide open, particularly since Hungary had made such a bad start. Lednev won comfortably with

1096 with Kancsal (990) and Bartu (TCH- 976) some way behind. The top scores were more widely spread than usual and consequently lower; this played into the hands of the British team whose usual 700+ scores did not do so much damage to their overall position. The shooting produced 23 190+ scores compared to only six in Munich. For the British team, Nightingale shot 191, Parker 188 and Fox 187. The West Germans, whose shooting had been awe-inspiring in previous years, did inexplicably badly as they had also done in the fencing event. This eliminated them from the team reckoning. The USA team also had a disaster in the shooting. Fitzgerald had a strong 194 but Burley (180) and Nieman (176) fell apart. Though tranquillisers were not on the list of banned substances in Montreal and were widely used, the Americans, all military personnel, had been threatened with court martial proceedings by their manager were they to use drugs.

After three events, then, the Czech team led with the British team back in 8th position. Individually, the British positions were Fox 18th, Nightingale 21st and Parker 23rd. Each member of the British team swam a personal best time: Parker 3:24.3, Nightingale 3:32.7 and Fox 3:44.2. The event was won impressively by Bob Nieman (USA) whose 3:13.5 went a little way to making up for his shooting performance.

With only the running to go, Great Britain, now in 5th position, had to run the 4000m course three minutes faster than the young Czech team, 75 seconds faster than Hungary, 50 seconds faster than Poland and 44 seconds faster than the USA if they were to win. Individually, the 21 year old Jan Bartu led the competition (4304) from Pavel Lednev (4242) and Janusz Peciak (4202). Peciak

(POL) had beaten a top field in Yerevan earlier in the year and was known as a strong runner. Adrian Parker, the first to go off in the one minute interval start, set an unbeatable winning time on a tough course of 12:09.5. He was comfortably ahead of strong runners, Mike Burley (12:26) and Janusz Peciak (12:29). Danny Nightingale (12:32) and Jim Fox (12:47) ensured a decisive British team win in the running but was it enough to win the competition?

At the time, it was usual to explain to others that the British were good at running because the event required no special sporting facilities and, since we had none, we ran instead. That, thankfully, has for many years now not been true. It raised the interest, however, of British 5000 metre bronze medallist, Brendan Foster, who promptly came round after the competition to invite Adrian Parker to go on a training run.

Details were slow to emerge. Eventually, the overall result actually gave victory to Great Britain by quite a margin: 15,599 to Czechoslovakia's 15,451 and Hungary's 15,395. Individually, Janusz Peciak's run took him past the hot-favourite Pavel Lednev to win individual gold and Jan Bartu took the bronze. The British placings: Adrian Parker 5th, Danny Nightingale 10th, Jim Fox 15th, surpassed all expectation. The victory turned the team competition upside down; it would be four years before the Soviet Union won again and eleven before Hungary did the same.

Individually, Fox was disappointed with his performance; he had clearly been upset by the Onischenko incident in the fencing and it showed in his subsequent results. It was widely reported that Fox and Onischenko were close friends; this was not the case, though it had been with Fox and Balczó, for instance. Fox and Onischenko had been rivals for many years, though, and the warm solidarity that exists between pentathletes of whatever nation meant that Onischenko's disqualification was a disappointment for everyone in the sport. As it turned out, Jim Fox was able to retire at the top of his game, bronze medallist in 1975 and the award of the Unesco Fair Play Trophy, gold medallist in 1976. Along the way, Fox had needed coaxing back into competition, particularly in 1970 when he had been a civilian for a year and returning to the army seemed to him, at the time, like taking a step backwards. One man credited for this coaxing was British coach, Ron Bright.

Ron Bright, BEM (1930-2002)

The expression 'larger than life' seemed to have been invented for Ron Bright. As a member of the 5th Iniskilling Dragoons he had won the team event alongside Peter Duckworth in the British Modern Pentathlon Championships as far back as 1950. He is best remembered, though, as coach in Mexico, Munich, Montreal and Moscow, and manager in Los Angeles and Seoul. After retirement as an Army Sergeant, he moved successfully into sports management with a particular skill in the setting up of new centres. A wheeler and dealer of great panache, he could turn his hand to practically anything and pentathletes needed to be quick off the mark if they wanted to avoid permanent injury in one of his post-event soothing massages. Ron Bright was at the centre of British Modern Pentathlon for twenty years and the Montreal gold medal was part of his legacy too.

The British victory was a healthy change for a competition dominated for so long by two countries, the

Soviet Union and Hungary. The remarkable sequence of events that took place in Montreal –unexpected failure by rival teams, unexpected successes for the British in individual events - had all had a powerful effect, none more so, though, than the disqualification of Boris Onischenko and, consequently, the Soviet team in the fencing event.

Onischenko and the 'faulty' epée

The most publicised act of cheating in Modern Pentathlon history was the 'fixed' epée of Boris Onischenko which led to his permanent disqualification from the sport. It was a front page news item around the world at the time and one wonders whether such an event could have the same impact in today's more globalised atmosphere. In 1976, the tension between Soviet communism and Western capitalism was almost palpable. To have a member of a Soviet team caught cheating in the heart of the western world at such a major event was a gift for the world's media. If anything proved the inherent evil of Communism, they proclaimed, this was it.

The two favourites for the individual title were both from the Soviet Union and Pavel Lednev had the most impressive record as world champion for the preceding three years. But Boris Onischenko, now 39 and in his final competition before retirement, was also a possible champion. He had been World Champion in 1971, Olympic silver medallist in 1972, 2nd in 1969 and 3rd on three occasions (1970, 1973 and 1974). Onischenko was, like Lednev, a Ukrainian but, while Lednev was based in Lvov, Onischenko was from Kiev where he held the role of Major in the Red Army which, so it was strongly rumoured, involved significant work for the KGB. He was also an important member of the Dynamo Sports Institute in Kiev. It was always interesting to watch the Soviet team together: whether it was the fact that Onischenko was rather older than the other team members or that his KGB responsibilities made the others wary of him, but he was certainly closer to the coaching staff than he was to the other team members.

The popular 'version' of the Onischenko story runs as follows:

'Soviet cheat Boris 'Dishonest-chenko' was caught out by wily Captain of the British team, Jim Fox. Our Jim, a James Bond lookalike and upholder of all things decent and British, realized what was happening in the first round of the day and shopped Onischenko to the authorities. The shame-faced Russian was whisked away to a Russian boat, given a stern dressing down by President Brehznev himself and, two years later, was found floating face down in a swimming pool, a victim of a KGB hit squad.'

This, of course, is nonsense. Jim Fox had no idea Onischenko was cheating, and Onischenko is alive and well and was, for all practical purposes, rehabilitated and happily at work within months of the Montreal Games.

It is necessary to have some understanding of the mechanics of the fencing event to know how Onischenko manipulated results. So, for those not fully acquainted with how the electrical epée works, here's a simple explanation. A hit is registered when the button on the tip of the epée is depressed. This makes the contact between the two wires that run down the groove on the upper side of the blade from the tip of the blade to the base inside the guard. From here the circuit continues from a linking plug next to the handle, down through the body wire which each fencer wears inside his jacket, through the electric spool, back to the scoring box. From the tip of the blade all the way to the electric box, the wires are insulated with a thin non-conductive coating. A red or green light on the electric box then illuminates to show which fencer has made the hit. In 1976, the light opposite the successful fencer would light up. In the modern sport, this process has been reversed, it being believed that a spectator will be more able to follow the scoring system if a winning light is physically closer to the fencer who actually scored the hit.

With such a basic system there are, inevitably, problems. The clash of blades often exposes wires. The insulation that should prevent the circuit being completed without the button being depressed is then ineffective. Additionally, spots of rust or dirt on the guard may well interfere with the earthing system and also bring the light on when the tip of an opponent's blade makes contact with them. So, it often happens that an unexplained light comes on and it is the Referee's task to decide if the hit was valid or not. A dirty guard is the responsibility of the fencer but that same fencer can hardly be required to prevent wires from becoming exposed. In the event of an unexplained light, the Referee seeks to repeat the error by beating the blades together or pressing the point of the epee repeatedly against the guard of his opponent. Sometimes, a faulty earthing system can be instantly corrected by applying spit to the earthing plug inside the guard. If the fault cannot be repeated, the Referee is obliged to award the hit.

What Onischenko actually did was to drill a hole in the orthopaedic handle of his epée so that he could push a wire through it. This wire was attached to a small plate at the head of the handle. When the wire was pushed forward with the thumb, it connected the electric circuit by making contact with the exposed wiring at the base of the blade. This simple mechanism was concealed by covering the orthopaedic handle with a thin layer of material. Although stringent, the testing methods used up to 1976 did not involve the dismantling of the epée. A pass sticker was attached inside the guard when an epée passed the relevant tests. Changing your own handle after testing was an easy task to perform and did not affect the legitimate status of the weapon. This is exactly what Onischenko did. After Montreal, the FIE changed the laws to take account of this loophole in the testing procedure.

Before the fencing event begins, all equipment is tested. Blades must be the right length and flexibility, the guard must not be too big, the tip must withstand a certain weight and travel a certain distance before electronic contact is made, and the wiring must be properly insulated. In Montreal the testing was particularly stringent. Thirteen of the seventeen epées submitted by the British team were initially rejected. The Soviet team's equipment would have been subjected to exactly the same stringent checks; to have presented a faulty weapon in the very first round of the day and claimed it was due merely to incomplete insulation, as Onischenko did, was careless.

During the fencing event, each pentathlete fights every other competitor in turn. The British team had begun the day by fighting each other as did every other team. This process takes place at the beginning of the day in order to mimimise the competitive impact later on but it is usually as hard-fought as any other bout during the day.

By 8.45am that morning in Montreal, the bouts against the Soviet Union began and the first to take on Onischenko was Adrian Parker. Both Parker and Onischenko were left-handed fencers. As in tennis, the relative infrequency of left-handedness might be seen to give a slight advantage (except of course in the event of all six finalists being left-handers as happened in one major British tournament of the time.). When two right-handers face each other, the blades are open to each other, that is to say, the targets are exposed. When a left hander meets a right hander, his main point of attack is outside the blade, usually prefaced with a beat on the blade to expose part of the opponent's arm. Since the extended arm holding the weapon is the most prominent target, it is common for hits to land in the area of the wrist and forearm, particularly when a left hander approaches a right hander. However, both Onischenko and Parker were left-handers with targets open to each other. What happened in the Parker-Onischenko bout was described by the Referee, Guido Malacarne in his letter to *The Sword*, Spring 1977:

'An attack from Onischenko made his light go on and I ruled that Parker had been hit. However, Parker took off his mask and assured me that the hit had not arrived. I pointed out that I had distinctly seen Onischenko's point go very close to his forearm, and that perhaps he had not felt the hit arrive because it landed in a fold of his glove or of his sleeve. Parker again assured me that no hit had arrived and I therefore proceeded to make a rapid examination of Onischenko's epée. The point was marked with the pass sign, as were the blade and coquille (guard), while inside the guard the two wires were separated by a sheet of plastic. I again told Parker that I had no reason to annul the hit, and I signalled to the score table that Parker had been defeated.'

This is a fair interpretation for a Referee to put upon the sequence. He followed the rules, found no fault and, despite Onischenko's point having only been described as having gone 'very close to his forearm' (not a convincing description of a hit, therefore), it is an acceptance that the human eye is frail in these matters and, in the absence of concrete proof to the contrary, the hit must have arrived. Adrian Parker was adamant that the hit had gone nowhere near him, the light having come on when Onischenko's blade was pointing skyward.

When Jim Fox came on the piste against Onischenko there was real tension in the air. Parker losing to Onischenko by fair means would not have been a surprise; no one knew then that Adrian would finish 5th overall, be the best British pentathlete and lead the gold medal victory. At this stage, however, Fox was embarking on a battle for individual glory and one of his biggest rivals would be Boris Onischenko. The result of this single bout would not only give the victor 24 points but deprive the loser of a similar score. The loser would have to swim six seconds faster or run sixteen seconds quicker to regain that lost ground. Since Malacarne was also now alerted to possible disputes involving Onischenko, there was a much improved focus on the bout. He declared in his report that he had made a special point of asking the name of the troublesome fencer: 'Onischenko. I would be on my guard'.

Jim Fox's account of his own bout runs as follows: 'When I fenced him I jumped in, deliberately opening myself for a stop-hit. (A stop-hit anticipates the forward movement of an opponent and the fencer merely holds the point in line with that approaching target). I was still outside hitting distance when I picked up Onischenko's blade – really high, before his point was anywhere near me. His blade was above my head and I smacked (my point) into his chest –but the light was already on (against me).' Onischenko was the first to insist that it had not been a valid hit and was eager to change the weapon for another. Jim insisted that the faulty weapon should not go back into Onischenko's bag. At that stage, he cannot possibly have known that Onischenko was cheating; his concern was simply that, later in the day, Onischenko may well bring out that faulty weapon again and gain easy points against other less-discerning pentathletes.

Malacarne's report is a model of correct procedure – he summons Tibor Szekely, a Hungarian official, to use his testing kit on the faulty weapon. At that point, a break in the insulation is found at the base of the weapon. Szekely's opinion is that there is no way of proving that such a break had been made deliberately and that, after a warning, a repetition of such an offence would result in a mere 10 point penalty rather than disqualification from the whole competition. It is the intervention of Carl Schwende and Rene Mercier that enabled no lesser person than Charles Debeur, President of the FIE, to actually dismantle the offending epée and expose the truth.

However, had it not been for the persuasion of Mary Glen Haig, Head of British Fencing who urged Michael Proudfoot, the British Team Manager, to submit an official protest, it would never have got to that level of testing. As already stated, faulty weapons are not rare in fencing so there was no particular reason to suspect foul play at any stage. Additionally, it being the first round of the day, Malacarne, like all the other referees would have been under some pressure to get things moving. A major investigation in the first round that may have come to nothing and held up the day's fencing would not have been popular. Richard Cohen points out in his history of Fencing *(By the Sword* -Macmillan 2002) that, it was Guido Malacarne, who had himself caused a sensation in the fencing world a few years earlier by disqualifying the Russian Women's World Foil Champion, Gorokhova, when she quite deliberately threw a bout to a lesser opponent. Certainly, procedures were followed to a logical conclusion in Montreal but the actual sequence was far more haphazard than Malacarne's report suggests. As it turned out, Michael Proudfoot's official protest (handwritten and submitted at 10.40am together with the requisite $25) did not need to be considered. By that time, the truth was out.

What is the most puzzling fact is that, despite being an outstanding fencer, Onischenko was hopeless at cheating. Even a mediocre fencer could have managed to make the light come on in circumstances described by Malacarne above. So much of one-hit fencing consists of picking away at the edges of the opponent's guard in the hope of catching an opponent on the wrist. It would not have been difficult to synchronise such a move with depressing a switch in the handle to make the light come on.

Why then, was Onischenko so useless at it? It shows, I think, that he had never attempted this before, that it was probably a last minute decision, and that he was very nervous about it. There are those who think that he had been cheating for years. Others consider that the whole team was in on the deception. I am quite convinced neither is true and so is Michael Proudfoot, who not only, as a Professor of Philosophy, has the advantage of a forensic attitude to fact and fiction but also had the good sense to record all his observations within hours of the event (good police practice). Malacarne considers a wider plot to be possible because the team were so resistant to surrendering the epée but there is an obligation on any team to try and support one of its members whether they fully understand his reasons or not. According to Richard Cohen, a senior official, Sandy Kerekes, believed that Onischenko was pressured into such actions by an unscrupulous coach.

Wille Grut in his memoirs tells of a meeting he personally had with an 'Armenian' official in Lvov. Having convinced himself that Grut wasn't secretly recording the conversation, the official then assured Grut that Onischenko had only cheated to enable his own retiring coach to obtain a better pension on the strength of the Olympic success. Janusz Peciak (POL), the Individual Champion in Montreal and a good friend of Pavel Lednev whom he pushed into 2nd place, is convinced the rest of the Soviet team would never have condoned the cheating, not least because of the advantage it would have given Onischenko over Lednev, the hot favourite. Peciak does believe, however, that Onischenko's elevated position as the elder statesman in the Soviet team may well have given him the chance to try to cheat before. So, he puts Onischenko's incompetent cheating in Montreal down to a nervousness over the heightened security and weapon testing.

On the way to the fencing event that morning, I sat next to Onischenko on the bus. We were both left-handers and I liked his epées very much. He used a modified orthopaedic grip which he filed down himself to combine strength of grip with some of the finesse of a French (or straight) grip. I was very happy to buy epées from him whenever possible and he had promised me several at the end of the day's fencing. Was he excessively nervous on that morning anticipating the dread deed he was about to perform? It didn't seem that way to me. To this day I wonder if I missed out on a significant sporting momento – the legendary doctored epée.

Jim Fox feels no animosity towards Onischenko for his actions. Other pentathletes agree. We feel sympathy for the conditions that pushed him over the edge to choose such an approach –a successful champion at the end of his career striving for one final triumph. It is good to know that Boris lives contentedly in Kiev, his home town, a grandfather with a successful career behind him in the administration of Kiev sport. Let's not overlook his impressive achievements in Modern Pentathlon either. And, from the British point of view, we have Boris Onischenko to thank for eliminating the unbeatable Soviet team and opening the way to an extraordinary British gold medal.

1977 World Championships: San Antonio (USA)

The World Championships returned to Texas in early October, six years after their first visit there but this time they involved Senior and Junior events. New participating nations were New Zealand, Republic of China, Ireland and Spain. Also, for the first time, a Women's event was held. This was not officially a World Championships (they began in 1981) but a test event in which 11 women took part (three Americans, three British, two Germans, two Canadians, and one Australian). The facilities in San Antonio were outstanding and it was the first time that the running event used the Handicap Start. This was an experimental system that became, for a time, the norm. It resulted in odd decimal points on the final scores for teams and the system was sufficiently difficult to operate that, though the individual finishing order was obvious, it took officials four hours to calculate the team results. One of the most striking effects of the British win in Montreal was that it had opened the field. No longer were the Soviet Union and Hungary allowed to dominate proceedings; new faces emerged triumphant from unexpected quarters. For instance, the Polish team, 11th in the fencing event in Montreal, won the fencing in San Antonio.

In the Senior event, the individual battle would clearly be between Janusz Peciak and Pavel Lednev, last year's gold and silver medallists. It was as tight a competition as might have been predicted. Both men opened with 1070 in the riding event. 36 riders scored 1000+ but only six scored 1100. All the others with the exception of one Republic of China competitor scored 900+. This prompted Dieter Krickow to wonder if there should be modifications to the riding event. Certainly, he felt, there was no longer any need to offer lower jumps for juniors and for women.

Lednev gained a single hit lead over Peciak in the fencing (1000 points to Peciak's 977). Jiri Adam (TCH) impressively won both the fencing and shooting events with 1023 and 1066 / 197 but his Czech team, silver medallists in Montreal, was destined to finish only 9th overall. The British team, too, would only finish 7th though Michael Proudfoot's eternally optimistic report pointed out that after three events, the team had a better score than they had had in Montreal. In shooting in particular they were far better (Nightingale 194, Parker 192, Archibald 192). Meanwhile, at the top of the leader board, Peciak had clawed back Lednev's lead with a 196 shoot over Lednev's 194.

Zbigniew Pacelt (POL) won the swimming as he had in Montreal although his time was five seconds slower (3:20.9). Indeed, the physical performances of those who had been in Montreal were markedly slower in San Antonio. Peciak's superior swim gave him an 81 point lead over Lednev before the final event, a lead he was unlikely to lose. The run, over a pleasant golf course but in baking temperatures allowed Mike Burley (USA) to show his true talent. He won the run comfortably in 12:08 ahead of Sergei Riabkin (URS – 12:37), Adrian Parker (12:48) and Andy Archibald (12:50). Next home were the champion and the runner-up overall – Peciak (12:55) and Lednev (12:56). Parker's marked loss of form in the running compared to his great wins in Mexico and Montreal was the result of a winter in which he was struck down by glandular fever. The pressure to earn a living also reduced possible training time.

Peciak's retention of his position as World No: 1 was proof that here was a man worthy to take on the crown from Lednev. The bronze medallist was another Pole, Slawomir Rotkiewicz who was just three points ahead of Daniele Masala (ITA). Masala had been 4th in Montreal, too, but would rival Peciak in years to come as another great champion. Rotkiewicz, interestingly, seized his chance to defect to the West a year later. The German team members, particularly the Berliners (who were, after all, living in closest proximity to the East /West divide) were particularly fine facilitators of this practice and happily assisted Rotkiewitz into his new life.

The team competition in San Antonio was a triumph for the Polish team who were, nevertheless, only two points ahead of the USSR. Hungary beat the USA to the bronze medal by an even smaller margin, 0.49 of a point. This goes some way to explaining why the US officials took four hours to produce the results! In the end, nine teams bettered 15,000 points. In the Junior event, Vasili Nefedov (URS) edged out Achim Bellmann (FRG) overall but Nigel Clark, in 7th position gave hope for Great Britain's future in the sport.

The new women's event differed only in that the swim was 200 metres and the run 2000 metres. There was also a slightly shorter riding course. The event was won by Virginia Swift (USA) but with the British competitors, who had already held their first British Championships that year, in 2nd (Kathy Tayler), 4th (Wendy Skipworth) and 5th (Sarah Parker), there was even more optimism about British prospects.

1978 World Championships: Jönköping (SWE)

Once again the popular combination of Senior and Junior events at the same venue took place in Jönköping. It was also the venue for the second of three Women World Cup legs, the others taking place in Zielona Gora and London. A team from Liechenstein entered the Men's event for the first and only time and among the spectators there were Bo Lindman (1924 Olympic Champion), Charles Leonard (1936 Silver medallist) and Andras Balczó (1972 Olympic Champion).

Although more than half the field scored 1000+, there were no 1100 scores and quite a few disappointing rides.

Tamas Szombathelyi (HUN) who had won a prestigious competition in Budapest earlier that year, scored only 672 on a difficult horse. Tarev (URS) had the same horse and also only achieved 738. A similar plight befell Danny Nightingale who managed 974 on a horse that Bohumil Starnovsky (TCH), a member of the Olympic silver medal team, rode for only 628. Nightingale was warned for overuse of the stick but he could find no other way of urging the horse round. He at least had the admiration of many riders in the crowd including the horse's owner. The big competition was, of course, between Peciak, the World Champion and the 35 year old Lednev. Both men began the competition with 1088 in the riding event.

Among the referees at the fencing were Sweden's world champion epéeists who were able to witness Jiri Adam (TCH) win the event once again (1057). Daniele Masala won the shooting with a perfect 200 while Zbigniew Pacelt once again won the swimming in 3:17.8 though not quite as fast as Britain's Chris Humpage (3.17.0) in the Junior event. The Senior World title was settled this year, however, in the shooting event. Peciak shot an inexplicably bad 189 while Lednev's 196 gave him more points than he needed to hold the Pole at bay. It was enough to enable Lednev to win the World Championships for the fourth time in six years. In the second year of the handicap start, Mike Burley once again won the running event in 12:09.5 although Neil Glenesk, his team mate, was only eight seconds behind with a run that won him the bronze medal overall behind Lednev and Peciak. This left Daniele Masala (ITA) in 4th place for the third year running. It was a fate that would have driven lesser men to despair but Masala's World and Olympic titles were yet to come.

In the team event, Poland retained the title it had first won the year before in San Antonio. In 2nd place was West Germany who succeeded in keeping the Soviet Union in bronze medal position. The British team had a very poor competition: Tony Woodall 34th, Danny Nightingale 36th, and Nigel Clark 38th between them came 12th and barely qualified for the following World Championship. The Junior team, however, came 4th, a best-ever position and the forerunner to success in the coming years. Two 17 year olds, Chris Humpage (13th) and Richard Phelps (14th) did best, the latter making his World Championship debut in a long and illustrious international career.

1978 Women's World Cup

The Women's World Cup, established this year, was a very successful precursor to the Women's World Championships begun in 1981. It consisted of three legs, one each at Zielona Gora, Jönköping and London. An equivalent Men's competition did not begin until 1990. Entries came from USA, Canada, Sweden, Denmark, GB, Germany, Poland and the Republic of China. The two Chinese women who competed in Jönköping were not yet riders but nevertheless managed to walk their horses through the start and salute the judges before retiring. Each of the three legs was won by Great Britain with Wendy Skipworth, a 16 year old swimmer, winning in Zielona Gora and London and Wendy Norman, a 13 year old Pony clubber winning in Jönköping.

1979 World Championships: Budapest (HUN)

The Senior Championships returned to Budapest at the end of the decade with the Hungarians determined to restore some of the lost dignity they had incurred by only finishing 5th in Jönköping. The World Champion, Pavel Lednev, was absent injured and so it was assumed Peciak would regain his lost title and that Poland would retain the team title for the third year running. But Peciak, too, was not in peak form having had a recent tendon operation. A massive field of 67 took part and there were new entries from Greece and Egypt. On home soil, Hungary had plumped for two of their Olympic trio, Tibor Maracskó and Tamas Kancsal, and kept Laszlo Horváth from the previous year's team. The Soviet Union included their teenaged World Junior Champion from 1978, Anatoly Starostin, alongside Oleg Bulgakov and Sergei Riabkin. The Poles retained Peciak and Pacelt and added Jan Olesinski, while the USA returned with their full 1976 Olympic team of John Fitzgerald, Mike Burley, and Bob Nieman. This selection left out the previous year's World bronze medallist, Neil Glenesk so that only Mike Burley had competed at this level in the intervening years.

The rankings revealed that the USA had had an excellent season and, rather surprisingly, topped the list ahead of the USSR. The UIPM decided that only the top 12 teams in Budapest would qualify for the Olympics the following year. This was short-sighted: illness and injury in the Bulgarian team ruled them out and the British only qualified by the skin of their teeth after a horrible riding experience. The horse that Danny Nightingale and Alan Williams (CAN) rode was called Anonymous and, according to Wille Grut's UIPM report, should not have been in the draw at all. It gave Danny his only zero ride and fiercely jeopardized British Olympic qualification. The vast majority of competitors, however, scored

1000+ with seven 1100s including Peciak, Kancsal and Britain's Peter Whiteside.

For the third year running, Jiri Adam won the fencing (1034) but he was only a single hit ahead of Bob Nieman whose astonishing 1019 was a world apart from his 784 score in Montreal. It gave him an unexpected lead over Peciak (932) and Masala (949). Even more astonishing was his 198 in the shooting (176 in Montreal). His US team mates, Burley and Fitzgerald both scored 194 with their best events still to come. Quite clearly the error of judgement they had made at the shooting event in Montreal had been well and truly resolved. The winner of the shooting with 199 was newcomer Janis Xenakis (GRE) while Peciak was still in the hunt with his score of 193.

With his best event still unswum, Nieman was experiencing one of those magic competitions in which 'if' didn't much figure. He had given Peciak a 60 point lead after the riding but now it hardly seemed to matter. Nieman swam 3:14.0 to give himself a lead of 174 points over Masala and 247 over Peciak. Even with a mediocre run of 14:01, he held off Peciak whose run of 12:44 was strong, given his injury, but still 33 seconds behind Mike Burley who won the running event for the third year in a row.

The crowning of Bob Nieman as World Champion was combined with a win, too, for the American team who held off Hungary by just seven points. Individually, Peciak was 2nd and Masala was at last on the podium in 3rd after his repeated 4th place of recent years. The Soviet team was 3rd. Though only 12th overall, as a result of Nightingale's zero ride, the two other Great Britain team members had acquitted themselves well in Budapest. Peter Whiteside took 16th place and Tim Kenealy 22nd. It was now four years since a Hungarian or Soviet team or individual had won a World Championship. This was a very healthy situation for the sport and encouraged teams from all over the world to value their chances in a big competition. The biggest competition of them all would take place in Moscow in a year's time. At this stage nobody realized the extent to which the Olympic Games would be undermined by the cynical political actions of Western governments.

1979 Junior Championship and Women's World Cup

The Junior event in The Hague saw a reverse of the previous year's top two. Christian Sandow (FRG) managed to beat Anatoli Starostin (URS) into second place. Best Briton, Richard Phelps came 10th. In the Women's World Cup series held in Warendorf, Zielona Gora and London, it was the British team that won overall from USA and West Germany. The top two individually were Kathy Tayler and Wendy Norman whose strong running lifted them above the field. Though these were still early days for the competition and absentees frequently hampered any sense of an overall pattern in performance, the British team was developing into a well-bonded hard-working squad with Eileen Tayler as manager and Jim Darby as coach. For both officials, team spirit and mutual support was the cornerstone of success in the squad – Kathy Tayler, Wendy Norman, Wendy Skipworth, Sarah Parker, Gill Suttle and Janet Savage. In 1979 Kathy Tayler was voted into 2nd place in the prestigious National Sportswriters' Association poll behind show jumper Caroline Bradley.

British developments in the 1970s

A somewhat myopic reviewer of the history of Modern Pentathlon in Britain might observe that our successful team in Montreal was made up of three civilians and a single soldier. This might imply that this new success was attributable to civilian development and that the military antecedents of the sport were now well and truly forgotten. Nothing could be further from the truth. The importance of the military in Modern Pentathlon has always been paramount and continues even to the present day. Without military facilities, coaching expertise and competition organisation, no civilian would have had the chance to compete at all. What happened in the 1970s was an integration of civilian and military organization so that, by the end of the decade, the Centre of Excellence at REME headquarters in Arborfield under the leadership of Capt. Jim Fox, was the hub of all Modern Pentathlon activities in Great Britain. It should also be pointed out that for the next 20 years after Montreal, our Olympic team was composed of 50% military / 50% civilian athletes, among whom were the 1988 bronze medal team in Seoul.

One of the driving forces of civilian development in the 1970s was Jim Darby. Jim had been in our 1972 Olympic team and, as a coach, he was an inspirational and extrovert leader. He organized weekend training sessions and competitions at Arborfield in the early 1970s which fed the steady flow of talent coming out of the excellent Biathlon Badge Scheme and National Biathlon Championship. Young athletes would come to Arborfield from all over the country and be given a common purpose through Jim Darby's technical and moral support. By the end of the decade he had sufficiently developed a coaching scheme so that every level of pentathlete was catered for.

For the first time, sponsorship from Skol enabled an annual home international to be held each year and for the MPAGB to employ a full-time Development Officer. This role was filled by Lt. Cdr Dick Sutton RN (Rtd), an extremely likeable enthusiast who spread the word widely throughout the country and who introduced many pentathletes to the delights of navy argot in the process. Shortly afterwards, Sports Council support enabled the MPAGB to run a full-time office in Purley organised by Adminstrative Secretary, Doreen Dew. Success in Montreal also brought training grants for international pentathletes via the Sports Aid Foundation, a fund generously supported by, among others, Elton John. By the end of the decade, the Centre of Excellence with its brand new shooting range became the fulcrum of all training plans. Money was, nevertheless, always tight, even after the Montreal victory. Cussons supported the 1973 World Championships and Debenham's financed some later internationals. Some support for the Biathlon Badge Scheme came from Alpine Double Glazing and the Sports Council funding usually made up the difference between sending a team abroad or not. It might seem extraordinary in the modern climate of strong financial support for Olympic medallists that, post-Montreal, the MPAGB was so poverty-stricken but, despite being the BBC Sports, Daily Express, and British Sportswriter's Team of the Year, there was no rush of sponsors.

British Championships for women began in 1977 when Sarah Parker won the opening competition. Wendy Norman won in 1978 and 1979. For the men, Jim Fox won every year from 1970 to 1974 by which year he had completed a record ten National Championship victories. In 1975 he was beaten by Adrian Parker by a margin of only three points and for the next three years, Danny

Nightingale was the Champion (1976, 1977, and 1978). The final championship of the decade was won by 18 year old Richard Phelps, the first of his astonishing thirteen victories.

Though military and civilian pentathletes worked together in every way, there was some tension over the team competition each year. Given some waning of support from military authorities under pressure to cut funding wherever possible, it became more and more urgent for military pentathletes to get good publicity. This certainly led to 'representational' military overtures being common at Selection and Management meetings. One fair gripe the military had was that civilians without a club tended to join together which gave them the advantage in team competitions. This led to clubs like Southern and Fiveways recruiting any new talent that came along and usually winning as a result. Meanwhile appeals to the MPAGB for Army, Navy and RAF representatives to come together as a Combined Services team were constantly rejected. Sqd Ldr Stuart Hocknell, as the Combined Services MPA Chairman, wrote several letters quite reasonably stating the case for military combinations but the old traditions of team entries coming from Army, Navy, RAF, or Royal Marines were slow to change.

For the period 1970 to 1974 it was a REME team that won the British Championship and it wasn't until 1975, with strong civilian opposition, that it was felt more prudent to enter as the Army. Throughout the 1970s, REME pentathletes –Jim Fox, Terry Bunyard, Peter Twine, Jim Darby, Steve Birley, Pete Younger, Bernie Moss and Tony Woodall –were strongly in evidence in British teams and only later did they make up Army teams with the help of Peter Brierley, Mike Mumford and Peter Whiteside. The Navy had internationals in Tim Kenealy and Mike Ellis with Eric Adlam and Harry Tate completing naval teams. The RAF could rely on Stuart Hocknell, Chris Wales, John Warburn, Alan Girlow and even elder statesmen like Peter Hart and Dave Gibbs.

Chapter Eight: 1980-89

'In this competition, it wasn't a case of the IF's and BUT's being "if I'd had another 350 points" (which is very "iffy"), but "if I'd had a 10 instead of a 9" (which is much less "iffy").' Michael Proudfoot, British Team Manager's Report 1983.

1980 Olympic Games: Moscow (URS)

One of USA President Jimmy Carter's final efforts to boost popularity against an ailing foreign policy was to lead a boycott by 61 nations of the Moscow Olympics over the Soviet invasion of Afghanistan. While more truly liberal countries allowed their athletes the choice of attending or not, the so-called 'land of the free' put down a blanket ban. In the light of Afghan history since that time, this boycott would now be laughable had it not deprived the current World Champion, Bob Nieman and his American teammates from defending their titles in Moscow. Other notable absentees were West Germany, Japan, and Italy. Often it was government employees who were denied the freedom of choice so the Italians, all military policemen and including top pentathlete, Daniele Masala, had to miss the event. One of the Italian team, Pierpaulo Cristofori, however, took leave of absence from his military role in order to compete as a civilian. In Great Britain, Thatcher's mean-spirited government required civil servants to take unpaid leave to compete but it was a triumph of the spirit of individualism that the MPAGB managed to put out a full team, including two military personnel.

With Nieman and Masala missing, the favourites would be Janusz Peciak, Olympic Champion and 1979 silver medallist, and Pavel Lednev, returning from injury and now, aged 37, in his final competition. For the British, Danny Nightingale had won a spectacular victory the year before in the Moscow Spartakiade beating both Daniele Masala (ITA) and the young Anatoli Starostin (URS). Starostin had grown up in Tajikistan, a distant Soviet republic bordering China and Afghanistan but, at the age of 14, his sporting prowess had been noted and he had been sent to Moscow to train. There, he joined with other athletes who themselves had left lives behind in distant parts of the USSR –Lvov, Kiev, Talinn, Yerevan – in order to train together. They lived in an enclosed world in which the team was the most important aspect of their lives. It explains the tremendous brotherly loyalty and support the Soviet athletes gave to each other – a loyalty which still remains evident in the Russian teams of today. At the age of 18, Starostin had been World Junior Champion, and now in 1980 at the age of only 20 he was competing to become the youngest ever Olympic Champion. Also making his debut in the first of four Olympic appearances was Jöel Bouzou (FRA), later to become World Champion and in present times the Secretary-General of the UIPM.

The riding event was kind to most of the top competitors. No fewer than 30 of the 43 scored 1000+ and the event was won by Bohumil Starnovsky (CZE) who had had such a difficult horse at the previous year's World Championships. Of those who would comprise the final top six, only Svante Rasmuson (SWE) and Tibor Marácsko (HUN) did poorly scoring 936 and 980 respectively. Ironically, in the British team it was the two Pony Club boys, Nightingale and Clark who fell below the 1000 mark while Peter Whiteside managed 1010.

The fencing event was won by Laszlo Horváth (HUN) with 1052. He otherwise had a poor competition unlike the other top scorers – Tamas Szombathelyi (HUN), Pavel Lednev (URS), both 1022 and the young Starostin (URS) 1000 – who established themselves at the top of the scoreboard. Peciak (POL), the defending champion, fenced poorly (844) and was dropping out of contention.

The standard in the shooting was so amazingly good that, from the time of the UIPM Congress that same year, plans were afoot to reduce the size of the target to make the event more of a challenge. George Horvath (SWE), the youngest in the competition, aged 20, won with an incredible 200. This was actually a greater achievement than the 200 scored by Charles Leonard back in 1936 because, since the war, the target had been made considerably smaller. Horvath was joined at the top of the shooting ranks by the other 20 year old, Anatoli Starostin who scored 199; the shooting event was clearly no longer the preserve of more stable older athletes. The young Swedish team won the shooting event with 200, 198, and 194. After three events, though, it was Hungary who led the team event from the Soviet Union and Sweden. Individually, Szombathelyi led from Starostin and Lednev.

Once again Sweden did well enough in swimming to be only two points adrift of the new leaders, the Soviet Union, after four events. The event was won by Ivar Sisniega (MEX) in 3:10.8. Sisniega went on to become Minister for Sport in his native Mexico and is now a member of the UIPM executive. In second place with 3:12.8 was the Swedish medical student, Svante Rasmuson. Rasmuson had competed for Sweden in the 100 metres Freestyle in the Montreal Olympics and his rapid accumulation of pentathlon skills showed particularly in his fine fence (922) and shoot (194) in Moscow. This was his first major competition and Sweden was experiencing a resurgence in the sport by taking a chance on him. George Horvath (SWE) stopped for several moments in the swim to readjust his goggles, a slip that, in the end, did not change the final team result. Twelve of the swimmers were faster than 3:30 and only two in the whole field swam slower than four minutes. After four events, Starostin led from Szombathelyi and the much improved Paul Four (FRA).

The final running event was held on a hot day (88F/ 31C) and the runners set off at minute intervals. The results service was held up for an hour when the Swiss timing system broke down. Fortunately, a back-up system came immediately into play and was able to confirm that the new Olympic Champion was 20 year old Anatoli Starostin. Tamas Szombathelyi (HUN) was 2nd and, coming back from 7th place before the running, Pavel Lednev, at 37, made his greatest effort and took the bronze medal with a time of 13:07.7. Svante Rasmuson was only nine points behind Lednev in 4th place with Maracsko and Peciak 5th and 6th. Great Britain's Danny Nightingale won the running event by two seconds from Pierpaulo Cristofori (ITA) in 12:55.6. In the team event the Soviet Union won ahead of Hungary with Sweden taking the bronze. The favourites, Poland, only finished 4th and the British team (Nightingale 15th, Whiteside 21st, Clark 33rd) finished 8th of the 12 teams competing.

Though Starostin's victory was a wonderful achievement for the young Tajikistani, now was the time to look back on the career of one of the greatest pentathletes ever, Pavel Lednev. Lednev had competed in four Olympic Games, winning three individual bronze medals and a silver and two team golds and a silver. He had also been World Champion four times. No pentathlete has achieved a greater haul of Olympic medals.

UIPM developments in the 1980s

At the Moscow Congress it was decided that, from 1981, the order of the shooting and swimming events would be reversed. At the 1982 Congress, there was sufficient confidence in testing procedures to put beta-blockers on the list of banned drugs. From 1983, it was believed that by holding the shoot and run on the same day, the use of tranquillisers for the shooting would lose their value since such use would adversely affect the running performances. There remained a fair gap of time between events, though, and there appeared to be no discernible drop in shooting scores. Indeed, quite the opposite effect showed with startlingly high scores. So, at the 1985 Congress, officials took the dubious decision to revert to the five day competition. At that same meeting, they decided to reduce the upper age limit for juniors from 21 to 20. Since this plan was scrapped two years later, it can't have been a popular change.

The issue of drugs would not, however, go away. The UIPM had had to gain some education in this field in a hurry but the world had moved on much faster. By the early 1980s, the range of useful drugs had proliferated almost exponentially. There were a huge variety of sedatives with much shorter half-lives (the time it takes to get the drug out of the system in readiness for running), there were effective masking agents that made detection more difficult and there was still the huge expense of testing to deter officials. The cost of testing meant that only a small number of the competitors would be tested at any one time and this was another loophole in the system. Now, too, it was realized that there were readily-available drugs that enabled the athlete to train harder for longer with far more efficient cardio-vascular development. Not yet on the banned list since it wasn't a drug was the so-called 'blood-doping' in which blood was extracted, oxygenated, and then returned to the body to increase haemoglobin levels and consequently enable the athlete to achieve even greater cardio-vascular feats. This was not a Modern Pentathlon problem alone; it was a fact of life in sport. Indeed, Modern Pentathlon did far more to put its house in order than many other sports whose officials persisted in denying the existence of such problems. In 1986, the UIPM seized the bull by the horns and made a number of disqualifications that established, in effect, an end to the matter.

For Wille Grut, though, who retired as Secretary-General in 1984 to be replaced by Thor Henning (1984-88) and then Dieter Krickow (1988-92), resolving the drug question was being approached in entirely the wrong way. He was outraged when the sport reverted to a five day competition in 1986. He was a strong advocate of introducing the very system that is used today –the combined shoot/run event – and was all for introducing the air pistol. In such an event, the use of tranquillisers would be counter-productive. Some people in our sport chose to play down the extent of drug use. They felt that the mere mention of drugs brought bad publicity to Modern Pentathlon. That may well have been true but such a defensive approach was not going to solve the problem. Strongly aware that the UIPM was spending $120, 000 per year on drug testing, Grut told Michael Coleman, the journalist: 'What an utter waste of money. Introduce the air pistol system (as a combined event), forget about the drugs problem and spend the money on spreading the sport, buying horses and sending out coaches.' Of course Grut was prescient in this respect. It was still going to be some time before a central IOC sporting agency (WADA) would have sufficient funding to take charge of drug testing in all sports.

There was a feeling among athletes in the 1980s that more needed to be done to make the competition more exciting to the public and UIPM officials were very alert to this. Wille Grut's proposal of a shift from 0.22 pistols to air pistols took this into account. Some countries had found themselves unable to take up the sport because of their severe anti-gun laws and this had been a block to the sports' wider development. Also, air pistol, with its much reduced safety risk, would enable the sport to be brought into mainstream sports centres and made visible to exactly the kind of young people the UIPM wanted to recruit.

In 1981, the riding speed was reduced from 400 metres per minute to 350 in order to further protect the horses. Rules came in to insist on tougher Kevlar materials for fencing clothing and for 'maraging steel blades'. Briefly, in 1988, the UIPMB became the UIPMBT, adding Triathlon to its remit. This arrangement lasted only a year, each organization then going its separate way.

In 1988, our President, Sven Thofelt, decided to retire after almost three decades at the helm. He and Wille Grut had developed the sport together through a relationship of great trust, intelligence, and flexibility, qualities not always found in such abundance in those who have been so long in power. Thofelt was replaced as President by Igor Novikov, the great pentathlete of the late 1950s, who had been his deputy for the previous 16 years.

Stimulating wider participation

In 1974, the IOC had required a minimum of 40 participating countries in order to justify inclusion in the Olympic Games. Widening membership was always on the mind of the UIPM and, at that time, it had 47 member countries, up from 17 in 1949. By 1982, the number had grown to 51 but there was something rather artificial about the total. A small number of countries on the list only participated in Winter Biathlon and there were countries like Tunisia, Venezuela and Cuba who had national bodies but never participated in any activities. The stimulus of the inaugural Europa Cup and Latin Cup in 1974 had produced some additional participation and a scheme whereby neighbouring countries tried to win over nearby friends was partially successful. Some such combinations were Australia with New Zealand; Great Britain with Ireland and Hong Kong; Japan with Korea and China; Spain with Portugal; and France with Belgium. By 1982, the list of member countries of the UIPM included Algeria,

Bahrain, Bermuda, Cuba, Cyprus, Greece, Iran, Malta, Norway, Peru, Senegal, South Africa and Venezuela – all with fairly limited involvement. However, Ireland and New Zealand were at the 1980 Games, and Bahrain, Egypt, South Korea, Portugal, Austria, and Chinese Taipei (TPE) were all at the 1984 Games. Indeed, entries for the big competitions were so overwhelming that an upper limit of 66 competitors was placed on World Championships in 1982 with preparatory qualification systems. Also team entries had grown from only seven in 1949 to 26 in 1979 with an even more rapid burgeoning of entries for Junior Men and Women in their competitions.

1980 World Junior and Women's World Cup

If Great Britain's seniors might have been lamenting a lack of success since 1976, there was no such mood amongst the Juniors and the Women's team. In Madrid, Richard Phelps and his teammates grabbed the first medals Britain had ever won in the Junior World Championships. Richard Phelps took the silver medal, just 16 points behind Alexei Khaplanov (URS) but ahead of Olympic Champion, Starostin. The team (Phelps, Peter Tayler, and Phil Royston) won the bronze medal behind the Soviet Union and West Germany. From today's perspective and with Richard Phelps' later achievements in mind, it seems extraordinary he could have been left out of the Olympic team that year. He had already become British Champion the year before. Too often it is argued that youthful inexperience (Phelps was 19) should bide its time when it is exactly that early experience that often creates later success. The women's team once again won the World Cup series with Wendy Norman the Champion, Sarah Parker 5th and Kathy Tayler 6th overall.

1981 Men's World Championships: Zielona Gora (POL)

Zielona Gora with 'the intimate charm of a small rural commune' had won the right to hold the Championships over the powerful Legia Warsaw. As it turned out, it was a wonderfully organised competition and the 10,000 that turned up to watch was certainly a bigger crowd than the sport would have found in the capital. A new fencing hall and swimming pool at the Drzonkow Sports Centre enhanced the events.

Defending World Champion from 1979, Bob Nieman (USA) sustained a groin injury in riding training and was unable to compete. World Junior Champion, Christian Sandow (FRG) was also injured and, of course, the great Pavel Lednev (URS) had retired. So the individual competition ought to have been fought between Olympic Champion, Anatoli Starostin (URS), Janusz Peciak (POL) who was competing on home soil, Tamas Szombathelyi, the Olympic silver medallist, and Daniele Masala (ITA), who had been absent from Moscow the year before. The order of events had been changed so that the swimming came before the shooting but each event was held on a separate day.

The riding presented few difficulties, though, with two jumps remaining, the choice offered of an approach through an open gate or over a hill caused some problems. Of the 55 entries, 43 scored 1000+ and 14 of those scored 1100. Daniele Masala then opened up an impressive lead by winning both the fencing (1000) and the shooting (199). Peciak and Szombathelyi fenced well

(1060 and 1040) but Starostin was slipping out of the picture with a 960 fence. The fact that 28 pentathletes shot 194 or better in this competition underlined heavily that the roof had almost been reached and a new challenge was required, either through smaller targets or through more effective drug control. The swim was once again won by Ivar Sisniega (MEX) in 3:14.2.

The tussle between Masala and Peciak was extraordinary. With only the run remaining, Masala appeared to have an unassailable lead, 164 points (55 seconds) ahead of Peciak. But Peciak was running on home soil and political events had raised the importance of the event. *Solidarity*, the Polish freedom movement was flexing its muscles and anti-Soviet feeling was strong. The event, unusually, was televised in Poland and Peciak and the Polish team seemed to be carrying the nation's aspirations on their backs. Peciak managed to catch the minute interval on Svante Rasmuson, immediately ahead of him, who, nevertheless, gave him a race over the final stretch. Incredibly, Peciak ran almost a minute faster than Masala and snatched victory by 13 points. He even beat Mike Burley (USA) by 14 seconds. The crowd went wild. The Poles also took the team gold medal and, almost as important to the Polish crowd, the Soviet team went away empty-handed with Hungary 2nd and Italy 3rd. Two weeks later, the Polish border was closed and the Soviet government reasserted its authority.

Individually, Szombathelyi won the bronze medal with Rasmuson (SWE) 4th, Bouzou (FR) 5th, and Starostin (URS) only 9th. The British team (Richard Phelps 12th, Mike Mumford 22nd and Steve Sowerby 26th) had finished a creditable 7th of the 21 teams, beating the USA who had been champions in 1979.

1981 and 1982 World Junior Championships: Berlin and London

Starostin made up for his poor showing in the senior event by winning the junior event for the second time. The British team (Phelps 5th, Royston 10th, Tayler 23rd) repeated their 4th place in the team event and, a year later in London, won the bronze medal in front of the home crowd. Richard Phelps also took individual bronze to add to the silver he had won in 1980. Behind the scenes, few knew how difficult it had been for the cash-strapped British to hold the event at all. When all seemed lost, a group of businessmen led by ex-Olympic pentathlete, Tom Hudson, raised just enough for it to go ahead.

1981 Women's (First) World Championships: London (GBR)

Only eight countries and a total of 30 competitors participated in these inaugural championships but they were remarkable for the number of big names still to make their mark in the sport some years down the line – Anna Bajan (POL), Pernille Svarre and Eva Fjellerup (DEN), Caroline Delemer and Sophie Moressee (FRA), and Lynn Chorobrywy (CAN). Indeed, in a triumph of sporting longevity, Svarre and Delemer both competed in the first-ever Women's Olympic event in Sydney in 2000. The British, having rather dominated the World Cup events of the previous years, duly won the team event ahead of USA and Sweden but it was Anne Ahlgren (SWE) who was the first-ever Women's World Champion with Sabine Krapf (GER) 2nd and Wendy Norman, Britain's strongest competitor, coming 3rd. There were only ten points separating the three medallists in a nail-biting finish and only 65 points between 1st and 6th.

Wendy finished with a fine run but was nevertheless well-beaten in that event by Joy Hansen (USA). French women won the fencing and the swimming events, the winner of the fencing (Christine Van Hyfte) also finishing 4th overall. Even in this first outing, there were 11 shooting performances over 190 though none better than 193. Wendy Norman's 192 was rather better than she ever managed again in World Championships. The rest of the British team finished 7th (Kathy Tayler), 13th (Sarah Parker) and 17th (Janet Savage).

1982 Men's World Championships: Rome (ITA)
The Curcio Manoeuvre

A most extraordinary riding scandal took place in Rome and was later uncovered by Michael Coleman, *The Times* correspondent. Michael made an enormously important contribution to supporting and publicising Modern Pentathlon in Britain during the years 1978 to 1994. Sadly, he died of a heart attack in his early sixties despite being a regular runner who took good care of himself. Like any journalist, the prospect of a real scoop in the midst of the daily diet of fodder for the chip wrappers was too much to turn down and, despite (or perhaps because of) the controversy, he followed this one to the very death.

At these World Championships, the riding event proved to be most unusual. Only 17 pentathletes out of 58 achieved 1000+ points in the riding event compared to twice that number in most years. Indeed, only four of the final top ten got 1000+ out of a possible 1100. Compare that with the previous year (1981) when 43 out of 55 riders gained 1000+ points and the 1980 Olympics where 30 out of 43 gained 1000+. Even stranger was the fact that, despite the obvious thoroughbred quality of the horses, the horse drawn by Janusz Peciak from Poland, the World and Olympic Champion, appeared to have become a donkey by the time he rode it. His mount refused at jump after jump and, in the end, Peciak retired from the entire competition in disgust. 'I feel that somebody gave something to my horse. When I hit it with a whip outside the arena there was no reaction. It was as if dead. We asked for a vet for a dope check, waited two hours, but nobody came', he complained. The horse 'Herrenwood' had been whisked away immediately after the draw and the attempts of the Polish team to follow it were thwarted. Their appeal was rejected by the committee. But Peciak was adamant. He was made further suspicious by the arrival of a large TV set, an elegant 18 carat gold model of a horse, and a pile of training equipment, delivered as 'consolation prizes' to his hotel room the next day by a priest who then spent two hours 'counselling' him.

The main beneficiary of Peciak's withdrawal was Daniele Masala, the Italian champion who went on to take his first World Championship before his home crowd. It should be pointed out right away that Masala would almost certainly have won the competition anyway even with Peciak unimpeded and on his best form – Masala's record in the preceding years was impressive: 2nd the previous year; 3rd in 1979; and 4th on no fewer than four occasions (1974, 1976 (Olympics), 1977, and 1978). As a military policeman he'd been prevented from competing in Moscow in 1980 but he went on to become Olympic Champion in 1984. He duly gained the maximum riding score of 1100 points in Rome but, even had there been no riding event, would still have won the competition comfortably. His closest rival in the end was Anatoli Starostin, the Soviet 1980 Olympic Champion and he was 250 points adrift of Masala. It's true Starostin rode only 948 points but had the misfortune to ride in the midst of a tumultuous thunderstorm, another of the hazards in pentathlon against which there is no appeal.

In 1982 in Rome, there were other complaints about the riding event. Oddly though, the complaints of the British, American, German and Finnish teams were not that the horses were sluggish but that they were too lively, having been kept cooped up since their trial round the day before. Prominent victims, all of them good riders, were Danny Nightingale of the British team and Mike Burley and Mike Storm of the USA. There was no doubt in Rome that the quality of the horses was very high. Too high, some thought. Fifty thoroughbred horses had been prepared for the event and been ridden round by a former Olympic Gold Medallist in the equestrian events, Sergio Albanese. He had single-handedly and successfully taken the horses over 800 jumps in a frenetic four hour display. He achieved a 1000+ score on 30 of them.

Yes, of course they were good horses but throroughbred horses are temperamental; they are more sensitive to their riders and more likely to become stubborn if they are not treated in the manner to which they have become habituated. Most horses provided for pentathlon events are of a much lower order – predictable, solidly reliable, unexceptional, in fact. A pentathlete is meeting the competition horse for the first time. He has a mere twenty minutes to become acquainted with it. There are times when a rider, used to driving an old nag forward, finds that he is now fighting for his life to hold a wild stallion back. And the way he learned to ride in Germany, USA or Britain may be quite different from the local styles of the host country. Highly eccentric quirks are more present in the thoroughbred horse than in a lesser beast.

Another consideration is that a horse can be a very different animal from one day to the next. The insistence of the Italian Federation that all their horses were of the highest standard and this had been proved by Sergio Albanese was entirely reasonable. However, Mr Albanese's expertise notwithstanding, any horse can behave entirely differently if it is penned up, filled with water, or drugged and such a radical change of behaviour can be effected in minutes.

It was to be 12 years before the 'truth' of what really happened that day in Rome fully emerged. In 1982, when Coleman wrote his piece about the riding event in *The Times*, it caused such a furore that the President of the FEI (International Equestrian Federation), Prince Philip himself, felt obliged to write a letter of complaint to the Editor of *The Times*, Mr. Charles Douglas-Home.

The Prince, naturally, relied on the reports of others, notably that of General Sandro Azais, the FEI's representative at the World Championship. Azais complained, in his report, that Michael Coleman's article headed 'Horses take the bit between their teeth' had been expressed by a journalist 'as keen in satire as in ambiguity'. By contrast, Azais stated, his own report was the view of an 'old Cavalry officer' who only deals with 'the reality of facts'. His report, though not a whitewash, was inevitably partial. He reiterated the success of the horses in practice, the conformity of the jumps to UIPM demands and his ultimate responsibility to the UIPM. He acknowledged that the violent downpour could have had an effect on some horses - 'though not considerably' so. He took Danny Nightingale's claim that the horses had been 'penned up for days' without comment, stating simply that they had been through the selection procedure and so had clearly had relatively recent exercise. He did not consider what happened to the horses after that trial, why the request for a dope test from the Poles had been turned down, or the discrepancy between the success of the pentathletes at this World Championship and other major competitions. But then, none of these were within his remit and would need to have been addressed by the UIPM committee.

What was seized upon by Prince Philip and his advisors was Azais' final comment: 'The riding level of many riders was definitely lower than the standard required by the UIPM International rules.' Azais attempts to explain further that 'Mr. Nightingale's trial was not very successful due to a continuous contrast between the mouth of the horse and a fixed support kept by the rider with no firmity, whereas the delicacy of the mouth of the horse and its nature would call for those qualities described in the article; unfortunately, the rider did not put them into practice.'

So, it is the ultra-sensitivity of the thoroughbred horse coupled with the legendary cack-handedness of the pentathlete that, apparently, was the problem. The fact that the stringent 'UIPM International rules' seemed to have worked perfectly well on every other recent occasion is conveniently overlooked.

In his letter to Douglas-Home, Prince Philip echoed concern over the 'lurid and satirical' nature of Coleman's article, reiterated the effectiveness of the trial rounds, and pointed out that Danny Nightingale, as well as gathering a mere 680 points in Rome had got a zero score in the riding event at the Budapest World Championships in 1979 (the implication being, therefore, that he didn't know how to ride). He re-heated Masala's past achievements, and then provided the following summary: 'My conclusion from all this is that there was little wrong with the horses but quite a lot to be desired in the riding ability of many of the competitors.'

As President of the FEI, Prince Philip's comments were proprietorial and provided some justification in guarding the role of the FEI. As Patron of the MPAGB, however, his comment about Danny Nightingale's riding ability seems unfortunate. Nightingale was always an excellent rider. He'd come to Pentathlon from the Pony Club and been around horses all his life. No pentathlete, no matter how magnificent a rider, can completely survive a sporting career without mishap in the riding event – that's much more to do with the nature of the horses than the fault of the pentathlete. We all know that, in those rare moments when pentathlon has been televised, the producers will seize upon riding gaffes as the most spectacular photo opportunities for their brief and inaccurate overview.

The final coda to this saga was a sensation. Twelve years later, in 1994, Michael Coleman, reporting on the World Championships being held that year in Sheffield, was approached by Janusz Peciak himself, then (and now) coach to the USA team. Peciak reminded Coleman of the strange events of 1982 and then revealed that he had been absolutely right to have suspected his horse had been drugged. The Head of the Italian Pentathlon Federation, General Roberto Curcio, had recently died of cancer. Igor Novikov, the great Soviet champion and then President of the UIPM, visited him on his deathbed in a Rome hospital. Curcio and Novikov had been old friends and sparring partners in sporting stadia and committee meetings. Curcio told Novikov 'Igor, I've a confession to make. Remember Rome 1982 and the horses? Well, I'm the guilty man. I arranged that the horses were tampered with and it's been on my mind ever since. I want you to know about it.' It was Novikov who passed this information on to Peciak.

Deathbed confessions may seem too melodramatic for the present age and more at home in a Dickens novel. Sadly, Curcio, Novikov and Michael Coleman are all now dead but Peciak, understandably, still has an axe to grind. Commenting on the Italian authorities' treatment of the protest he says 'They were guilty then and they are guilty now.' But there are puzzles remaining. Why drug only Peciak's horse? Surely Starostin, the current Olympic Champion, must also have presented a threat to Masala and yet his only handicap was an unexpected thunderstorm. Are we to assume Curcio was responsible for that too? Were those other overexcited horses featured in the appeal of other nations given stimulants rather than merely being kept cooped up? Certainly, Masala wouldn't thank anyone for tarnishing what, for sure, was a complete victory over all his rivals. And Curcio's reputation was impressive. Both as competitor and official he had had a long and dignified involvement with the sport. Was this cheating just one wayward decision borne of too much power? The world of politics (even sporting politics) is so often a tussle between the moral imperative and the expedient solution but if he carried that secret to his deathbed, then the long-term outcome weighed much more heavily on him than any glory he might have felt from the short-term solution.

Though the riding event rather overshadowed the whole competition, it couldn't entirely detract from Masala's convincing win. He beat Starostin (URS) and Jöel Bouzou (FRA) by 250 points. Other features of the competition were that 38 0f the 58 competitors shot 190+ with Nieman (USA), Dosymbetov (URS) and Santanen (FIN) tying for first place with 199. Paul Four (FRA) won the fencing with 1076, Christian Sandow (FRG) the swim and Mike Burley (USA) the run, though Alex Watson (AUS) pushed him close. Bob Nieman, the 1979 World Champion, had an indifferent ride (924) and fence (943) and finished in 6th place overall. In the team event, only 100 points separated the top three teams: USSR won ahead of Hungary and Italy with Great Britain in 8th place (Richard Phelps 24th, Danny Nightingale 30th and Mike Mumford 43rd).

1982 Women's World Championships: Compiègne (FRA)

The second annual World Championship for women was an unforgettable one for Great Britain. Among the 30 individual competitors, there were seven teams entered - Australia, France, Germany, Great Britain, Sweden, USA and, for the first time, USSR. Poland and Italy, present the previous year, were, sadly, absent. The competition took place over five days in mid-August in the order: ride, fence, swim, shoot, run, the last day's run being postponed until early evening because of the 90F heat. Kathy Tayler (GBR) was one of two clear rounds in the riding and, though Wendy Norman (GBR) fenced 1032, that event was won by Ameyalli Martinez (MEX) with 1114. Guylaine Berger (FRA) won the swimming (1244) and Sarah Parker (GBR) the shooting with 1000. Wendy Norman's storming run (1285 points) gave the

16 year old a comfortable World Championship victory by 175 points ahead of Sarah Parker and Kathy Tayler who took silver and bronze medals.

This clean sweep of the medals gave Great Britain a team victory by almost 800 points over West Germany and Sweden. British Team Manager, Eileen Tayler's report was a masterpiece of detached observation. She described the quest for sufficient Union Jacks for the medal ceremony and noted 'Finally, after scouring Compiègne, three were flying…although, in the hurry, two were upside down.' No gushing hyperbole, no admiring salutations, just the important recognition that the medals were accompanied by the presentation of 'very useful holdalls, put into use immediately on the return journey.'

There were many notable pentathletes in the field: the 1981 Champion, Anne Ahlgren (SWE) finished 4th; Lynn

1982 Compiègne: Great Britain's World Champion Team (l-r: Wendy Norman, Sarah Parker, Teresa Purton, Kathy Tayler).

Chornobrywy (CAN), who would become World Champion a year later, scored zero in the riding, just as four-times World Champion (1990, 1991, 1993, 1994), Eva Fjellerup (DEN), had done the year before. Pernille Svarre (DEN) finished 6th, 19 years before she would become the 2000 World Champion. Like Pernille, Caroline Delemer (FRA) would still be competing 20 years later and would take the bronze medal in 1988 and 1989; Sabine Krapf (FRG) would take bronze in 1986 and 1987; and Sophie Moressee would win the silver in 1986 and become a member of France's Olympic Gold medal winning Epée team in 1996. Though only 19, this was the final competitive season for Great Britain's Kathy Tayler who went on to become a popular TV presenter, her rigorous pentathlon training equipping her well for an early morning start on the breakfast show.

1983 Men's World Championships: Warendorf (FRG)

With Daniele Masala absent and Janusz Peciak somewhat off-form (he finished 8th), the way was open for Anatoli Starostin to become World Champion. He did this without any single outstanding event but with consistent strength throughout –Ride (1040), Fence (984), Swim (1228), Shoot (1044), Run (1210). In fact, given that the running was held on a tough course with times as much as a minute slower than the previous year, his run was outstanding in comparison with the leading runners – Sisniega (1264), Watson (1243), and Sowerby (1240). Starostin's nearest rival at the end was Tamas Szombathelyi (HUN) who took the silver medal. Yevgeny Zinlevski (URS), another strongly-competent all-rounder, took the bronze. The team event was won by the USSR with Hungary and France 2nd and 3rd. Individually,

Szombathelyi won the fencing (1080) while Gabor Pajor (HUN) and Ahmed Nasser (EGY) jointly won the shooting (198). Sisniega (MEX) and Sandow (FRG) both swam 3:14 and Ivar Sisniega's 12:47 run made it clear that he was the best pentathlon run/swimmer in the world. The next best, incidentally, were two British athletes, Steve Sowerby and Richard Phelps.

In his final Team Manager's Report, after more than a decade leading the British Team, Michael Proudfoot adopted a very pragmatic and psychological approach to the team's preparations. He made clear after the many disappointments since the Montreal victory that in the world of 'If' there was a distinction. He argued that 'If I'd had 350 points more…' was a very 'iffy' statement whereas to say 'If I'd shot a 10 instead of a 9…' was 'much less "iffy" '. On this basis, he urged the athletes to set realistic individual and team targets. The British team in Warendorf largely achieved those aims. In finishing 7th they were only 71 points short of their target (5th) and the individual achievements –Richard Phelps 6th, Mike Mumford 24th and Steve Sowerby 27th – were well in keeping with the pre-competition estimate. In the World Ranking List at the end of the previous year, Phelps had been only 33rd and Mumford 68th. Proudfoot's insistence that 'Medals are won, not by exceptional performances but by not making mistakes' is a mantra that pentathletes may know to be a truism but one on which constant focus is, nevertheless, required.

1983, 1984, and 1985 World Junior Championships: Los Angeles, Bucharest, and Kiev

In 1983, the Soviet team was inexplicably absent from Coto de Casa in California, for the Olympic test event.

This opened the way for Hungary to finish 1st, 2nd and 3rd individually (Fábián, Demeter and Bardi) and, of course, win the team event ahead of Poland and the USA. Only Peter Tayler remained from the successful British team of recent years and he finished 14th.

In 1984, USSR reasserted its position in Bucharest with individual gold and bronze medals (Igor Shvarts and Vaho Yagorashvili) and beat Hungary and Rumania to the gold medal in the team event. The competition also witnessed the beginnings of a British resurgence over the coming years in Dominic Mahony's 8th individual position. Dominic, like Mike Mumford, had been a student at Millfield School and also followed him into officer training in the army. Behind Richard Phelps, he was the best British pentathlete of that era and, since retirement, has taken a full role in the sport as British Team Manager.

In 1985, Yagorashvili moved up to top place with his compatriot, Alex Makeev in 2nd place and the Bulgarian, Velizar Iliev, who was later to compete for the USA in the 2000 Olympics, 3rd. Dominic Mahony came 6th with an outstanding fencing score – 1092. Yagorashvili was to have an extraordinary career in Modern Pentathlon, competing in Olympic Games for three different countries – in 1988 for USSR, in 1996 for Georgia, and in 2004 for USA.

1983 Women's World Championships: Göteborg (SWE)

Numbers were now growing fast. There were 47 competitors and 15 teams represented in Sweden, including new team entries from Taiwan, China, and Italy. The Soviet team, reported to be arriving in style by submarine from Leningrad, finally failed to attend.

Poland, however, missing in 1982, did return. In 1984, Pernille Svarre (DEN) would become World silver medallist. But, in Göteborg, it was her turn to get a zero ride. Eight others suffered the same ignominy despite 21 of the field scoring 1000+. Another casualty was the World Champion, Wendy Norman, whose difficult ride gave her only 566 points and left her in a humiliating 24th place overall. The organisers had carelessly left some plastic sheeting flapping in the wind on some nearby scaffolding and this spooked a number of the horses. Lynn Chornobrywy (CAN) had led throughout the first four events and the final run was held in front of 20,000 spectators as a curtain-raiser for a big football match. Lynn took 2nd place in that in front of the crowd. The comfortable winner of the run, however, was Britain's Teresa Purton who took herself into an impressive 5th place overall with that performance. Lynn Chrnobrywy had done quite enough, however, to win the overall victory comfortably from Anne Ahlgren (SWE) whose record so far -1st, 4th and 2nd in successive World Championships was outstanding. Sarah Parker took the bronze medal. So, even without Britain's reigning World Champion, Wendy Norman, counting in the team result, Great Britain still managed to retain the title with Vicky Sowerby finishing 8th in her first World Championship. As they had done the previous year, West Germany and Sweden took silver and bronze medals.

1984 Olympic Games: Los Angeles (USA)

Pentathletes in the Communist Bloc countries were only told in May of 1984 that they would not be going to Los Angeles because of the boycott. All the World Championship individual medals had been won the previous year by Communist Bloc athletes and the Communist boycott was a kick in the teeth for great champions like Anatoli Starostin, Tamas Szombathelyi and Janusz Peciak. To make a fuss would have been suicidal in the political climate of the time but Peciak was incensed. 'Nobody will remember a boycott but everyone remembers an Olympic Champion,' he argued. As World and Olympic Champion, Peciak knew what he was talking about; he had twice been Poland's Sports Personality of the Year. But his team mates and trainers held their breath in fear of retribution from governmental offices. What actually happened showed surprising ingenuity on the part of the Polish authorities. The Polish Olympic Committee relied heavily for its survival on donations from its wealthy expatriates in the USA. So, instead of castigating Peciak for his outburst, they promoted him to Vice-President. The American Poles were more than willing to fill the coffers of the Polish Olympic Committee in support of Peciak's rebel stance! And Peciak was absolutely right; nobody pays attention to the absentees. A gold medal is a gold medal without reference to who's missing.

The Los Angeles Olympic Modern Pentathlon was actually held 50 miles away at Coto de Casa. This had considerable advantages: travel between events was kept to a minimum and the full security measures of such travel were made clear on the trip to the swimming event which was held in Irvine, 20 miles away. The three buses travelled in convoy with two motor-cyclists, four police cars and two helicopter gunships overhead. Despite the boycott, the event drew 52 competitors and marked the return to form of Daniele Masala after his year's absence. He also had hopes that the Italians might outperform the French who had won bronze the previous year.

The riding event enabled 35 of the field to gain 1000+ and, among the eventual top performers, Daniele Masala, Carlo Massullo (ITA) and Richard Phelps all scored 1100. Among the unlucky was Steve Sowerby of the British team. He drew a horse on which Daniel Esposito (AUS) had scored zero in the first round. In the collecting ring, Sowerby was actually making progress but the horse's owner felt that the morning problem had been that the horse had been asked to jump too big a jump too early and was unsettled. So she and Ron Bright, the British manager lowered one of the poles on the oxer in the practice paddock. The German coach objected and put in a protest that Sowerby was 'rapping' the horse (concealing one pole behind another to wake the horse up by 'rapping' its shins) and this was a disqualifiable offence. Steve went on to ride a creditable 755 on the horse but by evening discovered he had been eliminated. A counter protest from the British camp reduced this to a 200 point penalty but, with only 555 points, Sowerby and the British team were now out of the running. Ron Bright's own report of the event described his contretemps with the German coach thus: 'Utilising my best knowledge of the German language, I informed him that it was my right to lower the fence and continued to do so.' Many of us, acquainted with Ron Bright's negotiating skills in such situations, would gladly have bought tickets to witness this exchange.

The fencing event was won by Achim Bellmann (FRG) with 1066 though Svante Rasmuson's 1022 put him in a strong position after two events, especially with a 3:16 swim still to come. Mike Storm (USA) won the shooting with 198 (Masala 193, Rasmuson 190, Massullo 197) but it was the event that put paid to Richard Phelps' hopes. He shot only 184 and started the handicapped run in 9th position. Amazingly, he moved up the field so that, with 400 metres to go, he was in bronze medal position. It was almost inconceivable that Carlo Massullo (ITA) could overtake him but Richard had run himself into the ground and had nothing left when Massullo came past him in the final stretch. An almost identical situation had taken place up ahead. Though he started eight seconds behind Masala, Svante Rasmuson came past his rival and was destined to win the gold medal when he fell on the sandy course, thoroughly exhausted. Masala could hardly believe his good fortune as he passed Rasmuson in the final stretch to become Olympic Champion.

Italy won the team event and the USA ran so well that they outdid the French by just three points to take the silver. Some small consolation for Richard Phelps was that his victory in the running event sustained a great British tradition; Jim Fox had won in Munich Adrian Parker in Montreal and Danny Nightingale in Moscow. His overall 4th place equalled Jim Fox's 4th position in Munich as the best British Men's individual Olympic effort so far. The British team came 7th with Mike Mumford 24th and Steve Sowerby 37th.

In the months after these Olympics, press rumours about drug use in Los Angeles abounded. Beta-blockers had been banned by the UIPM since the 1982 Congress but the IOC allowed such use where medical conditions (epilepsy, hypertension) required it. The pentathlete merely had to provide a doctor's certificate. This, Wille Grut considered dishonest (Why would a fit young athlete have hypertension?) and wrote to clarify the situation with Prince de Merode, President of the IOC Medical Commission. Details of testing had been destroyed but de Merode's team were able to confirm that the Italian winners had shown no positive tests and, according to Michael Coleman, *The Times* journalist, the only two athletes providing medical certificates were Mike Storm (USA), who won the shooting and whose team finished 2nd and Peter Minder (SUI) whose team came 4th. When Coleman approached the USMPA about this situation, Ralph Bender, their treasurer, fearing the loss of the USA silver medal, claimed 'Our team was one of the cleanest there.' Such a statement is reflective of the deep mistrust and suspicion surrounding drug use at the time. The Drug Commission in Los Angeles blustered that it was impossible to mask drugs and that no one could possibly have evaded their tests. But drug development was moving fast and testing procedures were unlikely to have been perfect. Blood doping wouldn't be banned until 1986 and competitors in Los Angeles were seeing physical performances in their rivals out of all proportion to previous achievements. In his autobiography, Wille Grut stated the position quite clearly. He wrote:

'Daniele Masala had competed against Svante Rasmuson many times before and always been beaten by him in the run by more than half a minute. That Rasmuson did not manage to catch the seven-second lead the Italian had at the handicapped start was because the Italian was 'blood-doped.' This is not an argument without solid foundation. One of my oldest friends in the pentathlon world, the now deceased Roberto Curcio has given me written confirmation that Masala and his teammates were 'blood-doped.'

Grut regarded this as a kind of moral cheating but, since blood doping was not a banned activity in 1984, the Italians and anyone else who had the medical technology were perfectly entitled to use this assistance at the time. Also, in the Modern Pentathlon, only the top five in each event together with two others randomly chosen were tested. While this was a practical approach to time and cost, should a positive test be found, there would constantly be speculation, justified or otherwise, about the rest of the untested field. Such a situation made for an uneasy atmosphere of doubt and suspicion.

1984 Women's World Championships: Hörsholm (DEN)

The venue, a suburb of Copenhagen, brought a World Championship to Denmark for the very first time. By now the entry had swollen to a remarkable 18 countries and 57 competitors. The Soviet team, after a hesitant start in Women's Modern Pentathlon now established control. Svetlana Yakovlova won individually and the USSR took the team competition ahead of Poland and West Germany. Pernille Svarre took the silver medal in her home country and, now long-established at the top, Sabine Krapf (FRG) won the bronze, despite illness. The British team (Norman 4th, Sowerby 8th, Parker 37th) finished 6th overall and their perennial weakness in fencing and shooting this time kept them out of the medals. Wendy Norman, however, continued to be our top performer. She recovered from the previous year's disappointment by finishing 4th overall with a 187 shoot. Wendy's fencing was always the exception to the British team's malaise. In Hörsholm, she fenced 1022.

1985 Men's World Championships: Melbourne (AUS)

A return of the big event to Melbourne for the third time brought many more pentathletes to Australia than the long journey had allowed in the past. 17 teams and 55 competitors participated. How would Olympic medallists Italy, USA, and France fare against USSR, Hungary, and Poland now that the Eastern bloc was returning to the fold?

The hard riding course provided only 18 1000+ rides out of the field of 55. The only 1100 went to Attila Miszér (HUN) and it was a lead he wouldn't concede for the rest of the competition. He fenced 1000, shot 195, and was right up there with the leaders in the swim and run. By contrast, his rivals, the two Soviet competitors, Anatoli Starostin, 1983 World Champion, and young Igor Shvarts, rode only 972 and 904 respectively. It was enough to settle the final result. Mizsér won by 20 points overall from Starostin with Shvarts 3rd, some way behind after a mediocre run. The Olympic Champion, Daniele Masala, finished 6th, having won the shoot (198) but having fenced only 860. His compatriot, Carlo Massullo fenced only 760 and yet still managed to finish 4th overall. This gave USSR a clear victory over Hungary with Italy, the Olympic Champions, coming 3rd and France 4th.

The British team chose to leave Dominic Mahony on the bench and fielded Richard Phelps, Graham Brookhouse, and Jim Nowak, fourth man for the previous two years. The team had a poor start in the riding (Phelps 950, Brookhouse 842, Nowak 982) and then all fenced only 640 each. However, Graham Brookhouse swam 3:13 to win the event in a field in which seven others broke 3:20 and Richard Phelps was just five seconds behind the winner of the run, Milan Kadlec (TCH). But with 33 of the competitors shooting 190+, the British performances of 189, 189, and 186 just weren't good enough and the team finished 8th overall. Richard had already proved he was world-class and it was a team that would go on to far better performances but not in Melbourne.

1985 Women's World Championships: Montreal (CAN)

The appeal of the women's event saw 17 countries and 44 competitors making the flight to Montreal and, just when it looked like the Soviet Union had things sewn up, Poland triumphed in the team and, through Barbara Kotowska, the individual event. Irena Kiseleva (URS), in 2nd place, would become champion for the next two years and Anna Bajan (POL) won bronze. In the team event, the Soviet Union placed 2nd and Sweden 3rd. Great Britain (Norman 5th, Purton 28th, Parker 36th) were 8th. Wendy Norman's 5th place included a 182 shoot. This was Sarah Parker's final World Championships. Sarah had been an important presence in the sport for the previous ten years, as swimming coach to the winning Montreal men's team including her brother, Adrian, and then as a central member of the women's team throughout their most successful period as World Champions. She continued to act as coach to the women's team after retirement.

Problems in the USA in the 1980s

Apart from their silver medal in Los Angeles in 1984, the USA Men's team in the 1980s never reproduced the splendid form of their 1979 team and individual victory.

This was, in part, the result of tension between the US Army authorities and the USMPA. Fort Sam Houston in San Antonio was the home of Modern Pentathlon and military and civilian pentathletes alike enjoyed the marvellous facilities provided by the US Army. However, the publicity given to the use of tranquillisers in the sport and the American tendency towards litigation as the first step towards solving problems made for an ugly sequence of events. In the early 1980s, the US Army conducted a formal investigation in which pentathletes and officials alike at Fort Sam were accused of 'possession and distribution of controlled substances', 'false swearing', 'bribery', 'wrongful disposal of government property' 'smuggling' etc. Essentially, the daily and reasonable activities of a thriving Pentathlon centre were held under a very misanthropic microscope. It left a sour taste. The US Army officials were determined to remind Modern Pentathlon of just who paid the bills and who had the final say. The rift became more serious in 1986 when, as a result of litigation within the pentathlon camp, the US Army refused to support the centre any longer.

After the 1986 USMPA trials, Blair Driggs and Rob Stull, 1st and 2nd in the competition, were found to have taken a banned drug. They protested that they had not been notified that this drug (glutamine) was on the banned list. Thus, the USMPA decided to suspend the six month ban they had initially imposed. Other pentathletes were outraged and Laszlo Beres and Harvey Cain took the matter to court. There followed a bizarre attempt by their lawyer to serve an injunction on Driggs and Stull at New York airport en route to the World Championships in Italy. This attempt was foiled by 'a burly association official'. Mutual restraining orders were served. Beres and Cain travelled incognito to Montecatini in the hope of preventing the participation of Blair and Driggs but to no avail. The US Army hierarchy were appalled at the publicity given to these events and were keen to distance themselves from the sport. All this coincided with the appointment of Janusz Peciak as US coach who, having played no part in these events, must have wondered what he had got himself into. That he is still the US coach 26 years later is a very good sign that such troubles were temporary.

1986 World Championships: Montecatini (ITA)
Men

In May 1986, a major pentathlon event had taken place in Birmingham as part of the city's Olympic bid. The British authorities, unusually, decided to test every one of the competitors for drugs after the shooting event. This was a very expensive and thorough approach. Usually, if tests were done, they were only done on the top few in the event. The Birmingham tests cost £100 per sample, in total as much again as the cost of mounting the whole competition. But Great Britain, congenitally disposed to see herself as 'the virgin in the whorehouse', was at the forefront of drug testing in the world and was determined to do it properly. As it turned out, only the Polish team proved positive.

Montecatini was the last venue to host all three World Championships –Men, Junior Men and Women – all at the same time. It meant there were 156 competitors in all (63 men, 45 junior men, 48 women) - rather too many for comfortable organization.

In the men's competition, the riding event was a hard one. Only 13 out of the 63 entries cleared 1000 points and 11 scored zero. Among those zeros were Anatoli Avdeev (URS) and Blair Driggs (USA). One of only two 1100 riders was Carlo Massullo (ITA) but his rivals were not so far behind –Masala (1030), Starostin (1004) and Kadlec (1034). For the British, Peter Hart was our only success with 950. The other members of the British team appeared to be pushing dead meat around a field (Phelps 676, Mahony 722).

The fencing was won by Starostin (1068) while Ruer (FRA) and Toraldo (ITA) both swam 3:13. Jan-Erik Danielsson (SWE) shot 199 and Milan Kadlec (TCH) and Peter Hart (GBR) both ran 12:16. The other British runners were not far behind; both Phelps and Mahony ran 12:30 which took Mahony into 21st place overall, Hart 33rd and Phelps 35th. Starostin won the competition comfortably, 100 points clear of Massullo and Masala with reigning World Champion, Attila Mizsér (HUN) back in 10th place. But Starostin wouldn't be World Champion for long.

The results of the drug testing at Birmingham and Montecatini were not released until November 1986. Starostin was the most high-profile of a number of disqualifications for beta-blocker use. Of the 15 athletes disqualified in November, he was one of only three disqualified in the men's competition but the other two, Driggs (USA) and Donov (BUL) had finished well down the order. So, still only 26 years old, Starostin was the high-profile scalp, the sacrifice to the Gods that proved the UIPM meant business. None of the athletes concerned came to Stockholm for the inquiry. In a rather embarrassing conflict of loyalties between his own Soviet federation and his duty to the UIPM, Novikov protested that the drugs concerned were not clearly on the banned list and abstained in the vote. All 15 athletes from the three World Championships and the Brimingham International were banned for two and a half years.

It is common these days to talk about 'drug cheats' as though such people are a breed apart riddled with calumny and deceit. This may be a morally comforting stance for some to take but is, I believe, grossly distorting. The UIPM had been under pressure to resolve a very unsatisfactory status quo regarding drug use. There is no doubt that new drugs were becoming available so rapidly and their addition to the banned list made so suddenly, that it was very likely that some athletes would make the mistake of assuming a drug was not on the banned list when it was. It was not inspiring to the notion of thorough testing that only the top four in each event together with two others chosen at random were tested. How many more athletes among the 67, then, had taken similar drugs and got away scott-free? As Grut said afterwards, the banned athletes were only 'the tip of the iceberg'. Starostin had tested negative in Birmingham and still won the competition. His disqualification in Rome, therefore, was, in large part, the result of carelessness by the Soviet officials in whose charge he was placed and yet he, in the prime of a successful sporting career, was forced to bear the brunt. When asked how he feels about this now, he smiles, shrugs his shoulders, and with Dostoyevskian resignation says 'That's life.' It is a mark of the greatness of Starostin that, instead of retiring, he continued to train hard. He had been robbed of a second Olympic title in 1984 by the boycott and now the ban took away his chances for 1988 as well. Yet still he made a comeback –

8th in 1989, 2nd in 1990, and finally 4th place and a team silver medal at his final Olympic competition in 1992.

Starostin rose to the rank of Colonel in the Soviet Army and then worked in the Russian Customs and Excise Department. Though he was willing to offer his expertise to the new Russian Modern Pentathlon Federation, he was constantly and inexplicably overlooked. It took someone with the foresight of current President, Vyacheslav Aminov, to realize Starostin's potential as a coach and to bring him on board.

So history was immediately rewritten. Massullo was surprised to find he was the new World Champion with Masala 2nd and Lajos Dobi (HUN), 3rd. Unaffected by the disqualifications, Italy won the team competition, 16 points ahead of Hungary with France taking the bronze. Avdeev's zero ride had kept the USSR out of medals even without Starostin's disqualification.

In the Junior Championships, the toll was greater: two Bulgarians, two Poles and two Soviet athletes were disqualified. Among them was World Junior Champion, Velizar Iliev (BUL) so the revised result gave Franck Guilluy (FRA) the title with Madaras (HUN) 2nd and the only remaining Soviet athlete, Gutsevich 3rd. In the team event, Hungary won ahead of France and Italy with a rather surprised and pleased Great Britain team (Jason Lawrence, Greg Whyte and Kevin Griffiths) moving into 4th place. It remains a puzzle that there is no apparent consistency in the pattern of disqualifications. Why would only one or two members of the team show positive while the third did not? It seems unlikely that competition preparations would have been left entirely up to the individual when coaches had such high levels of responsibility as was the case in most Eastern European teams of the time.

Women

The three women disqualified after this competition were the two Soviet athletes, Tatiana Tchernetskaya and 1984 World Champion, Svetlana Yakovleva, who had placed 3rd and 4th in the competition. The other was Lori Norwood (USA) who would, nevertheless come back to become World Champion in 1989. The outright winner was Irina Kiseleva (URS) who would go on to repeat this feat the following year. With two experienced pentathletes, Moressee (FRA) and Krapf (FRG), taking silver and bronze, the outcome was popular enough. In the absence of her disqualified teammates, Kiseleva was unable to add a team medal to her tally; France moved up a place to win ahead of West Germany and Italy. Though the British team was out of the medals they were the heroes of one remarkable event: Great Britain beat the USSR into 2nd place in the fencing event! This is a quite extraordinary achievement given the mediocrity of most British fencing performances in the past. Indeed, Teresa Purton finished 2nd in the event (1046), one hit behind Kiseleva (1069) and one in front of Sophie Moressee (1023) who would later win a gold medal in the Women's Epée team in the 1996 Olympics. Wendy Norman won the running event but her 177 shoot compared very unfavourably with the eight competitors who shot 194 or better. Wendy finished 18th, Teresa 20th and Louise Ball 29th. This competition also marked the debut of a Hungarian team. Given that Hungary is such an accomplished Modern Pentathlon nation, it is rather surprising that the Hungarian women took so long to appear in the World Championships. It was a slow start for them; it wasn't until 1989 that they would win any kind of medal.

1987's new developments

1987 was the first year of the European championships and also marked a new innovation, the brainchild, apparently, of Oleg Chuvalin –the relay event. A first attempt had been made at this event at the Spartakiade as far back as 1979 so it was appropriate that the USSR should be the first champions in 1987 beating the ten other teams. The event consisted of teams of three each of whom rode over 9 jumps in relay form with the clock running and penalties made in the usual way, a fencing event in which each member of a team fought his opposite number in each of the other teams, then, 10 shots each for an accumulated team shooting score, a 3 x 200m swimming relay and a 3 x 2000m run. Great Britain made a very good start in the European Championships, finishing 2nd in the team event behind USSR. Another important development in the same year was that the Asian Modern Pentathlon Federation was formed with the resolve to hold Asian Championships annually.

1987 Men's World Championships: Moulins (FRA)

With only a year to go before the Seoul Olympic Games, there were 73 individuals and 30 countries entered in Moulins, each of which had had to qualify through a series of competitions. In the riding event, 31 of the 65 who made it to the competition scored 1000+. Not the Hungarians though. They scored a miserable 2449 total (Fábián 980, Martinek 749, Mizsér 772) and yet still, astonishingly, won the overall team competition. Two years later, each member of this team had in turn become World or Olympic Champion but here was a test for only the toughest of pentathletes and this great team showed what was possible when faced with adversity. The same team fenced 2904, a result which included Fábián's winning score of 1128 ahead of Jöel Bouzou's 1080.

Cesare Toraldo (ITA) won the swim in 3:11 with Graham Brookhouse only a second behind. Mizsér (HUN) and Danielsson (SWE) both shot 199 though, since the previous year's drug disqualifications, the overall standard had dropped markedly. Only seven scored 1000 points or better. For the record, the number of 1000+ shooting scores in the 1980s Championships was as follows:

No drug tests:	1981 (27); 1982 (23); 1983 (24).
Olympic testing:	1984 (9).
Some testing:	1985 (15); 1986 (15).

After four events, Jöel Bouzou (FRA) was in the lead and giving the home crowd something to shout about. He led from Fábián (HUN) and Avdeev (URS). The run took place on an extremely hot August day and was a tough course. It was so hot, in fact, that Christophe Ruer (FRA) and Martin Lamprecht (SWE) fainted en route and were unable to finish. Milan Kadlec's (TCH) marvellous winning run took him up into the silver medal position but he couldn't catch Jöel Bouzou who became World Champion in the best of all places, his home country. Laszlo Fábián got a deserved bronze ahead of Carlo Massullo (ITA). In the team event, Hungary won heroically ahead of the USSR and, with France out of the competition as a result of Ruer's collapse, the bronze medal was taken by Great Britain. The British team had a couple of highlights- Mahony's 968 fence and Brookhouse's 1336 swim. Even with Phelps running below par, an average ride of only 980, average fence of 800 and average shoot of only 187, they still took the bronze medal. In a hard-fought competition, the British knew they could only get better in Seoul the following year.

1987 Women's World Championships: Bensheim (FRG)

The entry for the women's event was now up to 52 individuals with 22 countries represented. 28 of the field scored 1000+ on the riding and Paula Salminen (FIN) won both the riding and swimming events (1100 and 2:16.7). Unfortunately, though just behind the World Champion, Kiseleva (URS) after three events, Paula was unable to score in the shooting and dropped out of contention. Meanwhile, Moressee (FRA) won the fencing from Kiseleva (1066) and Wendy Norman (1044). But Wendy shot only 173 compared to Sabine Krapf's (FRG) 195. Though she fought back in the running event (6:41) behind Janna Gorlenko (URS) who finished in 6:30.1, there was no way back from that shoot. Irina Kiseleva retained her World title ahead of 1984 Champion, Barbara Kotowska (POL) and Sabine Krapf (FRG). For Sabine, this was her fourth individual World Championship medal. Though the title eluded her, she continued to be a force in the sport right up to 1992. The team medals were won by USSR, West Germany and Poland with Great Britain in 4th place (Wendy Norman 11th, Louise Ball 22nd and Mandy Flaherty 27th).

1988 Olympic Games: Seoul (KOR)

The competition took place, as had been the tradition in Modern Pentathlon, in the first week of the Games but, unlike in 1984 when the competition was a four day event, each event was on a different day, the order remaining ride, fence, swim, shoot, run. There were 19 teams and 26 countries represented.

Given the riding experiences of 1982 and 1986, there was some trepidation among the pentathletes over the fact that the horses in the riding event had been imported from Italy. The course had, however, by now been reduced to 400 metres in length. Certainly, 22 of the 66 entries managed 1000+ but there were four zero rides and quite a few others whose hopes were dented after the first day: Fábián (HUN) 876; Yuferov (URS) 716; Avdeev (URS) 680; Stull (USA) 470; Gostigian (USA) 0. Graham Brookhouse, however, managed to get 986 points out of Rob Stull's horse and, with Mahony (1036) and Phelps (964) avoiding disaster, Great Britain was well-placed in 4th. The only two 1100 rides were from Alex Watson (AUS) and Mohamed Abdou El Souad (EGY).

Fábián won the fencing (1051) ahead of his compatriot, Mizsér and Christophe Ruer (FRA) won the swim in 3:10.58 with 20 of the field, including Brookhouse and Phelps, swimming faster than 3:20. After the swimming event, then, Great Britain was in 2nd place despite Dominic Mahony having damaged ligaments in a right knee which required strapping. His 898 fencing score (the same as Phelps) was very sound in the circumstances. In all three events so far, the British had scored higher than they had the previous year and Richard Phelps had now moved up to 4th place individually.

The shooting event was won by Khalid of Bahrain with 198, one target point ahead of Masala (ITA) and Kim (KOR). 15 competitors scored 1000+ but only two of the final top six managed to score well –Massullo (ITA) 196 and Yagorashvili (URS) 192. Janos Martinek (HUN) appeared to be throwing away his lead by scoring only 188. The British team averaged 188, slightly better than the previous year, but still dropped to 5th overall. After four events, Italy had a 24 point lead over Hungary with USSR now in 3rd place, a great achievement for the Soviet team after their terrible riding experience.

The final run was won by Attila Mizser (HUN) in 12:37 with Milan Kadlec (TCH) running 12:46. Janos Martinek (HUN), however, by managing 5th place in the run, made up for his poor shoot and rather surprisingly took the individual title ahead of Carlo Massullo (ITA) and Vaho Yagorashvili (URS). In their wake were some great names: Mizsér (HUN) -1985 World Champion - 4th; Bouzou (FRA) -1987 World Champion- 8th; Masala (ITA) –defending 1984 Olympic Champion- 10th; Kadlec (TCH)- 1987 silver medallist – 11th; Nieman (USA) - 1979 World Champion- 18th; Rasmuson -1984 Olympic silver medallist – 22nd; and making his debut, Arkadiusz Skryzpaszek (POL) – the future 1992 Olympic Champion - 23rd. It was also good to see two Koreans, Kim Myeong-Geon and Gang Gyeong-Hyo, making their mark by coming 12th and 13th respectively in their home country.

Hungary won the running event ahead of Mexico. The British team without fourth man Peter Hart only finished 3rd in the running event (Brookhouse 9th, Phelps 11th, Mahony 29th) but it was enough to pull them up to 3rd place overall to win the bronze medal behind Hungary and Italy and eight points ahead of France. Jöel

1988 Seoul: Great Britain's bronze medal team (l-r: Graham Brookhouse, Dominic Mahony, Richard Phelps).

Bouzou very generously congratulated the British team by saying 'I do not mind losing to you because I know you are sportsmen.' However, two days later, when Mahony and Phelps were called before the IOC Medical Commission over drug test discrepancies, Bouzou was changing his mind and suddenly becoming interested in the prospect of the French taking the bronze by default for the second time in Olympic history (they took the bronze when Sweden were disqualified in 1968). Fortunately for the British, there was no evidence at all of drug use, the team retained its bronze medal and Bouzou his faith in British sportsmanship. The only two disqualifications, in fact, were Jorge Quesada (SPA) for using beta-blockers in the shooting (an event in which he only came 59th with a score of 184) and Alex Watson (AUS) who was deemed to have had too much caffeine in his blood.

1988 Women's World Championships: Warsaw (POL)

With a big turnout of 55 athletes representing 22 nations in Warsaw, Poland and Dorota Idzi (POL) won team and individual events on home soil. World Champion for the previous two years, Irene Kiseleva (URS), came 2nd and other experienced athletes filled the other top places – Caroline Delemer (FRA) 3rd; Sabine Krapf (FRG) 4th; Eva Fjellerup (DEN) 6th. Italy and France took the other team medals and Great Britain (Wendy Norman 15th, Louise Ball 20th, and Sarah Cox 21st) finished in 6th place. This marked the end of an 11 year career for Wendy Norman. She had first made her mark coming 5th in the 1978 World Cup as a 13 year old schoolgirl. She was a leading world competitor throughout the 1980s, having been World Champion in 1982. Wendy's big 'if' was always her shooting event and frequently, had she shot a little better, no one would have come near her in the final standings. Appropriately, she finished her career by winning the last of her seven British Championships in 1988.

1989 Men's World Championships: Budapest (HUN)

The return to Budapest for the World Championships was a big occasion and was marked by several changes in the sport. Firstly, the competition reverted to a four day event in the order: fencing, swimming, shooting, running and riding with the swim and shoot being held on the same day. Fortunately, a strong field of Hungarian horses did not cause havoc on the final day. Secondly, it was the first year of the ring targets which were intended to make the shooting harder and open up the scores a little. Attila Mizsér's (HUN) startling winning score of 196, however, suggested that this was going to be a tricky job. The new target score for 1000 points was 182 +/- 15 points per target point. Finally, 1989 marked the introduction of the team relay which had been trialled in the European Championships.

A field of 66 representing 26 countries made for a tough competition. Fábián (HUN) won the fencing (1085), and Yagorashvili (URS) the swimming (3:14.2). Barely 100 points separated the top six at the end. The final order was: 1st Fábián 5654; 2nd Mizsér 5616; 3rd Peter Blazek (TCH) 5615. Iliev (BUL), back from his 30 month ban, scored 5588 for 4th place, just a single point ahead of Richard Phelps who was 5th with 5587; 6th was Yagorashvili. The next few finishers were all big names: Kadlec, Starostin, Massullo, Bouzou, and Olympic Champion, Martinek, the worst of the Hungarians in 11th place. Hungary won the team and the relay event to complete a very successful competition for the home country.

The British team had a full contingent in Budapest: Martin Dawe (Manager); Robbie Phelps (Coach); Andy Jackson (Physio); John Llewellyn (Fencing Coach); Jabina Maslin (Riding Coach); Keith Clark (UIPM Council Member); Terry Bunyard (MPAGB President); and Pat Chaffey (General Secretary). The pentathletes, fresh from success in the Nordic Cup consisted of Richard Phelps, Graham Brookhouse, and Greg Whyte with Peter Hart as fourth man. Dominic Mahony's military duties kept him out of the team. The team finished 7th in the team event (Phelps 5th, Brookhouse 20th, Whyte 36th) and, since the top ten teams qualified for the inaugural Team Relay event, came 9th in the relay. Of course, Richard Phelps' 5th place showed his continued world-class level (Ride 1040, Fence 932, Swim 3:16.4, Run 13:03). Unusually, the team only finished 6th in the running event but a strong swim (Brookhouse 3:16.6, Whyte 3:21.7) produced a team win in that event.

1989 Women's World Championships: Wiener Neustadt (AUT)

The new targets saw Temesi (HUN) score 192 to win that event but, despite having broken her wrist in May of that year and returning from a drugs ban, Lori Norwood won the running event and finished with a 1070 ride to become USA's first Women's World Champion. Hungary grabbed their first medal when young Iren Kovacs took the silver and the experienced Caroline Delemer (FRA) once again took the bronze medal. World Champion Dorota Idzi (POL) could only finish 6th but Poland retained the team event ahead of USA and Italy. The British team (Kath Young 19th, Sarah Cox 39th and Teresa Purton 40th) came 11th. Teresa Purton had been a powerful force in Women's Modern Pentathlon in the 1980s and this was her final competition. Always a good runner, over the years she attained a very high level in fencing, too. She later married Richard Phelps.

In the first-ever Junior Women's Championship, Iren Kovacs was undisputed champion, winning the fencing (1075) and the swimming (2:13) events. Her teammate Anita Heilig was 2nd and the Hungarian team, therefore, won its first major women's competition.

British developments in the 1980s

The British Championships, often won by someone other than the obvious favourite, were nevertheless dominated by two people in the 1980s. In the men's event, Richard Phelps won six titles and, in the women's event, Wendy Norman won five titles. Graham Brookhouse won two titles and Mike Mumford and Peter Whiteside confounded the opposition in 1980 and 1985 by winning while not being selected for the Olympic / World Championships that year. Teresa Purton won three titles and Ali Hollington and Janet Savage one apiece.

Administratively, on the domestic front, two major challenges perennially affect funding. Financial support comes as a result of either high membership numbers or successful international results. In the 1980s, MPAGB membership remained at about 550 and, with 133 clubs affiliated, this showed a very active presence in the sport. Of course the numbers were tiny compared to single sports like swimming or horse riding but that is an inevitable consequence of the multi-specialised nature of Modern Pentathlon and the Sports Council was sensitive to this fact. For individual athletes, the Sports Aid Foundation continued to give grants but only to world-class performers.

The weight of wrestling with these problems always falls on the shoulders of a relatively small number of people who make up the committees. Often such people come into the sport because they have children involved and then, when their children retire, out of a generosity of spirit find it difficult to extricate themselves from the useful roles they have been given. These are the great servants of Modern Pentathlon in every country around the world. In Britain by the end of the 1980s the titles 'President' and 'Chairman' had became interchangeable. Keith Clark took over the leadership of MPAGB from Errol Lonsdale in 1983 who, nevertheless, continued to edit the *Broadsheet*. Some form of magazine or yearbook is essential both for information and the maintenance of records and, at an approximate cost of £1000 per year, such a periodical was difficult to sustain.

By the end of the decade, Terry Bunyard, who had led the Coaching Committee, took over as President/ Chairman. Jim Fox was Vice-Chairman for five years before surrendering that position to Ron Bright and then Catie Banks. The post of Secretary was held by Martin Grieves, Bernie Moss and Eileen Tayler, all of whom had responsibilities with the national teams as well. John Felix took over the role of Treasurer and he was followed by Michael Proudfoot who brought in Grant Thornton as auditors for a more professional approach before handing over the post to Ian Stenhouse. The finances of the Association had been poorly handled in the early 1980s and the progress in MPAGB finances was very much due to careful stewardship of these tasks. From an annual loss of £434 in 1984, finances steadily accumulated so that, by 1987, there was actually a surplus of £21,302. Michael Proudfoot was at lengths to point out that, although an annual turnover of about £16,000 per year seemed a lot, the use of the money provided by the Sports Council and sponsors like Allied Breweries was always highly constrained and for very specific projects. It was not money that the MPAGB was free to spend as it wished. Long-term servants of the MPAGB like Bridget Robbie worked on membership numbers and our present Chairman, Tony Temple, was able to shape decisions made at the AGMs to a more logical conclusion thanks to his legal expertise. All these volunteers gave their services free of charge.

There was also a change in the MPAGB's professional staff. Doreen Dew, who married John and became Doreen Felix during this period, retired as Administrative Officer and was replaced by Pat Chaffey. This involved a move of the office from Purley to Baughurst. The post of National Development Officer was taken on by Danny Nightingale in 1986. It was a job that took him regularly into distant parts of Scotland and Wales as well as touring England extensively. In 1989, he passed on the post to Peter Hart who would add stability to the job, holding it for the next 20 years.

Among the decisions made during that period was approval for the UIPM's proposal to make the riding event the last of the five events. Ron Bright argued that competitors preferred this. The MPAGB strongly rejected an FIE proposal that Women's epée should be replaced by foil in Modern Pentathlon. The endurance demands of the Iron Man Triathlon competitions emerging in the early 1980s were attractive to pentathletes but the money prizes on offer had to be scrutinized carefully. Professionalism was still not part of our way of life.

Finally, a tragic event in 1983 should be recorded. John Warburn, an RAF Flight Lieutenant and long-time pentathlete was killed in a fencing accident when his opponent's broken blade slipped under his mask and severed his carotid artery. This, of course, shocked everyone in the sport and in part contributed to the tightening of laws during the 1980s regarding the strength and flexibility of epée blades used.

Chapter Nine: 1990-99

'If Richard Phelps in 5th place had gained only four more points he would have won a bronze medal, with five more he'd have won the silver, and with just 43 more he'd have been World Champion.' 1990 World Championships.

The 1990s was a crucial period for the survival of Modern Pentathlon. Its place in the Olympic movement was placed under scrutiny as never before. It was no longer sufficient to argue tradition and the sport's special place in the heart of Baron de Coubertin; the new face of the IOC was 'modernism' with an emphasis on being commercial at all costs. Those hard-working UIPM officials who fought tooth and nail for our sport's survival deserve our special thanks for their efforts and their ability to turn Modern Pentathlon into the exciting competition it is today. This was a decade in which a huge variety of new competitions filled the programme. Both men and women took part in a World Cup tour of competitions around the world for which sponsors provided cash prizes. Age group competitions proliferated as did regional events and the Team Relay became an essential component of Modern Pentathlon life.

The birth of the modern sport

In 1990, in an article in *Olympic Review*, Vitaly Smirnov, Chairman of the IOC's Programme Commission, explained how the IOC intended to cut back on the number of events in the Olympic Games. There had been no review of procedures since 1973 and, he argued, changes were long overdue. The comments in the article most pertinent to Modern Pentathlon were as follows: firstly, team events in which the scores were merely an accumulation of individual scores were regarded as less worthwhile than those based on 'collective efforts' like hockey or football. Secondly, the Olympic charter stipulated that multiple events which demanded the same skills and training methods, for instance, the many freestyle swimming and some individual gymnastic events, ought to be reduced in number. On both these counts, the team event in Modern Pentathlon was doomed.

Much less specific was the IOC argument that 'modern trends' demanded that Olympic sports should be 'popular, inexpensive, and accessible'. Modern Pentathlon had for many years been conscious of the need to recruit new members world-wide and to make the sport more easily understood by the public but now quite specific evidence was needed of these developments in our sport. Smirnov's report also pointed out that 90% of countries competing in the Olympic Games only took part in a maximum of five sports. Though wanting to achieve wider participation in other sports by these countries, the IOC would also need to be assured that high Olympic standards could be maintained everywhere. So, if Modern Pentathlon was going to win hearts and minds around the world, it would need to show that its burgeoning number of global participants could also compete at the highest standards.

The UIPM was already preparing plans for a one-day event for both men and women to increase spectator interest and 'telegenicity'. Anticipating the threat to the men's team event, they brought forward plans to substitute the team event with the relay which was already proving successful in World Championships. Most persuasive of all was the UIPM's eagerness that a women's event be included in the Olympic Games. The UIPM committee members were well aware that adding women would inevitably result in a reduction in the number of men allowed to compete, but the IOC requirement that a sport be popular and accessible played directly into the UIPM's case for the inclusion of women.

However, a devastating letter arrived at UIPM headquarters on 28th August 1990. It was addressed to UIPM President, Igor Novikov and written by Gilbert Felli, IOC Sports Director. Felli regretted that, in the 1996 Olympic Modern Pentathlon, there would be no men's team event, no women's event and no relay team event. This was a huge disappointment for Modern Pentathlon and even elicited a letter to the IOC from retired President, Sven Thofelt, expressing his dismay.

All the points raised in Smirnov's article had been dealt with admirably by the UIPM. Very conscious that their own athletes were among the most strident in their demands for modernisation, they went back to the drawing board and began providing clear evidence of their modernising process.

New events, new rules

Firstly, in decisive changes agreed at the crucial General Assembly in Amelie les Bains in November 1992, the competition would, from 1993 onwards, be a one-day event for both men and women. As soon as it was possible to arrange, air pistol or laser gun would be used for shooting, swim times would be seeded so that the best swimmers raced together in the final heat, the length of the fencing bout would be reduced to one minute, and the running would be either a handicap or pack start. Riding would take place over a simplified course of only 350 to 400 metres in length with a bogey time of two minutes. There would be 12 jumps, including a double and a treble. The proposals for the Team Relay answered the demand that team events be 'collective efforts' and certainly increased the spectator excitement.

Finally, Ivan Popov's persuasive article put a convincing case for the inclusion of women in the Olympic Modern Pentathlon. He emphasized the rapidly increasing numbers, the high standards, and the wide participation with detailed statistical backing. The most convincing argument of all was that the addition of a women's competition would, given the proposed one-day event for each competition, require no extra time, no additional numbers, facilities, horses or officials. The Olympic competition, as proposed, would still only be four days long even with a men's and women's individual event and team relays for men and women.

Klaus Schormann became UIPM President in 1993, replacing Igor Novikov and the interim Anders Besseberg, who oversaw the formal separation of Modern Pentathlon and Biathlon to its completion in July 1993. Immediately, Schormann's energy and business acumen were evident in the plans made by the UIPM. He initially worked with Erik Boek and Eivind Bo Sorensen who each took the role of Secretary-General for a time but, when ex-World Champion, Jöel Bouzou took over the post at the Congress in Budapest in 1996, the UIPM established a successful working partnership that has endured until the present day.

After the first one-day World Championship in Darmstadt (Schormann's home town) in 1993, the new President was able to proclaim that both men's and women's events had had an entire hour's coverage each on Eurosport TV, that links to the media were more effective than ever before and that the rapid promotion of youth events in the sport was clear evidence of the future success of Modern Pentathlon. He urged the participation of all concerned in this brave new world with this exhortation:

'I appeal to all member associations of the UIPM, in solidarity to our athletes, to use every possibility to open the eyes of the 'Olympic World' and to prove with convincing arguments that Modern Pentathlon must have its place in the Olympic family as a permanent Olympic Sport.'

1990 Men's World Championships: Lahti (FIN)

This was the first return to Finland for Modern Pentathlon since the 1952 Olympics and 65 competitors from 26 countries were represented in a competition that was held over three days. This compression was the result of a plea from the organisers of the Goodwill Games in Seattle which had intended to feature many of the leading pentathletes and was due to begin just a few days later. It meant that the fencing took place on day one, the swim and shoot on day two and the run and ride on day three. The most extraordinary feature of this competition was that, by the end, only 100 points separated the top 11 competitors. If Richard Phelps in 5th place had gained only four more points he would have won a bronze medal, with five more he'd have won the silver, and with just 43 more he'd have been World Champion. When you consider that he shot only 185 and rode only 980 points, these wafer-thin points differences would be enough to give permanent insomnia to anyone but a seasoned pentathlete.

Rob Stull (USA) won the fencing with 1075, Vaho Yagorashvili (URS) won the swim in 3:13.4 with the two Italians, Gianluca Tiberti and Cesare Toraldo, just behind. Gozdziak (POL) won the shoot with 195 ahead of Starostin (194) and Mizsér (193). Manuel Barroso (POR) won the first of three consecutive running events (1990, 1991, 1992) in 12:38 with Kadlec (TCH) running 12:48. The horses for the final riding event were a mixture of Finnish and Russian mounts. There were only three zero scores but there was also a wide range of scores between 600 and the six who scored 1100. The fact that the Soviet Union team had a lead of over 600 points before the ride and finally won by just six points gives you some idea of the topsy-turvy world created on the final day. Among the 1100 rides was Gianluca Tiberti who jumped from 10th position after four events to take a thoroughly unexpected gold medal.

The final totals were: Tiberti (ITA) 5441; Starostin (URS) 5403; Kadlec (TCH) 5402; Mizsér (HUN) 5401; and Phelps (GBR) 5398. Zenovka (URS) scored only 728 in the riding and dropped from top position out of the reckoning. The USSR clung on to team victory ahead of Italy and Poland. Hungary dropped to 4th position with a riding disaster comparable to that of the USSR. The final individual positions for Hungary, a team made up entirely of ex-World and Olympic Champions, were Mizsér 4th, Martinek 26th and Fábián 29th. This gave them only 12 points more than the British team who finished 5th overall (Phelps 5th, Mahony 24th, Brookhouse 30th). Immediately afterwards, Martin Dawe, the British Manager, and Richard Phelps along with a number of other competitors, jumped on a plane to get to Seattle for the Goodwill Games. Indeed, with the inaugural Men's World Cup Series having begun this year and won in 1990 by Peter Steinmann (SUI), the fixture list was becoming very crowded and was rapidly introducing pentathletes and officials to a new jet-set lifestyle.

Eduard Zenovka

The young Russian, Eduard Zenovka, was one of the most extraordinary pentathletes of the 1990s. He had come to prominence by winning a silver medal (1988) and then a gold medal (1989) in the World Junior Championships. He, more than anyone in Modern Pentathlon, must have had a poor opinion of the decision to make riding the final event since, in both the 1990 and 1991 World Championships and in the 1992 Olympic Games, he led the field after four events and on each occasion saw that lead slip away as a result of his poor riding scores. The third of these losses cost him the Olympic title in 1992 when he scored only 736 in the final riding event. A few months after that sporting disaster, in February 1993, this hugely talented but accident-prone athlete made the worst mistake of his life. He had been drinking heavily, even though it was only noon, when he drove his car into the path of an oncoming truck. His passenger, Oksana Kostina, the 1992 World Rhythmic Gymnastics Champion, was killed and Zenovka was in a coma for some time and lost a kidney.

Somehow, Zenovka recovered and in Atlanta in 1996, despite having handled his horse well, produced the top score in the shooting, and been the best runner in the field, he stumbled in the final stages to let slip his almost-certain grip on a second Olympic gold medal as Alex Parygin, the Kazakhstani athlete, overtook him in the final strides. Zenovka continued to compete for the rest of the 1990s and, indeed, his final tally of medals was impressive: Olympic individual silver and bronze (1996 and 1992); Olympic team gold (1992); World Championships team gold (1990, 1991), team bronze (1997) and Relay silver (1999).

1990 Women's World Championships: Linköping (SWE)

One woman dominated Modern Pentathlon in the early 1990s: Eva Fjellerup put Denmark on the sport's map by winning four of the next five World Championships. In the inaugural 1981 World Championships, Eva had scored an ignominious zero in the riding to finish last and, throughout the 1980s, had hovered at about 13th in the final rankings but for her, as for so many of the top women of the time, this long apprenticeship proved enormously valuable. Her teammate, Pernille Svarre also scored a zero in her ride in 1983 but went on to become World Champion, too, in 2000. In Linköping, the riding event presented no problems for all but three of the 44 competitors. In winning, Fjellerup pushed the previous two champions, Lori Norwood (USA) and Dorota Idzi (POL) into silver and bronze medal positions. In the team event, Poland established a similar domination during this period by beating, in 1990, USSR and West Germany for the gold medal in the team event.

1991 Men's World Championships: San Antonio (USA)

San Antonio jumped in at the last minute to rescue the event when Spokane, the original host city, withdrew. Italian, Cesare Toraldo had followed Gianluca Tiberti's World Championship victory by taking the 1991 World Cup series but 1991 would not be the Italians' year for World Championship success. Frenchmen, Clergeau and Ruer won the fencing and swimming events (1030 and 3:15.49). There was a kind of *déjà vu* of 1990 in the other events with Gozdziak (POL) winning the shoot with 195 again and Barroso (POL) beating Kadlec (TCH) by a similar margin in the run as he had the previous year. This was a final outing for the great Czech runner and 1990 bronze medallist, Milan Kadlec, who was unable to qualify for the 1992 Olympics and soon retired. Sadly, Kadlec died at the very early age of only 41 and a youth competition is held annually in his memory in the Czech Republic each year. Once again, Zenovka (URS) led before the final riding event but could only finish 5th overall with a riding score of 868.

The World Champion in this critical pre-Olympic year was Arkadius Skrzypaszek (POL) who took the title ahead of Peter Steinmann (SUI) and Adam Madaras (HUN). Once again the USSR, in the final year of competition before the Soviet Empire dissolved, hung on to take the team title from Poland by 10 points. Hungary took the bronze medal with Madaras 3rd, Fábián 21st and Mizsér 31st. The British team had a disappointing final World Championships before the Barcelona Olympics: Phelps 20th, Whyte 39th, and Brookhouse 40th.

1991 Women's World Championships: Sydney (AUS)

53 competitors from 16 countries took part in Sydney. Though Sophie Moressee (FRA) convincingly won the fencing (1126) and Wang Li (CHN) shot 194, Eva Fjellerup's margin of victory was almost 600 points over Caroline Delemer (FRA) who improved on her 1988 and 1989 bronze medals by taking the silver in Sydney. Cristina Minelli (ITA) won the bronze medal and her team won 2nd place behind the victorious Polish team while France took the team bronze medal.

1992 Olympic Games: Barcelona (ESP)

Perhaps the formation of the European Modern Pentathlon Union in 1991 came about partly because the new Olympic qualifying rules sought to encourage participation from every corner of the world. This meant, to some extent, that the European pentathletes, by far the strongest and most numerous of the world's top performers, had to take part in many competitions before Barcelona in an effort to accumulate points for the world rankings list. This was their best means of qualifying. For Great Britain, Graham Brookhouse's win in the Corby World Cup meeting turned him into our first qualifier and in the same competition, the British team (Brookhouse, Phelps, Mahony) hinted at possible Olympic success by finishing a single point behind the Hungarian winners.

The advent of Triathlon in the Olympic programme, with its more instantly accessible events, put more pressure on Modern Pentathlon to develop into an exciting spectator sport as quickly as possible. Barcelona was the last occasion in which an Olympic team event would be contested and the upper limit of 66 individuals would be more than halved four years later. However, in Barcelona, 30 nations were represented including Peru, Guatemala, South Africa, China, and Uraguay. With the break-up of the Soviet Union, a Commonwealth of Independent States (EUN) formed a team of the larger Soviet republics while the Baltic states, Estonia, Latvia and Lithuania all entered separately. This meant that no fewer than ten former Soviet Union athletes were competing in Barcelona and, by 1994, this number had doubled, increasing the overall standard considerably.

The competition retained its position at the beginning of the Olympic programme for the final time and took place over four days: fence, swim/shoot, run, and ride. The leading contenders were the reigning World Champion, Skrzypaszek (POL), Steinmann (SUI), Starostin (EUN) in his final competition after 14 years at the top, Zenovka (EUN), Mizsér (HUN) and Phelps (GBR). Such was the Hungarians' strength in depth that neither Adam Madaras, the previous year's bronze medallist, nor Akos Hanzély, the 1992 World Cup winner, was included in their team. Instead, Hungary opted for Miszér, Fábián and Kálnoki Kis. The CIS / EUN team had Starostin, Zenkova, and the 20 year old 1991 World Junior Champion, Dmitry Svatkovsky. Two ex-World Champions in the field retiring after the Games were Jöel Bouzou (aged 36) and Carlo Massullo (aged 34) who finished 17th and 12th respectively.

In the cavernous Palau Metallurgia on day one, Fábián (HUN) showed his experience by winning the fencing (1034) ahead of Skrzypaszek (1000). On day two, Gintaras Staskevicius (LTU) won the swimming in 3:10.4 and Zenovka won the shoot with 198. Poor

Fábián dropped from 1st position to 18th after the shooting with a dreadful 170 score. On day three, Manuel Barroso, for the third year in succession, won the run (12:26). On day four, the final riding event was held at the elegant Club Real Polo. With only the riding remaining, Zenovka had a 106 point lead over Skrzypaszek and 171 over Mizsér. The horses, though largely competent, were not consistently so and there were some riding disasters – Phelps 900, Fábián 800, Kálnoki Kis 798, and Ruer (FRA) 605. By far the most shocking, though, was Eduard Zenovka's 736. After a number of refusals and knockdowns, he failed to put his helmet back on after a fall and continued to ride, for which many felt he should have been eliminated. His feeble final score was, nevertheless, enough to win him the bronze medal, so superior had he been in the other events. The new Olympic Champion, however, was Arkadiusz Skrzypaszek (POL), the first reigning World Champion to win the Olympic title the following year since Lasse Hall (SWE) had done so in 1952. At only 24, Skrzypaszek then retired with two Olympic gold medals, the Polish team (Skrzypaszek 1st, Gozdziak 10th and Czyzowicz 19th) having beaten the Commonwealth of Independent States (EUN) and Italian teams into 2nd and 3rd places. Hungary's disastrous riding score dropped them out of the medals into 5th place behind USA and one place ahead of Great Britain. Individually, Attila Mizsér (HUN) took the silver medal ahead of Zenovka and 1980 Olympic Champion, Anatoli Starostin, in his final competition, who finished 4th.

For Great Britain, Graham Brookhouse's 8th position was outstanding. He retained a consistency across the other events that enhanced his strong swim and was followed by Richard Phelps in 13th place and Dominic Mahony in 36th. The team had all swum season's best times in Barcelona and Phelps had recorded his best ever time of 3:15.3 but had lost six place positions with his 900 riding score.

1992 Women's World Championships: Budapest (HUN)

Having won the previous three World Junior titles, Iren Kovács (HUN) ought to have been a strong contender on home soil. Somehow, though, she never quite fulfilled that early promise. Iren finally finished 6th behind an impressively experienced field. Eva Fjellerup unexpectedly dropped out of contention this year and Iwona Kowalewska (POL) won the fencing (1088) ahead of experienced German pentathlete, Sabine Krapf (1066) and the equally experienced Frenchwoman, Sophie Moressee (1022). Kovács won the swim in 2: 14.9 and Zhana Dolgacheva (BLR) won the run in 6:46.6. In the final reckoning, it was Kowalewska who took the gold medal ahead of Dolgacheva and Dorota Idzi (POL). In 4th and 5th places were Sabine Krapf and Caroline Delemer. Of course, Poland once again won the team event but Hungary made the most of home advantage and took the silver ahead of Germany. The British team (Sara Cox 21st, Kate Houston 23rd, Liz Kipling 26th) finished 5th. Sophie Moressee (FRA) had been a major force in women's pentathlon throughout the 1980s as well as winning her Team Epée Olympic gold medal in Atlanta in 1996.

1993 World Championships: Darmstadt (GER)
Men - Richard Phelps is World Champion

The turmoil of rule changes persisted and this was the first World Championship to take place on a single day.

Richard Phelps (GBR): World Champion 1993.

It also marked the beginning of joint Men's and Women's World Championships being held at the same venue, a tradition that persists to the present day. For one athlete in particular, however, the greater the chaos the more he felt at home. Richard Phelps had begun the year with success in Australia but, at the European Championships ride, he had fallen badly and torn the ligaments in his shoulder. Though he was the only British qualifier of the 32 competing in Darmstadt, he spent six weeks without training in four of the five events and went on holiday to Majorca, keeping generally fit with a little triathlon. When he arrived in Darmstadt he was fully expecting to achieve nothing. True, of the 12 who had beaten him in Barcelona the year before, only Mizsér (HUN), Gostigian (USA) and Deleigne (FRA) were present in Darmstadt but Fábián (HUN), Toraldo (ITA) and Ruer (FRA) were all having good seasons.

The radical reduction of competitor numbers from 66 (1992) to 32 in Darmstadt was made more complex by each country being allowed a maximum of only two competitors. There was no team event and the team relay prefaced the individual competition. Though the relay event was destined to become a way of giving second-strings a run out, in Darmstadt, the medallists - Hungary, France and Italy – fielded strong teams. Phelps, meanwhile, watched from the stands. Later he was to appreciate the low-key nature of his experience in Darmstadt. He had had the benefit of psychologists, masseurs, and a whole support team at the Olympics but such backing can also bring added expectation and therefore pressure. With only his uncle, Robbie Phelps as coach and Martin Dawe as manager with him in Darmstadt, he was able to relax more.

The first event was the shooting, an event that had often let him down in the past, and Phelps shot 193. Only Ismo Marjunen (FIN) shot better (194). Though Ruer and Toraldo swam better than Phelps and Staskevicius (LTU) swam 3:11.5, Richard's 3:21.5 kept him in touch. Despite being six seconds down on his 1992 performance, his lack of expectation lent a far better sense of pacing to both his swim and his run in this competition. His 880 fencing score fell below his fine Olympic effort the previous year and Laszlo Fábián's winning 1120 gave the Hungarian a 148 point lead over Phelps after three events. The running event was a pack start (a major deviation from de Coubertin's intention) and this played directly into the hands of a strong runner like Phelps. He finished 2nd in 12:21, just one second behind Peter Steinmann (SUI) thus reducing Fabian's overall lead to 40 points.

Concluding with the riding event is a concession to spectators but not to pentathletes. Richard drew a difficult horse which had not gone well in the first round. The advice he got from Uncle Rob proved to be excellent and he rode a clear round for 1100 points. There have been many family coaching relationships in Modern Pentathlon and family tensions can often prove detrimental to such a set-up. In the early years of Richard's international career, such a relationship was not always helpful but by 1993, Richard is the first to admit, it was a coaching relationship that really worked well and one for which he is grateful. Though 20 out of the 32 competitors scored over 1000 points in the ride, Lazslo Fábián wasn't one of them. He scored 974 and slipped into the silver medal position, ahead of Sebastien Deleigne but behind Great Britain's first and only male World Champion, Richard Phelps.

In an interview after Darmstadt with Andrew Longmore in *The Times*, Richard was quoted as saying 'I just don't rate full-time training'. Realising that driving all over the place in a hectic rush to gain experience was not for him he added, 'Stuff it, I'm going to stay where I am, relax and train at the level I enjoy.' For all those coaches who might throw up their hands in horror at such a concept, it should be noted that Richard Phelps' career in Modern Pentathlon was a very long one. By the time he became World Champion in 1993, he had been competing for 21 years. He was to continue in the sport for a further seven years. Though the tale behind his becoming World Champion against all the odds is the stuff of boys' comic books, when he climbed on to that podium in Darmstadt, he was carrying the experience of many years at the highest level, not the training of just the past few weeks. His position as a World Champion has been underrated in the history of British sport and that is as much to do with Richard's self-effacing, good-humoured nature as it is with the appalling neglect of his achievements by the British press.

Women

The women's and men's competitions were held at the same venue in 1993 thus establishing a tradition which remained for the following years. Both were experiencing the limit of 32 competitors and the absence of a team event. Darmstadt represented a return to dominance for Eva Fjellerup who elbowed the 1992 Champion, Kowalewska, back into 2nd place with Dorota Idzi continuing to be a force in the bronze medal position. Kowalewska had begun impressively by winning the fencing with 1150 points but Fjellerup edged ahead to reclaim her title. In the absence of a team event, the all-conquering Polish team surprisingly only finished 8th in the Relay which was won by Russia.

Further modernisation

In November of 1993, IOC President Juan Samaranch, attended the UIPM Executive meeting in Lausanne and was warmly enthusiastic about the hard work the UIPM had put in to make the necessary changes to the sport. But there was much more to come. 1994 was the inaugural year for Youth A (18 and under) and Youth B (16 and under) competitions and the first year of the annual Asian Championships. The evidence that these new competitions would produce lasting benefits was there in the very first year. Finishing 3rd and 5th in the Youth B competition were two future Senior World Champions, Viktor Horvath (2007) and Michal Sedlecky (2002).

1994 also marked significant changes to the World Championship structure. For the first time, in both men's and women's events, there would be semi-finals in which there would be no riding event. For the women this involved two semi-finals of 31 and 32 athletes with the top 16 in each qualifying for the final. In the men's event, the 96 athletes were divided into four semi-finals with the top eight in each qualifying for the final. This latter division proved rather unsatisfactory since, with only eight to qualify, the luck of the draw was more in evidence. Indeed, one man eliminated by this method was 1985 World Champion and 1992 Olympic silver medalist, Attila Mizsér. Relay and team events also accompanied the individual competitions. The other major change to the sport was the replacement of 0.22 pistols with air pistols. After 82 years of turning targets, the new targets would be static throughout at a distance of ten metres. The competitor had 40 seconds in which to fire each shot and, since the test still involved 20 shots, the new 1000 point bogey was 172 with +/- 15 points per target score.

Great Britain's role in the changes

Klaus Schormann's appeal to all to participate in these changes was well-received in Britain. The MPAGB felt it had much to offer international developments and no fewer than six of our most experienced officials stood for election to UIPM committees: Terry Bunyard (Information), Eileen Tayler (Women), Dominic Mahony (Athletes), Martin Dawe (Marketing), Martin Grieves (Technical) and Keith Clark (Statutes).

Furthermore, in 1994, as Chairman of the Athletes' Committee, Dominic Mahony, together with World

Champion, Eva Fjellerup, were given the privilege of addressing the IOC Centennial Congress in Paris. Dominic explained how 'eager for modernisation' the athletes were and urged the IOC to consider ways of managing rather than reducing the number of Olympic sports. He argued that 'the greatest good is done when the greatest number take part.' Eva spoke movingly of the discrimination against women that still existed in sport though not, in her experience, in other aspects of life. Both athletes' speeches were well-received.

This success was played against a bleaker background in Great Britain in the mid-1990s. The Sports Council cut MPAGB's funding significantly, threatening, for a time, its very survival. Constantly aware that funding was the lifeblood of any sport, MPAGB officials fought hard to keep the ship afloat. The hard-pressed chairmen during this difficult period were Terry Bunyard and Catie Banks and then, in 1996, Jim Fox was persuaded to take on the role.

Jim's public profile was so strong in Great Britain that it was a critical move. Newspaper interviews with Fox portrayed the sport which he embodied as slightly old-fashioned and delightfully eccentric, qualities which appealed to the British public. People outside the sport were becoming aware of the warm, diffidently heroic nature of the pentathlete and celebrating it. Respected sports journalist, Simon Barnes in an article entitled 'Cinq or Swim?' clarified what the sport represented in contrast to the increasingly materialist calculations of the IOC: 'Without such daftness, the Olympic Games has no heart, no soul, no depth, no bottom. And central to Olympic credibility is Modern Pentathlon.'

As so often happens, the silver lining to the cloud under which the MPAGB had been labouring was just around the corner. Lottery grants arrived for many sports in 1998 and this marked the beginning of sustained international success for British Modern Pentathlon. Jim Fox and his team had done their work admirably. Forced at the end of the 1990s, to relinquish his role as MPAGB Chairman because of the increasingly debilitating effects of his illness, the sport continued in a far better condition as a result of his leadership.

Military difficulties in the 1990s

The military organisations, too, were experiencing 'a wind of change' that was threatening the use of facilities including the Centre of Excellence at Arborfield. Cutbacks in military spending meant that military personnel were rarely free to pursue sport in the way they had in the past. Recruitment to the sport was a problem and, despite REME having bathed in the publicity of its pentathletes' success for many years, Modern Pentathlon was in danger of being side-lined. In 1993, a meeting of the Army MPA set out a strategy for recruitment and publicity. The Army Chairman, Colonel Allen, and the REME Chairman, Colonel Selby formulated the new approach but Major Bunyard and Capt Fox were, of course, so central to Modern Pentathlon that their views were sought. Though away on exercise and unable to be at the meeting, Capt Dominic Mahony sent an interesting letter to Mike Selby. In it he suggested an approach that had been at the heart of the very origins of the sport in Sweden way back in 1912: 'If Pentathlon can be established at key training units through which all soldiers (officers and other ranks) pass we should be able to restore the essential value of the sport to the military…' He cited Sandhurst as the obvious first venue for such an enterprise. Sandhurst had been central to the running of competitions and training for pentathletes for decades and the shift in emphasis to Arborfield had perhaps reduced Sandhurst's importance. As it turned out, by the end of the decade, developments had pushed the centre of gravity of Modern Pentathlon to Bath University where it still remains. However, a major event in September 2011 held under the auspices of ex-pentathlete, General Sir Peter Wall, brought many pentathletes old and new to Sandhurst to celebrate the possibility that it may well return to some of its former glories as a Modern Pentathlon venue.

1994 World Championships: Sheffield (GBR)
Men

Great Britain had been entrusted with hosting the second consecutive joint Men's and Women's World Championships in 1994 in Sheffield. The British men, Greg Whyte, Richard Phelps, and Graham Brookhouse all did extremely well to qualify for the final. Of course, everyone was hoping for Phelps to repeat his 1993 success but, as many in Modern Pentathlon know, the pressure of a home crowd is not always conducive to good performance. Add to that the entirely new experiences of semi-finals and static air pistol, and nobody could be certain who would perform the best. The new order in the final was shoot, fence, swim, ride, run though there had been no riding event in the semi-finals. Some felt, therefore, that this was not a proper test of the pentathlete since the 64 eliminated competitors would not even have attempted the riding phase. It has, however, become a pragmatic solution to the achieving of an efficient one-day event. A survey of pentathletes in

1994 revealed that there was extremely strong support for the UIPM's modernising changes. However, a fair majority also felt that they would prefer the run to conclude the competition and not the ride. From 1994, this desire was sensibly put into action.

In Sheffield, the top shooting score with the new weapons was 182. Fábián (HUN) and Tiidemann (EST) won the fencing with the surprisingly low score of 940 and Frontier (FRA) won the swimming in 3:10.5. But it turned out that the first World Champion in the new format would be 22 year old Moscow law student, Dmitri Svatkovsky. An excellent runner, he strode confidently to victory in the final event (12:16) to hold off Christophe Ruer (FRA) who took a deserved silver medal thus erasing the bitter memory of his 605 point ride two years previously in Barcelona. Janos Martinek who hadn't even been included in the official Hungarian team, confounded this selection decision by taking the bronze medal individually while the nominated team member, Attila Mizsér, surprisingly failed to even make the final. Peter Steinmann (SUI), Lazslo Fábián (HUN) and Sebastien Deleigne (FRA) completed the top six. Both Fábián and Mizsér retired in 1994.

The British team all swam strongly and were consistent enough in the other events to win the silver medal in the team event behind France. Their individual positions were Whyte 12th, Brookhouse 20th and Phelps 22nd. In the riding, Phelps only scored 844 and Brookhouse 969 so there was some room for improvement but the French team was sufficiently strong for these setbacks not to have made any difference. The qualification system rather threw the cat amongst the pigeons as far as the team event was concerned – Belarus took the bronze medal and Russia and Hungary only finished 4th and 6th. Hungary did, however, win the Relay event ahead of Poland and Russia.

Women

Eva Fjellerup confidently regained her World crown with 1000+ scores in all five events including a 1030 victory in the fencing. Zhana Dolgacheva (BLR), the winner of the running, came 2nd overall and Ernese Köblö (HUN) took bronze. Another Hungarian, Eszter Hortobagyi, came 4th only two weeks after becoming World Junior Champion. Other established names didn't fare so well. Despite winning the World Cup and coming 2nd in the World Junior event, Elizaveta Suvorova (RUS) finished only 25th. Dorota Idzi (POL) shot only 153 with her new air pistol and finished 16th behind Kowalska (POL) in 12th place and Delemer (FRA) in 15th.

The success of the two Hungarians only won them the bronze medal in the team event, however. The top two teams, Italy and Poland both finished with exactly 15, 352 points. Initially, Italy was awarded the win. Poland protested and a tie was declared. So Italy protested and finally became the acknowledged champions. The rules on sorting out such an eventuality had been in place for some time. For both individual and team events, in the event of a tie, the individual/team that wins the most events is the winner. In this case, Italy won the ride and Poland the fence. So then the positions in each event are calculated in a return to the pre-1954 placing method of scoring. This solution gave Italy the title.

No British woman pentathlete made the final in Sheffield which was a little embarrassing in front of a home crowd. The early 1990s had been a quiet time for British women but changes were underway. In the Junior World Championships the year before, the British team of Michelle Kimberley, Julia Allen and Liz Kipling had won a silver medal in the Relay. In 1994, the winner of the bronze medal in the Junior World Championships in Toledo was Kate Allenby who was to lead the revival of British fortunes in the modern sport.

Kate Allenby

Kate Allenby's decade-long (1994-2004) presence at the top of the sport encompassed no fewer than 23 medals – eight gold, seven silver and eight bronze –in Olympic Games, World Cup, European, and World Senior and Junior Championship Individual, Team and Relay competitions. She also won Commonwealth silver and two bronze medals in Fencing. She was, therefore, the central figure in the rise to power of a women's team that, by 2000, was the best in the world.

Kate came into the sport via the Pony Club as did all Great Britain's other Olympic women medallists, Steph Cook, Georgina Harland and Heather Fell. That riding background makes her less sceptical than others about the merits of the riding event and well aware that, despite the occasional scoring setback, it is a skill that needs to be developed. She believes that, in the short period that the pentathlete is in charge of a horse, it must be given confidence to perform at its best. Pentathletes also have a responsibility for the welfare of the horse and good riding demonstrates that concern to the world. That also provides essential publicity to help ensure a steady supply of competition horses.

Today, Allenby gives greatest credit for the eventual success of the women's team in the 1990s to Istvan Nemeth, the Hungarian former film stunt man, who has been a mainstay of British women's coaching ever since. By coordinating the disparate training regimes of athletes around the country in the early 1990s, he gave a central purpose to the women pentathletes and thus a focus for success. When Jan Bartu arrived in 1998, access to financial support and centralized training turned that early work into a medal-winning machine. Competition success became, if not quite a check-list, at least a manageable itinerary and the team spirit was never in any doubt.

With a hard-working team, injuries are an inevitable risk – Kate's Olympic bronze medal was won despite a bad shoulder injury. Some of Bartu's strategies for avoiding injury included winter skiing training on soft snow to avoid the jarring that running on hard ground causes. High-altitude training was also given great value in this period. Despite eyebrows being raised over its value as preparation for the heat of a Greek summer, our pentathletes arrived in Athens in 2004 in the peak of fitness as a result of this strategy.

After retiring in 2004, Kate was snapped up by Whitgift School with a brief to revive Modern Pentathlon there. John Felix, who had started the sport there in 1959 and produced a number of Junior internationals had, through illness, been forced to retire in the early 1980s. Kate sowed the seeds for the school's current success in international Youth A and B competitions.

Like many former international pentathletes, Kate Allenby is still very much involved in the sport.

She will be in evidence as an organiser of the fencing event in London 2012 where she hopes to witness the continuation of British women's unbroken run of medals in every Olympics.

1995 World Championships: Basel (SUI)
Men

The Swiss organisers managed to provide sufficient strong horses for the riding event to be part of the semi-finals as well as the final. Considering that, for the third year running, the Men's and Women's Senior Championships were held together, this horse provision was an astonishing achievement and not one that other hosts could possibly repeat in future years. One interesting feature of the riding in Basel which is difficult to explain was that, in the semi-finals 76 of the 96 participants rode 1000 points or better and yet in the final of 32, only 12 achieved the same feat. The run also reverted to a handicap start which was the system preferred by the athletes. The venue, the Centre des Sports St Jakob, had the great benefit of enabling all five events to take place within a few hundred metres of each other. This was a feature greatly sought after by the UIPM in order to make real sense of the continuous nature of the one-day event. It was also a feature notably absent from the following year's Olympic Games.

The 1995 Championships were also the first step in the new Qualification system for those precious 32 places in Atlanta for the Olympic Games the next year. The first three would automatically qualify for Atlanta and the next six finishers would qualify their countries for the same event. There would be further qualification opportunities in the Mexico City, Seoul and Rome legs of the World Cup.

While 4700 points was the minimum qualifying score for a World Championship, this figure was raised to 5100 for the Olympic Games. It was a difficult balancing act to encourage worldwide participation while maintaining a good standard of performance.

Dmitri Svatkovsky, the reigning World Champion and winner of the World Cup series in 1994, 1995 (and, for that matter, 1997 and 1998) was able to retain his title in Basel, winning the fencing event with 1000 points and producing a decisive all-round performance. Akos Hanzély (HUN) was 2nd and Cesare Toraldo (ITA), always a leading swimmer in the sport and a World Cup final winner in 1991 and 1992, was now the individual bronze medallist, squeezing out Peo Danielson (SWE) by just nine points.

By 1995 it was evident that the team event was becoming rather unusual as a result of the semi-final system. Indeed, the winner, Hungary, was the only country from which three competitors qualified for the final. This meant that their scores would naturally be superior because all three of their members would have a riding score. Elimination in the semi-final ensured only a four-event total. Hungary was followed by Italy and Poland (who won the relay event) for the other medals.

The British team managed to qualify two pentathletes for the final, Richard Phelps and Greg Whyte, though Simeon Robbie failed to get through. In finishing 8th, Phelps won himself a qualifying place for the Olympic Games the following year while Greg Whyte finished 25th. Other notable placings outside the medals were Parygin (KAZ) 10th, Deleigne (FRA) 21st, and the two Hungarians, Martinek and Kálnoki Kis, 22nd and 29th.

Andrejus Zadneprovskis

The winner of both the swimming and running events, Andrejus Zadneprovskis (LTU) (3:15 and 12.15) amassed a total of 2672 points for those two events in his first Senior World Championship. His pentathlon career was to be one of the most impressive in our history. Retiring in 2010, Zadneprovskis has amassed, in his career, numerous World Cup, European, World and Olympic medals, most significantly his two World titles (2000 and 2004) and his Olympic silver (2004) and bronze (2008) medals. He and his compatriot, Edvinas Krungolcas, who still competes today, were members of the winning Lithuania team at the 1994 World Junior Championships. The sporting longevity of these two athletes and the impact that Lithuania has made on the world of Modern Pentathlon as a result of their efforts is outstanding. Zadneprovskis is married to top female pentathlete, Laura Asadauskaite.

Women

Of course, all the qualifying procedures and competition changes which the men had experienced applied equally to the women. Despite winning the World Cup that year, Eva Fjellerup could only finish 8th, fencing just 760 points. Zhana Dolgacheva-Shubenok (BLR) and the eventual winner, Kerstin Danielsson (SWE) both fenced 1030 and Elizaveta Suvorova won the shooting with 182. Danielsson's win was something of a shock victory. She had finished 7th in the previous two years but made no significant mark in World Cup events or later World Championships. The final order was Danielsson (SWE), Dolgacheva-Shubenok (BLR), Idzi (POL), Hortabagyi (HUN) and Kowalewska (POL). Great Britain's only finalist was Kate Allenby who finished 25th although the British trio (Allenby, Andrews, Allen) did manage to finish 5th in the Relay. The team event was won by Poland.

A month later in Usti nad Labem, the Junior World Championships were won by Suvorova (RUS) who had finished 11th in the Senior competition after a riding score of only 871. The semi-finals in the Czech Republic had a peculiar structure over two days, designed to accommodate all competitors efficiently so that, in some cases, pentathletes shot immediately after fencing. In the final, the silver medal was won by Kate Allenby. She had conceded 60 points to Suvorova on both the fencing and riding events but a further 130 points in the final running event. Gwen Lewis finished 20th.

1996 Olympic Games: Atlanta (USA)

All the developments of the previous four years now came to the great stage itself to see if the world would approve. Preparations by the UIPM had been rigorous. In an effort to reduce IOC costs, the UIPM paid for the shipping of horses to the venue and were also prepared to pay part of the costs for the building of a swimming pool at Emory University on the understanding that all the events would be held there. They had also agreed with NBC that the final running event would be shown live on prime time television. In addition, the IOC belief that Modern Pentathlon was not a spectator sport was crushed when it became the first sport to be oversubscribed with 26,000 applications for tickets.

Disappointingly, ACOG, the Atlanta Organising Committee, refused to allow the Emory single site plan and that decision, though no fault of the UIPM, proved very problematic. It is one thing to visit different venues on successive days but with five events in one day, it was unreasonable to assume that huge numbers of spectators could travel from venue to venue easily. Even worse, the extreme security measures being applied by the organisers meant that several thousand spectators were refused permission to use vehicles to travel the five miles to the riding event. They would be obliged to walk, an impossible demand in the 90 F degree heat. Many were also mistakenly directed to the wrong venue for the shooting event.

Despite all these problems, when the competition actually took place, one dramatic event suddenly turned Modern Pentathlon into the most talked about sport in the Olympic Games. *The Times* correspondent, David Miller, reported: 'Money could not buy the publicity given to modern pentathlon by the unfortunate Eduard Zenovka of Russia...NBC Television was running live for this million-dollar tumble.' He was referring, of course, to the incredible finish of the final running event in which Zenovka had moved from 6th position after four events to lead the run with only metres remaining. His rival Alex Parygin (KAZ) had even thrown up his hands to acknowledge defeat when Zenovka stumbled and fell and Parygin found himself unwittingly the new Olympic Champion. The US journalist, Richard Sandomir, quoted Parygin as saying: 'I didn't have any power and I felt "Let Eduard win," I'll be second and thank God, but then you saw what happened. And I found the power. I don't even, can't even believe I'm a champion.' All Zenovka could mutter was 'Maybe I'll remember what happened tomorrow.'

It was a long day with the timings (including added travel): 7am Shoot, 8.30am Fence, 1pm Swim, 5.15pm

Ride and 7.30pm Run. Philipp Waeffler (SUI), who later became a member of the British coaching staff, won the shooting with 185. Other shooting scores included: Toraldo 181, Zenovka 179, Parygin 178, Svatkovsky 173, Martinek 172, Phelps 166 and Zadneprovskis 163. Yagorashvili, now competing for Georgia, won the swimming with 3:15.04. Parygin won the fencing with 970 with Martinek scoring 910, Svatkovsky 880 and Zenovka 820. Richard Phelps and Janos Martinek both scored 1100 in the riding and, for once, Zenovka had a reasonably successful 1016 score. Other leaders were Parygin 1040, Toraldo 1040, and Svatkovsky 1010. With only the running to come, it was Cesare Toraldo (ITA) who led with 4324 points chased by Parygin (KAZ) 4278 and Martinek (HUN) 4258. Back in 6th and 9th places were the best runners in the field, the two Russians, Zenovka (4188) and Svatkovsky (4150).

Toraldo slipped to 8th place by the end of the run, well behind the winning runners, Zenovka (12:21) and Svatkovsky (12:22). The final battle for the gold has already been described but Martinek took the bronze medal just 12 points ahead of the disappointed double World Champion Dimitri Svatkovsky.

Richard Phelps was Great Britain's only representative and he finished 18th. It had been a hard year for him with illness and injury being constant worries. This was his fourth Olympic Games and, now aged 35, his worst finishing position. Would he go on to 2000 and make it five? 'Maybe,' he replied. Then with his usual wry understatement he added, 'That would be like Steve Redgrave....but without the medals.'

For the home crowd, there was only Mike Gostigian to cheer. He finished 16th but in keeping with the media style of the Atlanta Olympics, there were other US stories connected with Modern Pentathlon in 1996. Firstly, rapidly becoming one of the main publicists for the sport in the USA was the famous beefcake filmstar, Dolph Lundgren. He had made a film called 'Pentathlon' in 1994 which was a rather absurd thriller - East German pentathlete frees himself from the curse of Communism and finds happiness in the USA. There may be one or two pentathletes, however, whose own experience might lead them to disagree that this is an unbelievable scenario. Nevertheless, Lundgren's interest in and support for Modern Pentathlon were absolutely genuine and a valuable link to media interest. Another supporter in the news that year was John E DuPont, the wealthy owner of Foxcatcher Farm in Pennsylvania which, for almost 30 years had been a training base for many sportsmen including pentathletes. In 1996, after increasing mental problems, DuPont shot dead Olympic wrestler, Dave Schultz, one of his closest friends, and was jailed for life. He died in 2010. DuPont had had a long-established enthusiasm for Modern Pentathlon and Mike Gostigian was one of many to have benefitted from his support.

Despite the travelling difficulties, the Modern Pentathlon competition in Atlanta was a huge success. Gilbert Felli, IOC Sports Director, the very man who had sent that gloomy plan for the winding down of Olympic Modern Pentathlon to Novikov in 1990, was the first to acknowledge that 'the one-day event is very good.' 'But,' he added, 'it is obvious now that the event in future must be staged at one venue.' Since that was exactly the view of the UIPM, there was great hope that this would be achieved. Furthermore, the organisers of the 2000 Sydney Olympics had already indicated that they were keen on the inclusion of a women's competition in their programme for 2000.

Nico Motchebon

Many pentathletes have become top fencers but an even more extraordinary sporting transition was achieved by Nico Motchebon (GER). Nico had won a bronze medal as a member of the German relay team in San Antonio in 1991 and had been 5th and 6th respectively in the previous two World Junior Championships. In 1995, however, switching sports, he broke Sebastian Coe's European Indoor 800 metres record and in Atlanta finished 5th in the 800 metres final.

1996 Women's World Championships: Siena (ITA)

Despite the young Elisaveta Suvorova (RUS) retaining her World Junior title and winning the World Cup, she was beaten in Siena by the more experienced Zhana Dolgacheva-Shubenok (BLR) and Dorota Idzi (POL). Suvorova and Kowalewska (POL) had both fenced 1000 points but the final order was: Dolgacheva-Subenok, Idzi, Suvorova, Fjellerup (DEN) with Kate Allenby (GBR), who won a bronze medal at the World Cup Final this year, moving up to 6th place. The Team event was won by Russia with Germany and Poland taking the other medals. Great Britain finished 5th in both the Team and Relay events.

1997 World Championships: Sofia (BUL)
Men

1997 marked another significant change in the Modern Pentathlon programme; the distance of the men's swim and run were brought in line with the women's so that both competitions involved a 200 metres swim and a

3000 metres run. The 1000 point mark for swimming was faster than for the women (2:30 compared to 2:40) with one point for every tenth of a second over or under that mark. In running, the men's 1000 point marker was 10.00 (compared to 11:20 for women) with 2 points added or deducted for every half second. The swimming event was seeded so that the best swimmers always swam together in the final heat.

Even though each country was limited to a maximum of three competitors each, there were still 102 individual entries. Those eager for a recreation of the epic battle between Parygin and Zenovka in Atlanta were disappointed. Though they both rode 1100 points, Parygin's 820 fence and Zenovka's 157 shoot put them in 7th and 10th position by the end. The real battle was between 1994 and 1995 World Champion, Dmitri Svatkovsky of Russia and Sebastien Deleigne of France. Though Svatkovsky won the fencing with 1000 points, he couldn't come close to Deleigne's 186 shoot or, surprisingly, his 8.59 run. Deleigne won his first World title, Svatkovsky was 2nd (despite having won the World Cup again that year) and Zadneprovskis (LTU) took the bronze medal, the first of many Senior successes for him in the coming years. Some big names – Phelps, Ruer, Toraldo –failed to qualify for the final. Vaho Yagorashvili, now competing for his third country, USA, won the swimming in 2:03.3 and featured in another significant event. In the Relay, the organisers had miscalculated the USA's riding score and thereby the running was falsely handicapped in such a way that the error could not be resolved without repeating the running event. It meant that Russia beat USA for the gold medal. However, shortly afterwards, Sergeev of the

Russian team was disqualified for failing a drug test. So, USA was awarded the gold medal after all. In the main team event, only Hungary and Belarus had three men in the final and so took the first two places with Russia 3rd.

Women

Despite some poor organization and with Fjellerup and Idzi missing, Elizaveta Suvorova (RUS) made certain of victory this year, winning the shoot with 183. The silver medallist and winner of the fencing (970) was Fabiana Fares (ITA). Lucie Grolichova (CZE) took the bronze medal and Zhana Dolgacheva-Shubenok (BLR) was 4th. The British women were developing a strong squad now with Kate Allenby winning the European Championships this year. They won a bronze medal in the Relay (Allen, Allenby, Houston) but even more excitement took place at the World Junior Championships where Georgina Harland took the silver medal behind Zsuzsa Vörös (HUN) and ahead of Yelena Rublevska (RUS). The team (Harland, Bright, Lewis) placed 6th. The surprise winner of the World Cup in 1997 was Jeanette Malm (SWE).

1998 Jan Bartu becomes Great Britain's Performance Director

The arrival of Jan Bartu was a major step forward for British pentathlon. In the 1970s, Bartu and his Czech teammates had had to travel long distances to train on very little financial backing. Compared to the support given to the Soviet and Hungarian teams in their own countries, the success of the British and Czech teams in Montreal in 1976 had been built on quite flimsy ground. When Bartu arrived in Britain in 1998, he knew that minimising travel and having a centre for training was essential to success. His years as coach to the Mexican and USA team had also taught him another great lesson. Though he had made Mexico a world force in Modern Pentathlon (Ivan Ortega won the World Junior in 1993 and Horacio de la Vega in 1995 when the Mexicans also won the team event), his move to the USA was a sometimes frustrating experience. The San Antonio base was a successful training centre, but Bartu was at the beck and call of national committees who sent out conflicting messages. Despite winning the Men's Team Relay at the 1997 World Championships, the US committee remained unsatisfied.

So when lottery money allowed for new appointments, it is to the very great credit of the MPAGB that Bartu was allowed to take complete charge of the training and competition programme. No longer would selection committees debate the merits and possibilities of the latest new face or old lag; a strict rankings list gave an indisputable indication of who deserved a team place. Athletes knew where they were and the support of the MPAGB allowed Bartu to think long-term in his preparations rather than live from day to day. It wasn't an easy task though. Those early days saw Bartu travel many miles trying to coordinate the training of pentathletes from all corners of the country. All the time he was seeking out a centre that could become his base and at which a real training programme could be implemented. Among the places he visited was Bath University and he could see the possibilities there even though they were undeveloped. What Bartu was looking for was a base where, for the critical five years of good development, a pentathlete could train without wasting time and energy on travel, could study towards a future career, and could be helped to plan life as an elite athlete and beyond. Funding was growing; and the success of Steph Cook and Kate Allenby in Sydney in 2000 gave the sport immense prestige.

In his book *Bounce* (Fourth Estate 2010), subtitled 'the myth of talent and the power of practice', the table-tennis player, Matthew Syed makes clear that success in most things is a combination of hard practice and opportunity. It is never simply the result of talent. In a sport as diverse as Modern Pentathlon, practising long hours (Syed suggests 10,000 of them to become expert) without the distraction of travel is essential. Give the pentathlete 'opportunity' as well – good coaches, financial support, a competitive environment – and success will come. This has very much been Bartu's plan and it is clearly working. Another of Syed's arguments is that practice cannot simply be a process of going through the motions but must be 'purposeful'. This approach requires a coach to vary the challenges and make demands that a pentathlete training on his or her own would not be able to provide. It is difficult to accommodate those who go their own way in the Bath training regime but attempts are still made to do this where necessary and preparations for a life beyond sport are always included in the long-term planning.

1998 World Championships: Mexico City (MEX)
Men

The entry was slightly reduced to 90 competitors as a result of the cost of travel and Richard Phelps was the only British entry. He was injured in the riding and was unable to complete the competition. Despite the altitude, Sebastien Deleigne (FRA) retained his World title with a

177 shoot and a sound 10:00 run. The silver medallist was Vaho Yagorashvili (USA) and Andrei Smirnov (RUS) took the bronze medal with a fine run of 9:26. Other event winners were Tiidemann (EST) who shot 189, de la Vega (MEX) who fenced 1000 points and Kourousu (JAP) who swam 2:04.9. Svatkovsky, despite winning the World Cup for the fourth time this year, could only finish 9th. The home team, Mexico, achieved a great triumph by beating Hungary to the team gold medal while France took the bronze.

Women

Delays and errors caused further frustration at these championships although it should be pointed out that Mexico had taken on the running of the event at a late stage after France's withdrawal. However, the outcome of the final women's event was a delight for all. Anna Sulima, who had already been a member of the Polish gold medal team on eight previous occasions since 1988, won her first World Individual Championship. The other medallists were Zsuzsanna Vörös (HUN) and Sulima's Polish teammate, Paulina Boenitz. Since Paulina still competes today, the Polish tradition of success covers virtually the whole history of women's Modern Pentathlon. Vörös won the shoot with 186 but Sulima's excellent fencing score of 1120 secured her the victory. She also had the pleasure of a tenth gold medal in winning the team event ahead of the Great Britain team of Allenby, Lewis and Cook. Kate Allenby also won the gold medal in the World Cup this year and a British set of medals was completed with the team silver medal and the Relay bronze at the World Championships.

1999 World Championships: Budapest (HUN)
Men

Hungary, for many the home of Modern Pentathlon, was able to celebrate a double victory when the 1996 World Junior Champion, Gabor Balogh became Senior World Champion and his team took the gold medal in the team event. Balogh had a masterful competition: Shoot (1132), Fence (1000), Swim (1230) Ride (1040) Run (1166) for a total of 5568 which left him 58 points clear of the Czech athlete, Libor Capalini, and 136 better than Dmitry Svatkovsky (RUS). The reigning World Champion, Sebastien Deleigne (FRA) could only finish 5th. British pentathletes, Richard Phelps and Giles Hancock, who registered a fine 6th place at the World Junior Championships this year, failed to qualify for the final. Greg Whyte finished 30th with three good events combined with a 670 fence and a limping run of 892 to conclude. This placed the team 14th, some way behind the medallists, Hungary, Lithuania and Belarus.

Women

Zsuzsa Vörös took her first World title in front of a home crowd in a superbly organized competition. With a women's Olympic competition confirmed for Sydney the following year, Olympic prospects looked good for the young Hungarian. She finished ahead of Elizaveta Suvorova (RUS) and Kim Raisner (GER) who took the other medals. Not far behind was an impressive squad of British women: Georgie Harland 7th, Kate Allenby 8th, Gwen Lewis 12th and Steph Cook 13th. All four had performed consistently well but their obvious Achilles' heel was the fencing with scores of 730, 730, 640, 610 respectively; improving this event would be the measure of future success. Two major disasters were suffered in the riding event. Firstly, the reigning World Champion, Anna Sulima, scored a zero ride and finished last (32nd) and the 1998 World Junior Champion, Claudia Corsini rode only 628 points and finished 31st. Pernille Svarre in her 19th World Championship narrowly beat Steph Cook to win the running event. There were some big names among the also-rans, too: Caroline Delemer was 17th overall and Dorota Idzi, who had had a baby the previous year but still won the 1999 World Cup (where Allenby and Cook came 3rd and 4th), came 25th. In the team event, Russia beat Great Britain (Allenby, Cook, Lewis) into 2nd place but Great Britain won the gold medal in the Relay.

The British decade – from rags to riches

The general woe over Modern Pentathlon's Olympic survival, compounded in Great Britain by financial problems, was transformed by the end of the decade to a new world full of potential for future success. The only sadness was that Jim Fox's ill health had forced a premature resignation in 1999. Jim's contribution had been enormous and he was immediately voted Vice-President. Mike Goodall took on the difficult task of seeing through the exciting developments that new financial support had brought –a professional coaching set-up under Jan Bartu and wider grass roots participation. Even the income from membership fees, that perennial index of good health, had risen to £19,000.

The important work of submitting appropriate applications to the Sports Council was done by Dominic

Mahony, Martin Dawe and Nigel Frost, the MPAGB Treasurer. Nigel reported that in the past year turnover had increased from £100,000 per year to £500,000 with a projected further increase to £1,000,000 in the year ahead. A new Chief Executive Officer, Elaine Shaw, was appointed and the dissemination of information was enhanced when the association's first website (www.mpagb.easynet.co.uk) took flight.

With such a busy international programme, it wasn't always possible to run a British Championships with a full turn out. In the men's event, Richard Phelps won six more times in the 1990s to take his grand total to 13, and Dominic Mahony and Greg Whyte each won twice. The women's event, however, was a much more egalitarian affair; nobody had the audacity to win twice so the long list of winners included Sara Cox, Helen Nicholas, Kate Houston, Vicky Rowe, Rachael Wilmot, Julia Allen, Helen Griffiths, Liz Kipling and Sian Lewis.

The list, interestingly, omits Olympic medallists Kate Allenby, Steph Cook and Georgie Harland. This is not as unusual a feature as one might think; there are a number of Olympic and World Champions the world over who have never won their own National Championships. International standards in Great Britain, at least for the women, were vastly improved by the end of the decade but who could have anticipated the enormous success that would come their way in the new century?

Chapter Ten: 2000 -2012

'If Kate, the better fencer, had won her single bout against Steph in Sydney, she might have been Olympic Champion instead.'

Despite the excellent modernising programme of the 1990s, the IOC refused to be satisfied. In August 2002, the IOC Programme Commission recommended the exclusion of three sports from the Olympic list – Modern Pentathlon, Baseball and Softball. The UIPM were disappointed not to have been asked to present an updated account of developments in the sport to the commission before they made this recommendation. Since only the IOC membership could vote on such a decision and a simple majority would decide the outcome, everyone in the sport set about the necessary lobbying.

There were four counts made against Modern Pentathlon's inclusion:

    its lack of global participation
    its significant expense
    its operational complexity
    its relatively low broadcast and press coverage.
    The UIPM response to each claim in turn was:

There are 94 member nations from five continents. Major competitions take place on all five continents.

Recent development work had taken place in North Korea, Cameroon, Australia, Russia and Cuba.

We are no more expensive than other sports. We use the same venues and compact sites so do not add to costs for the IOC. The cost of fencing and shooting events has even been reduced. Riding costs are very flexible. Competitors do not pay for riding costs.

As above. Same venues used as other sports and all sited within a short distance of each other. The full competition is over in seven hours.

All major UIPM events (1995-2002) have been covered by various media. UIPM has its own website, journals and magazines.

In addition, the UIPM argued that Modern Pentathlon was 'education by essence'. While swimming and running were the basic physical skills, shooting demanded stress control and precision, fencing-adaptability and intelligence, and riding - flexibility, self-control and courage.

At the IOC meeting on 27th November 2002, Modern Pentathlon was retained by majority vote though the decision was to be reviewed yet again after the Athens Olympic Games in 2004.

2000 Spectator Survey

In an interesting guide to the public response to Modern Pentathlon, Norbert Muller and Manfred Messing conducted a survey among the Sydney spectators at the pentathlon events. Almost 1700 people filled in questionnaires from which the following information was gleaned: For 80%, this was their first view of the sport; more women than men attended; most had done some running and swimming and about half had been riders but almost no one knew about fencing and shooting. Reasons given for attending were: a five-in-one ticket is a bargain; the riding and running were the biggest attractions; the chance to see multi-talented athletes was interesting; and the fact that the final winner only emerged at the very end was exciting.

These observations speak well for the public reaction to the Modern Pentathlon modernisation programme in the past decade. Increasingly, as sympathy grew for the plight of Modern Pentathlon and its great struggle for survival, journalists more and more looked for the positive effects of attending the Olympic event. In consecutive BOA Olympic reports there are enthusiastic justifications for the wonders of a sport that, frequently, as with the Sydney spectators, the journalist is discovering for the first time. In 2000, one noted: 'Modern Pentathlon has one great advantage as a spectacle over the Heptathlon and Decathlon: positions in the final event determine prizes.' Even more glowingly, in Athens in 2004, Andrew Baker, the *Daily Telegraph* journalist reported:

'The grandstands at Goudi were crammed to bursting, and this is exactly the kind of sport the Olympics should be about. No one is in it for the money, the spirit among the competitors is tremendous and the variety of skills and strengths required render doping absolutely pointless.'

This was exactly the kind of support Modern Pentathlon needed when preparing to face the IOC for yet another round of scrutiny after Athens.

2000 World Championships: Pesaro (ITA)
Men

This first World Championships to occur in Olympic year was necessitated by the very limited number of competitors (24 men, 24 women) allowed to compete at the Olympic Games, the absence of team and relay events in Sydney, and the need to give everybody a final chance to qualify for one of those priceless remaining Olympic places. Though it was an important feature of the complete UIPM calendar, the World Championship held in Olympic year was not necessarily a predictor of Olympic performance; it functioned largely as a final qualifier for those not yet part of the Olympic entry list.

The choice of Pesaro, a sunny beach resort, must have detracted a little from the tension though, perhaps, more easily healed the wounds of those who missed out. Andrejus Zadneprovskis (LTU) was the winner, 26 points ahead of 1999 World Champion, Gabor Balogh (HUN) and the winner of the fencing, Nicolae Papuc (ROM), took the bronze. Against the odds, the USA won both team and relay events. Their team of Chad Senior, Velizar Iliev, Vaho Yagorashvili and James Gregory saw off Poland and Sweden in the team event and Russia and Hungary in the relay.

Women

As was the case with Anna Sulima (POL) two years before, Pernille Svarre's (DEN) triumph as World Champion in Pesaro was the culmination of long and hard experience in the sport as a World Championships competitor over the previous 19 years. Svarre had begun badly with only a 169 shoot compared to silver medallist, Paulina Boenisz's (POL) 185. Boenisz had first made her mark as Youth 'A' World Champion back in 1995 and 1996 and is one of only two contenders hoping to compete in her fourth consecutive Olympic Games in London in 2012. The other is Elena Rublevska (LAT).

Svarre's strong fence (970) and her final run secured the title ahead of Boenisz. Elena Rublevska (LAT) won the bronze and Great Britain's Kate Allenby (6th) Steph Cook (8th) and Georgina Harland (17th) secured the silver medal in the team event behind Poland but giving little hint of what was to come in Sydney. Steph and sisters, Gwen Lewis-Kinsey and Sian Lewis also took silver in the relay. Steph Cook had also placed 2nd in the European Championship behind Zsusza Vörös (HUN) but the Hungarian, who was also 1999 World Champion, could only finish 18th in Pesaro.

2000 Olympic Games: Sydney (AUS)
Men

With only 24 competitors in each of the Men's and Women's competitions, rivalry for places was intense and the qualifying process regionalized in accordance with UIPM and IOC strategies. Only five countries succeeded in qualifying two pentathletes –France, Hungary, Mexico, Ukraine and USA. No British competitor qualified, Richard Phelps' 29th position in the World Championships being his swansong. There were four World Champions in the Sydney competition – Andrejus Zadneprovskis (2000), Gabor Balogh (1999) Sebastien Deleigne (1997 and 1998) and Dimitry Svatkovsky (1994 and 1995) with Balogh, on current form, probably the favourite. Deleigne, at 33, was the oldest competitor and Emad El-Geziry (EGY) was the youngest at 18.

All eyes were on Modern Pentathlon in Sydney. Everything had to be better than perfect so every nuance of organization was scrutinised. The Baseball Stadium formed the hub of the pentathlon events in the Olympic

Park and the final ride and run took place entirely inside the Baseball Stadium in front of 18,000 spectators.

On 30th September, a 6.45am start on the shooting range created a suitably somnolent tone for the mental stress to come over the ten hour programme. Pavel Dovgal (BLR) won the event with 186, opening up a good lead on Balogh (181), Svatkovsky and Deleigne (both 176). With only 24 fencers, every hit had a value of 40 points– a critical quantity in the final analysis. The only 1000 point fence was achieved by Oliver Clergeau (FRA) ahead of Balogh (920) and Deleigne and Svatkovsky (both 880). Eric Walther (GER) won the swim in 2:00.71, the sub-two minute target for 200 metres coming closer at a much speedier rate than the first 300 metre swim in under four minutes had all those years ago. Zadneprovskis and Dovgal swam 2:14.3 and 2:14.6 but after three events, it was the American, Chad Senior who led the field.

SOCOG (the Sydney organising committee) and the UIPM had bought 25 horses for the Modern Pentathlon in Australia. Charles Sturt University and the Australian MPA would prepare them for the event in return for their use after the competition. Ex-Olympian, Alex Watson and Riding Director, Hunter Dogherty worked very hard to provide a suitably challenging course which appeared, nevertheless, to be a relatively straightforward inner loop /outer loop plan with the jumps all between 1.0 and 1.2 metres high. As is frequently the case, there was some discrepancy in the standard of horses and there were four zero rides. Perhaps most noticeable to spectators, however, was the number of knockdowns there were which resulted in no maximum 1100 scores at all.

On paper, there is nothing very unusual about the riding scores in Sydney; there have been far less equitable rides in major competitions and it would be wrong to suggest the course builders were at fault in any way. After all, *Wantabadgery*, on which Qian (CHN) scored zero, was ridden for 1070 points by Svatkovsky. Only *Cookardinia*, on which de la Vega (MEX) and Hantov (BUL) both scored zero, was withdrawn for the following day. Of the top men, only Balogh (HUN) and Zadneprovskis (LTU) dropped significant points in the riding (980 and 955 respectively). However, so under pressure were the UIPM to be seen to get everything right that an urgently convened Technical meeting at 8.30am the following morning decided to reduce the height of some jumps by five centimetres for the Women's event.

With only the running remaining, Clergeau (FRA) and Iliev (USA) led the field (Chad Senior's 890 ride had dropped him to 8th) with Dovgal, Balogh and Svatkovsky in 3rd, 4th and 5th places. Deleigne was in 9th and Zadneprovskis 11th. Sebastien Deleigne's marvellous 9:10.69 run brought him up the field but not into the medals. He finished 4th overall, three seconds short of Pavel Dovgal (BLR) who, despite a 760 fence, had a strong competition and took the bronze medal. The 2000 World Champion, Zadneprovskis (LTU) could manage only 7th place despite his 9:14.31 run. The favourite, Gabor Balogh (HUN) ran 9:29.49 but could not beat Dimitri Svatkovsky (RUS) who had gained a decisive 90 points over Balogh in the riding event. Though not the favourite in 2000, with his run of 9:21.79 Svatkovsky hauled himself from 4th place to become Olympic Champion, four years after everybody had expected him to do it. On that previous occasion he had missed the mark; this time he got it right.

Women – Steph Cook is Olympic Champion

For Great Britain, the gold and bronze medals won by Steph Cook and Kate Allenby in this event provided the stuff of legend. There was ample evidence from the recent team medals at major events that our women were in with a chance but the outcome was beyond dreams and for Steph Cook, turned her into the kind of media celebrity from which only her experience as a level-headed doctor could ever allow her to escape. Six countries had qualified the maximum two competitor each – Great Britain, Hungary, Italy, Poland, Russia and USA.

The day (1st October) began with Emily de Riel (USA) opening up a strong lead by shooting 185 compared to Cook's 178 and Allenby's 175. Though Kate fenced a strong 920, Steph only managed 760 and was six seconds

Steph Cook (GBR): Olympic Champion 2000, World Champion 2001.

down on Kate in the swimming, an event won by Zsusza Vörös in 2:15.8. The riding event was, with the lowered fences, kind to the final top six, all of whom scored 1040 except de Riel who scored 1070, but hard on some big names. Former World Champion, Elizaveta Suvarova (RUS) scored only 827, 2000 World Champion at 38 years old, Pernille Svarre (DEN) scored 702, and 1999 World Champion Zsusza Vörös scored 830. Fabiana Fares (ITA), silver medallist in 1997, and Nora Simoka (HUN), at 19, the youngest competitor, both scored zero.

Steph Cook started the run in 8th place with 49 seconds to catch on Emily de Riel. Ahead of her was also team mate, Kate Allenby. Steph was, of course, in the great tradition of British pentathletes, a fine runner. She had placed 7th in the National Cross-Country Championship in 1997 and gone on to represent Great Britain in that sport as a result. At the halfway stage, Steph had closed the gap on Emily to 15 seconds. With 750 metres to go, she overtook Kate and then, with 300 metres remaining, overtook Emily. Her final time of 10.03 was 19 seconds ahead of another fine runner, Pernille Svarre and 51 and 55 seconds ahead of de Riel and Allenby respectively who took the silver and bronze medals. Mary Beth Yagorashvili (USA) and Paulina Boenisz (POL) placed 4th and 5th. Suvarova finished 7th, Vörös 15th and three very experienced pentathletes, Delemer (10th), Idzi (16th) and Svarre (17th) were at least able to become true Olympians after years of being denied the opportunity.

The celebrity world

Both British women responded admirably to the rush of press interest. It is common to hear athletes express as much happiness for rivals' success as for their own. In a highly individual sport this stance often seems a little disingenuous. However, Kate Allenby and the British women's team of that time appeared to be entirely sincere in expressing such enthusiasm for each other's successes. If Kate, the better fencer, had won her single bout against Steph in Sydney, she might well have been Olympic Champion instead. But such a thought seems never to have crossed her mind. Indeed, Kate praised Steph for being a 'training demon' and inspiring her to greater efforts herself.

In the months that followed the Olympic Games Steph Cook was, according to Neil Wilson in the *Daily Mail,* driving a sponsored Mercedes, designing celebrity cars, attending Buckingham Palace, having dinner in Monte Carlo, doing a photo-shoot for Vogue, posing in the window of an Oxford Street shop and featuring in numerous TV quiz shows and interviews. Her press secretary was, apparently, receiving 80 enquiries per day. Only a tough and decisive person can handle all this and keep sight of what she really wanted in life. She told Neil Wilson:

'I don't think I've changed. Others may view me as a celebrity now but that's not how I see myself....For the moment I am more athlete than doctor but I am keen to get back to medicine next year and then I'll probably look back on this whole episode as something surreal. I'm under no illusions. It's going to change me in some ways but I shall still retain the same principles and values.'

This is very reminiscent of the interview given by Wille Grut after the 1948 Olympics in which he made clear that the Olympic title was something he'd prepared for properly but now it was time to get on with life. Once

2001 dawned, Steph was happy to cut back on the celebrity lifestyle and prepare for the 2001 World Championships being held in her home country. This would be her final effort before returning to her true vocation as a doctor, something which she had already planned to last much longer than her sporting career.

The Oxbridge connection

Newspapers made much of the fact that not only was Steph Cook an Oxford graduate but silver medallist, Emily de Riel, had taken her M.Phil. in Medieval English Literature there, too. Both women had started the sport while at Oxford. As Steph told Simon Turnbull of *The Independent*, 'OUMPA has a lot to answer for'. Theirs was an achievement of which, understandably, Oxford and Cambridge graduate pentathletes are proud. Both universities have sustained an annual Varsity match every year since 1958 and, every year, sponsorship is found and the match is well-organised and has a family-like charm about it. Among British international pentathletes from Oxbridge have been Julia Allen, Matt Barnes, Ed Egan, Kate Houston, Ben Measures, Mike Proudfoot, Simeon Robbie, Keith Shindler, Peter Wall and Lisa Willcocks. It is a fact, though, that high-powered graduates from such universities are unlikely to remain pentathletes for long since, as in Steph Cook's case, career ambitions inevitably call. So, it is often Oxbridge officials rather than athletes that give more lasting evidence of the universities' influence – Tony Temple is Chairman of MPAGB, Michael Proudfoot was British Team Manager for many years, Ed Egan was Technical Director for both the 2000 Olympics and the 2001 World Championships, and Tristan Robbie has been the commentator at World Championships and Olympic Games since 2001. Finally, Cambridge founder, Colin Peace, was British Team Manager, developer of Pony Club Tetrathlon and continues to provide support for the Canadian MPA.

2001 World Championships – Millfield (GBR)
Men

The choice of Millfield School in Somerset as a venue enabled the competition to take place within a very small area once again. Millfield School, like Whitgift, had a long tradition of school pentathlon – British Team Manager, Dominic Mahony was one of many pentathletes produced there. The MPAGB was determined not to repeat the financial errors of the 1994 Championships in Sheffield and set up a separate company to finance the event.

In 2001, Edvinas Krungolcas (LTU) won the World Cup Final ahead of 2000 Junior World Champion, 18 year old Andrei Mosieev (RUS). Krungolcas' team mate Zadneprovskis beat him into 2nd place in the European Championships but none of these took medals at Millfield. Victor Horvath (HUN) opened with a 191 shoot and Gabor Balogh (HUN) and Tzanko Hantov (BLR) both fenced 1000 points. These were the final medallists. Moiseev won the swimming in 2:08.3, all swims being rather slow compared to the Olympic times the year before and Sergio Salazar (MEX) won the run in 10:34. As in Sydney, the leading competitors held their own in the riding though, once again, there were no 1100 scores. Zadneprovskis, in 4th place finally, lost his World title with a 950 ride. Sebastien Deleigne (FRA) and Andrei Moiseev, former and future World champions, rode 511 and 449 respectively to finish in the last two places overall behind Britain's only qualifier, Giles Hancock, who was in 30th place.

Gabor Balogh (HUN) won the World title for a second time ahead of team mate Viktor Horvath and Tzanko Hantov (BLR). Lithuanians, Zadneprovskis and Krungolcas were 4th and 5th. In 2001, Great Britain had managed to qualify three athletes for the World Cup Final – Alex Buirski, Giles Hancock and Matt Barnes – but, before a home crowd, they were less successful and we had no finalists. Hungary won both team and relay events with Lithuania and Russia taking the other team medals.

Women

Steph Cook had decided to keep going for another year after the Olympic Games because the World Championships were being held before a home crowd but, perhaps more importantly for her, the women's team was so strong that she wanted to be a part of their success. Unlike her performances before Sydney in 2000, Steph dominated other competitions in 2001. She was European Champion in Sofia and won the home leg of the World Cup tournament. But other members of the British team were extremely strong too. Sian Lewis won the World Cup Final in 2001 and with Kate Allenby and Steph Cook, the three of them comfortably won World and European team competitions. It is some small irony that Georgina Harland, who had won the World Cup leg in Mexico, took the individual bronze medal at Millfield when she hadn't even been nominated for the team. The UIPM requirement to nominate team members in advance is a puzzling one, particularly since any nation that succeeds in qualifying four athletes for a major final deserves to benefit from such strength in depth. A similar anomaly occurred in the 2010 Men's World Championships in Chengdu when Sergei Karyakin (RUS) was not nominated for his team yet became World Champion in the same competition!

In 2001 both Steph Cook and Kate Allenby had to miss the British Championships because they were injured, Steph with a stress fracture to her foot and Kate still having problems with a torn shoulder muscle. So to have a full team for the World Championships was a bonus and they duly won both team and relay events. To have four women in the top five in the world at one point was quite exceptional.

Though Paulina Boenisz (POL) shot better, Steph began the competition with a strong 180 shoot and, with 860 in the fencing, held Boenisz to a 68 point lead. Kate Allenby had fenced well (972) to stay among the leaders and Georgina Harland's 2:16.0 swim was a good eight seconds ahead of her team mates. As in the men's event, there were no 1100 scores in the riding and also quite a few disappointments. Steph Cook managed a top score of 1070 but Harland and Allenby each had to settle for 980 and Sian Lewis only 890. Disappointed ex-World Champions were Vörös (HUN) with 812 and Suvarova (RUS), who was nursing a knee injury in her final competition, only 784. Pernille Svarre (DEN) was forced to withdraw after the shooting event. For once, the great running of Steph Cook was eclipsed by Georgina Harland who ran 10:11 to Steph's 10:18 but Steph Cook didn't need an all-out effort to take the World title. She finished more than 150 points ahead of the rest of the field with Boenitz 2nd, Harland 3rd, Claudia Cerutti (ITA) 4th, and Kate Allenby 5th. Further down the list were Rublevska (9th) Vörös (10th) Caroline Delemer (FRA) and celebrating 20 years since her first World Championship (11th), Sian Lewis (GBR (14th) and Suvarova, a disappointing 28th. It was a magical competition for Great Britain to dominate so fully in front of a home crowd and, for Steph Cook, a deserved fairytale finish to her sporting career. The press was full of rumours that, if the relay became an Olympic event in 2004, Steph might return to take part again but it was all optimistic dreaming. Steph Cook had done exactly what she set out to do, both individually and as a member of a hugely talented team, and then went off to do the important job for which she was always destined. A thoroughly charming person to everyone who meets her, Steph, now a mother of two, is just as likely to be spotted spending the day helping out at some minor competition as attending celebrity occasions. In both situations she manages to be completely herself.

There was more success for Great Britain in 2001 in the Junior Women's World Championships where Emily Bright took the individual silver medal and the team (Emily Bright, Jo Clark and Sarah Langridge) won bronze in the team event and silver in the relay.

Riding changes

As a result of what he saw as the poor riding standard in the 2000 Olympic Games, in 2002 James Allenby submitted a paper to the UIPM. In it he asked the question: 'Should the aim be to improve the image of Modern Pentathlon by making sure the top athletes are competent or should the standard be compromised and lowered to help those athletes who are not competent in riding?' This is, of course, a loaded rhetorical question. Allenby clearly believed that the standard wasn't good enough. Others of us disagreed, believing that the only way to limit the injustices of the riding event was to simplify it. However, the paper contained some very sensible practical proposals. By suggesting that there should be time penalties for being faster than the bogey time as well as slower, he was being sensitive about the careful treatment of the horses. Though the UIPM did not think this a suitable line to follow, Allenby's point was partly acknowledged when a rule was included that declared that the winner of the ride should now be the rider closest to the bogey time rather than the fastest. He also believed that a refusal or run out was a more serious demonstration of the rider's lack of control than a knockdown and that this should be reflected in the relative penalty score allotted to each. The current difference (20 points for a knockdown, 40 points for a refusal) is more sympathetic to that view than the former points score. For the 2002 World Championships, the UIPM Congress had decided to increase the maximum total for riding from 1100 to 1200 in order to keep the event in line with the increasingly high scores in shooting, swimming and running. Other more recent developments have been to require only two refusals rather than three before proceeding to the next jump and to penalise an eliminated rider 100 points for each jump not completed. This actually means that a rider, if eliminated, is rewarded for the number of jumps completed rather than the elimination resulting in a zero score.

2002 World Championships: San Francisco (USA)
Men

Stanford University played host to the 2001 competition. Imre Tiidemann (EST) won the shoot with 189 and Libor

Capalini (CZE) the swim in a relatively slow 2:10.0. Unusually, the top fencer, Jefremenko (LAT) finished well down the overall field despite his winning score of 1084. After three events, Zadneprovskis (LTU) was in the lead but a riding score of 876 dropped him down to 16th place by the end of the day. Four of the top final seven managed to score 1200 in the riding event and 26 of the 32 competitors scored 1000+. The final running event, held in rain and in very slippery conditions was slow but Matt Barnes (GBR) won the event with a time of 10:26 to finish 24th overall.

This was an era in which the winner of the Men's event constantly changed. Only Zadneprovskis won the World Championships twice in the entire decade. The final winner in San Francisco was 23 year old Michal Sedlecky (CZE) who thus announced the beginning of a period of great strength for the Czech male pentathletes; they won the team silver medal five times between 2002 and 2009. Erik Johansson (SWE) took the individual silver medal having fenced 1028, and Eric Walther (GER) beat Imre Tiidemann (EST), who won the European and World Cup titles in 2002, for the bronze medal. Hungary won the team event ahead of Czech Republic and Lithuania.

Women

With Steph Cook retired and Kate Allenby unavailable, it was going to be hard for the British women to retain the team title at Stanford. The team had already won the European team event and Georgina Harland and Sian Lewis were performing strongly. Individual favourite, Zsusza Vörös (HUN) was the World Cup winner in 2002 ahead of Claudia Corsini (ITA) who, in turn, had won the European title that year.

The outcome was a surprise. Bea Simoka (HUN) who had not qualified for the 2000 Olympic event and had had a baby the year before was the new World champion. She led the field after events three and four and barely hung on to that lead with a mediocre run, one and a half minutes slower than the British runners Harland and Lewis who ran 10.01 and 10.03 respectively. But Simoka's strong other events, particularly her winning 1112 score in the fencing secured the gold medal ahead of her team mate, Zsusza Vörös. Georgina Harland ran her way into the bronze medal for the second year in a row, having started in 13th place after four events. For the British team, however, Sian Lewis' disappointing 540 ride enabled Hungary to take the team title ahead of Italy and Russia. Sian finished 27th while Emily Bright came 22nd. Other pentathletes falling short of their past standards were Boenisz (POL) 7th, Rublevska (LAT) 11th and Corsini (ITA) 13th.

2003: MPAGB becomes Pentathlon GB

As early as the 2001 AGM, there was a proposal to make the MPAGB a 'Company Limited by Guarantee'. This would replace the General Council as a decision-making authority with a Board of Directors. The main purpose of this change was to protect officials of the MPAGB from personal liability in an increasingly litiginous world. It would also, by decreasing the 'layers of organisation', speed up decision-making and enable the day-to-day affairs of the association to proceed more efficiently. It wasn't until 25th October 2003, however, that this momentous change took place and the appointed Board of Directors consisted of Andy Ripley (Chairman), Martin Dawe and Dominic Mahony (Vice-chairmen) and David Langridge (Treasurer). Andy Ripley, the famous British Lions rugby player had been persuaded to take the chair at the beginning of the decade. His attitude was that it was his job, as someone new to the sport, to facilitate but not to interfere without taking advice from those who knew more about the subject. Dawe and Mahony were very experienced officials and were able to guide Ripley in any area in which he temporarily lacked knowledge.

David Langridge was Treasurer for the critical years of the new era, a period he describes as 'a golden decade of sport funding'. The money for MPAGB was coming from three main sources –Lottery UK, UK Sport and Sport England, the latter of these being mostly concerned with grassroots development. Unlike the 1994 Sheffield World championships, the 2001 Millfield World Championships had made a profit of £40,000 thanks to some astute accounting. Funding was partly influenced in this period by the international success of the athletes and for MPAGB, this was a golden decade, too, which raised the profile of Modern Pentathlon in the funding world. Whereas, in the past, unspent sponsorship funds had to be returned each year, the grant bodies no longer insisted upon this and this enabled the MPAGB to build assets.

Funding grants are generally made on a four year cycle and related to the Olympic preparation period. MPAGB was able to get extra funding for running the 2009 World Championships at Crystal Palace and, with 20 employees and a wage bill of £650,000 p.a. the MPAGB ('Pentathlon GB' is largely a re-branding title) is a well-organised company with board meetings held every six weeks. The current funding cycle comes to an end in March 2013. Will further funding be dependent on our pentathletes sustaining the success of the past three Olympic Games? In a harsher economic climate, there may be cuts ahead but for funding bodies to place all financial considerations on the outcome of two one-day events in August 2012 would be unfortunate behaviour. A look at the wider picture is essential.

2003 World Championships: Pesaro (ITA)
Men

The championships returned to Pesaro only three years after the Italian town had previously been host and it was a useful though distant preparation for the Olympic heat of Athens a year later. Zhenhua Qian (CHN) opened with a 191 shoot and Michal Michalik (CZE) shot 190. Erik Johansson (SWE) once again dominated the fencing with a 1084 score though Michalik and Eric Walther (GER) on 944 were within striking distance. Riding scores were almost uniformly good. Walther's strong swim/run (2:08 and 10.37) were slower than the event winners, Moiseev (RUS) with 2:06 and Valentini (ITA) with 10.27, but good enough to win the title overall pushing Johansson once again into 2nd place. Michalik took the bronze medal ahead of Sergio Salazar (MEX) and Andrea Valentini (ITA). Though Balogh was only 6th and Horvath 16th, Hungary won the team gold medal ahead of Germany and Czech Republic. Other notable individual placings were: Qian 7th, Yagorashvili 8th, Moiseev 10th, and reigning World Champion, Sedlecky 13th.

Women

The competition began with Olessia Velitchko (RUS) winning both the shooting (183) and the fencing (1028).

She had competed in the previous two years' championships but had only placed 20th and 30th. Now she amassed a significant lead over Vörös (HUN) and the British women, Allenby and Harland. Georgina, though both European and World Cup Champion in 2003 shot a truly awful 161 to begin the competition in the worst possible way. Kate was coming back into form after missing the 2002 Championships. Both women fenced well (Allenby 916 and Harland 944 compared to Vörös' 860) and kept to within five seconds of Vörös' winning time of 2:10.6 in the swimming. Meanwhile Velitchko could only manage 2:29.0. The riding was unchallenging with hardly any differentiation established so it was left to the running event to settle the final score. Zsusza Vörös ran an excellent 10:41 to take the title from Velitchko (10:55) and Allenby (10:59). Georgina Harland, used to steaming through the field in the final event had to dig even deeper after her bad start in the shooting. She ran an incredible 10:16 to finish 4th overall. It also clinched the team gold for Great Britain (Allenby 3rd, Harland 4th, Sian Lewis 11th) over Russia and Hungary. It was a great relief to gain the title again after the previous year's disappointment. Sarah Langridge finished 25th to complete the British effort. The 2002 World Champion Bea Simoka (HUN) could only come 10th. Meanwhile, in 27th position, the 2011 World Champion, Victoria Tereshuk (UKR) was making her debut in the World Championships.

2004 World Championships: Moscow (RUS)
Men

There were two notable absentees at this final Olympic qualifier at the end of May: World Champion, Eric

Walther and his runner-up Erik Johansson, who, having already qualified for Athens, both decided to continue with their Olympic preparations instead. Andrejus Zadneprovskis (LTU) repeated his 2000 pre-Olympic triumph to take the title once more. He achieved this with a surprisingly low fencing score of 792. Zhenhua Qian (CHN) shot 187 to finish 4th overall and with Korea's Lee Choon-Huan coming 2nd overall, these were results that signalled a strong future Asian presence in all major world competitions. Lee, though never having repeated his silver medal success in 2004, continues to compete and is still a contender in 2012. Libor Capalini (CZE) took the bronze medal ahead of Denis Cerkovskis (LAT) and Andrei Moiseev (RUS) was 7th. With only Akos Kallai (6th) and Gabor Balogh (11th) in the final, Hungary had to surrender their team title to Russia with Czech Republic and Italy taking the other medals. There were no British finalists but 2004 marked a gold medal for Nick Woodbridge in winning the World Youth 'A' Championships.

Women

As a final qualifier for Athens, this event was critical to many of the competitors. The increase in the Olympic allowance from 24 to 32 competitors clearly helped. For once, this competition was a strong predictor of Olympic success. 2003 World Champion, Zsusza Vörös (HUN) comfortably retained her title, though Kate Allenby came through strongly for the silver medal with a 182 shoot, a 944 fence, a 2:20 swim and 10:56 run. Nobody scored the 1200 maximum in the riding but only five of the 32 finalists rode less than 1000. Tatyana Mazurkevitch (BLR) won bronze and Georgina Harland, who started poorly with a 164 shoot and 692 fence, placed 5th, though winning the run in 10:00. Great Britain's Jo Clark finished 23rd which was enough, with Kate's and Georgina's scores, to win the team event for Great Britain over Belarus and Russia. Other individual results were: Tereshuk 6th, Corsini 7th, Rublevska 10th and Boenitz 11th. Making her World Championship debut in 30th position was future triple World Champion, Amelie Caze (FRA).

Meanwhile, at the Junior World Championships in 2004, Mhairi Spence placed 5th and the team of Spence, Fell, Livingston and Rowell won silver in the team and bronze in the relay.

2004 Olympic Games: Athens (GRE)
Men

Among the 32 competitors, it was difficult to select a favourite. As recent World Champion, Zadneprovskis (LTU) was a contender, as was 2003 World Champion Eric Walther (GER). Would twice-silver medalist, Erik Johansson (SWE) go one better in Athens? Perhaps we would see the first Asian Olympic Champion in either Lee Choon- Huan (KOR) or Zhenhua Qian (CHN). Qian opened with a 185 shoot, only bettered by Dzmitry Meliakh (BLR) with 186 but then, much against the odds, Andrei Moiseev (RUS) won the fencing and, more predictably, the swimming. It meant that after three events, Moiseev led from Marcin Horbacz (POL) and Denis Cerkovskis (LAT).

The riding event proved more challenging that expected. Nobody scored 1200 points and amongst the leaders there were some very varied scores. Moiseev rode only 1032 on a small horse that seemed to rush round knocking down a number of poles as a result. His nearest rivals, however, did much worse: Horbacz had a disastrous ride and dropped completely out of contention and Cerkovskis scored 1004. So, with only the running remaining, Moiseev had a 44 point lead on Michal Michalik (CZE) and Dzmitry Meliakh (BLR). The 25 year old Russian had little trouble holding off the field, even finding time in the final stages to stop and pick up a Russian flag to wave as he finished the race. The strong runners moved through the field; Zadneprovskis won a slow run in 10.51 ahead of Chad Senior (USA). This gave the Lithuanian the silver medal in front of another strong runner, Libor Capalini (CZE) who overtook Denis Cerkovskis to take the bronze medal. Former World Champions Walther, Balogh, and Deleigne finished 7th, 8th and 15th respectively. Asian stars, Qian and Lee were a disappointed 16th and 21st and double World silver medallist, Johansson was 23rd. The World Cup winner for 2004 was Edvinas Krungolcas (LTU) but, hampered by an injury in the run in Athens, he finished only 31st.

Women

The Gaudi Complex provided the perfect setting for the Modern Pentathlon with big crowds watching intense competition. The favourite was three-times World champion Zsusza Vörös (HUN) but Kate Allenby and Georgina Harland were strong contenders. There was some hanging about for competitors before the shooting began which tested mental strength. Lean Dong (CHN) won the event with a strong 189 well ahead of Vörös' 182 and the 15 year old Aya Medany's (EGY) 181. Kate Allenby shot 169 and Georgina Harland, a disastrous 156. In her diary of the event Georgina recorded: 'I knew after I shot a 3 for my second shot that the gold I had sought after would not be mine today.' But bouncing back is proof of the mental toughness of the pentathlete and the fencing went well for both British women. Kate fenced 972 and Georgina's 832 was better than she had expected. The experienced Elena Rublevska (LAT) won the fencing with 1028 but Vörös' 916 was enough to put her in the lead after two events, a position she would never surrender. Vörös swam 2:15.3 but the British women were close to their best times and just behind –Harland (2:14.3) and Allenby (2:17.3). This enabled Kate to move into 2nd place after three events, 124 points behind Zsusza Vörös.

Seven riders out of the 32 competing scored below 1000 points but among the leaders, everyone scored above 1100 except Kate Allenby. She commented 'My horse behaved like an emu. He had his head up so high he couldn't see his feet.' Even for an experienced rider like Allenby, it was almost impossible to prevent such a horse from knocking down almost everything in his way. She ended with a score of 1004 and, now in 7th place, was unlikely to catch the leaders, Vörös, Rublevska and Corsini (ITA). Harland, however, was in an even worse position, 14th with 50 seconds to catch on Corsini if she was to have any hope of a medal.

Harland's 10:17 run was an astonishing 27 seconds ahead of her nearest rival, Victoria Tereshuk (UKR). Even though she was running with a stress fracture of the foot, she caught Corsini with 300 metres to go to win a spectacular bronze medal behind Vörös and Rublevska. Georgina recalled afterwards: 'I do like to keep people hanging on. I knew on the last lap I had got a medal.' When asked if she considered the gap too much to catch she replied: 'It's never too much in the Olympics.' After such a dreadful beginning in the shooting, this really was a triumph of the spirit. Kate Allenby placed a disappointing 8th, thwarted in a riding event in which she was one of the most skilled. This was not the retirement competition she had deserved after a year in which she had won two gold medals (Individual World Cup Final winner and World Team Champion) and one silver (Individual World Championships). Other interesting placings in Athens were: Tereshuk (UKR) 7th, Boenisz (POL) 10th, Caze (FRA) 12th, and Medany (EGY) 28th.

2004 onwards: later MPAGB developments

Late in 2004, Tony Temple replaced Andy Ripley as Chairman and continues in that role to the present day. As a QC, Tony has the ability to get to the nub of every problem with utter clarity. As a Chairman, this enables him to speed up decision-making and guide his team with great efficiency. In the same year, MPAGB moved its headquarters to Bath, alongside the athletes' training centre which enhanced communication still further. A Selection Panel of Jan Bartu, Stuart Mason, Clive Townend and National Development Coach, Bernie Moss, was set up. Over the coming years, Clive Hawkins (Regional Development), Lawrence Moss (Statistics), Howard Jones and Geoff Lewis all served as directors and, by 2008, membership of the MPAGB had swollen to 4,800. A target of 15,000 by 2015 was proposed.

At the UIPM Congress in Guatemala in 2008, Great Britain was represented by the Chairman, Tony Temple, Peter Hart (Technical Committee) and Georgina Harland (Chairman of the Athletes' Committee) and in

2009, Terry Bunyard was awarded the UIPM Medal of Honour for his important contribution to the world of Modern Pentathlon over many years. Former Chairman, Andy Ripley battled with prostate cancer throughout the rest of the decade and, sadly, lost his fight in 2010. Despite his insistence that he knew less about the sport than his fellow officials, his final farewell as Chairman showed an astute sense of the essence of Modern Pentathlon. He wrote: 'Five events, stay brilliant but stay humble 'cos one of them is going to bite you.' No other epithet sums up the predicament and the temperament of the pentathlete more succinctly.

2005 World Championships: Warsaw (POL)
Men - The First Asian World Champion

In a year in which Modern Pentathlon survived yet another IOC vote thus ensuring its participation until 2012, it was all change once again at the top of the scoreboard in the men's event in Warsaw. Surprisingly, Moiseev, the Olympic Champion had been the only Russian to qualify for Athens. All this changed in 2005; Russian pentathletes placed 2nd, 3rd, and 4th and the winner, Zhenhua Qian (CHN) brought Asia its first World Championship. Qian had a dream competition, winning both the shooting (191) and the fencing (1028) and also being one of the five 1200 rides in the competition. By the final running event, he was so far ahead, his rather mediocre 11:27 run made no difference at all to the final standings.

Aleksei Turkin (RUS) pushed Olympic Champion, Andrei Moiseev, who won the swim in 2:07.3, into 3rd place and the winner of the run (10:23), Ilya Frolov, completed the Russian success by coming 4th. The post-

Olympic year is usually a time for new faces but there were plenty of established stars still competing. Capalini (CZE) was 8th, Horvath 9th, Krungolcas 13th and Lee (KOR) 20th. Former World Champions in the field were Walther 16th, Sedlecky 17th, and Balogh 19th. Team winners, as expected, were Russia ahead of Czech Republic and Germany.

Women

It was also the experienced pentathletes who lead the field in the women's event. Claudia Corsini (ITA) made up for her 4th place in Athens by beating the World and Olympic Champion Zsusza Vörös into second place. Corsini began with a winning 189 shoot and held Vörös to three seconds in the swimming. Grolichova (CZE) won the fencing with 1028 and the riding was not a major discriminator – Mouratova (RUS) was the only sub-1000 score in the whole field. A 10:32 run gave Corsini the title over Vörös and Elena Rublevska (LAT) took the bronze medal. The competition marked the debut of Laura Asadauskaite (LTU) who won the run and came 8th overall and to 2009 World Champion, Qian Chen (CHN) who placed 18th. Other significant positions were Tereshuk (UKR) 12th, Caze (FRA) 16th, and Boenisz (POL) 20th.

The British women, now missing their Olympic stars, nevertheless, all qualified for the final. Sarah Langridge was 26th, Mhairi Spence 30th and Katy Livingston 31st. Though they failed to win a team medal behind Russia, Hungary and Poland, the young team had their glory at the Junior World Championships where Mhairi took the bronze medal and the British team (Spence, Livingston, Gomersall) won the team gold medal.

2006 World Championships: Guatemala City (GUA)
Men

A mid-November World Championships made for a long season. World Champion Zhenhua Qian (CHN) couldn't have had a more different start to his title defence. He shot 181 and fenced 692 compared to 191 and 1028 the previous year and could only finish 26th overall. Olympic Champion, Andrei Moiseev (RUS) won the swim as usual but finished 11th overall. The new World Champion was Edvinas Krungolcas (LTU) whose 185 shoot was only just short of the winners, Horbacz (POL) and Kukshin (UKR), who both shot 187. Krungolcas' relatively lowly score of 972 in the fencing was still enough to win that event. Only four athletes failed to score 1000 points in the riding and Ilya Frolov (RUS) was the winner on a very slow running course on which nobody broke 11 minutes. Viktor Horvath (HUN) took the silver medal ahead of Krungolcas' Lithuanian team mate, Zadneprovskis who was back to top form after a year's break. Capalini (CZE) was 4th, Turkin (RUS) 7th and Britain's Nick Woodbridge, in coming 18th, produced the best British men's result in ten years. Not surprisingly with individual 1st and 3rd, Lithuania won the team event ahead of Hungary and Czech Republic.

Women

Guatemala was witness to some strange events in the women's competition. Victoria Tereshuk (UKR) began with a feeble 162 shoot and 692 fence and yet her swim/run was so strong (2604 points) that she won the silver medal. The winner, with steady unspectacular scores throughout, was Marta Dziadura (POL) who had placed 5th in her debut the year before but never rose again to such heights as she did in 2006, even failing to qualify for the 2008 Olympics. Omnia Fakhry (EGY) won the bronze medal, the first for the African continent. Surprisingly, the fencing scores of the three medallists were 776, 692, and 748, which went entirely against tradition. Indeed, Zsusza Vörös' winning fencing score was only 944. The Hungarian rode only 980 points, though, and finished 10th overall. Georgina Harland, after her post-Olympic break, finished 7th, also beginning poorly with a 160 shoot and a 736 fence. Mhairi Spence was 12th and Katy Livingston, who rode 916, came 18th. Other notable positions were Rublevska (LAT) 6th, Boenisz (POL) 8th and Caze (FRA) 22nd. In 20th place making her debut in the World Championships was future Olympic Champion, Lena Schöneborn (GER), who rode only 928 points. The British team took silver medals in both the team and relay events behind Poland.

In the Junior World Championships, The Great Britain team (Spence, Helyer, Gomersall) won both the team and relay gold medals and Mhairi Spence won the individual silver medal. Mhairi also won a bronze medal in the Senior European Championships where the British team took gold and silver medals in the team and relay events respectively.

2007 World Championships: Berlin (GER)
Men

This competition continued the trend of even scoring in the fencing event (highest score 976 – lowest 688) and few could complain about the riding event with a score of 1020 for the last-placed rider. Zhenhua Qian (CHN) shot 190 to open a lead of two target points over Viktor Horvath (HUN). Michal Michalik (CZE); Steffen Gebhardt (GER) won the fencing with 976; Eric Walther (GER) swam 2:00.42 to Moiseev's (RUS) 2:00.79; and then Ilya Frolov (RUS) won both the riding event and the running (9:02.1). Frolov's fine run took him past several leading pentathletes into 2nd place overall, just eight points behind the new Champion, Horvath.

It was a very tight finish with only 12 points separating the top four. Indeed, Robert Nemeth (HUN) got the same score as 4th placed Gebhardt but had run faster so claimed the bronze medal. In 5th and 6th places were current Olympic Champion, Andrei Moiseev (RUS) and his runner-up, Andrejus Zadneprovskis (LTU), Moiseev having lost a higher placing with his 176 shoot. The 2006 Junior World Champion, David Svoboda (CZE) finished 8th and former World Champions placed as follows: Walther (GER) 10th, Sedlecky (CZE) 12th, Balogh (HUN) 14th, and Qian (CHN) 20th. World Champion, Edvinas Krungolcas (LTU) was unable to defend his title in Berlin but he won the World Cup Final in 2007 for the fourth time. Though placing 1st and 3rd individually, Hungary were punished for not qualifying a third team member in the final and only finished 3rd in the team event behind new winners, Germany (4th, 10th and 16th) and Czech Republic.

Women

In pre-Olympic year, a clear signal came out from Berlin as to the leading contenders for Beijing. Amelie Caze (FRA) won the first of her three World Championship titles by just 16 points from Lena Schöneborn. Caze fenced 1000 and swam 2:12.3. Both Schöneborn and Laura Asadauskaite (LTU), the bronze medalist rode the maximum 1200 and ran much faster than Caze but the Frenchwoman managed to hold them off as they closed fast on her lead. With only one year to Beijing, the British women performed disappointingly. Georgina Harland was 8th but with a rather better shoot / fence (164/ 952) than the year before, Mhairi Spence was 18th and Heather Fell 20th. Katy Livingston, after a nightmare 460 ride finished 35th. Elsewhere, the team had managed to win the relay and come 2nd in the team event at the European Championships.

Sheila Taormina

In 9th place in Berlin was the American, Sheila Taormina, making her World Championship debut with a 2:07.42 swim and a 10:14.6 run. Sheila had a most extraordinary history. She had been a member of the USA gold medal-winning Olympic 4 x 200m Freestyle team in 1996 in Atlanta. Not content to rest on her laurels, she then represented USA in the Triathlon at the Sydney Olympics in 2000, where she placed 6th, and then again in 2004 (23rd). Now she was trying for a unique achievement –four consecutive Olympics in three different sports!

2008 World Championships: Budapest (HUN)
Men

Once again, this final Olympic qualifier was not much of a predictor of Olympic glory. Olympic Champion, Andrei Moiseev (RUS), despite winning the European Championship in 2008, ruled himself out of contention with a 172 shoot at the start of the day. The only 1000 score in fencing was Andrea Valentini (ITA) while the two Russians, Frolov and Moiseev fenced 952 and 928 respectively. For the first time in a World Championships, three swimmers broke two minutes: Moiseev who won in 1:58.19, 2005 Junior World Champion, Adam Marosi (HUN), and Jean Maxence Berrou (FRA). With increasingly tight finishes in final pentathlon results, the marked increase in overall swimming speeds this year showed where the heavy training work had been done over the winter.

Nicola Benedetti (ITA) was the only 1200 ride and then he went on to win the run in 9:10.25, six seconds ahead of Ilya Frolov. However, it was Frolov who became the 2008 World Champion by a good margin over David Svoboda (CZE) and Igor Lapo (BLR) who took the silver and bronze medals. Jean Berrou (FRA) was 4th, Moiseev (RUS) 5th, Zadneprovskis (LTU) 9th, Krungolcas (LTU) 13th, Marosi (HUN) 19th, Walther (GER) 22nd, and Balogh (HUN) 23rd. Viktor Horvath (HUN), the defending champion, was unable to run and so finished 36th.

For Great Britain, Sam Weale, in 25th position, was able to secure an Olympic spot. Nick Woodbridge, however, needed the help of MPAGB Chairman, Tony Temple, to get his Olympic place. Nick had been listed one place away from qualification on the rankings list. However, 1996 Olympic Champion Alex Parygin, now competing for Australia, had been admitted to the Olympic list without having achieved the minimum score imposed by the UIPM. The case went to the Court of Arbitration for Sport (CAS) and Nick was rightfully included in the Olympic line-up instead of Parygin.

Women

The final fraught qualifying competition for Beijing brought most of the top names to Budapest. Amelie Caze retained her World title, with a 1024 fence and 1368 points in the swim. Once again, her relatively weak (1040) final run caused some nervous glances over her shoulder at the rapidly closing field. She won by 20 points from Aya Medany (EGY) who, like her team mate, Omnia Fakhry, had a strong swim and had been threatening to challenge the field since her Olympic debut in Athens at only 15. To the delight of the British contingent, the disappointment of the previous year was laid to rest with Katy Livingston taking the bronze medal and Heather Fell finishing 4th. Lena Schöneborn (GER) was 5th. Heather had begun with a strong 182 shoot and Katy had followed that with a 1000 fence. Indeed Heather had the upper hand in all the remaining events so only lost out to Katy overall as the result of her poor fencing score (712).

Further back in the field, Mhairi Spence came 19th and Georgina Harland 30th. For Georgina it was a miserable final competition. She had never recaptured the form that won her the Olympic bronze in 2004. In Budapest she shot only 153 and fenced 784. Even for the most determined pentathlete, recovery after a start like that was unlikely. Other top competitors down on their luck were Claudia Corsini (ITA) 15th, Zsusza Vörös (HUN) 17th and 2006 World Champion, Marta Dziadura (POL) 24th. In the team event, Poland beat Great Britain and Hungary into 2nd and 3rd places.

At the Junior World Championships in 2008, the British team (Ferguson, Grandfield, Prentice) won the silver medal.

2008 Olympic Games: Beijing (CHN)
Men

The Men's event took place on 21st August. The oldest competitor, at 35, was Edvinas Krungolcas (LTU) and there was nobody below the age of 21 competing. Andrei Moiseev (RUS) became only the second man in history, after Lasse Hall (SWE – 1952 & 1956) to retain the Olympic title. In the modern era, when predicting the winner of any competition is a risky move, this was a marvellous achievement. Moiseev effectively won the title in the first event when he shot 186, a far better score than any of his recent performances. This kept him within striking distance of Zhenhua Qian (CHN) who, boosted by the home crowd, won the shoot with 189 and then shared top spot in the fencing with Moiseev (1024). Moiseev gained five seconds over Qian in the swimming despite a relatively slow 2:02.55, That event was won by Amro El-Geziry (EGY) in 1:55.86, just a tenth of a second ahead of Britain's Nick Woodbridge.

The riding event was something of a disaster. It had rained heavily and the area was a muddy quagmire. The situation was made worse by a large crowd that had never experienced horses before and made the kind of noise that only unsettled the horses further. As is often the case with the riding event, the overall scores seem reasonable enough until you look at the lower half of the table. Among the top 15, although nobody rode 1200, six rode better than 1100 and the other nine better than 1000. However, a look at the rest of field reveals some very big names with insultingly low scores: Walther 892, Horvath 896, Frolov 828, Balogh 852, El-Geziry 484, Svoboda 184 and Lee 84. The withdrawal of five of the worst horses before the women's event revealed the depth of the damage and, considering the intense scrutiny given Modern Pentathlon by the IOC on every Olympic occasion, there must have been many officials with their heads in their hands.

For the leaders, however, the battle continued. Moiseev, leading after three events, rode 1048. However, his nearest rival, Qian, rode only 984 to leave Moiseev, the stronger runner, with an almost unassailable lead. Qian, a poor runner, brought further misery to the home crowd by slipping out of the medals into 4th place by the end of the run. He was overtaken by the two Lithuanians, Krungolcas and Zadneprovskis who took the silver and bronze medals. Fastest runner of the day was Nam Dong-hun (KOR) with a fantastic time of 8:55.57. Final positions for the unlucky riders were: Walther 16th, Horvath 19th, Frolov 20th, Balogh 26th and Svoboda 29th.

For Great Britain, with Sam Weale in 10th position and Nick Woodbridge in 25th, this competition marked a comeback for British men after too long an absence. They were now hoping to establish the kind of standards that British women had been enjoying for several years.

Women

There was a strong belief, generated by Great Britain's 3rd and 4th placings in the recent World Championships that a medal could be on the cards for the third consecutive Olympics. The main focus was on Amelie Caze (FRA), the World Champion, and her runner-up, Lena Schöneborn (GER). Among the 36 competitors were four women who were competing in their third Olympic Games - Paulina Boenisz (POL), Elena Rublevska (LAT), Zsusza Vörös (HUN) and Tatiana Mouratova (RUS). Sheila Taormina (USA) was already setting a multi-sport record in her fourth Olympics but she added another by being, at 39, the oldest-ever Olympic competitor in the women's event. At the other end of the age scale, there were three 16 year olds competing – Margaux Isaksen (USA), Marlene Sanchez (MEX) and Rita Sang-Agero (GUA).

On 22nd August in an air-conditioned hall, Belinda Schreiber (SUI) won the opening shooting event with 188 but Heather Fell's 185 gave her a strong lead over her rivals, Caze and Schöneborn (both 177). Katy Livingston and Victoria Tereshuk (UKR) both scored 178. However, Lena Schöneborn's winning fencing score of 1072 gave her a lead which she would not give up for the rest of the competition. Tereshuk and Caze both scored 928 while Fell and Livingston kept in touch with the leaders with 880 and 808 respectively. Poor Sheila Taormina (USA) won only four of her 35 bouts for a score of just 496. However, she predictably won the swim (2:08.86) while Caze swam 2:11.29, Fell 2:12.77 and Schöneborn 2:16.91. Less predictably, Taormina won the ride as well, only three women riding 1200, the other two being Qian Chen (CHN) and Laura Asadauskaite (LTU). There had been a number of withdrawals of horses after the men's event the day before. This meant that 11 of the horses had to ride the course three times. This actually turned out to be a sensible solution with better performances all round. However, Tereshuk and Caze gave 90 points away to Schöneborn and Livingston (both 1172) and a valuable 60 points to Fell (1144). After four events, then, Schöneborn led by 76 points from Fell. Schreiber was 3rd, Caze 4th and Chen 5th.

Though Heather Fell cut the gap on the German athlete by half in the run, Schöneborn, the ex-swimmer from Bonn, was not to be denied her gold medal. A strong run from Heather (10.19.2) gave her the silver

Lena Schöneborn (GER) 2008 Olympic Champion. (Photo courtesy of Paul J Roberts/Roberts Sports Photos)

medal ahead of the rapidly closing Victoria Tereshuk who took the bronze medal. Schreiber dropped to 10th, Caze to 9th while Katy Livingston moved up to 7th place. The winner of the run, Anastasia Samusevich (BLR) raced through the field to 4th place overall with a time of 10.04.4 ahead of Chen in 5th and Boenisz (POL) in 6th place. Aya Medany (EGY) was 8th and Taormina, 19th, just one place ahead of defending Olympic Champion, Zsusza Vörös, who had never managed to attain the high standard of her victory in Athens since.

So a second Tavistock Pony Club member won an Olympic medal eight years after Kate Allenby had. For Heather, preparation hadn't been easy going; in 2006 she had very nearly given up after injury problems and a shortage of money. At that time, she was holding down three part-time jobs and 'fitted the swimming, riding and running around working.' In such circumstances, two British athletes in the top seven was a fine result.

2008 UIPM Congress –Guatemala
The birth of the combined event

At the post-Olympic Congress, the decision was taken to replace the shooting and running events with a combined event in which each athlete would run 3000 metres interspersed with firing sufficient shots to hit five targets before every 1000 metres. An initial 2000 point bogey for this event was set at 14 minutes with +/- 4 points per second for all of the Senior, Junior, Youth A and Youth B competitions –men and women. After the 2009 World Championships, acknowledging the rapid adaptation to the new task by the pentathletes concerned, this bogey time was reduced to 12:30 with the same points allocation per second.

Like virtually all innovations throughout the history of Modern Pentathlon, there was some resistance to this change. The MPAGB, assigned the task of organizing the first World Championships using the new combined event, declared they would 'make the best of' the situation. As it turned out, the combined event has become a very exciting conclusion to the competition. True, it takes a skilled commentator to draw the audience's attention to the rapid change of leadership often experienced in the shooting phase and some athletes have clearly adapted to the new event much better than others, but the new format is working very well so far.

2009 World Championships – Crystal Palace (GBR)
Men

A special grant of £40,000 enabled Great Britain to host the World Championships once more, only months after a major upgrading of the Crystal Palace facilities. The event was excellently organized by John Woodbridge who was also skilled in improving small details as the competition progressed and deal with the challenge of how, for instance, competitors and spectators alike could get a clear view of the shooting phase in the combined event. The final ran smoothly but there remained a problem of standardisation of the horses, particularly for the men's event.

Olympic Champion, Andrei Moiseev, failed to qualify for the final. He was certainly the most high profile of a number of athletes who were having trouble adjusting to the new combined event. Moiseev had been further hampered by a serious injury incurred when he had been hit by a truck when winter training in Colorado after the Beijing Olympics. His team mate, World Champion, Ilya Frolov (RUS), however, adapted excellently to win the combined event in 10:30.82. Frolov also won the fencing with the only 1000 score and swam a good time of 2:02.23. He was, however, thwarted by a riding event in which eight competitors failed to score 1000 points. Frolov scored only 804 which made his final combined event effort the more impressive. He finished in 9th position. Another bad riding experience was had by double World Champion, Andejus Zadneprovskis (LTU) who scored only 788 points.

The winner of the 2009 title was Adam Marosi (HUN). Marosi, too, had suffered a setback when he had broken his leg during the winter. Hungary had not included him in their pair selected for the Olympic Games so it was a triumph for the young Hungarian to win in London. He fenced 904, swam 2:01.94, rode

1128 and had a combined event of 10:49.07. The runner-up was David Svoboda (CZE) whose combined event was just two seconds behind Frolov's. Dimitri Kirpulyansky (UKR) took the bronze medal. Great Britain's Nick Woodbridge won the swimming event in 1:56.4, fenced an impressive 952 but fell back in the field with a riding score of 996 and a poor combined event time of 11:34.64. Nevertheless, he finished in 13th place overall. Hungary won the team event ahead of Czech Republic and Lithuania. Marosi also won the World Cup Final in 2009 but could only finish 3rd behind Polivka (CZE) and Frolov (RUS) in the European Championships.

Women – First Asian Women's World Champion

2009 marked a popular win for Asia's first-ever World Champion. Qian Chen (CHN) surprised everyone by beating Laura Asadauskaite (LTU) who won the combined event in 11:34.76, and Olympic Champion, Lena Schöneborn (GER) into 2nd and 3rd places. Chen began by fencing 1000 points. This opened a margin of 96 points on Laura and 120 on Lena giving Qian the critical advantage since there was little to choose between the three on the other events. Qian put in a strong combined event, just five seconds behind Asadauskaite, and won the competition by more than 100 points. Polina Struchtkova (RUS) won the swim in 2:09.76 and Sylvia Gawlikowska (POL) was the only 1200 ride.

Great Britain was well-represented in the final but positions were a little disappointing: Heather Fell 9th, Mhairi Spence 14th, Freyja Prentice 15th and Katy Livingston 23rd. The year had begun with Heather Fell and Katy Livingston at the top of the world rankings in 1st and 3rd places and they had gone on to win the team event at the European Championships. But Great Britain was beaten into 2nd place in the team event at Crystal Palace by Germany with Hungary finishing 3rd. The most outstanding performance among the British girls was Katy Livingston's magnificent score of 1096 in the fencing, an event which she won comfortably. It was quite clear, however, that neither the British men nor women were ready for the combined event yet, final times being notably weak. Other significant individual placings at Crystal Palace were: Amelie Caze (FRA), who had beaten Heather Fell for the European title, 11th, Zsusza Vörös (HUN) 22nd, and Elena Rublevska (LAT), whose 708 riding score didn't help her position at all, 28th.

2010 World Championships: Chengdu (CHN)
Men

China hosted the Championships at a brand new £80 million purpose-built centre. Such opulence, however, could not control the weather and the running course was flooded throughout the semi-finals and dried out only in the nick of time for the final. No British men qualified for the final despite Sam Weale having earned a silver medal at the European Championships behind David Svoboda (CZE) earlier in the year. The relay team did, however, narrowly miss out on a medal in Chengdu, coming 4th overall. At the World Junior Championships, Jamie Cook's 5th place gave optimism for the future.

The new sensation on the Senior circuit was Alex Lesun, a long, lean young Belarussian who had shot to prominence during 2010 in a World Cup event at Great Britain's newest venue, the Medway Centre. Alex had represented Belarus at the World Junior Championships and then been told that he had a heart condition and his training would no longer be supported by his national body. Lesun then moved to Moscow and became part of the Russian team - the rest would soon be history. At the European Championships that year, Moiseev (RUS) had begun the combined event in the lead but slipped to 5th place, a full minute slower on the final event than the four who overtook him. In Chengdu, he failed to qualify for the final and it was commonly felt that Moiseev would never adjust to the new format and, once sufficiently humiliated, would quietly retire. Though we couldn't know it in 2010, Andrei Moiseev has a layer of steel inside him that can resist all blows and his triumphant comeback would be just around the corner. Meanwhile, he was biding his time.

The Chengdu competition had an extraordinary outcome. Alex Lesun was indeed pushing for victory in his first Senior World Championships but it was 2008 World Junior Champion, Sergui Karyakin (RUS) who took the title, despite not having been considered good enough to be included in the official Russian team of three. Lesun fenced 1000 to Karyakin's 928 but swam slower than Karyakin's 2: 04.13 swim, an event won by Amro El-Geziry (EGY) in 2:00.21. The 80 points Lesun dropped to Karyakin on the riding event proved critical. Karyakin held on to the 12 second lead he had at the start of the combined event to keep Lesun in 2nd place and Justinas Kinderis (LTU) took the bronze medal just ahead of the home crowd's man, Zhongrong Cao (CHN). Two surprisingly poor combined events came from Ilya Frolov (RUS) who had won that event the year before in 10:30 and yet was only timed at 11.49.36 in

Chengdu to finish 12th overall. Secondly, World Champion, Adam Marosi (HUN), who won the World Cup Final in 2010 ahead of Frolov and Svoboda, was timed at only 11:38.15 in Chengdu and finished 13th.

Women

2010 was Amelie Caze's (FRA) year once again. In the European Championships she beat Lena Schöneborn (GER), who won the World Cup Final, and Donata Rimsaite (RUS) and then repeated that victory in Chengdu. Aya Medany (EGY) won the fencing event with 1048, one hit ahead of Caze and Elodie Clouvel (FRA) won the swim in 2:07.9. In the riding event, 16 of the competitors scored below 1000 points, the only leader to be thus affected being Medany who scored 992. Margaux Isaksen (USA) won the combined event in 11:56.41 but it was Donata Rimsaite (RUS)'s time of 11:59.21 that took her past Lena Schoneborn and Aya Medany to take the silver medal, Caze's lead before the combined event having been solid enough to secure her gold medal. World Champion Qian Chen (CHN) only finished 19th in front of her home crowd.

There were three British women in the final: Heather Fell 8th, Freyja Prentice 9th, and Samantha Murray 22nd but this performance was still enough to give them the silver medal in the team event behind France but ahead of Germany who had beaten them the year before and who had won the European team event in 2010. In the Junior World Championships, Frejya Prentice won the individual silver medal with Kate French placing 5th. The team (Burke, Murray, Prentice, French), however, won both team and relay gold medals.

2010 UIPM Congress: Riga (LAT)

The use of laser pistols for the shooting phase of the combined event was the central issue at this congress. The argument in favour of using laser pistols rather than air pistols is that it enables the event to take place virtually anywhere –shopping centres, gymnasia, car parks, etc. Since there is no need for a back wall to catch the pellets and protect the public, the shooting phase can be viewed by spectators from any angle, even facing those firing the laser pistols. This is a tremendous boost to making the sport spectator-friendly. The UIPM also suggested that laser shooting was more 'environmentally-friendly' than air pistol though that seems a more modish than pragmatic stance. Opponents of the change felt the laser systems being used were still in their infancy and to rush acceptance through in order to make the system available for the 2012 Olympic Games was too hasty. It also had to be recognized that the introduction of the combined event only two years before had made major demands on the athletes; for them to accept laser shooting as well so soon afterwards seemed to be asking for a little too much. Laser shooting is also expensive and, according to top coaches, has a different feel from air pistol, making it unsuitable as a learning weapon.

The laser shooting proposal was twice put to the vote in Riga and twice rejected by Congress of whom a two-third majority vote was required. Nevertheless, the UIPM Executive was determined to implement laser shooting at all costs. Since, in anticipation of such developments, the rules already stipulated that laser shooting could be used as an alternative, the Executive declared that the Technical Committee would be justified in making such a change to the event without the support of Congress and a press release was promptly issued proclaiming laser shooting as accepted.

Among the many wishing to proceed more slowly, British officials made their position clear: 'If a case can be made for laser we will support its introduction on a timely basis. If the case cannot be made, we will resist it. For the time being it appears to us that laser is not an appropriate way forward for the Olympic Games in London in 2012.'

As they did with the combined event, the MPAGB had to make 'the best of' the implementation of the laser pistol whatever their doubts. Since the European Championships and World Cup Final were both to be held in Great Britain in 2011 in anticipation of its hosting the Olympic Games in 2012, the best solution was to join in with all efforts to try to make the system work.

2011 was an interesting year for the laser pistol plan. The 2010 Youth Olympics in Singapore had used laser in the Modern Pentathlon competition there, seemingly without a hitch. However, problems, it appeared, could be caused by sunlight and by rain, and by systems that could not block outside interference. Most important of all, when a laser shot missed its target, it was essential to know where it went. Nothing was more frustrating than to fire a missing shot and to have no idea whether the problem lay with the shooter or the system used. During 2011, the sight of huddled officials debating system problems became quite common but, by late in the year, it seemed that the best system had been selected. Most successful laser events had taken place in Moscow at both the Kremlin Cup and the World Championships.

The result is that each pistol is now linked to a computer which gives a clear indication of where every shot 'lands' and the system is suitably protected against outside elements and interference.

As we approach the Olympic events in 2012 there is no reason to feel that the laser pistol element of the Modern Pentathlon is as underdeveloped as, perhaps, it was when proposed as the working system in Riga in late 2010. Once again, athletes have had teething problems with the change as they did initially with the combined event but there is now considerable confidence in the new systems.

2011 World Championships: Moscow
Men

This was the year in which double Olympic Champion, Andrei Mosieev (RUS) was truly back in business. Lesser mortals would have given up in the face of such an inability to get the combined event right but Moiseev has finally succeeded, raising the real possibility that he might achieve an unprecedented third consecutive Olympic title in 2012. When Moiseev crossed the line in Medway in August to take the European Championship, the roar of relief that he gave was a true reflection of the man's struggle with the event changes. Once again, he'd failed to make his mark at the World Cup Final in London in early July at the Olympic venues but, in front of his devoted home following in Moscow in September, Moiseev became World Champion, surprisingly for the first time, but at a critical point in his career from a psychological point of view.

Moiseev opened with a winning fencing score of 1024, a swim of 2:01.89 and a 1180 ride. With only the combined event remaining he had a good lead on team mate Alex Lesun and the riding winner, Adam Marosi (HUN). He had been in a similar position in the past and blown it on the combined event but this time, though at least half a minute slower than his nearest rivals, his time of 10:45.33 was enough for a 20 point victory over Lesun and 40 points over Marosi. The competition was something of a return to older traditions with the first six places being entirely filled by Russians and Hungarians: Ilya Frolov (RUS) was 4th, Robert Kasza (HUN), the World Cup Final winner, 5th, and Bence Demeter (HUN), the World Junior Champion, 6th. The winner of the combined event was another Hungarian, Robert Tibolya, whose time of 10:01.2 compared well to Riccardo De Luca's (ITA) record time of 9:51.37 set in the European Championships.

The marked increase in combined event performance skills was noticeable amongst everyone, even in the British team. Britain's best men's performance in Moscow was Sam Weale's 12th place which was a great achievement for him after a season hampered by injury. It placed him just ahead of defending World Champion, Sergui Karyakin in 13th place. 20 year old, Jamie Cooke, who had astounded everyone by finishing 4th at the European Championships, thereby becoming the first British Olympic qualifier, had a 692 ride in Moscow and, with a strapped-up leg, finished 35th overall. Jamie burst upon the scene in a world in which only Nick Woodbridge and Sam Weale of the British men had made any impact for the previous few years. A protégée of 1988 Olympic Modern Pentathlon team bronze medallist, Graham Brookhouse, at the Gloucester Swimming Club, Jamie's great strength is in the swimming event. In Moscow he won the swim in

1:55.47 but at the European Championships in Medway his time was a world record 1:49.59. Most impressively of all, in Buenos Aires in November 2011, he became World Junior Champion, beating the holder, Bence Demeter. Included in his performance was another world record time of only 30 seconds for the shooting phase of the combined event. Though failing to qualify for the final in Moscow, Nick Woodbridge's greatest achievement in 2011 was his 3rd place behind Kasza and Lesun at the World Cup Final. It was a competition in which he finally showed he could handle the pressure of the combined event on the big occasion. The results of the 2011 season indicated that Great Britain now has three real male contenders for Olympic success in London 2012.

Women

With Amelie Caze (FRA) injured and Lena Schöneborn (GER) not at her best, this important hint of the possible Olympic outcome in 2012, was won spectacularly by Victoria Tereshuk (UKR). She began with a poor fencing score of 784 in an event won by Evdokia Gretchinikova (RUS) with 1000. Leading the competition comfortably after three events was World Junior Champion, Sarolta Kovacs (HUN), who beat Tereshuk in three of the four events. But Tereshuk's winning combined event time of 10:50 was a minute better than Kovacs who still managed to finish 2nd. Laura Asadauskaite (LTU), returning to the sport after having a baby, won the bronze medal from Gretchinikova and Schöneborn in 4th and 5th positions. The swim was won once again by Elodie Clouvel (FRA) in 2:08.33. Yanyan Wu (CHN) was one of only two 1200 riders, the other being silver medallist, Sarolta Kovacs.

For the British women Moscow was a disappointing competition. Mhairi Spence finished 8th with a good fence (928), Katy Burke 10th, Freyja Prentice 16th and Heather Fell only 27th. It meant that the British team slipped out of the team medals for the first time in four years, finishing 4th behind Germany, Hungary and Russia. However, at the Junior World Championships in Buenos Aires, Freyja Prentice won the bronze medal, Lydia Gosling was 5th and Kate Burke 8th. Together they also won both team and relay gold medals.

Who will win in 2012?

The complex qualifying system ensures that all continents will be represented in London. So, for instance, Andrei Gheorge (GUA), whose father was an Olympic pentathlete in 1992, will be there. He is among the continental quota (Europe 8 places, Asia 5, Pan-America 4, Oceania and Africa 1 each) that suddenly makes the pre-Olympic competition on each continent all important. For the remainder, the world rankings list on 1st June 2012 will largely fill the rest of the quota. This means that every World Cup event and the World Championships in 2012 will be an opportunity to climb higher on that vital list.

That, however, is not the end of the selection problem. Each nation can have no more than two athletes qualified in each of the men's and women's competition. Though not a tricky selection problem in some countries, for the Russian men, for instance, only two of Moiseev, Lesun, Frolov and Karyakin can be included. It is likely, therefore that two recent Russian World Champions will not be selected. For Great Britain who, as host, is automatically allowed one place per competition, the world rankings will decide such ordering.

In the World Cup series in 2011 nobody, man nor woman, won twice. Before the World Cup Final in London, the men's winner, Robert Kasza (HUN) was 34th in the rankings list. This makes predicting an Olympic winner a difficult task. Four of the top seven ranked women at the end of 2011 were British, none of them yet achieving the top place even though Mhairi Spence had been in the top three twice in World Cup competitions and Heather Fell and Freyja Prentice had also been among the medals.

In the men's event, it would be a magnificent achievement (and very good for Modern Pentathlon publicity) for Andrei Moiseev (RUS) to win the Olympic title for the third time. A year ago this was unthinkable. Now, he must be the favourite. Does Alex Lesun (RUS), top of the rankings list at the end of 2011, have the grit and determination to take the gold medal from his compatriot? Among others in the current top ten, 2009 World Champion, Adam Marosi (HUN) must be a possibility for the gold medal, too. Pavlo Tymoschenko (UKR), who, like his compatriots, the Kirpulyansky brothers, Dimitri and Pavlo, is the son of an ex-pentathlete, is 4th in the world rankings and may well surprise everyone. We should not exclude the powerful contingent from Asia; Jinhwa Jung (KOR) and Zhongrong Cao (CHN) are both in the world top ten. Though having a relatively quiet year in 2011, the two Czech athletes, David Svoboda and Ondrej Polivka, when fresh, are dangerous. For Great Britain, Nick Woodbridge is 11th in the rankings list and current World Junior Champion, Jamie Cooke, 14th. Sam Weale would also be high on the list if his season had not been curtailed by injury. It is very hard to predict which two will qualify. A medal is a real possibility for the successful qualifiers.

In the women's event, the favourite is surely defending Champion, Lena Schöneborn (GER). Her great rival, Amelie Caze (FRA) was injured for most of 2011 but may well be back stronger than ever. Other possible winners are current World Champion, Victoria Tereshuk (UKR), Laura Asadauskaite (LTU), and the up-and-coming World Junior Champion, Sarolta Kovacs (HUN). Great Britain has four athletes in the top twenty of which Olympic silver medalist, Heather Fell, has the most experience, but is not as well-placed as Mhairi Spence. As with the men's team, it is pleasing to know that selection will involve choosing from a strong contingent which includes Freyja Prentice,

Jamie Cook (GBR): 2011 World Junior Champion. (Photo courtesy of Paul J Roberts/Roberts Sports Photos)

Katy Burke and Samantha Murray. Medal prospects are strong.

The Future of Modern Pentathlon

The sport that began life as a part of military training is now widely practiced among large numbers of people from all over the world and from many varied backgrounds. With smart offices in Monaco, the UIPM is at the hub of Olympic sporting life. President Klaus Schormann and Secretary-General Jöel Bouzou are indefatigable in their zeal to spread the word to every corner of the globe. In the modern world, effective public relations skills are essential and Modern Pentathlon is justified in being proud of its public image. The internet is invaluable in spreading the message via an outstanding UIPM website from which enormous quantities of information can be sourced, and via Facebook where videos are posted and pentathletes from all over the world can share ideas. The link between Modern Pentathlon and 247tv is particularly valuable. No longer must we rely on a poorly informed outsider giving the briefest of summaries of our major events. Now every major competition is 'streamed' to the internet so that we can watch the excitement wherever it takes place in the world. It is also accompanied by intelligent commentary by people who know the sport – top pentathletes and others who have taken the trouble to get to understand Modern Pentathlon.

Modern Pentathlon's place in the Olympic movement ought to be assured but will always be vulnerable to the transient tastes of perceived public opinion. Fortunately, the IOC members who are the final arbiters of participation are imbued with more lasting values and have thus far supported our cause. Nobody who knows anything about the modern sport can ever accuse Modern Pentathlon of being anachronistic. Every such charge against us has been patiently remedied and Modern Pentathlon remains, in every way, the most searching test of the sporting all-rounder.

Acknowledgements

Firstly, I am indebted to Mike Egan who was the inspiration for this history. Mike was the prime mover in establishing the MPAGB archive and his own expertise in research, particularly on the earliest British pentathletes, advice about military matters and his careful reading of every stage of the manuscript have been invaluable. He located and introduced me to many retired competitors that I would otherwise never have had the pleasure of meeting. In the writing of this history, when my opinions have overstepped the mark, he has usually reined me in. When I have, occasionally, charged on regardless, he has shown great restraint in stepping aside.

Terry Bunyard's important roles as MPAGB and Army Chairman and his membership of the UIPM Cultural Commission have given him access to papers and documents that I would never have seen without his help. I am well aware that, had his health been better in recent years, he would surely have written an informed history himself. I hope that I have not fallen short of his aims in my own version.

In my bibliography I have attempted to acknowledge all sources. There were times, however, when my information came from photocopied scraps and photos by people it has been hard to identify. I apologise to anyone whose contribution to our history had not been properly acknowledged and will be eager to amend this situation given the opportunity.

One book in particular has been my friend throughout the writing of this history. The Hungarian Modern Pentathlon Association has a proper respect for the history of our sport and the Souvenir History produced by István Mészáros and his team for the 1999 World Championships is a delightful compendium of facts and photographs. It was produced in a limited edition and is not as widely available as it deserves to be. I would also like to thank Ferenc Benedek who, in 1997, organized a Hungarian MPA 75th anniversary competition in Budapest to which I was lucky enough to be invited. There I met many of the great names of Modern Pentathlon, champions all, who spanned more than five decades of experience. In researching their sporting careers for this book, I fully understand what a privilege it was to have met them.

I am grateful to the archivists that have helped me find materials: Lizzie Richmond, our MPAGB archivist at Bath University; Caroline Lam at East London University's Olympic Archive; and Bob Kelly of the Army PTC Museum. MPAGB officials Tony Temple, Martin Dawe, and John Woodbridge have been a great help in supporting the archive and enabling me to meet important contacts. Matt Pound at the UIPM has readily supplied me with materials and support.

I am also grateful to those who have supplied materials for the archive or been happy to chat about their pentathlon experiences. In particular, I'd like to thank: Kate Allenby, Jan Bartu, Gina Bochmann, Nigel Clark, Steph Cook, Peo Danielsson, Peter and Ann Duckworth, Mike Ellis, Jim Egan, Ed Egan, Les

Farrington, John and Doreen Felix, Jim Fox, Alan Girlow, Giles Hancock, Sandra Heck, David Langridge, Bruce Lumsdaine, Michael and Catherine Lumsden, Dominic Mahoney, John and Christine Majendie, Danny Nightingale, Adrian Parker, Sarah Parker, Colin Peace, Janusz Peciak, Richard Phelps, Robbie Phelps, Seb Pollington, Mike Proudfoot, Frank Quinn, Bridget Robbie, Tristan Robbie, Veikko Salminen, Steve Sowerby, Anatoly Starostin, Chip Stidolph, Pavel Tymoschenko, Eduardo Valle, Vikki Vielvoye, Guy Walters, and Anthony Wieler. I apologise to anyone omitted from my list in error.

Finally, I am grateful to everyone in the great family of Modern Pentathlon. Over the two years of writing this history I have been privileged to meet many pentathletes, past and present. Even in writing about pentathletes now long dead, I felt a personal bond with each of them that stems from our shared love of a sport that has always demanded patience, resilience and, above all, good humour. I am very conscious that, in focusing on World Championships and Olympic Games in particular, I have given less importance to the many other competition levels within Modern Pentathlon. I hope those not mentioned by name in this history will, nevertheless, feel represented.

Bibliography

Bailey, Steve (1997), 'A Noble Ally and Olympic Disciple: The Reverend Robert S. de Courcy Laffan, Coubertin's 'Man' in England' in *Olympika: The International Journal of Olympic Studies* Volume VI – 1997.

Bergvall, Erik ed. (1913), *The Fifth Olympiad, The Official Report of the Olympic Games of Stockholm 1912,* Wahlstrom & Widstrand, Stockholm.

Blacker, Gen. Sir Cecil (1993), *Monkey Business,* Quiller Press, London.

Boustead, Col. Sir Hugh (1971), *The Wind of Morning,* Chatto & Windus, London.

Blumsen, Martin (1972), *The Patton Papers* 1885-1940 vol.1 (Boston): Houghton, Mifflin.

British Medical Assn (2002), *Drugs in Sport,* BMJ Books, London.

Cohen, Richard (2002), *By the Sword,* Random House, New York.

Coote J & Goodbody J (1976), *Olympic Report 76,* Kemps Group Ltd, London.

Dávid, Sándor (1973), *Balczó,* Sport, Budapest.

Greenburg, Stan (2003), *Whitaker's Olympic Almanack 2004*, A & C Black Ltd, London.

Grut, Wille (1994) *On jag minns ràtt? (If I remember correctly)*, Strömbergs Bokförlag AB, Malmö.

Hampton, Janie (2008), *The Austerity Olympics*, Aurum Press, London.

Hegedüs, Frigyes (1968), *Modern Pentathlon*, Corvina, Budapest.

Hill, Christopher R (1996), *Olympic Politics Athens to Atlanta 1896-1996*, Manchester UP.

Horrocks, Lt. Gen. Sir Brian (1960), *A Full Life*, Fontana Books, London.

Hunn, David (1980), *Smelling of Roses- A Biography of Jim Fox*, Ward Lock Ltd, London.

Hunt, Thomas M (2007). 'Sport, Drugs and the Cold War – The Conundrum of Olympic Doping Policy 1970-1979' in *Olympika: The International Journal of Olympic Studies*, Vol. XVI - 2007.

Llewellyn, Matthew P (2008). 'Olympic Games are an international farce': the 1920 Antwerp games and the question of GB's participation.' in *Olympika: The International Journal of Olympic Studies*, Jan 1 2008.

Mészáros, István ed.(1998) *Modern Pentathlon Souvenir edition 1998* Hungarian Modern Pentathlon Association, Budapest.

Miller, David (2008), *The Official History of the Olympic Games and the IOC*, Mainstream, Edinburgh.

Morgan WJ, Meier KV, & Schneider A (2001), *Ethics in Sport*, Human Kinetics, Champaign.

Mottram, David R, ed. (1996), *Drugs in Sport, 2nd edition*, E & FN Spon, London.

Syed, Matthew (2010), *Bounce*, Fourth Estate, London.

Wallenchinsky, David & Loucky, Jaime (2008), *The Complete Book of the Olympics* (2008 Edition), Aurum Press, London.

Walters, Guy (2006), *Berlin Games: How the Nazis Stole the Olympic Dream*, John Murray, London.

Wilson, Harold E. Jr (1997), 'A Legend In His Own Mind: The Olympic Experience of General George S. Patton, Jr.' in *Olympika: The International Journal of Olympic Studies* Volume VI – 1997.

UIPM Bulletins
MPAGB yearbooks and magazines
Official Olympic Reports
BOA Olympic Reports
Olympic archive documents
Various newspaper and magazine articles
www.sports-reference.com
www.la84foundation.org
www.wikipedia.org
www.Sports123.com
www.pentathlon.org (UIPM website)
www.pentathlongb.org (MPAGB website)

Abbreviations

IOC National abbreviations

ARG	Argentina
AUS	Australia
AUT	Austria
BEL	Belgium
BLR	Belarus
BRA	Brazil
BRN	Bahrain
BUL	Bulgaria
CAN	Canada
CHI	Chile
CHN	People's Republic of China
CUB	Cuba
CZE	Czech Republic
DEN	Denmark
EGY	Egypt
ESP	Spain
EST	Estonia
FIN	Finland
FRA	France
GBR	Great Britain
GEO	Georgia
GER	Germany
GRE	Greece
GUA	Guatemala

HUN	Hungary
IRL	Ireland
ITA	Italy
JPN	Japan
KAZ	Kazakhstan
KGZ	Kyrgyzstan
KOR	(South) Korea
LAT	Latvia
LIE	Liechtenstein
LTU	Lithuania
MAR	Morocco
MEX	Mexico
NED	Netherlands
NOR	Norway
NZL	New Zealand
PER	Peru
POL	Poland
POR	Portugal
ROM	Romania
RSA	South Africa
RUS	Russian Federation
SUI	Switzerland
SWE	Sweden
SVK	Slovakia
TUN	Tunisia
UKR	Ukraine
URU	Uruguay
USA	United States of America

Former states

DDR	East Germany
EUN	Former Soviet Union States
FDR	West Germany

TCH   Czechoslovakia
URS   Soviet Union/USSR

Other abbreviations in text

APTC   Army Physical Training Corps
ASCB   Army Sports Control Board
BOA   British Olympic Association
CAS   Court of Arbitration for Sport
CIPMO   Comité Internationale du Pentathlon
            Moderne Olympique
FEI   Fédération Équestre Internationale
            (world riding)
FIE   Fédération Internationale d'Escrime
            (world fencing)
FINA   Fédération Internationale de Natation
            Amateur (world swimming)
IOC   International Olympic Committee
NCO   Non-Commissioned Officer
RAC   Royal Automobile Club
UIPM   Union Internationale de Pentathlon
            Moderne
WADA   World Anti-Doping Agency

Olympic and World Championship Results

Men's Olympic Games: Results

YEAR	HOST	GOLD	SILVER	BRONZE	TEAM WINNERS
2008	Beijing	A. Moiseev (RUS)	E. Krungolcas (LTU)	A. Zadneprovskis (LTU)	LTU*
2004	Athens	A. Moiseev (RUS)	A. Zadneprovskis (LTU)	L. Capalini (CZE)	CZE*
2000	Sydney	D. Svatkovsky (RUS)	G. Balogh (HUN)	P. Dovgal (BLR)	FRA*
1996	Atlanta	A. Parygin (KAZ)	E. Zenovka (RUS)	J. Martinek (HUN)	HUN*
1992	Barcelona	A. Skrzypaszek (POL)	A. Mizsér (HUN)	E. Zenovka (EUN)	POL
1988	Seoul	J. Martinek (HUN)	C. Massullo (ITA)	V. Yagorashvili (URS)	HUN
1984	Los Angeles	D. Masala (ITA)	S. Rasmuson (SWE)	C. Massullo (ITA)	ITA
1980	Moscow	A. Starostin (URS)	T. Szombathelyi (HUN)	P. Lednev (URS)	URS
1976	Montreal	J. Peciak (POL)	P. Lednev (URS)	J. Bártu (TCH)	GBR

1972	Munich	A. Balczó (HUN)	B. Onischenko (URS)	P. Lednev (URS)	URS
1968	Mexico City	B. Ferm (SWE)	A. Balczó (HUN)	P. Lednev (URS)	HUN
1964	Tokyo	F. Török (HUN)	I. Novikov (URS)	A. Mokeev (URS)	URS
1960	Rome	F. Németh (HUN)	I. Nagy (HUN)	R. Beck (USA)	HUN
1956	Melbourne	L. Hall (SWE)	O. Mannonen (FIN)	V. Korhonen (FIN)	URS
1952	Helsinki	L. Hall (SWE)	G. Benedek (HUN)	I. Szondy (HUN)	HUN
1948	London	W. Grut (SWE)	G. Moore (USA)	G. Gärdin (SWE)	SWE*
1936	Berlin	G. Handrick (GER)	C. Leonard (USA)	S. Abba (ITA)	USA*
1932	Los Angeles	J. Oxenstierna (SWE)	B. Lindman (SWE)	R. Mayo (USA)	SWE*
1928	Amsterdam	S. Thofelt (SWE)	B. Lindman (SWE)	H. Kahl (GER)	SWE*
1924	Paris	B. Lindman (SWE)	G. Dyrssen (SWE)	B. Uggla (SWE)	SWE*
1920	Antwerp	G. Dyrssen (SWE)	E. de Laval SWE)	G. Runö (SWE)	SWE*
1912	Stockholm	G. Lilliehöök (SWE)	G. Asbrink (SWE)	G. de Laval (SWE)	SWE*

Men's World Championships: Results

YEAR	HOST	GOLD	SILVER	BRONZE	TEAM WINNERS
2011	Moscow	A. Moiseev (RUS)	A. Lesun (URS)	A. Marosi (HUN)	RUS
2010	Chengdu	S. Karayakin (RUS)	A. Lesun (URS)	J. Kinderis (LTU)	LTU
2009	Crystal Palace	A. Marosi (HUN)	D. Svoboda (CZE)	D. Kirpulyansky (UKR)	HUN
2008	Budapest	I. Frolov (RUS)	D. Svoboda (CZE)	I. Lapo (BLR)	RUS
2007	Berlin	V. Horváth (HUN)	I. Frolov (RUS)	R. Németh (HUN)	GER
2006	Guatemala	E. Krungolcas (LTU)	V. Horváth (HUN)	A. Zadneprovskis (LTU)	LTU
2005	Warsaw	Z. Qian (CHN)	A. Turkin (RUS)	A. Moiseev (RUS)	RUS
2004	Moscow	A. Zadneprovskis (LTU)	C-H.Lee (KOR)	L. Capalini (CZE)	RUS
2003	Pesaro	E. Walther (GER)	E. Johansson (SWE)	M. Michalik (CZE)	HUN
2002	San Francisco	M. Sedlecky (CZE)	E. Johansson (SWE)	E. Walther (GER)	HUN
2001	Millfield	G. Balogh (HUN)	V. Horváth (HUN)	T. Hantov (BUL)	HUN
2000	Pesaro	A. Zadneprovskis (LTU)	G. Balogh (HUN)	N. Papuc (ROM)	USA

1999	Budapest	G. Balogh (HUN)	L. Capalini (CZE)	D. Svatkovsky (RUS)	HUN
1998	Mexico City	S. Deleigne (FRA)	V. Yagorashvili (USA)	A. Smirnov (BLR)	MEX
1997	Sofia	S. Deleigne (FRA)	D. Svatkovsky (RUS)	A. Zadneprovskis (LTU)	HUN
1995	Basel	D. Svatkovsky (RUS)	A. Hanzély (HUN)	C. Toraldo (ITA)	HUN
1994	Sheffield	D. Svatkovsky (RUS)	C. Ruer (FRA)	J. Martinek (HUN)	FRA
1993	Darmstadt	R. Phelps (GBR)	L. Fábián (HUN)	S. Deleigne (FRA)	not held
1991	San Antonio	A. Skrzypaszek (POL)	P. Steinmann (SUI)	A. Madaras (HUN)	URS
1990	Lahti	G. Tiberti (ITA)	A. Starostin (URS)	M. Kadlec (CZE)	URS
1989	Budapest	L. Fábián (HUN)	A. Miszér (HUN)	P. Blazek (CZE)	HUN
1987	Moulins	J. Bouzou (FRA)	M. Kadlec (CZE)	L. Fábián (HUN)	HUN
1986	Montecatini	C. Massullo (ITA)	D. Masala (ITA)	L. Dobi (HUN)	ITA
1985	Melbourne	A. Miszér (HUN)	A. Starostin (URS)	I. Schwartz (URS)	URS
1983	Warendorf	A. Starostin (URS)	T. Szombathelyi (HUN)	Y. Zinkovsky (URS)	URS
1982	Rome	D. Masala (ITA)	A. Starostin (URS)	J. Bouzou (FRA)	URS
1981	Zielona Góra	J. Peciak (POL)	D. Masala (ITA)	T. Szombathelyi (HUN)	POL

YEAR	HOST	GOLD	SILVER	BRONZE	TEAM WINNERS
1979	Budapest	R. Nieman (USA)	J. Peciak (POL)	D. Masala (ITA)	USA
1978	Jönköping	P. Lednev (URS)	J. Peciak (POL)	N. Glenesk (USA)	POL
1977	San Antonio	J. Peciak (POL)	P. Lednev (URS)	S. Rotkiewicz (POL)	POL
1975	Mexico City	P. Lednev (URS)	T. Kancsal (HUN)	J. Fox (GBR)	HUN
1974	Moscow	P. Lednev (URS)	V. Shmelev (URS)	B. Onlschenko (URS)	URS
1973	Crystal Palace	P. Lednev (URS)	V. Shmelev (URS)	B. Onlschenko (URS)	URS
1971	San Antonio	B. Onlschenko (URS)	Z. Villányi (HUN)	A. Balczó (HUN)	URS
1970	Warendorf	P. Kelemen (HUN)	A. Balczó (HUN)	B. Onlschenko (URS)	HUN
1969	Budapest	A. Balczó (HUN)	B. Onlschenko (URS)	B. Ferm (SWE)	URS
1967	Jönköping	A. Balczó (HUN)	S. Shaparnis (URS)	B. Ferm (SWE)	HUN
1966	Melbourne	A. Balczó (HUN)	V. Mineev (URS)	F. Török (HUN)	HUN
1965	Leipzig	A. Balczó (HUN)	I. Novikov (URS)	F. Török (HUN)	HUN
1967	Jönköping	A. Balczó (HUN)	S. Shaparnis (URS)	B. Ferm (SWE)	HUN
1966	Melbourne	A. Balczó (HUN)	V. Mineev (URS)	F. Török (HUN)	HUN

Year	Location				
1965	Leipzig	A. Balczó (HUN)	I. Novikov (URS)	F. Török (HUN)	HUN
1963	Macolin	A. Balczó (HUN)	F. Török (HUN)	I. Novikov (URS)	HUN
1962	Mexico City	E. Sdobnikov (URS)	I. Novikov (URS)	F. Török (HUN)	URS
1961	Moscow	I. Novikov (URS)	I. Deryugin (URS)	A. Balczó (HUN)	URS
1962	Mexico City	E. Sdobnikov (URS)	I. Novikov (URS)	F. Török (HUN)	URS
1961	Moscow	I. Novikov (URS)	I. Deryugin (URS)	A. Balczó (HUN)	URS
1959	Hershey	I. Novikov (URS)	A. Balczó (HUN)	A. Tarasov (URS)	URS
1958	Aldershot	I. Novikov (URS)	K. Lindeman (FIN)	A. Tarasov (URS)	URS
1957	Stockholm	I. Novikov (URS)	A. Tarasov (URS)	N. Tatarinov (URS)	URS
1955	Macolin	K. Salnikov (URS)	O. Mannonen (FIN)	A. Kovácsi (HUN)	HUN
1954	Budapest	B. Thofelt (SWE)	W. Vetterli (SUI)	I. Szondy (HUN)	HUN
1953	Santo Domingo	G. Benedek (HUN)	I. Szondy (HUN)	W. André (USA)	SWE
1951	Helsingbörg	L. Hall (SWE)	L. Vilkko (FIN)	T. Lindqvist (SWE)	SWE
1950	Berne	L. Hall (SWE)	D. Brignetti ITA	L. Vilkko (FIN)	SWE
1949	Stockholm	T. Bjurefelt (SWE)	L. Vilkko (FIN)	V. Platan (FIN)	SWE

Women's Olympic Games: Results

YEAR	HOST	GOLD	SILVER	BRONZE	TEAM WINNERS
2008	Beijing	L. Schöneborn (GER)	H. Fell (GBR)	V. Tereshuk (UKR)	GBR*
2004	Athens	Z. Vörös (HUN)	E. Rublevska (LAT)	G. Harland (GBR)	GBR*
2000	Sydney	S. Cook (GBR)	E. de Riel (USA)	K. Allenby (GBR)	GBR*

Women's World Championships: Results

YEAR	HOST	GOLD	SILVER	BRONZE	TEAM WINNERS
2011	Moscow	V. Tereshuk (UKR)	S. Kovacs (HUN)	L. Asadauskaite (LTU)	GER
2010	Chengdu	A. Caze (FRA)	D. RImsaite (RUS)	L. Schöneborn (GER)	FRA
2009	London	Q. Chen (CHN)	L. Asadauskaite (LTU)	L. Schöneborn (GER)	GER
2008	Budapest	A. Caze (FRA)	A. Medany (EGY)	K. Livingston (GBR)	POL
2007	Berlin	A. Caze (FRA)	L. Schöneborn (GER)	L. Asadauskaite (LTU)	BLR
2006	Guatemala	M. Dziadura (POL)	V. Tereshuk (UKR)	O. Fakhry (EGY)	POL
2005	Warsaw	C. Corsini (ITA)	Z. Vörös (HUN)	E. Rublevska (LAT)	RUS
2004	Moscow	Z. Vörös (HUN)	K. Allenby (GBR)	T. Mazurkevich (BLR)	GBR
2003	Pesaro	Z. Vörös (HUN)	O. Velichko (RUS)	K. Allenby (GBR)	GBR

2002	San Francisco	B. Simóka (HUN)	Z. Vörös (HUN)	G. Harland (GBR)	HUN
2001	Millfield	S. Cook (GBR)	P. Boenisz (POL)	G. Harland (GBR)	GBR
2000	Pesaro	P. Svarre (DEN)	P. Boenisz (POL)	E. Rublevska (LAT)	POL
1999	Budapest	Z. Vörös (HUN)	E. Suvorova (RUS)	K. Raisner (GER)	RUS
1998	Mexico City	A. Sulima (POL)	Z. Vörös (HUN)	P. Boenisz (POL)	POL
1997	Moscow	E. Suvorova (RUS)	F. Fares (ITA)	L. Grolichova (CZE)	ITA
1996	Siena	Y. Shubenok (BLR)	D. Idzi (POL)	E. Suvorova (RUS)	RUS
1995	Basel	K. Danielsson (SWE)	Y. Shubenok (BLR)	D. Idzi (POL)	POL
1994	Sheffield	E. Fjellerup (DEN)	Y. Shubenok (BLR)	E. Köblö (HUN)	ITA
1993	Darmstadt	E. Fjellerup (DEN)	I. Kowalewska (POL)	D. Idzi (POL)	not held
1992	Budapest	I. Kowalewska (POL)	Y. Dolgacheva (BLR)	D. Idzi (POL)	POL
1991	Sydney	E. Fjellerup (DEN)	C. Delemer (FRA)	C. Minelli (ITA)	POL
1990	Linköping	E. Fjellerup (DEN)	L. Norwood (USA)	D. Idzi (POL)	POL
1989	Wiener N'stadt	L. Norwood (USA)	I. Kovács (HUN)	C. Delemer (FRA)	POL
1988	Warsaw	D. Idzi (POL)	I. Kiseleva (URS)	C. Delemer (FRA)	POL
1987	Bensheim	I. Kiseleva (URS)	B. Kotowska (POL)	S. Krapf (FRG)	URS
1986	Montecatini	I. Kiseleva (URS)	S. Moressee (FRA)	S. Krapf (FRG)	FRA

YEAR	HOST	GOLD	SILVER	BRONZE	TEAM WINNERS
1985	Montréal	B. Kotowska (POL)	I. Kiseleva (URS)	A. Bajan (POL)	POL
1984	Hørsholm	S. Yakovleva (URS)	P. Svarre (den)	S. Krapf (FRG)	URS
1983	Göteborg	L. Chernobrywy (CAN)	A. Ahlgren (SWE)	S. Parker (GBR)	GBR
1982	Compiègne	W. Norman (GBR)	S. Parker (GBR)	K. Tayler (GBR)	GBR
1981	London	A. Ahlgren (SWE)	S. Krapf (FRG)	W. Norman (GBR)	GBR

An asterisk indicates an unofficial calculation. There was no official team competition in these events but team results have been calculated by adding together the best three scores from each nation. In the case of the 2000-2008 Olympic Games where each nation was allowed a maximum of only two competitors, the result is calculated from adding the scores of those two competitors.

UK Modern Pentathlon
Roll of Honour

Top 6 finishers in Olympic Games, World Championships and World Cup Finals

2011			
Junior World Championships	Jamie Cook	Individual	Gold
Junior World Championships	Freyja Prentice	Individual	Bronze
Junior World Championships	Lydia Rosling	Individual	5th
Junior World Championships	**French, Prentice, Rosling**	**Women's Team**	Gold
Junior World Championships	**Prentice, Rosling**	**Women's Team Relay**	Gold
Junior World Championships	French, Myatt	Mixed Team Relay	4th
World Championships	Burke, Prentice, Spence	Team	5th
World Cup Final	Nick Woodbridge	Individual	Bronze
World Cup Final	Mhairi Spence	Individual	5th
2010			
Senior World Championships	Fell, Murray, Prentice	Women's Team	Silver
Junior World Championships	**Burke, Murray, Prentice**	**Women's Team**	Gold
Junior World Championships	**Burke, French, Prentice**	**Women's Team Relay**	Gold
Junior World Championships	Freyja Prentice	Individual	Silver
Junior World Championships	Kate French	Individual	4th

Junior World Championships	Jamie Cooke	Individual	5th
2009			
Senior World Championships	Fell, Livingston, Spence	Women's Team	Silver
Senior World Championships	Weale, Woodbridge	Men's Team Relay	4th
Senior World Championships	Fell, Spence	Women's Team Relay	4th
2008			
Olympic Games	Heather Fell	Individual	Silver
Senior World Championships	Katy Livingston	Individual	Bronze
Senior World Championships	Fell, Harland, Spence	Team	Silver
Senior World Championships	Fell, Livingston, Spence	Team Relay	Silver
Junior World Championships	Ferguson, Grandfield, Prentice	Women's Team	Silver
Youth World Championships	Jamie Cooke	Individual	Silver
Youth World Championships	Cooke, Legon, Worrall	Team	Bronze
2011			
Junior World Championships	**Jamie Cook**	**Individual**	**Gold**
Junior World Championships	Freyja Prentice	Individual	Bronze
Junior World Championships	Lydia Rosling	Individual	5th
Junior World Championships	**French, Prentice, Rosling**	**Women's Team**	**Gold**

Junior World Championships	Prentice, Rosling	Women's Team Relay	Gold
Junior World Championships	French, Myatt	Mixed Team Relay	4th
World Championships	Burke, Prentice, Spence	Team	5th
World Cup Final	Nick Woodbridge	Individual	Bronze
World Cup Final	Mhairi Spence	Individual	5th
2010			
Senior World Championships	Fell, Murray, Prentice	Women's Team	Silver
Junior World Championships	Burke, Murray, Prentice	Women's Team	Gold
Junior World Championships	Burke, French, Prentice	Women's Team Relay	Gold
Junior World Championships	Freyja Prentice	Individual	Silver
Junior World Championships	Kate French	Individual	4th
Junior World Championships	Jamie Cooke	Individual	5th
2009			
Senior World Championships	Fell, Livingston, Spence	Women's Team	Silver
Senior World Championships	Weale, Woodbridge	Men's Team Relay	4th
Senior World Championships	Fell, Spence	Women's Team Relay	4th
2008			
Olympic Games	Heather Fell	Individual	Silver
Senior World Championships	Katy Livingston	Individual	Bronze
Senior World Championships	Fell, Harland, Spence	Team	Silver
Senior World Championships	Fell, Livingston, Spence	Team Relay	Silver

Event	Names	Category	Medal
Junior World Championships	Ferguson, Grandfield, Prentice	Women's Team	Silver
Youth World Championships	Jamie Cooke	Individual	Silver
Youth World Championships	Cooke, Legon, Worrall	Team	Bronze
2007			
Senior World Championships	Livingston, Spence, Weedon	Women's Relay	Gold
2006			
Senior World Championships	Harland, Spence, Weedon	Women's Team Relay	Silver
Senior World Championships	Harland, Spence, Livingston	Women's Team	Silver
Junior World Championships	Mhairi Spence	Individual	Silver
Junior World Championships	Spence, Helyer, Gomersall S	Women's Team	Gold
Junior World Championships	Spence, Helyer, Gomersall S	Women's Team Relay	Gold
2005			
Junior World Championships	Spence, Livingston, Gomersall S	Women's Team	Gold
Junior World Championships	Mhairi Spence	Individual	Bronze
2004			
Junior World Championships	Spence, Fell, Livingston	Women's Team Relay	Silver
Junior World Championships	Spence, Fell, Rowell	Women's Team	Bronze
Junior World Championships	Mhairi Spence	Individual	5th
Olympic Games	Georgina Harland	Individual	Bronze
Youth World Championships	Nick Woodbridge	Individual	Gold
World Cup Final	Kate Allenby	Individual	Gold

	Allenby, Clark, Harland	Women's Team	Gold
World Championships	Kate Allenby	Individual	Silver
World Championships	Georgina Harland	Individual	5th
2003			
World Cup Final	Georgina Harland	Individual	Gold
World Cup Final	Kate Allenby	Individual	5th
World Championships	Kate Allenby	Individual	Bronze
World Championships	Allenby, Harland, Lewis S	Women's Team	Gold
Junior World Championships	Heather Fell	Individual	Gold
Junior World Championships	Lindsey Weedon	Individual	Bronze
Junior World Championships	Fell, Livingston, Weedon	Women's Team Relay	Silver
Junior World Championships	Fell, Livingston, Weedon	Women's Team	Gold
2002			
World Cup Final	Georgina Harland	Individual	Gold
World Championships	Georgina Harland	Individual	Bronze
Junior World Championships	Clark, Fell, Langridge	Women's Team	Silver
2001			
World Cup Final	Sian Lewis	Individual	Gold

World Cup Final	Georgina Harland	Individual	5th
Junior World Championships	Emily Bright	Individual	Silver
Junior World Championships	Bright, Clark, Langridge	Women's Team	Bronze
Junior World Championships	Bright, Clark, Langridge	Women's Team Relay	Silver
World Championships	**Steph Cook**	**Individual**	**Gold**
World Championships	Georgina Harland	Individual	Bronze
World Championships	Kate Allenby	Individual	5th
World Championships	**Allenby, Cook, Lewis S**	**Women's Team**	**Gold**
World Championships	Allenby, Cook, Harland	Women's Team Relay	Gold
2000			
World Cup Final	Georgina Harland	Individual	5th
Olympic Games	**Steph Cook**	**Individual**	**Gold**
Olympic Games	Kate Allenby	Individual	Bronze
Junior World Championships	Bright, Clark, Langridge	Women's Team Relay	Bronze
Junior World Championships	Emily Bright	Individual	6th
World Championships	Kate Allenby	Individual	6th
World Championships	Allenby, Cook, Harland	Women's Team	Silver
World Championships	Cook, Kinsey, Lewis S	Women's Team Relay	Silver

1999			
World Championships	Allenby, Cook, Lewis S	Women's Team	Silver
World Championships	Cook, Harland, Lewis G	**Women's Team Relay**	**Gold**
World Cup Final	Kate Allenby	Individual	Bronze
World Cup Final	Steph Cook	Individual	4th
Junior World Championships	Giles Hancock	Individual	6th
1998			
World Championships	Lewis S, Cook, Allenby	Women's Team	Silver
World Championships	Allen, Allenby, Cook	Women's Team Relay	Bronze
World Cup Final	**Kate Allenby**	**Individual**	**Gold**
1997			
World Championships	Allen, Allenby, Houston	Women's Team Relay	Bronze
Junior World Championships	Georgina Harland	Individual	Silver
Junior World Championships	Harland, Bright, Lewis G	Women's Team	6th
1996			
World Championships	Kate Allenby	Individual	6th
World Championships	Allenby, Lewis G, Wilmott	Women's Team Relay	6th
World Cup	Kate Allenby	Individual	Bronze
Junior World Championships	Lewis, Leach, Harland	Women's Team	5th
Junior World Championships	Lewis, Leach, Harland	Women's Team Relay	6th

1995			
World Championships	Allen, Allenby, Andrews	Women's Team Relay	5th
Junior World Championships	Kate Allenby	Individual	Silver
1994			
World Championships	Phelps, Brookhouse, Whyte	Men's Team	Silver
Junior World Championships	Kate Allenby	Individual	Bronze
Junior World Championships	Allenby, Kimberley, Lewis	Women's Team	6th
Junior World Championships	Allenby, Kimberley, Kipling	Women's Team Relay	6th
1993			
World Championships	Ric Phelps	Individual	Gold
World Championships	Macfadden, Houston, Rowe	Women's Team Relay	5th
Junior World Championships	Allen, Kimberley, Kipling	Women's Team	Silver
1992			
Olympic Games	Phelps, Mahony, Brookhouse	Men's Team	6th
World Championships	Cox, Houston, Kipling	Women's Team	5th
Junior World Championships	Allen, Kimberley, Kipling	Women's Team Relay	5th
1991			
Junior World Championships	Kimberley, Kipling, Nicholas	Women's Team Relay	4th
1990			
World Championships	Ric Phelps	Individual	5th

World Championships	Mahony, Phelps, Brookhouse	Men's Team	5th
Junior World Championships	Nicholas, Macfadden, Kimberley	Women's TeamRelay	6th
Junior World Championships	Nicholas, Macfadden, Kipling	Women's Relay	6th
1989			
World Championships	Ric Phelps	Individual	5th
1988			
Olympic Games	Ric Phelps	Individual	6th
Olympic Games	Mahony, Phelps, Brookhouse	Men's Team	Bronze
World Championships	Norman, Ball, Cox	Women's Team	6th
1987			
World Championships	Dominic Mahony	Individual	6th
World Championships	Mahony, Phelps, Brookhouse	Men's Team	Bronze
World Championships	Norman, Ball, Flaherty	Women's Team	4th
Junior World Championships	Whyte, Ball, Chaffey	Men's Team	5th
1986			
World Championships	Norman, Purton, Ball	Women's Team	6th
World Championships	Mahony, Hart, Phelps	Men's Team	6th
Junior World Championships	Lawrence, Whyte, Griffiths	Men's Team	4th
1985			
World Championships	Wendy Norman	Individual	5th

Junior World Championships	Dominic Mahony	Individual	6th
1984			
Olympic Games	Ric Phelps	Individual	4th
World Championships	Wendy Norman	Individual	4th
World Championships	Norman, Sowerby, Purton	Women's Team	6th
1983			
World Championships	Sarah Parker	Individual	Bronze
World Championships	Teresa Purton	Individual	5th
World Championships	**Parker, Purton, Sowerby**	**Women's Team**	**Gold**
World Championships	Ric Phelps	Individual	6th
1982			
World Championships	**Wendy Norman**	**Individual**	**Gold**
World Championships	Sarah Parker	Individual	Silver
World Championships	Kathy Tayler	Individual	Bronze
World Championships	**Norman, Parker, Tayler**	**Women's Team**	**Gold**
Junior World Championships	Ric Phelps	Individual	Bronze
Junior World Championships	Phelps, Royston, Tayler	Men's Team	Bronze
1981			
World Championships	Wendy Norman	Individual	Bronze
World Championships	**Norman, Tayler, Parker**	**Women's Team**	**Gold**
Junior World Championships	Ric Phelps	Individual	5th

Junior World Championships	Phelps, Tayler, Royston	Men's Team	4th
1980			
Junior World Championships	Ric Phelps	Individual	Silver
Junior World Championships	Phelps, Tayler, Royston	Men's Team	Bronze
1978			
Junior World Championships	Phelps, Humpage, Brodie	Men's Team	4th
1976			
Olympic Games	Parker, Nightingale, Fox	Men's Team	Gold
Olympic Games	Adrian Parker	Individual	5th
Junior World Championships	Clarke, Tolfree, Mumford	Men's Team	5th
1975			
World Championships	Jim Fox	Individual	Bronze
1974			
World Championships	Jim Fox	Individual	6th
1973			
Junior World Championships	Wall, Nightingale, Mullis	Men's Team	5th
1972			
Olympic Games	Jim Fox	Individual	4th

1967			
World Championships	Jim Fox	Individual	5th
1966			
World Championships	Jim Fox	Individual	5th
1957			
World Championships	Don Cobley	Individual	6th
1951			
World Championships	Lumsdaine, Percy, Blacker	Men's Team	4th
1950			
World Championships	Lumsdaine, Duckworth, Marsh	Men's Team	5th
1949			
World Championships	Lumsdaine, Duckworth, Brooke	Men's Team	4th
1928			
Olympic Games	David Turquand-Young	Individual	6th

British Representatives
at Olympic Games

1912   Ralph Cliverd, Douglas Godfree, Hugh Durant.

1920   Edward Gedge, Edward Clark, Thomas Wand-Tetley, Hugh Baustead.

1924   Brian Horrocks, Frederick Barton, David Turquand-Young, George Vokins,
Henry Churcher (Manager), S.Usher (Trainer).

1928   David Turquand-Young, Lance East, Alfred Goodwin, WA Turner,
WP Bradley-Williams (Manager), TS Hill (Trainer) .

1932   Percy Legard, Vernon Barlow, Jeffrey MacDougall, Henry Churcher (Manager), Roger Ames (Judge).

1936   Percy Legard, Jeffrey MacDougall, Archie Jack, Roger Ames (Manager), Thomas Wand-Tetley (Chef d'equipe).

1948   Geoffrey Brooke, Michael Lumsden, Andy Martin, Peter Duckworth,
Geoffrey White (Manager), Leslie Wieler (Chef d'equipe).

1952   Jack Lumsdaine, John Hewitt, Jervis Percy, George Norman, Errol Lonsdale (Manager).

1956   Don Cobley, Tom Hudson, George Norman, Michael Howard, Geoffrey White (Manager).

1960   Pat Harvey, Don Cobley, Peter Little, Len Collum, Peter Duckworth (Manager).

1964   Micky Finnis, Rob Phelps, Jim Fox, Paul Stevenson (Manager).

1968   Jim Fox, Barry Lillywhite, Rob Phelps, Mike Howe,
Monty Mortimer (Manager), Ron Bright (Coach).

1972   Jim Fox, Barry Lillywhite, Rob Phelps, Jim Darby,
Monty Mortimer (Manager), Ron Bright (Coach).

1976   Adrian Parker, Danny Nightingale, Jim Fox, Andy Archibald,
Michael Proudfoot (Manager), Ron Bright (Coach).

1980   Danny Nightingale, Peter Whiteside, Nigel Clark, Tim Kenealy,
Michael Proudfoot (Manager), Ron Bright (Coach).

1984   Richard Phelps, Mike Mumford, Steve Sowerby, Jim Nowak,
Ron Bright (Manager), Rob Phelps, Bernie Moss (Coaches), Keith Clark (Chef d'equipe),
Martin Grieves (Conference delegate).

1988   Richard Phelps, Graham Brookhouse, Dominic Mahony, Peter Hart,
Ron Bright (Manager), Rob Phelps, Danny Nightingale (Coaches),
Jabeena Maslin (riding), Tom Redhead (shooting).

1992   Graham Brookhouse, Richard Phelps, Dominic Mahony, Greg Whyte,

Martin Dawe (Manager), Rob Phelps (Coach), Jabeena Maslin (riding), Tom Redhead (shooting).

1996 Richard Phelps, Greg Whyte, Martin Dawe (Manager), Rob Phelps (Coach).

2000 Steph Cook, Kate Allenby, Dominic Mahony (Manager), Georgina Harland (Armourer),
Jan Bartu(Performance Director), Istvan Nemeth (Coach), Frici Foldes (Fencing).

2004 Georgina Harland, Kate Allenby, Dominic Mahony (Manager),
Jan Bartu (Performance Director) Istvan Nemeth (Coach), Frici Foldes (Fencing).

2008 Heather Fell, Katy Livingston, Sam Weale, Nick Woodbridge,
Dominic Mahony (Manager), Jan Bartu (Performance Director), Istvan Nemeth (Coach), Frici Foldes (Fencing), Jabeena Maslin (Riding).

Index of Names (by chapter)

Storm, M. (USA) 8
Stranne, J. (SWE) 1
Struchtkova, P. (RUS) 10
Stull, R. (USA) 9
Stull, R. (USA) 8
Sulima, A. (POL) 9, 10
Suttle, G. 7
Sutton, R. 7
Suvarova, E. (RUS) 9, 10
Svarre, P. (DEN) 8, 9, 10
Svatkovsky, D. (RUS) 6, 9, 10
Svoboda, D. (CZE) 10
Swift, V. (USA) 7
Syed, M. 9
Szabo (HUN) 5
Szekely, T. (HUN) 7
Szelestowski, S. (POL) 2
Szombathelyi, T. (HUN) 7, 8
Szondy, I. (HUN) 4, 5

T
Taalikka (FIN) 5
Tanaka, K. (JAP) 6
Taormina, S. (USA) 10
Tarassov, A. (URS) 5
Tarev, A. (URS) 7
Tasnády, K. (HUN) 5
Tatarinov, N. (URS) 5, 6
Tate, H. 7
Tayler, E. 7, 8, 9
Tayler, K. 7, 8

Tayler, P. 8
Tchernetskaya, T. (URS) 8
Tegner, T. (SWE) 4
Temesi, K. (HUN) 8
Temple, A. 6, 8, 10
Templer, G. 6
Tereshuk, V. (UKR) 10
Thade, H. (FRG) 7
Thatcher, M. 8
Thofelt, B. (SWE) 5, 6
Thofelt, S. (SWE) 1, 2, 3, 4, 5, 6, 7, 8, 9
Thomas, M. 6
Thompson, D. 5
Thorpe, J. (USA) 1
Tiberti, G. (ITA) 9
Tibolya, R. (HUN) 10
Tiidemann, I. (EST) 9, 10
Tindall-Carill-Worsley, G. 3
Todt, H-J. (FRG) 6
Tonnet, C. (NED) 2
Toraldo, C. (ITA) 8, 9
Török, F. (HUN) 6
Török, O. (HUN) 6
Townend, C. 10
Trost, R. (AUT) 6
Tscherner, H-J. (DDR) 6
Tuck, R. 4, 6
Tuma, K. (TCH) 2
Turkin, A. (RUS) 10
Turnbull, S. 10

PSIA information can be obtained
t www.ICGtesting.com
rinted in the USA
VHW01s0138071017
51545LV00001B/67/P

CPSIA information can be obtained
at www.ICGtesting.com
Printed in the USA
LVHW01s0138071017
551545LV00001B/67/P